EUROPEAN CUP &
CHAMPIONS
LEAGUE
THE ILLUSTRATED HISTORY

Scene: Istanbul's Ataturk stadium. **Occasion:** the 2005 Champions League Final, Liverpool versus Milan. **Time:** 45 minutes to kick-off. Alongside me is Jacques Ferran, last survivor of the *L'Equipe* editorial team who created the European Cup. He is transfixed by a magazine picture of the teams lining up at the first, 1956 final. **I ask:** "Did you ever envisage where that would lead?" Ferran waves towards the TV screens and sponsor banners. **He says:** "Personally, I don't like it but that's not important. What really matters is what happens on the pitch: the players and the football... and that remains as good and as dramatic as ever."

KEIR RADNEDGE

First published in 2005
Updated editions in 2006, 2007
This edition published in 2015

10 9 8 7 6 5 4 3 2 1

A CIP catalogue record for this book is available from the British Library.

ISBN: 978-1-78097-686-0

PREVIOUS PAGE: **LIONEL MESSI CELEBRATES WITH THE EUROPEAN CUP AFTER BARCELONA'S VICTORY OVER JUVENTUS IN 2015.**

Managing Editor: Martin Corteel
Editorial Assistant: David Ballheimer
Project Art Director: Luke Griffin
Picture Research: Paul Langan
Production: Maria Petalidou

Printed in Dubai

EUROPEAN CUP & CHAMPIONS LEAGUE
THE ILLUSTRATED HISTORY

KEIR RADNEDGE

Featuring **exclusive** contributions from:

**SIR BOBBY CHARLTON • ALFREDO DI STEFANO • EUSEBIO • FRANZ BECKENBAUER
IAN RUSH • PAOLO MALDINI • ZINEDINE ZIDANE • LIONEL MESSI**

CARLTON
BOOKS

Contents

RIGHT: **CRISTIANO RONALDO SCORED HIS SIDE'S FOURTH GOAL AS REAL MADRID BEAT CROSS-CITY RIVALS ATLETICO IN THE 2014 FINAL**

SIR BOBBY CHARLTON

Country: England

Position: Inside-forward

Born: 11 October 1937

Club: Manchester United
(England)

SIR BOBBY CHARLTON

Call it the European Cup – as we did in the early years – or the Champions League now that it has expanded to move with the times but, whatever the label, it remains the competition any big club with ambition wants to win.

The English football authorities would not let Chelsea enter in the first season, and they tried to stop us at Manchester United after we won the league in 1956. But Matt Busby, United's manager, knew better. He had vision. He believed that the European Cup represented the future of the game and he wanted United to be right in at the start. He got his way, we played and the rest, of course, is history.

Consider the identities of some of the other pioneers: Real Madrid, Milan, Juventus, Benfica, Barcelona... the biggest names both then and now. Of course it was a very different world then. The only live football on TV in England was the FA Cup Final once a year. Now we have live football almost every day. Worldwide broadcasting technology was in its infancy and satellite television was not even dreamed of.

I remember watching an early European match involving Real Madrid – it was the first time I'd seen them – on a tiny black-and-white set, and the picture kept breaking up. It was primitive compared with today, but for me, back then, it was like opening a window into another world.

The two-leg knockout system was successful because of the drama it brought, and playing under floodlights was also new. Those were always the most exciting matches either to play in or watch. There was nothing like it. As a young player, you never knew quite where you were going or what players or styles you would come up against – or what conditions.

I remember going to Hungary once to find that the Danube had flooded and the pitch was under water. It meant that we had to come all the way home and then go back again the next week. You would not have that now. Football today is so much more professional in every area, from communication and organization to nutrition and training.

English clubs learned a lot from going into Europe, and I'm sure the continental clubs and coaches learned things from us about attitude and so on. We all helped each other improve.

Off the pitch, we have seen enormous commercial progress. Football has exploded from being just one of several popular games into the majority game for the entire world. That has brought other responsibilities. You see it with all the big clubs and the leagues in France, Germany, Italy, Spain and England: professional football has to be run as a proper business. The increasing power and influence of television and sponsors has made itself felt but, on the plus side, their investment in football helps keep ticket prices at a level most fans can afford.

But it's romance, not profit, that sticks in the memory. For me, the pinnacle was winning the European Cup against Benfica at Wembley in 1968. It was such an emotional achievement, for Sir Matt in particular, because of what had happened to the club and so many of his players at Munich.

Yet when it comes to drama I would look elsewhere – a few weeks further back to the second leg of our semi-final that season against Real in Madrid. At Old Trafford, we had beaten them 1–0, but when we went back to Spain we were 3–1 down at half-time. The world seemed to be collapsing around us. But English teams always keep going, and somehow we got back to 3–2 and then 3–3 to reach the final. That was the most dramatic game I ever played in.

Can you imagine football without the European Cup and now the Champions League? Of course not. This book is about 60 years which have changed the game for ever.

OPPOSITE: **BOBBY CHARLTON SURVIVED THE MUNICH DISASTER TO WIN THE EUROPEAN CUP IN 1968 WITH SIR MATT BUSBY'S REBUILT MANCHESTER UNITED**

THE EARLY DAYS

In the beginning... only the football mattered when 22 players, one referee, two linesmen and a few thousand fans populated the wooden stands at grounds in Vienna, Budapest and Prague

That was the essence of association football, not yet compromised by the twisting gaze of the commercial and media lens. Television was still an inventor's dream. Radio was primitive. Sponsorship was a word yet to be coined on 14 August 1927.

This was the founding date of pan-European international competitive club football. The UEFA Champions League it was not; the European federation did not exist. Nor was it the Coupe Européenne des Champions; the French sports newspaper *L'Equipe*, which was to be instrumental in the formation of the competition, did not exist either.

Various one-off tournaments had been cobbled together in the previous 20 years to define club supremacy in one corner of Europe or another. FIFA, the fledgling world football federation, had tinkered with the concept of a world club championship rather than a national team tournament. However, lacking money and the means of transport – motorways, jet aircraft, high-speed trains, the product of future decades – it gave up on the idea for the best part of a century.

It was love of football alone that breathed life into the Mitropa Cup, whose title was a contraction of Mitteleuropa, the German name for Central Europe; indeed, its reach

RIGHT: **VALENTINO MAZZOLA (SECOND RIGHT) CAPTAINS ITALY AGAINST PORTUGAL IN GENEVA, 1949. HE WAS TO DIE A FEW MONTHS LATER WHEN THE PLANE CARRYING HIM AND OTHER MEMBERS OF THE TORINO SQUAD CRASHED OVER TURIN**

TOP RIGHT: **FERENC PUSKAS WHO MOVED FROM HONVED TO REAL MADRID TO TEAM UP WITH THE GREAT ALFREDO DI STEFANO**

owed everything to the historic Austro-Hungarian Empire and nothing to the nation-state jigsaw created in its place by the First World War.

The Cup's instigator was one of the greatest of the forefathers of international football. Hugo Meisl was born in what is now Ostrava but was the scion of a Jewish banking family and wealthy enough to live the dream in an age before lofty idealism was transformed into a term of derision.

Meisl became both general secretary of the Austrian federation and manager of its fabled 'Wunderteam'. He was an internationalist. That, for Meisl, was the only way forward. He mixed happily with counterparts and sometime rivals from Germany, Czechoslovakia, Switzerland, Italy and England, from where he imported the legendary coach Jimmy Hogan.

Meisl had more ambition than football had money. And the clubs, in the early years of continental professionalism, had more money than the federations. Logic thus dictated that the Mitropa Cup took off in the late 1920s and 1930s in a way that even the World Cup could not match.

An organizing committee was created by a founding meeting in Venice in July 1927. Two clubs each from Austria, Czechoslovakia, Hungary and Yugoslavia were entered: the champions and either runners-up or cup-winners.

Initially, Meisl wanted to run it on FA Cup lines. But, after consideration, he decided that the English formula did not meet his concept of sporting equality. Thus, he devised the now familiar home-and-away system, with victory decided on aggregate over two legs.

Meisl could not think of everything. In the goal-glut days immediately after the change in the offside law, he had not foreseen that clubs might end up all square. Sparta Prague and Hungaria of Budapest (later Voros Lobogo/Red Banner and then MTK) drew their 1927 semi-final 2–2, 0–0. A frightened referee tossed a coin and Hungaria, to their fury, were eliminated. Sparta went through to beat Rapid Vienna and become the first holders of the Mitropa Cup.

Sparta won 6–2 in Prague and lost 2–1 in Vienna, where their rugged tackling provoked a hail of stones, fruit and bottles from the crowd. Centre-half Karel Kada was carried off after being knocked out by one such missile, and demonstrations continued long after the final whistle. Familiar fury, indeed.

The Mitropa grew just as the Champions Cup would grow. Initial critics from neighbouring nations recognized the error of their ways and hurried on board. The Cup grew both in size and in status. The richer clubs went fishing in

foreign oceans for their players. Juventus, with one eye on Serie A and one on the Mitropa, imported a bevy of Argentines in vain; Bologna went scouting in Uruguay and were rewarded with success in 1932 and 1934: they were Italy's only inter-war winners.

Winning mattered with an intensity to match today's standards. It was more about glory than financial rewards. FK Austria's Matthias Sindelar, his country's greatest-ever player, is said to have travelled to the winning finals of 1932 and 1936 on the same tram as his adoring fans. Sparta meanwhile had raised the largesse to persuade Belgian forward Raymond Braine to sacrifice a World Cup opportunity in 1934 because his own federation frowned on professionalism.

The idyll faded after a decade. Meisl died in 1937, which was also the last year in which Austrian clubs competed before independence was forfeited the following spring in Hitler's Greater German Anschluss. One further year and Sindelar, artistic, free-scoring symbol of Mitropa football, died in his home after a mysterious gas leak.

The Mitropa Cup lived on in name but not spirit. It was 'captured' by the communist-controlled federations of post-war Soviet eastern Europe and, even before slipping away in 1992, had been reduced to an embarrassing joust between the reluctant reserve teams of second division champions.

But the legacy was priceless. The Mitropa spelled international club glamour, 'defining the market' long before bright young things talked in such terms, demonstrating that great clubs need the grand stage for which domestic duelling is insufficient.

Four years after the end of the Second World War – and a year before FIFA had revived the World Cup – the federations of Italy, Spain, France and Portugal launched their own club competition. European clubs could not afford hefty travel costs, so the Latin Cup was staged at the end of every season in each country by turn. Direct knockout was the system: two semi-finals, a third place play-off and a final. Every four years, the competition points were totalled per nation. Spain took overall honours in 1949–52 and 1953–57.

That was immaterial. What lives on, even beyond the fading memory of outstanding matches, is the Latin Cup's legacy of an interim international stage for the likes of Real Madrid, Milan, Benfica, Barcelona and Reims. Also there is the regret that the greatest club team of the era never competed.

Torino, champions of Italy five seasons in a row, sent a mixture of reserves and youth-team graduates to the 1949 Latin Cup. One month earlier their entire first-team squad had been wiped out. Some 12 Italian internationals were among the 18 players killed when the plane bringing them home from Lisbon, after a warm-up testimonial against

Benfica, swooped through mist and rain into the perimeter wall of Turin's Superga basilica.

The deaths of Italy's captain Valentino Mazzola and his team-mates was only the first such tragedy. But football would never be daunted from breaking down its own – and politicians' – international barriers. Post-war technology, an ironic byproduct of the demands of battle, provided the means for revolution with high-powered focused floodlighting. Football could now be played both day and night.

Pioneering promotional work in England was led by Wolverhampton Wanderers. Manager Stan Cullis, a former England centre-half, was a devoted proponent of the physical long-ball game, but he recognized that the future was international. Hence Wolves invited Moscow Spartak and Hungary's Honved to Molineux for prestige friendlies in November and December 1954.

Honved brought all their star soldiers, including the great inside-forwards Ferenc Puskas and Sandor Kocsis as well as right-half Jozsef Bozsik. They led 2–0 then lost 3–2 on a pitch which Cullis, deliberately, had half-flooded before the game. Next morning's headline in the *Daily Mail* hailed Wolves as 'Champions of the World'.

L'Equipe editor Gabriel Hanot, sitting at his desk in Paris, was not amused.

RIGHT: **BEFORE THE DAYS OF PRIVATE JETS AND SLEEK COACHES, PLAYERS USED TO ROUGH IT, WHILING AWAY LONG JOURNEYS PLAYING CARDS. THIS IS WOLVES IN 1963**

OPPOSITE: **WOLVES STALWART STAN CULLIS LEADS OUT HIS SIDE AT MOLINEUX. AN ADVOCATE OF THE LONG-BALL GAME, HE HAD HIS OWN WAYS OF DEALING WITH 'FANCY' FOREIGN FOOTBALLERS**

1950S

FOOTBALL'S NEW HORIZONS

The 1950s were a mere half-decade as far as the European Champions Cup was concerned. But it laid a foundation for a sporting edifice which changed the game, its balance of power and its finance. Out in front, on and off the pitch, were Real Madrid. They won the Cup for the first five years of its existence, including those four initial seasons of its inaugural decade. The most powerful initial challenge came from two of Spain's Latin neighbours. Reims from France were twice runners-up, in 1956 and 1959, with the Italian clubs Fiorentina and Milan the silver medallists in the intervening seasons. Alfredo Di Stefano was the defining individual.

RIGHT: **THE VERY FIRST FINAL: REAL MADRID VERSUS REIMS IN THE PARC DES PRINCES IN 1956. THE FRENCH SIDE RACED INTO A 2-0 LEAD, THEN IT WAS 3-1, BUT MADRID STORMED BACK TO WIN 4-3, SETTING THEIR BENCHMARK FOR THE FUTURE**

ALFREDO DI STEFANO

Country: Argentina and Spain

Position: Centre-forward

Born: 4 July 1926

Died: 7 July 2014

Clubs: River Plate, Huracan, River Plate (Argentina), Real Madrid, Espanyol (Spain)

ALFREDO DI STEFANO

No one believes me now when I tell them that Real Madrid, when I joined in 1953, had gone so many years without winning the league that hardly anyone could remember the last time. Not that it bothered me. I just thought this was the club of the capital of Spain, with a fantastic stadium and lots of great players before me. We had a duty to be the best.

I was determined to do something very special. I did not come for the money, I came to achieve.

When I had arrived in Barcelona from South America that May, no one knew whether I was to play there or for Real Madrid. They both claimed to have bought me. At one stage, there was even talk of loaning me to Juventus. I got fed up with it all. I told Barcelona I was getting the next flight back to Buenos Aires. But then in the September, Santiago Bernabeu, the Real president, pulled some strings somewhere, so I went to Madrid. I went to play for two years, signed initially for four and stayed all my life.

The day we arrived, I had to dump my family on the steps of the hotel and go straight to the stadium for a spot of training, a steak for lunch and a game that afternoon against a French club, Nancy.

I was not too keen. I had been sitting around in Barcelona for three months. In all that time, I had not trained properly and I had played only three friendlies. The stadium was being redeveloped and you would not believe the state of the pitch! On top of that, I was worried about what had happened to my family. It was all a bit of disaster and we lost 4–2. Still, I scored a goal with a header.

That was on the Wednesday and, four days later, I made my league debut at home to Santander. We won 4–2 and I scored again, though I still felt disorientated because I knew about as much about my team-mates as I did about the opposition – nothing.

Of course, that changed. We won the championship both in that first season and then in my second, which qualified us for the new European Champions Cup. This was a big deal

and we made it even bigger by winning it for the first five years. Joan Gaspart, who was briefly president of Barcelona years later, said that our first five European Cup wins were worthless because the opposition in the 1950s and early 1960s was so weak. But what did he know? He did not have to play against them.

In the first campaign, we played Partizan in the snow in Belgrade. When we beat them, the fans threw snowballs at us. One hit our coach, Pepe Villalonga, on the back and knocked him over. There was a stone in the snowball. If it had hit him on the head, it would have killed him.

Against Nice next season, we started to develop our style. Villalonga told me to stay up in attack, but we knew it was not working. We used to talk a lot on the pitch about the state of the game and what had to be done. I dropped

LEFT: **ALFREDO DI STEFANO IN THE COLOURS OF ESPANYOL AFTER LEAVING REAL MADRID IN 1964**

back towards midfield, but because I was quick we did not lose anything in attack.

I remember the final against Milan in 1958 when Paco Gento scored the winner in extra time. I still don't know how the ball went in because there were so many people in the penalty area. Then Bernabeu signed Ferenc Puskas. It proved a wonderful choice, though Hector Rial did not like it much because he could not adapt to playing inside-right instead of inside-left.

It was in that 1958–59 season that I was sent off for the first time, against Besiktas, for dissent because I got fed up with their goalkeeper's time-wasting. We had to beat Atletico in a play-off in the semi-final – Kopa and Mateos were fantastic – and Reims again in the final, just as we had in the first cup in 1956.

We had an outstanding team with extraordinary individuals. We also had high standards. Nothing upsets me now as much as seeing a player applaud a team-mate who has missed a crucial pass. In my day, we would have killed for such an appalling mistake. We always had a core of South American players – myself, Rial, Santamaria and so on – so we had the ideal mixture of South American technique and European pace. We developed a distinctivestyle because we could keep the ball until something opened up for us.

That was why we were champions of Spain, Europe and the world. That was why for every home match the ground was full, with 125,000 spectators, which was the capacity then. People had laughed at Bernabeu when he planned the stadium in the 1940s. But he was proved right. He had built a stadium that big because he knew he could get the people to fill it.

Bernabeu was a great president – the best. He set the standard. For example, when I was at Barcelona, they gave me a nice car, but I had to give it up when I moved to Madrid. Real Madrid players were not supposed to own cars. No ostentation was allowed. Bernabeu was quite conservative:

no cars, no moustaches, no beards and later no long hair either. Every game we knew we were ambassadors for the club – and we played a lot of games.

People talk about world tours as if they're something new, but we used to do two or three every year. We'd play friendlies half a world away. We'd start in Uruguay and finish up in New York. We even went up as far as Vancouver one year. Then we would go back down to play River Plate or Boca Juniors. We used to fly in airplanes that took years off your life. I used to complain that I had signed a contract to play football, not to run rings around the world.

We did not get paid anything to compare with today, but I cannot complain. We earned what we were worth in different times. I can remember ex-players in my day saying how much more we earned than they did. It's always been the same.

People said that the team which beat Eintracht Frankfurt in 1960 was the 'team of Di Stefano and Puskas', but this was untrue. I have never changed my view: football is a team game and everybody in the side depends on everyone else. For example, in the 1960 semi-finals we beat Barcelona. They had better individuals than us, but we were the better team.

It's collective responsibility both when you win and when you lose – and in the end, of course, we lost, for reasons there is no point in pursuing now. But I have no regrets. I am delighted with all the titles and trophies I won – much more than I could ever have dreamed of. I had a wonderful career.

Later, it was a great honour when Florentino Perez invited me to be honorary president. But I still believe the strength of Real Madrid is the way the club maintains a pride in its history without losing sight of present-day priorities. Some clubs spend too much time looking back. Real Madrid is not like that.

Reputations do not win matches and trophies, only goals can do that.

LEFT: DI STEFANO WON
FIVE EUROPEAN CUPS AND
WAS SURELY ONE OF THE
GREATEST ALL-ROUND
PLAYERS EVER TO GRACE
THE COMPETITION

TOWARDS A BETTER TOMORROW

In the decade after World War II, the format for the brave new world of European football was open to discussion. At club level, Real Madrid had friends in high places and were able to pull strings

Alfredo Stefano Di Stefano Lauhle arrived in Madrid at 10.30 on the morning of 23 September 1953. With him, on the sleeper train from Barcelona, were wife Sara and their two daughters. Today the greatest footballer in the world would be enveloped in a locust swarm brandishing cameras, voice recorders and notebooks. Instead, at Atocha railway station, a tired and somewhat bewildered footballer and his young family were greeted by two reluctant officials from the local football club, Real Madrid.

Di Stefano had been born in Argentina, rose as a teenager with his father's old club River Plate, then took advantage of the explosive strike of Argentine players in 1949 to fly off and join Millonarios of Bogota in their pirate professional league in Colombia.

Later Millonarios took their 'blue ballet' to Europe to make money from prestige friendlies – which is how Real Madrid president Santiago Bernabeu came to spot Di Stefano at the club's 50th anniversary tournament in 1952.

His first season climaxed with Madrid winning the league title for the first time in 21 years. They repeated the magic a year later. This was the most significant league title in the history of the club, because it earned Madrid an invitation to Paris for the meeting which created the European Champions Club Cup.

Gabriel Hanot, former French international full-back and editor of the daily sports newspaper *L'Equipe*, had called the meeting. He had been irritated by the English media's assumption of world-dominating status for Wolves after their friendly victories over Hungarians and Russians. Along with colleagues Jacques Goddet, Jacques van Ryswick and future *France Football* editor Jacques Ferran, he went down the road pursued by Hugo Meisl in Vienna 30 years earlier.

Hanot was not alone in dreaming of a new international club competition. Swiss pools supremo Ernst Thommen and FA general secretary Stanley Rous had already put their heads together to create the International Inter-Cities' Fairs Cup. But Hanot had the advantage in that entry to his European Cup was based entirely on the sporting merit conferred by winning league titles.

Quickly Hanot and his assistants found the workload and the political complications too much to handle. With a mixture of pride, regret and relief, they ceded administrative authority to the one-year-old European federation, UEFA – whose first officers were delighted to be handed a ready-made *raison d'être*.

Not all the founder clubs had ended up as domestic champions and not all of them dived in. Chelsea had qualified

RIGHT: **HIBERNIAN GOALKEEPER TOMMY YOUNGER DIVES ON THE BALL UNDER PRESSURE FROM GLOWACKI AND LEBLOND OF REIMS DURING THE FIRST LEG OF THEIR SEMI-FINAL IN APRIL 1956**

as champions of England but were then forbidden to compete by the Football League for fear of fixture problems.

The first match was played on the sunny Sunday afternoon of 4 September 1955 in Lisbon between Sporting Clube de Portugal and the Yugoslav club Partizan Belgrade. The first goal was scored, after 14 minutes in front of a 30,000 crowd, by Sporting's Joao Baptista Martins in a tempestuous 3–3 draw. Four days later, Real Madrid launched themselves into football history by winning 2–0 away to Switzerland's Servette in Geneva. Madrid's first goal was scored by their right-half and captain, Miguel Munoz. Madrid cruised through comfortably with a 5–0 win back in their magnificent stadium, named after Bernabeu, their inspirational president. Di Stefano scored twice.

Other first-round winners were Reims, Milan, one-time Mitropa Cup-winners Rapid Vienna, Hibernian of Scotland, Djurgarden of Sweden and Hungary's Voros Lobogo. The quarter-finals saw victories for Reims over Voros Lobogo, Milan over Rapid, Hibernian over Djurgarden and Madrid over Partizan.

Madrid very nearly did not make it. The first problem was political. Franco's Spain had denied diplomatic relations to all Soviet bloc countries. Officially, Yugoslav passport-holders could not enter Spain. Bernabeu pulled more strings. Partizan's players and officials were smuggled into Spain through a side gate at Barajas airport, bypassing customs and passport controls. Their 'reward' was a 4–0 thrashing.

But in the snow and ice of Belgrade in late January the tables were turned. Partizan's inspiration was tearaway centre-forward Milos Milutinovic, elder brother of Bora, the future World Cup managerial mercenary. At 3–0, Milutinovic shot past Madrid goalkeeper Juanito Alonso only to see the

ball stick in the goal-line slush. Madrid scrambled the ball clear and went into the semi-finals. Their players rolled in the snow in delight. Inside-left Jose Hector Rial breathed an icy sigh of relief. His contribution in Belgrade had been to miss a penalty.

In the semi-finals Madrid came through against tougher opponents in Milan but who had needed two contentious penalties converted by Giorgio Dal Monte to win 2–1 in a largely-deserted Stadio San Siro. Madrid, 4–2 winners at home, reached the final 5–4 on aggregate.

Reims had beaten Hibernian 2–0, 1–0 in a tight semi-final but when it came to the final star forward Raymond Kopa laced his boots before the game with his head in a whirl. He, more than anyone else, had been responsible for the inevitably-labelled champagne football which had brought Reims to the inaugural final.

Yet, then and there in the Parc des Princes which would become a second home for Reims in Europe, he knew that next season he would be playing for the Madrid club he was about to face.

At first it was all Reims. Michel Leblond and Jean Templin struck two goals in 10 minutes. Reims paused to catch their breath only to be caught first by Di Stefano then by fellow Argentine Hector Rial: 2–2 after half an hour.

Just after the hour Kopa's free kick was turned in by Michel Hidalgo, future manager of France, to restore Reims' lead. Not for long. Marquitos charged forward out of central defence and thumped home another equaliser for 3–3. Electric-heeled left winger Paco Gento then set up the winner for Rial.

In Madrid, Di Stefano celebrated, on his return, by buying his first car; in Manchester, an enthralled Matt Busby determined to raise a challenge.

UNITED ENTER THE FRAY

The future of top-level football lay in Europe. This much was obvious to Matt Busby, who defied the Football League to take his team abroad in a year when revolution turned Honved into exiles

England's football commanded wide respect in the game in the late 1950s despite the thrashings by Ferenc Puskas's Hungary in 1953 and 1954 and the embarrassing World Cup defeat by the United States in 1950. All that was missing was English engagement in Europe: an old story and not only in football terms.

Manchester United had different ideas. Their manager, Matt Busby, felt he had been granted a glimpse into the future after the competition's first season. When his magnificent young team of so-called 'Busby Babes' won the Football League in 1956 he had no doubt that Europe was the route to follow.

The Football League told United not to enter. United defied this injunction. Busby said: 'We don't fear congestion of fixtures. We have at least 18 players who can play in the first team without noticeably weakening us.' The 18 included the left-back and captain Roger Byrne, wing-halves Eddie Colman and the magnificent Duncan Edwards, centre-forward Tommy Taylor, a record signing at £29,999, wingers John Berry and David Pegg plus inside- forwards Billy Whelan, Dennis Viollet and the teenage Bobby Charlton.

United proved Busby's point in their opening tie by thrashing Belgian champions Anderlecht, which made it a painful homecoming for their manager, the former Blackburn goalkeeper Bill Gormlie. United won 2-0 in Brussels and by an imposing 10-0 back at Maine Road, their temporary European home from home while Old Trafford's floodlighting was installed. Viollet scored four, Taylor three.

Borussia Dortmund were beaten next and then the Basque club Bilbao, who had previously seen off the ageing greats of Hungary's army team, Honved.

Bilbao, coached by Kubala's Slovak father-in-law Ferdinand Daucik, had won 3-2 at home. Before the return could be staged, however, the Hungarian revolution erupted back in Budapest.

Honved's players decided not to go back to Hungary and arranged for the return with Bilbao to be played in Brussels. But in the Heysel stadium everything went wrong. The weather was freezing and, early on, goalkeeper Lajos Farago was injured. Substitutes not being permitted, left-winger Zoltan Czibor had to go in goal, and the 10 men of Honved could only draw 3-3.

Bilbao then fell to United in a memorable quarter-final. In Spain, on a quagmire of a pitch, the Basques led 3-0 at half-time, then 5-2 before Whelan pulled one more back with a remarkable solo effort. With ominous presentiment, United's players helped clear snow and ice off their plane for the return journey. They then completed the comeback with a straightforward 3-0 dispatch at home.

The holders had not enjoyed an easy ride, particularly against Rapid Vienna in the second round. Madrid won 4-2 at home but lost 3-1 in the Prater stadium within sight of the giant ferris wheel made famous by Carol Reed's film *The Third Man*. Veteran defender Ernst Happel scored a hat-trick from two free-kicks and a penalty.

RIGHT: **MATT BUSBY, MANAGER OF MANCHESTER UNITED, AT RINGWAY AIRPORT, MANCHESTER, BEFORE LEAVING FOR COLOGNE AND THE DRAW FOR THE SEMI-FINALS OF THE CHAMPIONS CUP**

If away goals had then counted double, Madrid would have been dead and buried. Instead level aggregate scores meant a play-off.

Madrid 'persuaded' Rapid to play back in the Bernabeu and duly won 2–0. Nice were defeated home and away, so the semi-finals lined up the old masters from Madrid against the young pretenders from Manchester. The Madrid–Manchester semi-final was a duel between teams from very different footballing cultures, sharing enormous mutual respect: United marvelled at Di Stefano's relentless energy and vision, while Madrid took the young giant Edwards to their hearts. Greater experience – plus goals from Rial, Di Stefano and Enrique Mateos – brought Madrid a 3–1 win in the Bernabeu. United thought they could turn the tie around, as they had against Bilbao. But Madrid were in a different class. Within 32 minutes of the kick-off at Maine Road they led 2–0 through Kopa and Rial. United, true to their perpetual nature, fought back but only for a 2–2 draw.

Busby, while admiring Madrid and Di Stefano, remained fervently convinced that his young team represented the European Cup's future. United's average age had barely risen above the low 20s whereas Madrid and Italian rivals Fiorentina were on the other end of the scale as they lined up in the afternoon sunshine in the Estadio Bernabeu. The original rules and regulations had deemed that one year's winners should host the next final: Madrid's early dominance soon saw that idea dispatched to the dustbin of football history.

Madrid showed three changes compared with Paris 12 months earlier, with Kopa having arrived from Reims. Fiorentina's tactic was classic Italian. Coach Fulvio Bernardini relied on a safety-first defence, a hard-working phalanx in midfield and the attacking inspiration of Brazil's Julinho at outside right, 'Pecos Bill' Virgili at centre-forward – so-called for his love of cowboy comics – and the underrated Argentinian, Miguel Montuori, at inside left.

It was a system devised to win, not entertain. Now it managed neither. Di Stefano scored first from a penalty and Gento's pace earned himself and Madrid a decisive second.

THURSDAY 30 MAY 1957
BERNABEU, MADRID

REAL MADRID	**2**
DI STEFANO 70 PEN, GENTO 76
FIORENTINA	**0**

HT: 0–0. ATT: 120,000.
REF: HORN (HOL)

REAL MADRID:
ALONSO - TORRES, MARQUITOS, LESMES - MUNOZ*, ZARRAGA - KOPA, MATEOS, DI STEFANO, RIAL, GENTO.
COACH: VILLALONGA.

FIORENTINA:
SARTI - MAGNINI, ORZAN, CERVATO* - SCARAMUCCI, SEGATO - JULINHO, GRATTON, VIRGILI, MONTUORI, PRINI.
COACH: BERNARDINI.

*CAPTAIN

THE SHADOW OF TRAGEDY

Aggrieved at past defeat, Milan set their sights on overhauling Real Madrid with a furious campaign of recruitment. But this season will always be remembered for the death of the Busby Babes

Milan are the older of the two Milanese clubs, founded in 1899 and thus nine years senior to splintering Internazionale. In the inter-war years Milano – the name change enforced by Benito Mussolini's *fascisti* – were second best in the city. At the start of the 1950s, however, new money and renewed ambition revived *rossoneri* (red and black) pride.

President Andrea Rizzoli sent his scouts far and wide. Sweden provided the greatest inside-forward trio in the club's history in Gunnar Gren, Gunnar Nordahl and Nils Liedholm. As they aged, so South America filled the gaps through the Argentine left-wing partnership of Ernesto Grillo and Tito Cucchiaroni alongside the Uruguayan world record signing Juan Alberto Schiaffino, the 1950 World Cup-winner who cost a then staggering fee of £72,000.

The supporting cast was Italian and included a promising young full-back or central defender named Cesare Maldini.

Milan believed they should have beaten Real Madrid in the 1956 semi-finals and that Madrid's European crown rightly belonged to them. Their revenge campaign began falteringly; they needed a first-round play-off to beat Rapid

Vienna. Elsewhere Benfica marked their Champions Cup debut with a 3-1 aggregate defeat by Sevilla and Manchester United put nine goals past Shamrock Rovers over two legs. Real Madrid's holders were awarded a bye into the second round, where they beat Antwerp 2-1 away, 6-0 at home with a Rial hat-trick.

The other major players also marched on. Manchester United, featuring more youngsters in centre-half Mark Jones, right-winger Ken Morgans and inside-forward Colin Webster, overcame Czechoslovak army club Dukla Prague and their astute left-half Jozef Masopust; Grillo scored twice for Milan against Rangers at Ibrox on the way to a 6-1 aggregate success.

In the quarter-finals Milan, without the injured Schiaffino both away and home, overcame Borussia Dortmund 1-1, 4-1 with Grillo again on target; Madrid humiliated their fellow Spaniards from Sevilla 2-2, 8-0. Di Stefano struck four in the Bernabeu.

But the most memorable quarter-final was between Red Star Belgrade and Manchester United. Red Star were

COUPE DES CLUBS CHAMPIONS
EUROPESE BEKER DER LANDSKAMPIOENEN

1958

REAL MADRID - AC MILAN

STADE DU HEYSEL / HEIZELSTADION

28-05-1958: BRUXELLES
BRUSSEL

PROGRAMME OFFICIEL / OFFICIEEL PROGRAMMA · 5 BF

RIGHT: **THE BUSBY BABES AFTER BEATING RED STAR 2-1 AT OLD TRAFFORD. A NAKED DUNCAN EDWARDS (CENTRE) IS SHOWN WITH (FROM THE LEFT) TOMMY TAYLOR, DENNIS VIOLLET, ROGER BYRNE, EDDIE COLMAN AND MARK JONES**

an outstanding side with a ballet-dancer in goal in Vladimir Beara, a gypsy playmaker in Dragoslav Sekularac and a left-winger in Bora Kostic who packed one of the most thunderous shots in European football. United won only 2-1 at home after being 1-0 down at half-time and recovering with goals from Charlton and Colman. That match was played on 14 January 1958.

So to Belgrade. Back in December bad weather had seen United struggle to find flights back from Prague in time for their weekend league fixture. This time, to eliminate any such risk, United decided to charter their own plane.

It was Charlton's first European trip and he was the first-half hero, scoring two superb goals as United went 3-0 ahead. Red Star refused to concede. Kostic scored once, Lazar Tasic converted a penalty and Viollet deflected a Kostic free-kick past 'keeper Harry Gregg. But only two minutes remained and United clung on.

The next day, 6 February, United flew for home and stopped to refuel at Munich's cold, snowy Riem airport. They landed shortly after 2.00 pm and the party of club officials, led by Busby, players, journalists and crew returned to the plane half an hour later. Twice, accelerating down the runway, captain James Thain aborted the take-off. The passengers returned to the airport lounge while attention was given to a 'slight technical fault'.

The third attempt to take off saw the Elizabethan pass the point of no return without leaving the ground. It careered through the perimeter fence, striking two small huts and a tree on its deathly path.

The 23 dead included eight journalists, eight players – captain Byrne, Colman, Jones, Whelan, Taylor, David Pegg, reserve full-back Geoff Bent and, after fighting on for 15 days, Edwards – and United's secretary Walter Crickmer trainer Tom Crickmer and chief coach Bert Whalley.

No surprise then, that a patched-up team lost 2-1, 0-4 in the semi-finals to a Milan side who needed to win the European Cup not only for pride but to return the following season. No such worries for Madrid. They had beaten Vasas of Hungary in the semis and lined up in Brussels still celebrating the 2-1 win at Zaragoza which had secured a sixth league title.

The first half was all Milan but they found their progress towards goal thwarted at apparently every step by Di Stefano – the ultimate exponent of 'total football' long before the term was coined. The next day an Italian journalist wrote: 'For an hour he played Milan on his own. Is this man a god?'

The inevitable happened almost on the hour when Schiaffino climaxed a quicksilver interpassing move with Liedholm and Grillo to open the scoring. Di Stefano, naturally, levelled only for Grillo to restore Milan's advantage. As the Italians called to their bench to check the time so Rial punished the momentary lapse of concentration by equalizing again.

The European cup final thus went into an extra half-hour for the first time. Early in the second period, a fizzing drive from Gento surprised keeper Soldan at the near post. Years later Gento conceded: 'I just hit it and hoped.'

THURSDAY 29 MAY 1958
HEYSEL, BRUSSELS

REAL MADRID	**3**
DI STEFANO 74, RIAL 79, GENTO 107	
MILAN	**2**
SCHIAFFINO 59, GRILLO 78	

HT: 0-0. AFTER EXTRA TIME (90 MIN: 2-2). ATT: 70,000.
REF: ALSTEEN (BEL).

REAL MADRID:
ALONSO* - ATIENZA, SANTAMARIA, LESMES - SANTISTEBAN, ZARRAGA - KOPA, JOSEITO, DI STEFANO, RIAL, GENTO. COACH: CARNIGLIA.

MILAN:
SOLDAN - FONTANA, C MALDINI, BERALDO - BERGAMASCHI, RADICE - DANOVA, LIEDHOLM*, SCHIAFFINO, GRILLO, CUCCHIARONI. COACH: VIANI.

*CAPTAIN

THE YEAR OF REVOLUTION

It was Pele who coined the expression 'The Beautiful Game' and teams throughout Europe were inspired to emulate the Brazilians after their World Cup win. However, old enmities were not forgotten

The summer of 1958 marked a watershed in not only European but world football. In June Brazil became the first nation to win the World Cup outside their own continent when they triumphed in Sweden.

They prompted new tactical awareness with their 4-2-4 system and won new respect through the established talents of playmaker Didi and the explosive emergence of outside-right Garrincha and the 17-year-old inside-left Edson Arantes do Nascimento, aka Pele.

Europe's resistance was led by two Frenchmen: Raymond Kopa and Just Fontaine, the man Reims had bought to fill the gap left by the little man's departure for Madrid in the summer of 1956.

Kopa, restricted to the right wing at Madrid by Di Stefano's centre-field dominance, was the creative genius behind a majority of Fontaine's record-breaking 13 goals in Sweden. The sum total of French World Cup inspiration and

Champions Cup victory with Madrid earned Kopa the 1958 European Footballer of the Year prize. But he was a loser where Madrid's internal politics were concerned.

Ferenc Puskas, scorer of 83 international goals in 84 games from inside-left, was one of the three members of Hungary's 'magical Magyars' who had decided to stay in western Europe after the collapse of the 1956 revolution back in Budapest.

The Hungarian federation attempted to ban Puskas, left-winger Zoltan Czibor and inside-right Sandor Kocsis for life from signing anywhere else. But other forces were at work behind the scenes.

Ladislav Kubala, the darling of Barcelona, had fled Hungary almost a decade earlier and built an admired new football life in Spain. He persuaded Barcelona to sign Kocsis and Czibor, while Puskas was rescued by Emil Osterreicher, the former Honved technical director

RIGHT: **ATLETICO MADRID GOALKEEPER PAZOS MAKES AN AMAZING FLYING SAVE FROM REAL MADRID'S RAYMOND KOPA. IT WAS THE FIRST OF TWO MADRID DERBIES - 55 YEARS APART**

who was now on the Real Madrid payroll. It was a major gamble, as Puskas was now past 30 and overweight through inaction. The gamble paid off, however, when the Hungarian averaged nearly a goal a game in his first season in the Spanish league.

The European challenge to Madrid's crown appeared to be led by Italy's Juventus, by the Fontaine-fired Reims and by Madrid's neighbours and Spanish runners-up Atletico.

Football is a funny game, at all levels. Juventus expected to crush Austria's Wiener Sportclub. The attacking partnership of the outrageous Argentine showman Omar Sivori and the Welsh 'gentle giant' John Charles had overwhelmed the rest of Serie A. For good measure Sivori added a hat-trick in the opening 3-1 win over the Austrians, an unknown quantity at this stage of the competition. But Juve, complacent, collapsed 7-0 in Vienna. It took them years to recover European Cup confidence

There were no such problems for Reims and Fontaine. Later Fontaine would be forced into premature retirement after twice breaking a leg, but while he was fit he was lethal. He scored six goals against Ards, two against Palloseura Helsinki and two more against Standard Liege. Young Boys Berne concentrated so hard on stopping Fontaine in the semi-final that they forgot about two-goal Roger Piantoni and Armand Penverne. Reims, beaten 1-0 in Berne, turned the tables 3-0 at home.

Wolves were a disappointment despite benefiting from a first-round bye before being drawn against West Germany's Schalke. German football was part-time and lacked a national league, but the pace of winger Bernie Klodt was too much for Wolves both at Molineux and back in the mining citadel of Gelsenkirchen, deep in the heart of the Ruhr. Schalke matched two goals from Peter Broadbent to draw 2-2 away then won 2-1 at home. In the quarter-finals, however, they lost 0-3, 1-1 to Atletico Madrid.

Atletico had pounced, after the World Cup finals, to sign Brazil's pugnacious centre-forward Vava. He scored in both legs against Schalke and posed a major threat to Real when the neighbours were drawn together in the semi-finals.

Madrid had found this title defence the most bruising. Di Stefano was sent off in the opening win over Turkey's Besiktas, and Puskas was dismissed in the subsequent defeat of Wiener SK. The Hungarian, who had trained alone for months to sweat off most of the extra kilos, made amends with the first-leg winner when Real edged Atletico 2-1 in the Bernabeu stadium.

Not far across town, in Atletico's Metropolitano, left-winger Enrique Collar struck back painfully. As in 1956-57,

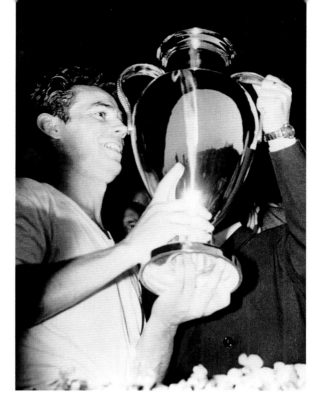

if away goals had counted double, Madrid would have gone out. Instead the play-off option provided the opportunity for a 2-1 win in neutral Zaragoza.

Di Stefano and Puskas scored the goals; Kopa would now face his old club in the final in Stuttgart. But unrest was stirring behind the scenes. Much of it swirled around Luis Carniglia, Madrid's Argentine coach.

Carniglia, a long-term sparring partner of Reims' Albert Batteux, had two selection issues. In goal Juanito Alonso had been taken ill so Rogelio Dominguez, after only five league games, was called in. In attack Puskas had a slight leg strain so, for all his 21 goals in 24 league games, he was omitted.

By contrast Reims came into the final with the advantage of fitness and a settled team.

Robert Jonquet was the commanding centre-back who had anchored France's defence in their run to third place at the 1958 World Cup; World Cup half-back partner Penverne wanted to make up for having missed the 1956 European final; Bruno Rodzik was a powerful raiding full-back; Rene Bliard and Roger Piantoni goalscoring inside-forwards; Jean Vincent an aggressive and pacy left-winger.

Not that it mattered. Madrid won comfortably, especially considering that they played half the match with 10 fit men after Kopa suffered a serious knee injury when taken down from behind by Vincent. Inside the second minute. Enrique Mateos opened the scoring. He also missed a penalty but Di Stefano shot Madrid decisively 2-0 ahead early in the second half.

WEDNESDAY 3 JUNE 1959
NECKAR, STUTTGART

REAL MADRID	**2**

MATEOS 2, DI STEFANO 47

REIMS	**0**

HT: 1-0. ATT: 72,000. REF: DUSCH (FR)

REAL MADRID:
DOMINGUEZ - MARQUITOS, SANTAMARIA, ZARRAGA* - SANTISTEBAN, RUIZ - KOPA, MATEOS, DI STEFANO, RIAL, GENTO. COACH: CARNIGLIA.

REIMS:
COLONNA - RODZIK, JONQUET*, GIRAUDO - PENVERNE, LEBLOND - LAMARTINE, BLIARD, FONTAINE, PIANTONI, VINCENT. COACH: BATTEUX.

*CAPTAIN

1960S

THE DECADE THAT SWUNG

The 1960s proved a decade of extremes for the European Champions Cup. Real Madrid began it wreathed in glory, only to be toppled by their old Spanish rivals Barcelona – who failed to capitalize on their achievement. Instead, it was Portugal's Benfica and the exciting Eusebio who briefly ruled the continent before being overtaken, in turn, by Italian pragmatism as represented by Milan and Internazionale. Latin Europe's domination then retreated in the face of a British invasion led by Celtic before Manchester United triumphantly sealed their own circle of fate. But already a new dawn was being promised by the Dutchmen of Ajax Amsterdam.

RIGHT: MATT BUSBY REVIVES MANCHESTER UNITED'S SPIRITS DURING THE 1968 FINAL JUST BEFORE EXTRA TIME BEGINS. IN THE BACKGROUND, YOU CAN SEE THE BENFICA PLAYERS. UNITED WON 4-1 IN THE END

EUSEBIO
(Eusebio da Silva Ferreira)

Country: Portugal

Position: Striker

Born: 25 January 1942

Died: 5 January 2014

Clubs: Sporting Lourenco
  Marques (Mozambique),
  Benfica (Por), Boston
  Minutemen (US), Monterrey
  (Mex), Toronto Metros
  (Can), Las Vegas Quicksilver
  (US), Beira-Mar (Por)

EUSEBIO

I am always surprised how many people continue to remember me, more than 40 years after winning the Champions Cup with Benfica.

A few years ago, the French presented me with the Borotra Trophy, which is a fair-play award in memory of their old tennis player. I was amazed. I thought my days for receiving trophies finished 30 years ago when the goals stopped.

Then, when Benfica built their new stadium for the European Championship finals in 2004, there was a suggestion that it might have been named after me – which would have been a great honour but not something I really wanted.

A football stadium is about a club and its fans; it's not just about one individual.

I had been proud enough, a few years earlier, when the club commissioned a statue of me to place at the stadium entrance. I had always associated such tributes in Portugal with our great statesmen and explorers.

Many great experiences came my way through football. The 1966 World Cup, when we reached the semi-finals in England, was a wonderful moment. But that was a one-off tournament. The prolonged high point was pulling on the red shirt of Benfica every week for a decade – once I had finally made it to Lisbon, that is.

Mozambique was still a Portuguese colony when I was a kid, and I played for Sporting Clube of Lourenco Marques, the capital, which is now known as Maputo. They were a sort of nursery club. We all knew that, if we were any good, one of the big Portuguese clubs would come in. The complication in my case was that both Sporting and Benfica wanted me.

Benfica made the first offer, and that was fine, but Lourenco Marques would not release me. So, even after I went to Lisbon and settled into the Benfica players' home, I could not play for them – even though I travelled to all their away games in the European Cup that season.

Finally, everything was sorted out eight days before we were to play Barcelona in the 1961 Champions Cup final. I thought I might have a chance of playing, but it turned out that UEFA had brought in a three-month transfer delay, so I was still ineligible.

In fact, I did not even go to the game. I had to listen to it on the radio because our coach, Bela Guttmann, wanted to keep me for a cup tie against Vitoria Setubal the next weekend. It's not a happy memory.

We lost and, though I scored a goal, I also missed a penalty which might have got us a play-off.*

My international baptism was not in the Champions Cup but in that year's end-of-season Paris Tournament, which was very prestigious in those days. We beat Anderlecht 2–1 in our semi-final – and I scored – and then we played the

LEFT: **EUSEBIO BEFORE PORTUGAL'S WORLD CUP QUARTER-FINAL AGAINST NORTH KOREA AT GOODISON IN 1966**

Brazilian club Santos, who had Pele playing for them, in the final.

Now, for me, Pele was the finest footballer of them all. He played in an era which had so many great players, yet he stood head and shoulders above them all.

He was the complete player in every respect, as well as being a very kindly human being. I have not seen anyone to compare, so imagine how I felt being on the same pitch with him for the first time.

Guttmann did not put me in the starting line-up. But after half an hour when we were losing 5-0 (!), he sent me on in place of Joaquin Santana. We would have needed a miracle, so I felt under no pressure and, perhaps because of that, I scored a hat-trick. In the end we lost 6-3, which was not so bad in the circumstances.

After that everything moved very fast. I scored again in the World Club Cup defeat against Penarol – we lost over there, in Uruguay, to a dubious penalty. Then I began my Portugal career in the qualifiers for the 1962 World Cup against Luxembourg and then against England at Wembley, the 'cathedral' of football.

Next we had the European Cup to defend, and this time I was in the team from the start.

I was lucky over the next 10 years to go all over Europe both as a player and just as me, Eusebio. But I have never met fans who are more passionate about football than the Portuguese. We soak up anything and everything about the game.

Look at the media here. We have three daily sports newspapers whose pages are mostly all about football. Not only that, but one daily sports paper sells more copies each day than any other newspaper of any sort.

Looking back, I think we built a lot of the legend of Portuguese football then. Before Benfica, Real Madrid had been the only club to have won the European Cup, so we were up at that level. We surpassed them, too, by beating them 5-3 in the 1962 final in Amsterdam. That was the game in which we were 3-2 down at half-time but Guttmann told us in the dressing room: 'Don't worry about a thing – we've got this all sewn up.'

That was when I was first called the Black Panther. Frankly, I did not like it, because there was a violent, revolutionary group in the United States with the same name. But it was meant as a compliment and I had no choice but to get used to it.

I did not like being called the 'European Pele' either. I thought that was disrespectful. Would Pele have appreciated being called 'America's Eusebio'? I doubt it somehow.

We should have beaten both Milan in the 1963 final and Inter in 1965. I have to say we could not begrudge Manchester United in 1968, even though my miss just before the end of the 90 minutes was probably the blackest moment of my career.

But with the Italian clubs it was different. Against Milan over-confidence meant we lost a game in which I scored first and which we had all but won; against Inter I needed a painkilling injection before the game and I played badly.

We also suffered crucial injuries during both finals in the days before substitutes were permitted. Luck was not with us.

Sometimes football is like that.

* The goalkeeper who saved Eusebio's first senior competitive penalty was Felix Mourinho, father of Jose Mourinho, the later Chelsea manager

LEFT: **KNOWN AS THE BLACK PANTHER, EUSEBIO WAS VOTED EUROPEAN FOOTBALLER OF THE YEAR IN 1965; HE WAS ALSO TOP SCORER IN THE 1966 WORLD CUP FINALS**

THE BRAIN GAME

The old-fashioned virtues of English football were put to the test as Barcelona took on Wolves. In a new tactical era, team play came to the fore as Eintracht Frankfurt stole almost unnoticed into the final

Wolverhampton Wanderers were back, determined to get it right this time. Their famous floodlit friendlies had prompted the creation of the European Champions Cup, but they had let themselves down badly the previous season. Manager Stan Cullis believed in the winning qualities of traditional English football, in spite of the evidence provided by Hungary and Real Madrid. For him, strength in defence, hard work in midfield, versatile inside-forwards and pacy wingers provided the hardware.

Wolves were changing. Billy Wright had retired, virtually overnight, after returning from England's summer tour to the Americas to find that Cullis was grooming George Showell to take his place in the heart of defence. The veteran left-winger Jimmy Mullen, one of the heroes against Honved and Spartak, had also been removed from the attacking equation.

Wolves started in East Germany against the army club, Vorwarts, from East Berlin. The communist takeover of eastern European had revolutionized sports administration. The main ministries and public utilities had either swallowed up the independent pre-war clubs or created new ones in their own authoritarian image. But the gain in financial subsidies was balanced, negatively, by the loss of foreign influences in both coaching and player sectors.

The ability of army clubs throughout eastern Europe to order conscripts into their playing ranks brought league titles aplenty for Vorwarts in the German Democratic Republic, Legia in Poland, Dukla in Czechoslovakia, CDNA (later CSKA) in Bulgaria, CCA (later Steaua) in Romania and Partizani in Albania, though not, oddly, CSKA in Russia.

Vorwarts played like good soldiers obeying orders: all discipline, no individual flair. They edged Wolves 2–1 at home and lost 2–0 at Molineux. The England inside-forward Peter Broadbent scored both away and home.

The next step was an emotional one: to Belgrade to play Red Star, last opponents of the Busby Babes before the Munich disaster. Six of the Red Star team who drew 3–3 with United now faced Wolves, including Beara, Sekularac, Tasic and Kostic. Again the outcome was a draw, this time 1–1, and Jimmy Murray scored twice as Wolves rampaged home 3–0 in the return.

That meant the quarter-finals and a meeting with Barcelona. The rest of the world had yet to fall for the Catalan 'romance' but their pedigree was clear.

They had triumphed in the first Fairs Cup in 1958, had won five Spanish league titles in nine seasons and boasted some of the world's finest players in the Hungarians Kubala, Sandor Kocsis and Zoltan Czibor, Brazil's Evaristo de Macedo and arguably Spain's greatest-ever player, Luis Suarez, who later played with Internazionale.

Wielding a demanding conductor's baton was a coach who had been born in Morocco, brought up in Argentina, played in France then made his coaching name in Spain: Helenio Herrera.

Now it was Wolves' turn to be intimidated by the four-square cliffs of the Nou Camp. Barcelona trounced them 4–0. It was a cosmopolitan collapse. Paraguayan winger Ramon Villaverde scored two, Kubala and Evaristo the others. Kocsis, one of the scourges of England in 1953 and 1954, scored four as Barça won 5–2 at Molineux. Barcelona,

RIGHT: **RON FLOWERS SHAKES HANDS WITH LUIS SUAREZ AFTER BARCELONA HAD BEATEN WOLVES 4–0 IN THE NOU CAMP IN FRONT OF A CROWD OF 80,000. WOLVES LOST THE SECOND LEG 5–2 AT HOME**

having earlier beaten Milan, considered themselves favourites to deprive Madrid of their European crown just as they had deposed Real as champions of Spain. Years later Di Stefano acknowledged: 'They had the better individuals,' then added after a pause, 'but we had the better team.'

Madrid duly won 3–1 both in the Bernabeu and in the Nou Camp. Furious Barcelona fans chased Herrera down the Ramblas and out of town.

In the final Madrid confronted the unconsidered, underrated Germans of Eintracht Frankfurt, first non-Latin team to progress thus far.

The clubs will be forever linked by events on that Glasgow evening of 18 May 1960. 'The greatest game ever played,' is the label which has sealed the legend of this match down the years. For later fans, flickering black-and-white TV images offer a dreamy, slow-motion quality. Oceanic expanses of pitch open up between players and protection for two hapless goalkeepers appears vague.

But greatness is born of context and nothing like it had been seen before. Without Real Madrid and the glamour of this one match the European Cup would not have sparked the international awakening of commercial and media giants.

The outcome was a surprise to the record 127,621 jamming Hampden. Frankfurt had pulverized Glasgow's own Rangers 12–4 on aggregate in the semi-finals.

In the final they even took the lead through veteran right winger Richard Kress. But Madrid struck back gloriously. The ball flowed from one white shirt to another with Di Stefano linking every phase of play and Puskas deadly at the attacking apex. Di Stefano scored three, Puskas four; in consolation, Stein replied with a late double for Frankfurt.

The game cast around desperately in search of new superlatives.

WEDNESDAY 18 MAY 1960
HAMPDEN PARK, GLASGOW

REAL MADRID   7
DI STEFANO 26, 29, 74,
PUSKAS 44, 56 PEN, 60, 71

EINTRACHT FRANKFURT   3
KRESS 18, STEIN 72, 76

HT: 3–1. ATT: 127,621.
REF: MOWAT (SCOT)

REAL MADRID:
DOMINGUEZ – MARQUITOS, SANTA-MARIA, PACHIN – VIDAL, ZARRAGA* – CANARIO, DEL SOL, DI STEFANO, PUSKAS, GENTO. COACH: MUNOZ.

EINTRACHT FRANKFURT:
LOY – LUTZ, EIGENBRODT. HOFER – WEILBACHER, STINKA – KRESS, LINDNER, STEIN, PFAFF*, MEIER. COACH: OSSWALD.

*CAPTAIN.

LEFT: **ALL-WHITE ON THE NIGHT: REAL'S PLAYERS CELEBRATE VICTORY ON THE LEGENDARY EVENING WHEN GOALS RAINED DOWN ON GLASGOW**

BELOW: **VAST NUMBERS OF FANS ROLL UP AT HAMPDEN PARK BEFORE THE CHAMPIONS CUP FINAL IN 1960. A RECORD CROWD OF 127,621 WAS TO SEE ONE OF THE GREATEST GAMES EVER PLAYED**

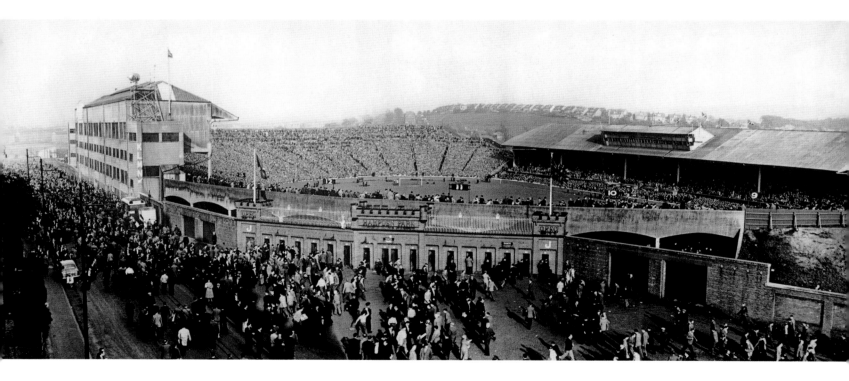

THE EAGLES HAVE LANDED

Football's spotlight turned further west with the arrival of Benfica as a major European power. They started as also-rans but picked up momentum as likely contenders dropped like flies along the way

Different times, different rules. Italy and Spain, increasingly concerned about the failings of their national teams, tightened restrictions on player imports. This trend was not one, however, to worry the champions of Portugal.

Benfica, the Eagles of Lisbon, had never signed a foreign player, but foreign coaches were a different matter. The man who led them into the 1960–61 Champions Cup was Bela Guttmann, a wandering Hungarian who had been on the coaching staff of the Magical Magyars in the early 1950s.

Guttmann had once, famously, been sacked by Milan while they were top of the table; during a spell in Brazil he claimed to have taught the future World Cup winners the 4–2–4 system. On arrival at Benfica, however, he decided his players were better suited to the traditional WM.

That did not go down well with players converted to 4–2–4 by Guttmann's Brazilian predecessor, Otto Gloria. In particular, it was not to the liking of midfield general Mario Coluna. He resented being 'restricted' to the inside-left channel. But Guttmann's gift was in knowing players better than they knew themselves; he also converted Jose Augusto from a creative centre-forward into the best right-winger in Europe after Kopa.

Real Madrid, as holders, had their usual bye through the opening round. The Merengues put the time to profitable use by winning the inaugural World Club Cup. Madrid held Penarol of Uruguay goalless in the Montevideo rain then thrashed them 5–1 back in Madrid. By that time, Di Stefano, Puskas and co were already thinking ahead to their Champions Cup defence: they would open against Barcelona.

Open... and close. Herrera having gone to Internazionale, Ladislav Kubala was restored to primacy at the Nou Camp. His creative partnership with Luis Suarez, in support of Kocsis and Evaristo up front, flared triumphantly. Suarez scored twice, once from a penalty, in the 2–2 draw in Madrid. Kubala then dropped back on the Barcelona right wing to smother the threat of Gento in the return. Madrid, with Pachin a limping passenger for much of the game, had three goals disallowed by referee Reg Leafe and lost 2–1.

'UEFA people didn't like us dominating "their" cup,' said a jaundiced Di Stefano later. 'That's why they got English referees to make sure we didn't. After all, English referees were supposed to be the best. No one would suspect anything.'

RIGHT: **ENGLISH REFEREE REG LEAFE DISALLOWS A GOAL TO THE VISIBLE DISBELIEF OF GENTO, PUSKAS AND VIDAL DURING THE SECOND-ROUND SECOND LEG AGAINST BARCELONA**

With Madrid gone, the cup was perceived as a shoo-in for Barcelona. The pyramid of power was built to their design. In the semi-finals Barcelona beat Hamburg, who had defeated the home-grown purists of Burnley – who had previously beaten Reims; injuries kept Fontaine out of the first leg, Kopa out of the second.

The signs were ominous for Barcelona in their semi-final. Hamburg were built on the bullish attacking fire of Uwe Seeler, the pace of left-winger Gerd Dorfel and the half-back support of Seeler's elder brother, Dieter.

Evaristo scored the lone goal in the Nou Camp, but goals from Peter Wulf and Uwe Seeler back in Germany put Hamburg on course for the final with 90 seconds left. Then Kocsis lived up to his nickname of 'Golden Head' to level the aggregate. The away-goals rule was yet to be adopted, so the teams had to play off at the Heysel stadium in Brussels. A lone goal from Evaristo settled it. All that was left for Barcelona was the academic matter of beating Benfica in the final in Berne.

Benfica possessed talented players who had grown in stature and confidence with each succeeding round as they dismissed Hearts, Hungary's Ujpest, Denmark's Aarhus and Rapid Vienna,

A number of Benfica's team, including Coluna, had been discovered in Africa, in Mozambique and Angola; but because these were colonies their footballers did not count as foreigners in Portugal. Another was Jose Aguas, the Benfica captain and centre-forward. In Angola he had earned local fame as a teenaged lion-hunter. Benfica had brought him to Lisbon and taught him to hunt goals.

Barcelona did not arrive in Bern for the final in the best of shape after coaching and cash confusion.

But worst of all was the superstition factor. Seven years earlier Sandor Kocsis and Zoltan Czibor had lined up in this same old wooden stadium for Hungary against West Germany in the 1954 World Cup Final. Hungary were far greater favourites then than even Barcelona now but they had lost 3-2; it was the Magical Magyars' first defeat in four years in the match which mattered the most.

History repeated itself. Barcelona led through Kocsis but Aguas, an own goal from 'keeper Antoni Ramallets and Mario Coluna put Benfica ahead. Barcelona fought back. Kubala saw a shot hit one post and ricochet back into play off the other upright; Kocsis had a header cleared off the line.

Quarter of an hour from time Czibor smacked home a second goal for Barcelona. But, as in 1954, he and Kocsis were again 3-2 losers.

THE NEW SOPHISTICATION

Formations were shuffled as European sides sought to capture a little of the magic Brazil had brought to the game. Real Madrid rang the changes as the draw set them on a collision course with Benfica

While the 1950s had been a golden age of creative football, the 1960s would prove an era of increasing negativity in which the importance of not losing outweighed the importance of winning.

Tactical shifts went into overdrive. Even England caught the trend. In the autumn of 1960 manager Walter Winterbottom adopted Brazil's 4-2-4 with a midfield run by right-half Bobby Robson and inside-left Johnny Haynes.

The results were remarkable. England scored 44 goals in eight games. Italian clubs took note. Welshman John Charles was an established legend in his own air space at Juventus. Now he was joined by England centre-forward Gerry Hitchens at Internazionale and Jimmy Greaves at Milan.

Workmanlike Hitchens stayed for a decade; Greaves, hating the dictatorship of coach Nereo Rocco, flew home after scoring nine goals in 12 games. A rising star at Chelsea, he returned for £99,999 to Tottenham; manager Bill Nicholson deliberately refused to make this goal-poacher supreme the English game's first £100,000 footballer.

Greaves strengthened a Spurs side who had, the previous May, become the first league and FA Cup double-winners of the twentieth century.

But he had to wait three months before he could play in the Champions Cup. UEFA had introduced a registration 'gap' to prevent any repetition of Real Madrid's overnight acquisitions of Miguel Torres in 1957 and Luis del Sol in 1960.

Even with Greaves in the stands, Tottenham did not do so badly, although it was far from easy. They were 4-0 down against Gornik in Poland in the first round but snatched back two late goals, then crushed the Poles 8-1 at White Hart Lane. Flying winger Cliff Jones scored a hat-trick on the first of the glory, glory nights.

Members of the Fleet Street press were not being immodest in suggesting that Spurs had the potential beating of all the rest.

Feyenoord lost 4-2 on aggregate, as did Dukla Prague in the quarter-finals. Nicholson and his loquacious Northern Irish captain Danny Blanchflower used reserve wing-half

Tony Marchi - back from a defensive education in Italy with Torino - as an extra defender for the away leg.

Joining Spurs in the semi were holders Benfica, former holders Real Madrid and the first Belgians to reach the last four, Standard Liege. The luck of the draw fell to Madrid, who snagged Standard; Tottenham drew Benfica.

Not that Madrid found it easy. After winning 1-0 away to Juventus in the quarter-final opener, they suffered their first European home defeat by the same margin in the return. Argentine Omar Sivori, Juve's European Footballer of the Year, scored the historic goal.

Sivori hated flying, so Juventus took the train from Turin to Paris for the play-off in the Parc des Princes. Ice and snow delayed their arrival and they appeared still half asleep when Felo put Madrid ahead within minutes of the kick-off. Santamaria gave Charles a 90-minute kicking and Madrid saw it out 3-1.

RIGHT: **THE GREAT EUSEBIO PLAYS KEEPY-UPPY DURING A BREAK FROM TRAINING AT THE WHITE CITY STADIUM BEFORE THE MATCH WITH TOTTENHAM HOTSPUR**

WEDNESDAY 2 MAY 1962
OLYMPIC, AMSTERDAM

BENFICA   **5**
AGUAS 25, CAVEM 34, COLUNA 61,
EUSEBIO 68 PEN, 78

REAL MADRID   **3**
PUSKAS 17, 23, 38

HT: 2-3. ATT: 68,000. REF: HORN (HOL)

BENFICA:
COSTA PEREIRA – MARIO JOAO,
GERMANO, ANGELO – CAVEM, CRUZ
– JOSE AUGUSTO, EUSEBIO, AGUAS*,
COLUNA, SIMOES.
COACH: GUTTMANN.

REAL MADRID:
ARAQUISTAIN – CASADO, SANTAMARIA,
PACHIN, MIERA – FELO, DI STEFANO,
DEL SOL – TEJADA, PUSKAS, GENTO*.
COACH: MUNOZ.

*CAPTAIN.

LEFT: **EUSEBIO KISSES THE CUP IN THE BENFICA DRESSING ROOM AFTER THE 5-3 VICTORY OVER REAL MADRID**

Standard's victims on the way to the semi-finals included Rangers, against whom Irish inside-forward Johnny Crossan scored twice. Crossan had built a continental career, first with Sparta Rotterdam, after being barred from the English game over a transfer wrangle. But his Belgians were no match for Madrid, losing both home and away and failing to score.

Benfica had started the season with defeat by Penarol in the World Club Cup but their attack had been powered up by the remarkable Eusebio. The youngster from Mozambique had made a stunning substitute's debut against Pele's Santos in the 1961 Paris tournament, then lit up Wembley for Portugal in a World Cup qualifier.

He scored his first Champions Cup goals in Benfica's opening defeat of FK Austria and followed up with two more against Nurnberg. He failed to score against Spurs in the semi-finals, but Aguas and Jose Augusto (twice) did the damage in Lisbon – despite the Marchi Plan – and Aguas struck early on back at White Hart Lane. Spurs, driven on heroically by left-half Dave Mackay, stormed back to win but only by 2-1.

Hindsight suggests that the 1962 final in Amsterdam was better even than 1960. Benfica benefited from stability plus the explosive arrival of Eusebio but Puskas caught them twice on the counter-attack.

Fortunately for Benfica, Aguas pulled one back almost immediately from close range and Domiciano Cavem equalised with a 25-yard drive which keeper Jose Araquistain blamed on poor floodlighting. No matter, Puskas completed his 21-minute hat-trick by restoring Madrid's lead.

At White Hart Lane in the semi-finals, it was Benfica who had born the brunt of a second-half rally. Now the boot was on the other foot. They answered the challenge superbly, raising the tempo and equalizing again, this time with another long-range thunderbolt from Coluna.

Madrid revived. Justo Tejada headed against the crossbar; referee Leo Horn turned down a penalty claim; and a Di Stefano shot rattled against the legs of the floundering Costa Pereira.

Benfica flew back down the other end and Eusebio thundered two match-winning goals beyond shell-shocked Araquistain in the space of three minutes: one from a penalty, one from a free kick. Benfica were European champions for the second and, as it turned out, last time.

ITALIANS ON THE COUNTER-STRIKE

Goals rained in as the strong mercilessly ripped apart the defences of the weak in the first round. Milan emerged at the head of the food chain as the Italians sought to win the European Cup for the first time

ABOVE: **IPSWICH TOWN'S TED PHILLIPS RISES ABOVE FLORIANA'S LOLLY DEBATTISTA TO SCORE ONE OF HIS TEAM'S FOUR GOALS**

Benfica were now recognized as worthy champions. The 1961 triumph had been considered a fleeting oddity. Now, even though Bela Guttmann had left and Aguas was winding down, they were accepted as the team to beat. Milan and Real Madrid were more challengers than contenders. Surprising Ipswich Town, pragmatically fashioned by future England manager Alf Ramsey, were not expected to last long. Similarly, little was expected of Scotland's Dundee, managed by Bob Shankly, whose brother Bill was south of the border breathing life and fire back into Liverpool.

Barely apparent at the time was the rising force of Benelux football. Feyenoord from Rotterdam returned for a second successive season. Eddy Pieters-Grafland in goal had been a Champions Cup pioneer in the late 1950s with Ajax; Coen Moulijn was a 'thinking' outside-left; Reiner Kreyermaat a steamrolling right-half.

Out of Belgium came Anderlecht. Few clubs had learned their lessons so avidly. This was not the naïve outfit put to the 12-goal sword by Manchester United in 1957. Now they had their own Hungarian émigré in goalkeeper Arpad Fazekas; outstanding home-grown defenders in Laurent Verbiest and Martin Lippens; a sharp-thinking, bespectacled general in Jef Jurion; and a striker in Paul Van Himst who was destined to become his country's greatest-ever footballer.

Anderlecht were bound together by French coach Pierre Sinibaldi, a pre-Kopa star at Reims, in a 4-2-4 system based on perpetual possession of the ball plus an offside trap. The surprise factor was immense, and beyond Real Madrid in the first round. The Spanish season had not started when rusty Real were shocked to be held 3-3 at home, then defeated 1-0 in Brussels. Jurion struck the late, late winner.

Elsewhere, goals rained in. Milan hit eight in their first leg against Union Luxembourg, with their Brazilian centre-forward Jose Altafini scoring five. Dundee put eight past the woeful West Germans of Koln at Dens Park. Ipswich topped that by smacking a round 10 past Floriana of Malta to complete a 14-1 aggregate; Ray Crawford scored two in Malta and five back at Portman Road.

Benfica and Reims alone were granted byes into the second round, where Kopa scored twice as the French hit back from first-leg defeat to overwhelm FK Austria. It was all down to Kopa now; Fontaine, having twice broken a leg, would never play again.

The holders eased gently into their defence, with Eusebio ever more greedy for goals. Against Norrkoping of Sweden he claimed his first European hat-trick.

The rest of the round went according to the status quo. That included Milan's beating of Ipswich by 3-0, 1-2. Left-winger Paolo Barison was their main man. He scored twice at the San Siro and once more at Portman Road. He also scored again in the 8-1 dismissal of Galatasaray which secured a semi-final against Dundee.

Feyenoord, meanwhile sprang a surprising away win over Reims courtesy of a long-range cracker from Kreyermaat which secured a semi-final against Benfica. Mario Coluna, now back as the fulcrum in Benfica's reversion to 4-2-4 under Chilean coach Fernando Riera, scored twice to see off Dukla Prague.

Portuguese skill proved too much for Dutch determination in the one semi-final, while Dundee had their own bubble punctured in the San Siro. Milan, held 1-1 in the first half, ran away after the break to win 5-1. Wingers Bruno Mora and the unstoppable Barison scored two apiece.

Milan thus challenged Benfica for their crown in Wembley's first hosting of the final. Riera's coaching reign had started ominously with a spectacular double-leg defeat by Pele's Santos in the World Club Cup. But he had promised to emulate Real Madrid's five-in-a-row European Cups and, in the midweek afternoon sunshine, the dream appeared reasonable.

On the opposite bench sat Nereo Rocco, a rough, tough sergeant-major of a coach. His disciplinary ferocity had driven Jimmy Greaves out of Milan early the previous season. But the Brazilian anchor Dino Sani and the classically gifted youngster Gianni Rivera coped equably.

Rocco's defence was marshalled by Cesare Maldini, now the captain and only survivor from Milan's beaten finalists of 1958. The attack was led by Jose Altafini, known in Brazil as Mazzola because of his resemblance to the captain of Torino who had died in the 1949 Superga air disaster.

Eusebio struck early in the first half and Milan grew more aggressive. Gino Pivatelli caught Coluna late and awkwardly. Benfica's captain limped through the rest of the match and Benfica lost their grip.

Rivera, whose half-share, as a teenager, had cost Milan £65,000 from Alessandria, glided into his own. His nimble footwork created both the equaliser and then the winner for Altafini, the Brazilian's record 13th and 14th goals of the campaign.

WEDNESDAY 22 MAY 1963
WEMBLEY, LONDON

MILAN	2
ALTAFINI 58, 66	
BENFICA	1
EUSEBIO 18	

HT: 0-1. ATT: 45,000.
REF: HOLLAND (ENG)

MILAN:
GHEZZI - C. MALDINI* - DAVID, BENITEZ, TREBBI - DINO SANI, TRAPATTONI, PIVATELLI - MORA, ALTAFINI, RIVERA.
COACH: ROCCO.

BENFICA:
COSTA PEREIRA - CAVEM, HUMBERTO, RAUL, CRUZ - SANTANA, COLUNA* - JOSE AUGUSTO, TORRES, EUSEBIO, SIMOES.
COACH: RIERA.

*CAPTAIN.

LEFT: **MILAN'S CESARE MALDINI TAKES THE BALL OFF BENFICA'S EUSEBIO ON THE EDGE OF MILAN'S PENALTY AREA**

THE SCIENCE OF SHUTTING UP SHOP

With Alfredo Di Stefano and Ferenc Puskas slipping into their footballing dotage, the game's philosophy took a defensive turn as Helenio Herrera's Inter Milan set foot on the road to success

Everton won the league in England, Real Madrid in Spain, Benfica in Portugal, Rangers in Scotland, PSV Eindhoven in Holland, Standard Liege in Belgium... and Internazionale in Italy for the first time in nine years.

What was important was not only securing the *Scudetto* but the manner in which it was achieved. Helenio Herrera may have pulled all the attacking strings at Barcelona, but in Italy he had become the high priest of defensive football.

To be fair, Herrera had not changed his mind the moment Barcelona fans chased him out of town and into the arms of Inter's oil tycoon owner Angelo Moratti back in 1960. But impatient Inter had gone through 13 coaches in five years before Herrera marched in, and he knew that something very different was needed: the ultimate in *catenaccio*, the bolt defence with a sweeper and single-minded man-for-man marking.

27. MAI 1964
EUROPACUP-FINALSPIEL

Preis S 3.-

F. C. INTERNAZIONALE MILANO –
REAL MADRID C. F.

HERAUSGEGEBEN VOM ÖSTERREICHISCHEN FUSSBALL-BUND
IM AUFTRAG DER U.E.F.A.

RIGHT: **MASTER OF** *CATENACCIO*, **HELENIO HERRERA, SMILES UNDER THE FLOODLIGHTS OF VIENNA'S PRATER STADIUM AFTER HIS INTERNAZIONALE TEAM HAD BEATEN REAL MADRID IN THE 1964 FINAL**

Everton's ill fortune was to be drawn against Inter in the first round. The first leg was at Goodison. Only two foreigners were permitted in Italian teams in Serie A and Herrera's first choices were Luis Suarez in midfield and Brazilian right-winger Jair.

Specifically for Europe, though, Inter had signed the rugged German wing-half Horst Szymaniak. He helped shut up shop for a goalless draw at Goodison; Jair scored the only goal of the tie back in Milan.

The financial support of the ruling Grimaldi family was not enough to save Monaco against Inter in the second round; the nucleus of what would be the 1966 runners-up team was not enough to save Partizan Belgrade in the quarter-finals; and a couple of future World Cup silver-medallists could not carry the day for Borussia Dortmund in the semi-finals.

Hans Tilkowski was the Dortmund goalkeeper, and Lothar Emmerich a goalscoring hammer of an outside-left. He hit Lyn Oslo for a first-round hat-trick.

Next time out Dortmund lost only 2–1 away to Benfica, then humiliated the ex-champions 5–0 back in the Ruhr at Rote Erde; this time centre-forward Franz Brungs scored the hat-trick.

The other ex-champions, Real Madrid, had better luck. Frenchman Lucien Muller, another Reims graduate, was now Di Stefano's aide-de-camp in midfield and Amancio Amaro a darting new outside-right.

But the old boys remained a danger: Di Stefano was being slowed by sciatica, but Puskas, despite some extra kilos, was still lethal in front of goal. He scored the lone winner away to Rangers at Ibrox in the first round and then a hat-trick in their 6–0 win back in Madrid.

Next up were holders Milan. But not the tight, confident Milan of the previous May. Rocco had been replaced as coach by Madrid's old boss, Luis Carniglia; Amarildo, Pele's World Cup-winning deputy with Brazil in Chile in 1962, had been added to the attack.

The mix had not worked against Santos in the World Club Cup, and it did not work against Madrid, even though the Spaniards had Felix Ruiz carried off with a fractured collar-bone during the first leg, which they won 4–1. Amancio, Puskas, Di Stefano and Gento scored the goals.

Injury robbed Milan of Gianni Rivera in attack and Cesare Maldini in defence for the second leg. They won 2–0 but it was not quite enough. Madrid cruised past Zurich in the semis to serve a very different challenge from Milan.

No romance about Inter. Where Milan's Gianni Rivera was a classical creator, his cross-town contemporary

Sandrino Mazzola was an attacking king of open spaces. Mazzola was five when his father, Italy captain Valentino, had been killed in the Torino air disaster. He was always considered destined for stardom and had the support to achieve it.

Giuliano Sarti, a European runner-up with Fiorentina in 1957, was an ice-cool goalkeeper; Tarcisio Burgnich and Giacinto Facchetti were pacy, ruthless full-backs; Aristide Guarneri an effective stopper; protecting them all was Armando Picchi, a ruthless sweeper rarely if ever to be found even level with his back line. Spaniard Luis Suarez provided the creative style.

In Vienna's Prater stadium the old boys of Madrid had more of the possession but none of the openings. Just before half-time Facchetti caught Amancio dawdling and fed Mazzola. His snap shot bounced awkwardly in front of keeper Jose Vicente and slithered through his grasp into the net.

Vicente was at fault again in the second half when a speculative shot from Aurelio Milani gave Inter a second goal. Felo pulled one back, breaching Inter's defence from a corner. But another slip, this time by Jose Santamaria, gifted Mazzola a third. Herrera and Suarez, at last, were champions of Europe.

ABOVE: **TARCISIO BURGNICH (LEFT) AND GIACINTO FACCHETTI, INTERNAZIONALE'S HARDBITTEN FULL-BACKS, POSE FOR A VICTORY PORTRAIT**

WEDNESDAY 27 MAY 1964
PRATER, VIENNA

INTERNAZIONALE 3
MAZZOLA 43, 76, MILANI 62
REAL MADRID 1
FELO 69

HT: 1–0. ATT: 72,000. REF: STOLL (AUS)

INTERNAZIONALE:
SARTI - PICCHI* - BURGNICH, GUARNERI, FACCHETTI - TAGNIN, SUAREZ, CORSO - JAIR, MAZZOLA, MILANI.
COACH: HERRERA.

REAL MADRID:
VICENTE - ISIDRO, SANTAMARIA, ZOCO, PACHIN - MULLER, DI STEFANO, FELO - AMANCIO, PUSKAS, GENTO*.
COACH: MUNOZ.

*CAPTAIN.

THE QUALITY OF MERSEY

Under the guidance of Bill Shankly with his Boot Room philosophy, Liverpool rumbled into life as a team to be feared in Europe. But the Reds had a lot to learn and were put to the sword in the semis

The blue half of the proud scouser city of Liverpool had already earned a crack at the European Cup and the Toffee Men of Everton had come unstuck at the first hurdle. Now the Reds had their chance. It was the era of Beatlemania and the Merseybeat and Liverpool, under the unique managerial leadership of Bill Shankly, caught the rhythm to perfection.

Indeed, long after the Beatles had all gone their separate ways, Liverpool would still be conducting the English football orchestra in continental competition. Shankly with his assistant and then successor Bob Paisley breathed a 90-minute fire into their teams and players which matched the new-fangled all-red strip.

Shankly's ferocious commitment was summed up by his most renowned aphorism: 'People say football is a matter of life and death. Well, they're wrong. It's more serious than that.'

Liverpool, in 1964, had won their first league title in 17 years. They lined up for the draw alongside a phalanx of European old boys: Rangers, Red Star, Rapid, Anderlecht, Dukla, Gornik, Real Madrid, Benfica and Internazionale.

In those days, long before seeding was introduced, the luck of the draw held sway. Thus Red Star went out immediately to Rangers, who then disposed of Rapid. Dukla saw off Gornik after a first-round play-off but lost to Madrid, whose new hero Amancio scored a hat-trick in the Bernabeu first leg. Madrid then crashed to Benfica, losing 5–1 in Lisbon and winning only 2–1 back in the Bernabeu, where Puskas missed a penalty.

Where was Di Stefano when they needed him? He had gone, at the end of the previous season, after refusing to concede to president Santiago Bernabeu that age had caught up with him. He had scored a record 49 Champions Cup goals in 141 games. Ironically, he left Madrid on a free transfer for a two-year spell with Espanol of Barcelona, where old rival Ladislav Kubala was player-coach.

Benfica scored five without reply in the semi-final against the Hungarians of Vasas Gyor, astutely guided by 1950s legend Nandor Hidegkuti. That lifted them into the final in Milan where, to Portuguese fury, they found Inter waiting – on their home ground.

Inter qualified for their title defence as holders. They had lost the Italian league crown in 1964 amid controversy. Bologna had led throughout the spring but were then

RIGHT: **LIVERPOOL'S ROGER HUNT FALLS UNDER THE CHALLENGE OF INTER MILAN'S ARISTIDE GUARNERI AND LUIS SUAREZ AS ARMANDO PICCHI APPEALS TO THE REFEREE**

LEFT: BENFICA'S EUSEBIO TRIES TO GET HOLD OF THE BALL AS ARMANDO PICCHI (6) PREPARES TO INTERVENE. EVERYTHING FELL APART FOR THE PORTUGUESE SIDE AS THEY SUBSIDED TO DEFEAT AMID TORRENTIAL CLOUDBURSTS

penalized nine points after half a dozen players failed dope tests. Bologna's lawyers ultimately had the charges and punishments thrown out, but the disruption cost them dear. Inter finished level on points before Bologna, spearheaded by Denmark's Harald Nielsen and West Germany's Helmut Haller, had the last laugh by winning a title play-off in Rome.

Ironically, Bologna were knocked out of Europe, by Anderlecht in a first-round play-off, before Inter had even started their campaign. Once they did, Dinamo Bucharest were crushed 6-0, 1-0 and Rangers outclassed 3-1, 0-1. Now it was Liverpool's turn to face Herrera's mystic machine in the semi-final.

Liverpool roared into the game fresh from their FA Cup Final triumph over Leeds. Injured heroes Gerry Byrne and Gordon Milne paraded the trophy around Anfield before kick-off, and the Kop greeted Inter with choruses of 'Go back to Italy' to the tune of 'Santa Lucia'.

Inter were experienced but this was something new. Roger Hunt swept Liverpool ahead on four minutes. Inter snapped back through Mazzola, but further home goals from Ian Callaghan and Ian St John were the least Liverpool deserved. Full-back Chris Lawler had a goal disallowed.

Inter's experience told, however, in the second leg. Corso scored on eight minutes, direct from what Spanish referee Jose Ortiz de Mendibil had signalled as an indirect free-kick. One minute later, Peiro punished 'keeper Tommy Lawrence's habit of bouncing the ball from hands held at head height; Peiro nicked the ball as it dropped and pumped it into the goal.

Level on aggregate, Inter had achieved the minimum of a play-off. It was not needed. Midway through the second half Facchetti strode up out of nowhere and ripped a superb, winning third goal beyond Lawrence.

By happy coincidence the final would also be staged in San Siro, to opponents Benfica's fury. As Elek Schwartz, the Romanian coach who had succeeded Fernando Riera, told friends: 'If we play in Milan they will not let us win, no matter how long the game has to last.' His fears were not only about intimidatory crowd pressure but about talk of Inter officials' close relationship with some eastern European referees.

UEFA refused to budge so the match went ahead despite storms which left the pitch looking like a quagmire. Both teams splashed hopelessly through most of the first half before Mario Corso and Sandro Mazzola put together a couple of passes and Jair's shot slipped through the hands and legs of keeper Alberto Costa Pereira.

Inter, as in the previous year, again went on to defeat Argentina's Independiente to retain the World Club Cup. Herrera appeared to have world football in an iron grip.

THURSDAY 27 MAY 1965
SAN SIRO, MILAN

INTERNAZIONALE   1
JAIR 42

BENFICA   0

HT: 1-0. ATT: 80,000. REF: DIENST (SWITZ)

INTERNAZIONALE:
SARTI - PICCHI* - BURGNICH, GUARNERI, FACCHETTI - BEDIN, SUAREZ, CORSO - JAIR, MAZZOLA, PEIRO.
COACH: HERRERA.

BENFICA:
COSTA PEREIRA - CAVEM, GERMANO, RAUL, CRUZ - NETO, COLUNA* - JOSE AUGUSTO, EUSEBIO, TORRES, SIMOES.
COACH: SCHWARTZ.

*CAPTAIN.

GATECRASHING THE BIRTHDAY BASH

As the competition entered its second decade, it was time for reflection: the old guard remained but there were new faces on the scene. And Manchester United made their first bow since 1958.

Matt Busby was back in charge. He had not shrunk from buying big before the time he needed to: hence the strengthening of the Busby Babes with Tommy Taylor and Harry Gregg. Now he had used the transfer market to help shortcut the rebuilding process, most notably with the £125,000 rescue of Denis Law from Torino.

Bobby Charlton and Bill Foulkes were stalwarts from the pre-Munich era, aided and abetted by a 20-year-old one-off from Northern Ireland named George Best.

Probably the greatest night of Best's entire career was 9 March 1966, in the Estadio da Luz in Lisbon, when he ran Benfica ragged. United, 3–2 winners at home in the first leg, scored a 5–1 triumph which ranks among the greatest single match displays in the history of all European club football.

Best scored twice in the first 12 minutes and John Connelly made it three in 15. Paddy Crerand and Charlton completed the 5–1 annihilation while, just for good measure, United even provided Benfica's only reply with Shay Brennan's own goal.

'When we drew Partizan in the semi-final we thought we were already in the final,' said Law, years later. But United had overlooked the Slavs' path to the last four. Many of their players had been battle-hardened in the 1960 Nations Cup and the 1962 World Cup: Yugoslavia had reached the

RIGHT: BENFICA'S TALL STRIKER JOSE TORRES HOLDS THE BALL ALOFT IN TRIUMPH AFTER SCORING IN THE 3–2 DEFEAT AT OLD TRAFFORD. UNITED WON 8–3 ON AGGREGATE

final in one, the semi-finals in the other.

To face United had meant beating the burgeoning youth of Nantes, the bad-tempered, hard-edged Germans of Werder Bremen and old Mitropa Cup heroes Sparta Prague. In Belgrade Law missed from the edge of the six-yard box and United lost 2–0. At Old Trafford, missing Best through injury, United won by an insufficient 1–0 after 'keeper Milutin Soskic pushed a Nobby Stiles cross-shot into his own net.

Partizan, having surprised themselves by reaching the final, were equally surprised to learn that their opponents would not be holders Inter, as expected – but Real Madrid.

Inter had made few changes once Herrera had established command. Gianfranco Bedin was now the 'attacking' wing-half, and hard-working Angelo Domenghini had ousted the erratic Brazilian Jair on the right wing, but Mazzola, Suarez and Corso had gone from strength to strength. Dinamo Bucharest and Ferencvaros – despite the graceful Florian Albert – proved easy meat en route to the semi-finals.

This was a very different Real Madrid – nicknamed the 'Ye-ye' team to suit the Beatle era.

These days Santamaria and Puskas were wheeled out chiefly for money-making prestige friendlies, though Puskas did score four times in the 5–0 first-round thrashing of Feyenoord.

After that initial flurry the baton was passed to energetic newcomers such as inside-forward Amancio, midfielder Pirri and a new deep-lying centre-forward in Ramon Moreno Grosso. Only full-back Pachin and skipper Gento, of the old guard, remained first choices with coach Miguel Munoz.

Gento was on target when Madrid beat Kilmarnock 5–1 in the second round and claimed two more in the quarter-final defeat of Anderlecht.

But few critics gave Madrid's mixture of the old and the new much chance against Inter in the semis – not even after a 1–0 win at home, in which Gento crossed for Pirri to score.

Madrid had their backs to the wall in Milan, where Hungarian referee Gyorgy Vadas resisted Inter pressure on and off the pitch. Real had lost the Spanish league crown to neighbours Atletico. Thus they had to win the Cup to maintain their record of perpetual entry. Gento again provided a lethal cross which Amancio converted. Facchetti levelled 13 minutes from time, but goalkeeper Jose Araquistain – making belated amends for his disastrous 1962 final – kept everything else out.

Inter's stultifying reign was over and Madrid's Ye-ye team went on to the Heysel Stadium in Brussels – scene of their 1958 triumph over Milan – to a victory repeat over Partizan, the first eastern European club to reach the Champions Cup final and only the second non-Latin contenders, after Germany's Eintracht Frankfurt in 1960.

Perhaps Partizan's seniors were distracted by thoughts of their lucrative and imminent transfers to the west. Either way, after taking the lead through raiding left-half Velibor Vasovic they relaxed and were hit twice in quick succession by Amancio and Fernando Serena.

The right-winger had promised the Spanish media in advance that he would score the winner amd he duly kept his promise from 25 yards with his 'wrong' left foot.

Real Madrid, for the sixth time, were champions of Europe and were allowed to keep the original trophy. Gento had won his record sixth cup, Pachin a second; Araquistain, Ignacio Zoco and Amancio had a winner's medal to offset their loser's baubles from 1962 or 1964.

Intriguingly, for a club who had leaned so heavily on star imports, Madrid had won with a team of 11 Spaniards. It was the first time a home-born team had won the European Cup.

ABOVE: **PARTIZAN'S GOALKEEPER MILUTIN SOSKIC LOOKS BACK IN ANGER AND DESPAIR AS AMANCIO'S EQUALIZER NESTLES GENTLY IN THE BACK OF THE NET**

WEDNESDAY 11 MAY 1966
HEYSEL, BRUSSELS

REAL MADRID	**2**
AMANCIO 70, SERENA 76	
PARTIZAN BELGRADE	**1**
VASOVIC 55	

HT: 0–0. ATT: 55,000.
REF: KREITLEIN (WG)

REAL MADRID:
ARAQUISTAIN – PACHIN, DE FELIPE, ZOCO, SACHIS – PIRRI, GROSSO, VELAZQUEZ – SERENA, AMANCIO, GENTO*.
COACH: MUNOZ.

PARTIZAN BELGRADE:
SOSKIC – JUSUFI, RASOVIC, VASOVIC*, MIHAJLOVIC – BECEJAC, KOVACEVIC – BAJIC, HASANAGIC, GALIC, PIRMAJER.
COACH: GEGIC.

*CAPTAIN.

GLASGOW'S PASSION PLAYERS

Celtic exploded from nowhere to power their way towards European football's most glittering prize, while Liverpool fell to an emerging Ajax side inspired by the precocious Johan Cruyff

In May 1967 Celtic became the first British club to win the Champions Cup, a high water mark to which the Bhoys have dreamed of returning ever since. But the Scottish game has changed beyond recognition and, arguably, for the worse where competition is concerned.

Celtic had qualified for the Champions Cup by winning the Scottish league title in 1966 for the first time in 12 years. They were the fifth different club to win the championship in seven seasons – after Hearts, Rangers (three times), Dundee and Kilmarnock – which says much about the competitive nature of Scottish football at that time. Of course, in Jack Stein they had the greatest modern manager in Scottish football.

He had gained an invaluable insight into what worked and what did not from a spell as reserve-team manager at Celtic in the early 1950s. That was where he first exercised his guiding control over ambitious young players such as Billy McNeill, later his captain. Impressive spells as manager in his own right at Dunfermline Athletic and Hibernian persuaded Celtic to bring him back as boss in the spring of 1965.

Celtic's progress from no one to someone in the Champions Cup within nine months shocked the continent. But beaten opponents along the way such as FC Zurich – for whom veteran player-coach Ladislav Kubala made his last European appearance – Nantes, Vojvodina Novisad and

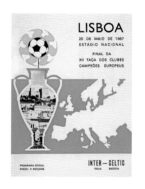

RIGHT: **THE NET BULGES AS BILLY McNEILL'S HEADER FLIES PAST VOJVODINA NOVISAD'S GOALKEEPER IN THE 90TH MINUTE TO GIVE CELTIC AN AGGREGATE LEAD. BOBBY MURDOCH (L) AND STEVE CHALMERS (2ND R) WATCH ON**

Dukla Prague, had only themselves to blame. Celtic had reached the semi-finals of the Cup-Winners' Cup in both of the two previous seasons and learned hard but significant lessons from last-four defeats by first MTK Budapest and then Liverpool.

Losing to MTK, after taking a three-goal lead to Budapest, had taught Celtic's players that nothing in Europe could be taken for granted; losing to Liverpool, after dominating the first leg, taught them that chances had to be taken with a ruthless efficiency unfamiliar to the Scottish League.

To that effect, Stein strengthened his team during the autumn of 1966 by splashing £30,000 on Hearts striker Willie Wallace. He envisaged Wallace replacing ageing Steve Chalmers and teaming up alongside top-scoring Joe McBride. But barely had Wallace arrived than McBride suffered a knee injury which was to blight his career.

To compound the blow, an administrative blunder meant that Wallace was not registered in time for the quarter-final against Vojvodina.

Undeterred, Celtic lost 1–0 in Yugoslavia and won 2–0 at home. Chalmers scored the first and McNeill headed the winner in the last minute to avert a Rotterdam play-off.

The quarter-finals also saw the exit of holders Real Madrid, who lost 1–0 away and 2–0 at home to Internazionale, with Helenio Herrera savouring vengeance for the previous season's semi-final defeat.

CSKA Sofia reached the semi-finals for the first time by cruising easily past Northern Ireland's Linfield, while further eastern European progress was attained by Dukla in defeating Ajax Amsterdam.

The Dutch, coached by their former centre-forward Rinus Michels, had sprung an earlier sensation by famously demolishing Liverpool 5–1 in the old Olympic stadium. The Reds' manager Bill Shankly, blaming Amsterdam fog rather than Ajax finesse, predicted hellfire vengeance back at Anfield.

The Liverpool floodlights, however, only lit up the enormous potential of young visitors such as Johan Cruyff and Piet Keizer. Roger Hunt scored twice, but so did Cruyff, and Liverpool fell 7–3 on aggregate.

Dukla then beat Ajax, after which their ageing legs creaked to a defeated standstill against Celtic, while Facchetti scored in both semi-final legs before Inter edged out CSKA in a play-off in Bologna.

Italian pragmatism would thus confront Scottish passion in Lisbon, where the European Cup had begun 12 years earlier.

Pride of place in Celtic's history will always go to that glorious moment when skipper McNeill – amid green-and-white mayhem – raised the new trophy over dictator Antonio Salazar's Estadio Nacional.

Herrera's luck had evaporated. The previous weekend Inter had lost their Italian league crown and thus the right to a Champions Cup return; they had lost Brazilian right winger Jair to a knee injury and Spanish playmaker Luis Suarez to a thigh strain, a major blow.

No such problems for Celtic. McBride remained a long-term absentee. But everyone else was there: from 36-year-old Ronnie Simpson in goal, via full-backs Jim Craig and Tommy Gemmell, 'Caesar' McNeill in the heart of defence, to the archetypal 'tanner ball-player' Jimmy Johnstone on the right wing.

Inter took the lead after six minutes in the mid-afternoon heat. Craig tripped Renato Cappellini and Sandro Mazzola converted the penalty.

Celtic had all the time in the world and nothing to lose. The green-and-white storm tide ultimately overwhelmed even Inter's flood barriers. Gemmell thrashed home a Craig cross from 25 yards and veteran leader Chalmers deflected home the winner with eight minutes left.

Two weeks later came the ultimate tribute: Celtic played, and beat, Real in Madrid in Alfredo Di Stefano's farewell testimonial match. Ring out the Spanish old, ring in the Scottish new.

ABOVE: (SHIRTLESS) CELTIC PLAYERS CELEBRATE WITH FANS AFTER THE GAME – (FROM THE LEFT), TOMMY GEMMELL, JOHN HUGHES AND BOBBY LENNOX. ALL CELTIC'S PLAYERS WERE BORN WITHIN A 30-MILE RADIUS OF CELTIC PARK

THURSDAY 25 MAY 1967
ESTADIO NACIONAL, LISBON

CELTIC 2
GEMMELL 62, CHALMERS 83

INTERNAZIONALE 1
MAZZOLA 6 PEN

HT: 0-1. ATT: 55,000. REF: TSCHENSCHER (WG)

CELTIC:
SIMPSON – CRAIG, MCNEILL*, CLARK, GEMMELL – MURDOCH, AULD – JOHNSTONE, WALLACE, CHALMERS, LENNOX.
MANAGER: STEIN.

INTERNAZIONALE:
SARTI – PICCHI* – BURGNICH, GUARNERI, FACCHETTI – BEDIN, BICICLI, CORSO – DOMENGHINI, MAZZOLA, CAPPELLINI.
COACH: HERRERA.

*CAPTAIN.

MATT BUSBY'S HOLY GRAIL

Innovative rule changes were the order of the day as UEFA attempted to slipstream the competition. And in the footsteps of Celtic, Manchester United made their bid for the European crown

Ten seasons after the Munich air disaster Manchester United were back yet again. They had fallen, to their own gaping disbelief, in the 1966 semi-finals. Now Matt Busby was once again in hot pursuit of his holy grail. But a significant change in the balance of power betweenEnglish and European football had occurred in the meantime.

England's double thrashing by Hungary in 1953 and 1954 had raised questions about everything from coaching to equipment. The awful realization that England no longer ruled the football waves was driven home by repeated failures in the fledgling European club competitions.

A London Select in 1958 and Birmingham City in 1960 had reached the finals of the Fairs Cup before Tottenham, in 1963, became the first English club to win a European

trophy, the Cup-Winners' Cup – carrying it off with plenty of goals and no little style.

The following year, 1964, Denis Law of Manchester United and Scotland became the first British winner of the European Footballer of the Year prize since Stanley Matthews in 1956. Even more significant was Bobby Charlton's Ballon d'Or in 1966, off the back of England's World Cup triumph.

English football was back at the world pinnacle, and command of the Jules Rimet trophy provided solid gold evidence of that fact. Celtic had broken a psychological barrier by proving that British clubs could beat Europe's best, and Manchester United duly squared the circle.

Celtic, never mind the seeding, lost their grip on the cup immediately. They lost 2–1 at home to Dynamo Kiev, the

RIGHT: **MANCHESTER UNITED'S LEGENDARY NUMBER 7 GEORGE BEST TURNS AWAY IN TRIUMPH AFTER SCORING THE ONLY GOAL IN THE HOME LEG OF THE SEMI-FINAL AGAINST REAL MADRID. THE AWAY LEG ENDED 3-3**

long-awaited first Soviet entrants, and drew 1–1 in Ukraine, from where they flew home to Glasgow grumbling about dirty tricks.

It was a poor omen for Celtic's even more painful defeat by Racing of Argentina in the mayhem of the World Club Cup.

The away-goals rule was of instant help to Benfica against Glentoran of Northern Ireland, while Real Madrid needed extra time to edge Ajax. Political sensitivities still raised the occasional complication: ultra-communist Albania refused to recognize West Germany, so Dinamo Tirana's withdrawal offered progress to Eintracht Braunschweig thanks to a walkover.

United had no problem in disposing of Hibernians of Malta 4–0, 0–0. The four goals were shared two apiece by Law and David Sadler.

But they had it tougher in beating Sarajevo: they drew 0–0 in Yugoslavia and won 2–1 at Old Trafford with goals from wingers John Aston and George Best.

That same 2–1 aggregate saw United past Gornik Zabrze, earlier conquerors of Kiev, in the quarter-finals, while Eusebio scored two in Benfica's defeat of Vasas Budapest. The Black Panther also managed one in each leg as Benfica beat Juventus in the semis to qualify for their fifth final in eight seasons.

United reached Wembley by the skin of their teeth and via a match which Charlton, years later, described as 'the most memorable individual match of my career'.

Old memories from different eras on both sides were renewed by the semi-final pairing of United with Real Madrid. Suspended Amancio missed the first leg at Old Trafford and Madrid, lacking his counter-attacking edge, conceded a lone goal to Best.

That did not appear enough as Madrid stormed back with three of their own in the first half in the Bernabeu. But when their storm blew over United raised one of their own: Ignacio Zoco had earlier put through his own goal, David Sadler scored a second, and Munich survivor Bill Foulkes – to the amazement of his team-mates – somehow found himself up in attack to level the scores at 3–3.

The demands of black-and-white television era meant that in the final neither United nor Benfica could play in their favoured red. Hence Wembley saw Benfica wearing all-white, United all-blue. But the blues at the end were reserved solely for the Portuguese.

Two years earlier England had beaten Portugal 2–1, also at Wembley, in the World Cup semi-finals. United brought to the party two of England's heroes in Charlton plus

combative half-back Nobby Stiles while Benfica fielded six of Portugal's line-up that day: Jose Augusto, Jaime Graca (whom they had signed after the World Cup) and Mario Coluna in midfield, plus forwards Eusebio, Jose Torres and Antonio Simoes.

United lacked the potent force of Denis Law through a knee injury but David Sadler stepped in to good tactical effect while left-winger John Aston played his finest game for United.

The first half ended goalless though Eusebio once set keeper Alex Stepney's crossbar twanging. Seven minutes into the second half United went ahead: Sadler's cross being glanced in for one of Charlton's rare headed goals.

Benfica, though significantly older, found fresh legs in pursuit of parity. Graca equalised and Eusebio, in the closing minutes, should have won the game only for his thunderous drive to strike Stepney full in the chest.

Thus Benfica heads went down ahead of destructive extra time. Three goals in seven minutes from Best, Kidd – celebrating his 19th birthday – and Charlton again brought the European Cup to England for the first time ... and to Manchester United amid tears of emotional, memory-scarred relief.

ABOVE: **MATT BUSBY PROVIDES WORDS OF INSPIRATION TO HIS PLAYERS AS THEY GET READY FOR ONE LAST EFFORT. SEVERAL PLAYERS WRITHE WITH CRAMP AS GEORGE BEST (7) PREPARES HIMSELF FOR DECISIVE ACTION**

WEDNESDAY 29 MAY 1968
WEMBLEY, LONDON

MANCHESTER UNITED   **4**
CHARLTON 54, 98, BEST 92, KIDD 95
BENFICA   **1**
JAIME GRAÇA 78

HT: 0-0. AFTER EXTRA TIME (90 MIN: 1-1). ATT: 100,000. REF: LO BELLO (IT)

MANCHESTER UNITED:
STEPNEY – BRENNAN, FOULKES, STILES, DUNNE – CRERAND, CHARLTON*, SADLER – BEST, KIDD, ASTON.
MANAGER: BUSBY.

BENFICA:
HENRIQUE – ADOLFO, HUMBERTO, JACINTO, CRUZ – JOSE AUGUSTO, JAIME GRAÇA, COLUNA* – EUSEBIO, TORRES, SIMOES.
COACH: GLORIA.

*CAPTAIN.

NO SUBSTITUTES FOR CLASS

Soviet tanks brought an end to the Prague Spring and football's administrators felt the chill when they had to keep East and West apart. But it was an Italian goalkeeper who stole the headlines...

In the international days before multiple substitutions, before overburdened qualifying schedules, and when friendlies were not meaningless but played for prestige and pride, many fine footballers were never rewarded even once with an appearance for their national team.

The expanding European club competitions thus offered an alternative route to international achievement and recognition. One such player to follow this route was the best goalkeeper never to play for Italy: Fabio Cudicini.

Cudicini had triumphed in the Fairs Cup with Roma in 1961 and then won the Cup-winners Cup with Milan in 1968 against Hamburg. Now he had the chance to become the first player to boast a winners' medal in all three European cups.

Politics intervened before even the start of term. Soviet tanks, supported by Warsaw Pact partners, had rolled into Czechoslovakia to bring an abrupt end to Alexander Dubcek's 'Prague Spring'. Celtic then refused to play Ferencvaros of Hungary in the first round, so UEFA organized a new draw, keeping eastern and western European clubs apart.

The Warsaw Pact federations announced that they were withdrawing their clubs in protest. In the event, Yugoslavia, by now a communist outsider, defied Soviet requests to toe the line and Red Star Belgrade played on. So did Steaua Bucharest from Romania as well as Czechoslovakia's Spartak Trnava – who beat Steaua 5-3 on aggregate in the first round.

Elsewhere, Manchester United put 10 goals past Waterford from the Irish Republic, with Denis Law making up for lost time by scoring all three in the first leg and four out of seven in the return. Neighbours Manchester City were not so fortunate. A fine side put together by Joe Mercer and Malcolm Allison went out narrowly but immediately to Turkey's Fenerbahce.

LEFT: **BRIAN KIDD LIES ON THE TURF AT OLD TRAFFORD AS NOBBY STILES REMONSTRATES WITH MILAN'S GIOVANNI LODETTI. MANCHESTER UNITED WON 1-0, BUT IT WAS NOT ENOUGH TO OVERHAUL THE 2-0 DEFICIT FROM THE SAN SIRO. TWO DAYS LATER, MATT BUSBY WALKED AWAY FROM THE CLUB FOR EVER**

Celtic averted an upset of their own against Saint-Etienne after losing the first leg 2-0 in France. Benfica put eight goals past Valur of Iceland, Ajax scored five against Nurnberg, Real Madrid 12 against Limassol and Milan five against Malmo: two for 1963 survivor Gianni Rivera, two for new striker Pierino Prati and one for the Italo-Brazilian centre-forward Angelo Benedetto Sormani.

The imbalance in the draw meant that Milan and Benfica benefited from byes through to the second round. Ajax won 2-0 both home and away against Fenerbahce, Law scored twice more in United's defeat of Anderlecht, and Jimmy Johnstone - a reluctant flyer - turned in a two-goal display which inspired Celtic's 5-1 home win over Red Star; manager Jock Stein had promised that Johnstone could skip the Belgrade trip if he turned on the first-leg style.

Ironically, the Czechoslovaks of Trnava thumped Finland's Lahden Reipas 9-1 away and 7-1 at home. They followed up with a quarter-final win over AEK Athens to reach the semis along with Milan (victors at Celtic on the tie's lone goal from Prati), United (3-0, 0-0 winners against Rapid) and Ajax (for whom Johan Cruyff scored at home and away against Benfica).

Ajax had the luck of the draw in the semi-finals. Trnava were well drilled and skilful, but Ajax boasted greater individual class, with the youth of Johan Cruyff, Wim Suurbier and Piet Keizer complemented by the experience of Henk Groot, Bennie Muller and the former Partizan Belgrade anchor, Velibor Vasovic.

Ajax won 3-0 at home, with Cruyff scoring his sixth of the campaign, and clung on at 2-0 down in Czechoslovakia for victory on aggregate.

Milan against United had been most observers' dream final. Milan had rebuilt since the 1963 victory over Benfica. Rivera, the inspirational playmaker, and wing-half Giovanni Trapattoni were the lone survivors from that side.

United had not had an easy time. They had lost a foul-strewn battle with the notoriously cynical Estudiantes de La Plata in the World Club Cup, when Stiles was sent off in the first leg and Best in the second. Best's consolation was to be voted European Footballer of the Year, the third United player to be so honoured in five seasons, Bobby Charlton in 1966 having followed Law in 1964.

Another expulsion was awaiting in Milan, where midfielder John Fitzpatrick's sending-off contributed to a 2-0 defeat by goals from Sormani and veteran Swede Kurt Hamrin. Milan brought a siege mentality to Old Trafford. Cudicini, once felled by a missile from the crowd, defiantly threw his huge frame left and right and was beaten only once, by Charlton.

ABOVE: AC MILAN'S BRAZILIAN FORWARD ANGELO SORMANI HOLDS UP THE EUROPEAN CUP IN THE BERNABEU BEFORE BEING ENGULFED BY JUBILANT FANS

Thus in Madrid, with five players edging 30 or more, Milan represented past and present while Ajax, the first Dutch club to reach the final, stood for the future. On this occasion experience had its way.

Gianni Rivera was at his peak, one of European football's greatest creative footballers bound later to become club president and a member of parliament. Before all of that he would be voted in as European Footballer of the Year.

In 1963 Rivera's passes had opened the way to goal for Jose Altafini. Now he played up to another Brazilian and a Swede.

Sormani had been brought to Italy from among the substitutes at Santos and was thus lumbered with the label of 'Pele's reserve.' Italian parentage helped earn him seven caps and a world record transfer of £250,000 from Mantova to Roma who almost went bankrupt over the fee.

Thus Sormani ended up at Milan alongside Sweden's Hamrin who had thought his trophy-winning days were over after a decade at Fiorentina had earned him a then club record 150 goals.

Ajax planned for Sormani and Hamrin but not for the virtuosity which hat-trick hero Pierino Prati brought to this one night in Madrid. Sormani scored the other goal. Velibor Vasosic, as with Partizan three years earlier, scored Ajax's lone goal and ended up again on the losing side.

WEDNESDAY 28 MAY 1969
BERNABEU, MADRID

MILAN 4
PRATI 7, 39, 74, SORMANI 66

AJAX AMSTERDAM 1
VASOVIC 61 PEN

HT: 2-0. ATT: 50,000. REF: ORTIZ DE MENDIBIL (SP)

MILAN:
CUDICINI - MALATRASI - ANQUILLETTI, ROSATO, TRAPATTONI, SCHNELLINGER - LODETTI, RIVERA* - HAMRIN, SORMANI, PRATI. COACH: ROCCO.

AJAX AMSTERDAM:
BALS - SUURBIER (MULLER 46), HULSHOFF, VASOVIC*, VAN DUIVENDOBE - PRONK, GROOT (NUNINGA 46) - SWART, CRUYFF, DANIELSSON, KEIZER. COACH: MICHELS.

*CAPTAIN.

1970S

THE NEW NORTH-SOUTH DIVIDE

The 1970s saw the European Champions Cup leave Latin Europe behind. Holland seized command for four years courtesy of Feyenoord and Ajax, but then the primacy of Johan Cruyff's vibrant 'total football' was usurped by the rule of law imposed by Franz Beckenbauer and Bayern Munich – the first German winners. German football proved internationally dominant. Beckenbauer also led his men to glory in both the European Championship and World Cup before England struck back at club level through Liverpool. But only Brian Clough's red-clad archers from Nottingham Forest, plotting their ambush through the English back door, proved capable of silencing the Kop.

RIGHT: AJAX WON THE EUROPEAN CUP THREE TIMES IN A ROW, THE FIRST TEAM TO DO SO SINCE REAL MADRID. HERE THEY LINE UP BEFORE THE FINAL WITH JUVENTUS IN 1973, THEIR LYRICAL SWANSONG BEFORE A LENGTHY FALLOW PERIOD

FRANZ BECKENBAUER

Country: Germany

Position: Sweeper

Born: 11 September 1945

Clubs: SC Munich 1906,
Bayern Munich, New York
Cosmos, SV Hamburg

FRANZ BECKENBAUER

'Please, don't let the ball fly out of the ground,' I was thinking in the last seconds of extra time in the 1974 final. We were losing 1-0 to Atletico Madrid and 'Katsche' Schwarzenbeck was bringing the ball through in midfield and setting himself to shoot. It was not his job and never his speciality. I feared it was all over. At least, if the ball stayed in play, we might have a few more seconds...

Of course he shot from more than 30 metres and somehow the ball flew past the goalkeeper and into the net for our equaliser. It had to be a fluke. But it was the perfect fluke because immediately afterwards the referee blew the final whistle. As it turned out, we would not have had any more time. It was that or nothing – and, of course, we were relieved to rescue the draw and the replay.

We won that 4-0, the first of our three Champions Cups. We were physically the stronger for the replay but the key to it was psychological. Atletico's players were mentally broken because they had put one hand on the trophy only to see it prised away at the last moment. For us, it worked the opposite way: we were still flying high after pulling it back.

There were no penalties to settle a drawn final in those days; UEFA only changed the rules afterwards. But we needed a penalty shoot-out to beat Atvidaberg when we launched our defence the next season. I even converted our last penalty, though I rarely got involved in the shootouts. We believed penalties were the responsibility of the forwards. Anyway, I was always too polite. I was content to step aside for whoever wanted to take a kick.

We had a wonderful side. Six of us were in the national team who won the World Cup that year: Sepp Maier, Gerd Muller, Schwarzenbeck, Paul Breitner, Uli Hoeness and myself. We were also German champions and would have won the cup final, too, if it had not been for the referee. More success than that is impossible. From then on, however, it was all downhill.

Internationally, we stayed on top of our game but back home we could not focus. Six weeks after we beat Holland

2-1 in the World Cup Final, we lost 6-0 to Offenbach on the opening day of the Bundesliga. We had a string of injuries and, because we had won so much, everyone was gunning for us.

In Europe, it was different. The return with Atvidaberg was one of our most memorable games. We had won 3-1 at home, then went 3-0 down in Sweden before Hoeness scored the all-important goal which earned us extra time and penalties.

Equally memorable were our games against Dynamo Dresden. It was the first time West and East German clubs had come out of the hat together. We won 4-3 in Munich and drew 3-3 in Dresden, which was only half the story.

An Italian club had warned us that, when they played over there, something was put in their food and they could hardly run during the game. So Wilhelm Neudecker and Robert Schwan, our president and manager, decided that instead of staying the night before the game in the GDR, we would stop on the West side of the border.

LEFT: BECKENBAUER
MODELLED HIMSELF ON
GIACINTO FACCHETTI,
INTER MILAN'S
ATTACKING LEFT-BACK

Our decision was a big issue at the time which went to the highest political and diplomatic levels. But Neudecker and Schwan refused to budge and we got our way. We did the same a year later against Magdeburg, also from the GDR, and then everyone was much more relaxed about it.

But we were not fooling ourselves. We knew we were past our best and needed to play a more tactical game because football is not only about using your legs, it's also about using your brain. That was how we managed to beat both Leeds in the 1975 final, then Saint-Etienne in 1976.

The key to it was our Bavarian axis of Maier in goal, myself as libero and Muller at centre-forward. Then we had a hard-running midfield with Franz Roth, Bernd Durnberger or Jupp Kapellmann, plus other world-class players like Hoeness. He and Conny Torstensson, or later Karl-Heinz Rummenigge, hung back a little deeper than Muller who was our attack leader.

Muller was sensational, a phenomenon. When I brought the ball out of defence, you could see the anticipation in the muscles in his legs. He had a speed off the mark I have never seen in any other player. He would have scored 80 goals a season in today's Bundesliga, twice as many as in his heyday. Back then, Muller always had two defenders trampling all over him but you never see double-marking nowadays. He would had much more room in which to work.

I had been developing my own role as libero since I was a youth player. I modelled myself on Giacinto Facchetti, the Internazionale left-back, who was always overlapping up the wing. That was revolutionary because 40 years ago everyone held his position much more rigidly than today.

The more I watched Facchetti, the more I realised that I could employ the same tactic through the middle. What he could do in a narrow corridor on the left I could do to better effect with so much more room in which to work through the centre of the pitch. So that is what I did whenever the state of the game permitted.

To make it work, I needed a loyal assistant to sit tight in defence and Schwarzenbeck did exactly that except, thankfully of course, against Atletico.

Our greatest rivals in the 1970s had been Ajax. They were world class in the three years before Johan Cruyff went to Barcelona. In the 1973 quarter-finals, they beat us 4–0 in Amsterdam. That was a black day. Maier made three mistakes in one match for the only time in his career and they punished each one.

In time, of course, Liverpool followed us which left the Latin Europeans out in the cold throughout the 1970s.

Twice I nearly went to play in Italy. First, Internazionale wanted me in 1966, but then Italy lost to North Korea in the World Cup and the federation blamed it on all the foreign players and shut the borders. I would have gone if I could have, not only because of the top-class players there, but also, of course, for the money. One Sunday I flew down from Munich to watch the Milan derby. It was fantastic to be in an 80,000 crowd for just a club game, while at Bayern we still played in the little old Grunwald stadium. Later AC Milan also tried to sign me, but it fell through. A pity. I would like to have tried the Italian experience.

Pele was the greatest player of my era and, in Europe, Bobby Charlton, Eusebio, George Best ... there were so many, unlike nowadays when I would pick out only Ronaldinho and Ronaldo.

Of course the game has changed. Players are fitter and far more professional in every aspect of their preparation. Also, the 'stage' has improved enormously. The footballs are better and so are the pitches. We played on potato fields which were green only in July and August; today's players have super pitches all year round.

But ... today's player must be conscious of his behaviour every waking minute. If he lets his guard slip for a moment, the media and public are on his case. Today's players live in glass houses, while we lived a comparatively normal daily life.

On balance, I am glad I played then rather than now.

LEFT: BECKENBAUER WAS THE PUPPET MASTER, PULLING THE STRINGS WHICH EARNED WEST GERMANY AND BAYERN MUNICH EVERY MAJOR PRIZE

HAPPINESS IS TROPHY-SHAPED

Under Ernst Happel, Feyenoord outstripped rivals Ajax to make the final. Their opponents were the winners of the Battle of Britain, as Celtic's Cavaliers took on the Roundheads of Leeds United

Headline-writers found easy alliteration to celebrate Feyenoord's achievement as the Cup's first Dutch winners in May 1970. The descriptive focus settled on their coach: Ernst Franz Hermann Happel.

He was, repeatedly, dubbed 'Happy Happel' in headlines, introductions and picture captions. But easy words bore little relation to reality: Happel was a dour disciplinarian, ever wary of the natural law balancing good fortune with bad, triumph with defeat.

Happel was Austrian, born in 1925, two years before the Mitropa Cup. As a boy, he supported Rapid Vienna and he grew up to become one of their most resolute players. He even became the first player to score a European hat-trick against Real Madrid, with two free-kicks and a penalty in a first-round tie in 1956 – only for Madrid to trump his hat-trick in the subsequent play-off.

Feyenoord had the easiest of starts: drawn against KR Reykjavik, they saved the Icelanders money by playing both legs in Rotterdam.

Sweden's Ove Kindvall scored a hat-trick in the opening

RIGHT: **AS A COACH AND PLAYER, ERNST HAPPEL WON 17 NATIONAL AND INTERNATIONAL TITLES AS WELL AS TAKING HOLLAND TO RUNNERS UP IN THE WORLD CUP IN ARGENTINA IN 1978. IN TRIBUTE, THE FORMER PRATER STADIUM IN VIENNA NOW BEARS HIS NAME**

12–2 win and two more in the 4–0 'return'. One of the opening dozen was struck by full-back Wim Van Duivendobe who had joined Feyenoord after collecting a runners-up medal four months earlier with Ajax.

'Ajax had the better individuals,' said Van Duivendobe later, 'but Feyenoord, just then, were the better all-round team.'

They were not the only first-rounders to hit double figures. Don Revie's Leeds United – prepared on a steady diet of dossiers and carpet bowls – put 10 past Norway's Lyn Oslo without reply at Elland Road. Mick Jones scored a hat-trick that night and added another when Leeds won 6–0 in Oslo.

Real Madrid – with Paco Gento still at No. 11 – put 14 past Olympiakos Nicosia over two legs while Celtic, showing only a modicum of change since Lisbon, saw off Basel more modestly. A goal from Tommy Gemmell in the 2–0 aggregate win proved that he had not lost his attacking flair.

Milan opened their defence with a 5–0, 3–0 win over Avenir of Luxembourg. The ties were moved forward to assist the Italians in their World Club Cup clash with Argentina's Estudiantes de La Plata, in which Milan triumphed but at heavy cost.

They won 3–0 in Milan easily enough, then held out in La Plata, despite losing a bruising battle 2–1, for a 4–2 aggregate win. Franco-Argentine centre-forward Nestor Combin had his nose broken and Pierino Prati was callously kicked in the back while lying on the pitch receiving treatment to a bruised ankle.

That battering to legs and morale lowered Milan's resistance for the European challenge of Feyenoord. Gianni Rivera was injured and substituted before half-time in the first leg in which the Rossoneri lacked the energy to press home the advantage provided by an early goal from Combin. Rivera missed the return and Feyenoord won more easily than the tallies of Wim Jansen and Wim van Hanegem suggest.

Italy's own champions, Fiorentina, survived one round further before falling to Celtic in the quarter-finals, where Feyenoord again scored a 2–1 overall win, this time against Vorwarts of East Berlin. Leeds got the better by 2–0 of

a Standard Liege side who had beaten Real Madrid 3–2 in the Bernabeu.

Feyenoord duly profited from an 'easy' semi-final draw against the Polish outsiders of Legia Warsaw, while Celtic squeezed out Leeds. The Bhoys won 1-0 at Elland Road then 2-1 at Hampden in front of a European record gate of 136,505. Jock Stein was jubilant. Celtic's manager had predicted in his programme notes that whoever won the 'Battle of Britain' would be favourites for the final.

But favourites do not always win. The media mimicked the Scots' over-confidence. Dutch clubs had won nothing and the rest of the continent was oblivious to the magical spell being conjured by Ajax in Amsterdam and the pacy pragmatism emanating from PSV in Eindhoven.

Celtic lined up seven Lisbon winners; Feyenoord responded with a goalkeeper in Eddy Pieters-Graafland who had been playing European cup football in the late 1950s, a resilient defensive rock in skipper Rinus Israel, two under-rated playmakers in Wim Jansen and Austrian Franz Hasil, plus Ove Kindvall up front and veteran Coen Moulijn on the left wing.

Moulijn, 33, was rated then as the greatest Dutch footballer since Faas Wilkes in the 1950s. His left-wing talent was not pure pace, in the manner of a Paco Gento or energy like Antonio Simoes, but guile. When he needed pace he could find enough but, above all, Moulijn had an eye for a gap and the passing accuracy to pierce it.

Not that this was instantly evident in Milan where Celtic went ahead inside the opening half-hour through Tommy Gemmell. But Israel headed home two minutes later and the wiles of Hasil, Moulijn and Co took its toll the longer the game ran on towards extra time.

A replay was looming when Kindvall chased a long, looping clearance. The ball might have eluded him and bounced away for a goal kick but a wavering arm of luckless Celtic captain Billy McNeill, stumbling back, arrested its pace. Referee Concetto Lo Bello allowed the advantage.

Kindvall's sixth goal of the campaign brought more than 200,000 onto the streets of Rotterdam the next day to welcome home the first Dutch champions of Europe. Even Happel almost smiled.

ABOVE: **RINUS ISRAEL (3) TURNS AWAY AFTER SCORING HIS SIDE'S OPENER IN THE SAN SIRO. ISRAEL WAS LATER PICTURED ON A DUTCH STAMP TO COMMEMORATE THE VICTORY**

WEDNESDAY 6 MAY 1970
SAN SIRO, MILAN

FEYENOORD	**2**
ISRAEL 32, KINDVALL 116	
CELTIC	**1**
GEMMELL 30	

AFTER EXTRA TIME, HT: 1–1. 90 MIN: 1–1.
ATT: 53,187. REF: LO BELLO (IT)

FEYENOORD:
PIETERS-GRAAFLAND – ROMEIJN
(HAAK 107), ISRAEL*, LASEROMS,
VAN DUIVENDOBE – JANSEN, HASIL,
VAN HANEGEM – WERY, KINDVALL,
MOULIJN.
COACH: HAPPEL.

CELTIC:
WILLIAMS – HAY, MCNEILL*,
BROGAN, GEMMELL – MURDOCH,
AULD (CONNELLY 77) – JOHNSTONE,
WALLACE, J. HUGHES, LENNOX.
MANAGER: STEIN.

*CAPTAIN.

HISTORY'S GOLDEN THREADS

Brazil had taken football to new heights when they won the 1970 World Cup final but now there was a new talent, the gawky son of a cleaner in Ajax's offices, to lead Europe's great revival

Threads of history weave an unbroken path through the tale of the Champions Cup. Ajax Amsterdam can trace their golden thread right back to Hugo Meisl, one of European football's leading administrators between the wars and founder of the Mitropa Cup.

Meisl's younger brother, Willy, had found his way to England as a refugee from the Nazis in the late 1930s after Hugo's death. In London, in 1955, this other Meisl published Soccer Revolution, which stands as a milestone among football books.

In it Meisl envisioned an end to the old rigidity of playing positions. Every player should be an all-rounder, said Meisl. 'A really fine footballer will be almost equally good in several positions and far from bad in all of them. He will have to be able to tackle any task workmanlike, because that will form the very basis of the new tactics.'

Meisl called his system of the future 'The Whirl'. Sadly he died in 1968, just too early to see it brought to life as 'Total Football' by Ajax.

Dutch football had embraced professionalism only in the mid-1950s, and even a decade later many of the stars who played in Europe for Ajax, Feyenoord and their domestic rivals were part-timers.

But the influence of European competition and the advent of television changed the focus.

Ajax appreciated the potential when they signed the English manager Vic Buckingham. In 1964 he gave a first-team debut to a gawky 17-year-old centre-forward named Johannes Hendrikus Cruyff, the son of a cleaner in the club offices.

Even as a teenager, Cruyff was opinionated and sharp-tempered. Early on, he incurred an international ban for lashing out at the veteran East German referee Rudi Glockner. But his talent was beyond compare; arguably Cruyff was the greatest footballer raised in post-war European football.

The 1968–69 European campaign, which saw a nervy Ajax conclusively beaten by Milan in the final, was a practice run. Between late 1970 and the summer of 1973 Ajax dominated European club football with a style and élan which earned comparison with the best of Real Madrid.

Not that they were among initial favourites in the late summer of 1970, when Europe was reeling from the World Cup-winning brilliance of a Brazilian team inspired by Pele, Tostao, Jairzinho, Gerson and Carlos Alberto. After that extravaganza, the subsequent opening round of the Champions Cup seemed very dull fare.

Easy starts were accepted as the norm by Everton for England (Alan Ball scoring a hat-trick against Keflavik), Borussia Monchengladbach for Germany, Celtic for Scotland (Harry Hood hitting three against KPV Kokkolan), Cagliari for Italy and Atletico Madrid for Spain; neighbours Real were absent for the first time.

Ajax began inauspiciously in edging the politically reclusive Albanians of Nendori Tirana, but Feyenoord were

RIGHT: **THE PORTLY FERENC PUSKAS TRAINING AT WEMBLEY WHEN HE WAS COACH OF PANATHINAIKOS. AS A PLAYER, HE SCORED 83 GOALS IN 84 MATCHES FOR HUNGARY AND WON THE EUROPEAN CUP FOUR TIMES WITH REAL MADRID**

not so fortunate. The holders were held 1–1 at home, to their own surprise, by UT Arad – an unfashionable side even by Romanian standards – and could only draw 0–0 away.

Thus Arad went through on the away-goals rule. Feyenoord could not even push them to the newly introduced settlement lottery of the penalty shoot-out.

The honour of being the Cup's first shoot-out winners went to Everton, who defeated Borussia 4–3 on penalties after 1–1 draws in Bokelberg and at Goodison.

Everton's inability to win matches then cost them dear in the quarter-finals, when they lost on away goals to Panathinaikos from Athens.

The underrated Greeks then achieved the shock of the season with a dramatic turnaround of their semi-final against Red Star, which they won on away goals after losing 4-1 in Belgrade. Ajax met them at Wembley, having beaten Basel 5-1, then both Celtic and Atletico Madrid by 3-1.

Cruyff had scored only one of their 15 goals along the way. Now the time had come for the new hero to cross swords with an old one.

Old Real Madrid icon Ferenc Puskas was coach of Panathinaikos on the Wembley stage, where he had written history against England in 1953 with Hungary. Though the Greek club was his first major European appointment as a coach, the 1971 final also proved the pinnacle of his managerial career.

The same could not be said of Rinus Michels, on the Ajax bench. Michels had been a powerful, if raw, international centre-forward for Holland in the mid-1950s. But Michels the coach was nothing like Michels the player; as a coach he was intuitive, sensitive, inventive and inspirational.

He and his headstrong young players did not always see eye to eye: they fell out frequently over issues from bonuses to training camps. But Michels knew their potential and all he wanted was to ensure they profited from the genius of the greatest single generation in Dutch football history.

Goals in each half from Dick Van Dijk and Arie Haan ensured a successful start. At last, third time lucky, Velibor Vasovic was a European Cup winner.

ABOVE: **GERRIT MUHREN OF AJAX RAISES HIS ARMS IN TRIUMPH AS ARIE HAAN (NOT IN PICTURE) SCORES THE CLINCHING GOAL AGAINST PANATHINAIKOS**

WEDNESDAY 2 JUNE 1971
WEMBLEY, LONDON

AJAX AMSTERDAM	**2**
VAN DIJK 5, HAAN 87	
PANATHINAIKOS	**0**

HT: 1-0. ATT: 90,000. REF: TAYLOR (ENG)

AJAX:
STUY - SUURBIER, HULSHOFF, VASOVIC*, RIJNDERS (BLANKENBURG 46) - G. MUHREN, VAN DIJK, NEESKENS - SWART (HAAN 46), CRUYFF, KEIZER. COACH: MICHELS.

PANATHINAIKOS:
EKONOMOPOULOS - TOMARAS, KAMARAS, SOURPIS, VLAHOS - ELEFTERAKIS, DOMAZOS*, GRAMOS, KAPSIS - FILAKOURIS, ANTONIADIS. COACH: PUSKAS.

*CAPTAIN.

PRESSING MATTERS FOR INTER

All hell broke loose when Inter played Borussia Monchengladbach and someone threw a Coke can from the crowd. Meanwhile, the magisterial Johan Cruyff was conducting play for a brilliant Ajax side

Roberto Boninsegna, centre-forward of the Italian national side who finished runners-up to Brazil in the 1970 Mexico World Cup, lay flat out as mayhem broke out in Borussia Monchengladbach's Bokelberg stadium.

Less than half an hour had gone in the first leg of the second-round match between Borussia and Internazionale. Near to Boninsegna lay a Coca-Cola can, blamed for the most controversial crowd incident thus far in the Champions Cup.

A steady rise in spectator unrest had been noted before the start of the season by UEFA's general secretary Hans Bangerter. A formal warning had been issued to all competing clubs that punishments ranging from fines to result-reversals would be imposed for further incidents. The warning, like many others issued by UEFA regarding the increasingly complex issue of hooliganism, had little effect. Telling the clubs seemed pointless to many when it was fans who were to blame.

Borussia, a fast-rising force in German club football, and Inter had both been unhappy with the second-round draw. The absence of effective seeding meant that one of these two clubs, both serious contenders for the trophy, faced a disappointingly early exit.

Borussia were leading 2-1 in the first leg after a rugged opening half-hour when Boninsegna was floored by a missile thrown from the crowd. Then all hell broke loose. In the end Borussia, while accusing Boninsegna of play-acting, won 7-1. Inter demanded a replay of the first leg, which they received, and went on to win 4-2 in Berlin's Olympic stadium to go through on a wave of

RIGHT: **HORST BLANKENBURG AND JOHAN CRUYFF PLAY CARDS ON THE EVE OF THEIR EUROPEAN CUP TIE WITH ARSENAL IN LONDON**

bad feeling. Borussia's luck was right out. They missed a penalty and lost centre-back Hartwig Bleidick in the opening half-hour with a broken leg after he mistimed a tackle on Boninsegna.

Inter then squeezed past Standard Liege on the away-goals rule in the quarter-finals and frustrated Celtic on penalties after two goalless games in their semi-final. 'Dixie' Deans, on as substitute for a youthful Kenny Dalglish, missed the crucial first spot-kick.

Buoyed by their previous success in persuading the authorities to intervene on their behalf, Inter launched another protest on finding that they would be playing holders Ajax in Holland, albeit in Rotterdam. UEFA, this time, was having none of it.

Ajax had beaten Dynamo Dresden 2–0, 0–0 in the first round, Marseille 2–1, 4–0 in the second, Cup newcomers Arsenal 2–1, 1–0 in the quarter-final, and Benfica 1–0, 0–0 in the last four.

Arsenal, winners of the Fairs Cup in 1970, had qualified for the Champions Cup for the first time by virtue of winning the English league and FA Cup double in 1971 under the low-key management of Bertie Mee.

They were absolutely delighted to return from Amsterdam with 'only' a 2–1 defeat, but that was before class told its own tale back at Highbury, though Ajax owed victory, oddly, to an own goal by Mee's sometime successor, George Graham.

Cruyff, crowned European Footballer of the Year the previous December after his emergent exploits in 1971, managed not one of Ajax's goals along the way – though his contribution, as he both led the line and faded back to organize play, was more magisterial than ever. He was saving his goals for the right occasion.

At the start of the season, Ajax's ego-edged young stars had been shocked rigid when president Jaap Van Praag had introduced Stefan Kovacs as coach in place of Barcelona-bound Rinus Michels. They had mixed feelings about Michels's departure; they had crossed swords with him, but he was also a father-figure they respected.

Kovacs was a scarcely-known Romanian, whose short grey hair and squat build marked him out as anything but a football man. 'How do you like the length of our hair?' the players asked him on his first day, ready to challenge some stereotypically authoritarian east European response.

'I've been employed as a football coach not a hairdresser,' Kovacs told them and he duly went on to take Ajax to new heights. In effect he completed the job Michels had started by bringing 'total football' to

its zenith. Crucially he allowed Cruyff to exploit all the pitch – as he did to perfect effect in the final against Inter in Rotterdam.

Inter, typically and traditionally defensive, reached half-time safely but the interval disturbed their concentration. Three minutes after the restart Wim Suurbier crossed from the right, goalkeeper Ivano Bordon fumbled and Cruyff stretched out a leg to jab home the opening goal.

Inter moved Sandro Mazzola forward behind Roberto Boninsegna, but the midfield imbalance left them dangerously exposed. Hence Piet Keizer eluded two defenders and crossed for Cruyff to rise and glance home his, and his team's, second goal.

The red-and-white banners were unfurled to hail the finest club team on the planet. Ajax were champions of Europe (again), champions of Holland as well as domestic cup-winners and duly added the World Club Cup and the new European Supercup to their rapidly-expanding trophy cabinets.

'Total football' meant total domination.

ABOVE: **THREE TIMES EUROPEAN FOOTBALLER OF THE YEAR, JOHAN CRUYFF HANGS ON TO THE CHAMPIONS CUP WITH HIS USUAL ELAN**

WEDNESDAY 31 MAY 1972
DE KUIJP, ROTTERDAM

AJAX AMSTERDAM	**2**
CRUYFF 48, 77	
INTERNAZIONALE	**0**

HT: 0–0. ATT: 61,000. REF: HELIES (FR)

AJAX:
STUY – SUURBIER, BLANKENBURG, HULSHOFF, KROL – NEESKENS, HAAN, G. MUHREN – SWART, CRUYFF, KEIZER*.
COACH: KOVACS.

INTER:
BORDON – BELLUGI – BURGNICH, GIUBERTONI (BERTINI 12), FACCHETTI – BEDIN, ORIALI, MAZZOLA*, FRUSTALUPI – JAIR (PELLIZZARO 58), BONINSEGNA.
COACH: INVERNIZZI.

*CAPTAIN.

THE GOLDEN DAYS OF CRUYFF & CO

'Total Football' continued to dominate as Ajax went for their third win in a row, disposing of Bayern Munich and Real Madrid in stylish fashion on their way to confront the Old Lady of Turin in the final

The climactic and concluding third term of Ajax's reign over world club football was marked by a clash of philosophies within the European game as the old guard came to increasingly tetchy grips with the new.

Ajax, on the one hand, underlined their class and confidence by dismantling both Bayern Munich (the future) and Real Madrid (the past) on the grand march to a European Cup hat-trick.

But Bayern's hunger was to be fuelled by a defeat which infuriated players such as Franz Beckenbauer, Gerd Muller and Uli Hoeness, all of whom had already attained the status of European champions at national team level in 1972.

Madrid had returned to 'their' competition for the first time in three seasons while Juventus were also back for the first time in five seasons, trying once again to exorcize their European demons. Record champions of Italy they may have been, but Europe was proving a perpetual puzzle for the Old Lady of Turin.

This season also saw the arrival on the Champions Cup scene of Brian Clough, manager then of newcomers Derby County. His was a household name in England, but so far nowhere else, and his idiosyncratic style and humour were lost on observers from the other side of the English Channel.

Ajax benefited from the holders' customary first-round bye to battle their way to victory in the World Club Cup. Their duel with Independiente of Argentina, however, left physical and mental scars which were still raw five years later when Holland reached the World Cup finals back in the land of the River Plate.

Regaining their composure, Ajax put three goals past CSKA Sofia both away and home in the second round. While Clough's Derby terorised Benfica, Eusebio and company hated the tight, noisy confines of the old Baseball Ground and were demolished 3–0. Roy McFarland, Kevin Hector and John McGovern scored the first-half goals which so comprehensively undermined Portuguese confidence that the Rams were able to claim a goalless draw in Lisbon after withstanding an initial 20-minute storm.

Now the going got tougher. Juventus edged Ujpest

on away goals, while Real Madrid beat a winter-rusty Kiev largely thanks to the defiant magnificence of young goalkeeper Mariano Garcia Remon in the first leg; for the rest of his playing career – and beyond, into coaching the club 30 years later – he would be known as 'the Odessa cat'. Derby found the unfashionable Czechoslovaks of Spartak Trnava a stiffer test than boastful Benfica. They lost 1-0 away but recovered at home with two second-half goals in 11 minutes from striker Hector.

LEFT: **DINO ZOFF DIVES BACK TOO LATE IN THE 47TH MINUTE. THE SCORER WAS JOHNNY REP (CENTRE)**

Ajax, meanwhile, thrashed Bayern 4–1, 1–2. The tie had been billed as the ultimate gladiators' duel between Johan Cruyff and Franz Beckenbauer, Bayern's skipper and creative sweeper. The first half in Amsterdam's Olympic stadium ended goalless but the second half was no contest. Arie Haan (two) and Gerrie Muhren scored three goals in 13 minutes, while Cruyff added a deft finishing touch of a fourth with two minutes remaining. Cruyff, claiming a minor knee injury, was thus free to absent himself from the second leg, which Bayern won by a merely academic 2–1.

Ajax maintained their domineering work in the semis when they beat Real 2–1 in Amsterdam and 1–0 in Madrid. The margin could have been greater in the Spanish capital, where Muhren undertook a keepy-uppy exercise to demonstrate exactly how much respect Ajax had for the history books.

For a second successive season they would face Italian opposition in the final. Juventus had qualified for the first time after beating Derby County in a controversial semi-final which prompted Clough into an angry, frustrated tirade about '****ing cheating Italians.'

He would have considered justice to have been served when Juve lost 1–0 to Ajax from the first Champions Cup final in eastern Europe, in the Yugoslav capital of Belgrade.

The opening 20 minutes saw Ajax at their best. They went ahead through Johnny Rep after barely four minutes and followed up with some of the most fluid, inventive football ever seen in a European final before or since.

Juve had a solid backbone. Dino Zoff would be Italy's goalkeeper-captain when they won the World Cup nine years later, Roberto Bettega would one day become chief executive and Fabio Capello a trophy-gathering coach with Juve, Milan and Real Madrid. But the here and now belonged to Ajax, albeit only by that single goal. They turned Juventus inside out, upside down and back to front.

It was the last such exhibition. Weeks later Cruyff was sold to Barcelona, rejoining Rinus Michels for a then world record fee of £922,000. The Spanish federation sanctioned the deal even though it was concluded after their own transfer deadline. Cruyff was that important – as Ajax's own, inextricable fall from grace would prove.

WEDNESDAY 30 MAY 1973
CRVENA ZVEZVA, BELGRADE

AJAX AMSTERDAM   **1**
REP 4

JUVENTUS   **0**

HT: 1–0. ATT: 93,000. REF: GUGULOVIC (YUG)

AJAX:
STUY - SUURBIER, BLANKENBURG, HULSHOFF, KROL - NEESKENS, HAAN, G. MUHREN - CRUYFF - REP, KEIZER*. COACH: KOVACS.

JUVENTUS:
ZOFF - SALVADORE* - LONGOBUCCO, MORINI, MARCHETTI - CAUSIO (CUCCUREDDU 78), FURINO, CAPELLO - ALTAFINI, ANASTASI, BETTEGA (HALLER 63). COACH: VYCPALEK.

*CAPTAIN.

GERMANY'S FOOTBALLING MIRACLE

The complexities of German history had held up the development of football but now the nation was firing on all cylinders with the emergence of Bayern Munich alongside the national side...

The scale of German achievement in 1973–74 – crowned by triumphs for Bayern Munich in the Champions Cup and West Germany in the World Cup – can be measured by historical reference.

Germany had been a modest power within the context of European football between the wars, when Italy, Austria, Hungary and Czechoslovakia were the finest of the non-British brigade.

In Germany, football had struggled initially to make inroads. The traditional sports culture clubs had long shut out the upstart footballers, while distance hindered the development of an integrated competitive structure.

Historic echoes of the span of German sport linger on. Today visitors to southern Poland find that Wroclaw's old stadium owes its 'Olympic' title to the matches the city hosted for the 1936 Berlin Games. Only then it was known as Breslau.

Adolf Hitler's national socialist regime added to the complexity by prohibiting professional sport. Ambitious clubs found ways and means. The heroes of Schalke, from the pit town of Gelsenkirchen in the industrial Ruhr, were paid as miners but never took the caged plunge below ground.

Leagues were organized in geographical regions, with the championship decided by a series of end-of-season play-offs. That system remained fixed in place after the war, partly because of Allied-imposed travel restrictions as well as the Soviet Union's decision to carve out the German Democratic Republic.

Such restrictive conditions only magnify the stunning achievement of the 1954 World Cup win. Regionalization meant that Germany could not afford full-time football, so its clubs could not compete effectively in Europe until 1963–64, when the launch of the unified, professional Bundesliga changed everything.

In 1966 Borussia Dortmund became the first German club to win a European trophy, the Cup-Winners' Cup. Bayern Munich, not Bundesliga founders but promoted two year later, emulated that example the following season.

No fewer than three of the players who scored a 1–0 extra-time win over Rangers in Nurnberg were in the Bayern side who won the Champions Cup in 1974 and also in the West Germany team who won both the 1972 European Championship and the 1974 World Cup: goalkeeper Sepp Maier, central defender Franz Beckenbauer and centre-forward Gerd Muller, possibly the greatest goal-poacher of all time.

By the time Bayern set out to avenge their crushing defeat by Ajax in the spring of 1973, their ranks had been strengthened by the arrivals of attacking left-back Paul Breitner, stopper Hans-Georg Schwarzenbeck and support forward Uli Hoeness.

When the draw was made in the mid-summer of 1973, Ajax were hot favourites.

By the time they took the field against CSKA Sofia, the glitter had gone. Johan Cruyff had been sold to Barcelona and the difference he made could be counted in goals. The holders had beaten CSKA 6–1 on aggregate in the previous season's second round; this time they lost 2–1. Ajax were history.

Bayern were not the only contenders for their crown. Among previous winners with an avenging hunger were Celtic who beat TPs Turku 9–1 overall, Vejle of Denmark 1–0 – after being held goalless at home – and Basel 6–5 after extra time to reach the semi-finals. Insufficient for the

Finale de la Coupe des Clubs Champions Européens
ACCORD DU CENTENAIRE,
A. BRUXELLES (HEYSEL)

Finale van de Beker der Europese Landskampioenen
KAMPIOENSTRIJD
TE BRUSSEL (HEYSEL)

Club ATLETICO de MADRID
F. C. BAYERN MUNCHEN

15 - 5 - 1974

PROGRAMME OFFICIEL
OFFICIEEL PROGRAMMA
ÉDIT. RESP. - VERANTW. UITG.
S.A. L'OISEAU B.V.

CASTEA — KAVA
PRIX 20 F PRIJS

RIGHT: **EVEN THE EAST GERMANS GOT IN ON THE FOOTBALLING BOOM AS JURGEN SPARWASSER SCORES HIS HISTORIC WORLD CUP WINNER AGAINST WEST GERMANY IN THE FAMOUS 1–0 VICTORY. IT'S A HAIR-RAISING MOMENT FOR GOALKEEPER SEPP MAIER**

Swiss were two goals scored in the first leg by a run-of-the-mill midfielder named Ottmar Hitzfeld.

Atletico had a powerful Argentine flavour. Coach Juan Carlos Lorenzo had led his country at the 1966 World Cup, where they lost notoriously to England in a quarter-final marked by the expulsion of captain Antonio Rattin.

Similarly at Parkhead, Atletico had Argentine Ruben Ayala and 'Panadero' Diaz plus substitute Quique all sent off while battling out (again literally) a goalless draw. Goals from Jose Eulogio Garate and veteran midfielder Adelardo collapsed Celtic late in the return.

Atletico were in the final for the first time. They even came within one minute of emerging from beneath the shadow of neighbours Real. But this was the start of the Bayern era. They had beaten the modest Swedish outfit of Atvidaberg and signed their best player, Conny Torstensson, to help fire them beyond East Germany neighbours Dynamo Dresden, Ajax conquerors CSKA and Ujpest Dozsa.

Torstensson had a poor game in the Heysel in Brussels. So did Hoeness, So did Gerd Muller. Hence, after Atletico had led in extra time through a curled free kick from Luis Aragones, it was rugged centre-back Schwarzenbeck who equalized with a desperate dip from 30 yards.

For the first time, the final went to a replay. It was also the last time since the replay option was scrapped within one more year. In truth, suspension-weakened Atletico had played above themselves in the first match. The replay, back in the Heysel two days later, was a step too far.

Hoeness and Muller each scored twice. Beckenbauer became the first German captain to hold aloft the Champions Cup just as, precisely 51 days later, and back in his Olympic stadium in Munich he would hoist, in similar fashion, the World Cup.

BELOW LEFT: **BAYERN MUNICH CAPTAIN FRANZ 'DER KAISER' BECKENBAUER LIFTS THE EUROPEAN CUP FOLLOWING HIS TEAM'S MAGNIFICENT 4-0 WIN. JOHNNY HANSEN AND GERD MULLER LINE UP BEHIND HIM**

WEDNESDAY 15 MAY 1974
HEYSEL, BRUSSELS

BAYERN MUNICH   1
SCHWARZENBECK 120
ATLETICO MADRID   1
LUIS ARAGONES 113

AFTER EXTRA TIME
HT: 0-0. 90 MIN: 0-0. ATT: 65,000.
REF: LORAUX (BEL)

BAYERN:
MAIER - HANSEN, SCHWARZENBECK, BECKENBAUER*, BREITNER - ROTH, ZOBEL, KAPELLMANN - TORSTENSSON (DURNBERGER 76), G. MULLER, HOENESS.
COACH: LATTEK.

ATLETICO:
REINA - MELO, HEREDIA, EUSEBIO, CAPON - ADELARDO*, IRURETA, SALCEDO (ALBERTO 91) - UFARTE (BECERRA 69), LUIS, GARATE.
COACH: LORENZO.

REPLAY
FRIDAY 17 MAY 1974
HEYSEL, BRUSSELS

BAYERN MUNICH   4
HOENESS 28, 81, MULLER 57, 70
ATLETICO MADRID   0

HT: 1-0. ATT: 23,000.
REF: DELCOURT (BEL)

BAYERN:
MAIER - HANSEN, SCHWARZENBECK, BECKENBAUER*, BREITNER - ROTH, ZOBEL, KAPELLMANN - TORSTENSSON, G. MULLER, HOENESS. COACH: LATTEK.

ATLETICO:
REINA - MELO, HEREDIA, EUSEBIO, CAPON - ADELARDO* (BENEGAS 61), IRURETA, SALCEDO - UFARTE (BECERRA 65), LUIS, GARATE.
COACH: LORENZO.

*CAPTAIN.

A CASE FOR THE FLYING DOCTOR

Bayern changed horses in midstream when they replaced Udo Lattek with Dettmar Cramer. Leeds were another club in uproar, having ended Brian Clough's reign at Elland Road after 44 days

For English football, the 1973-74 season had been depressing in the extreme. Liverpool had failed to live up to their own ambitions in the Champions Cup, Tottenham had lost to Feyenoord in a hooligan-marred UEFA Cup Final and England had failed to qualify for the World Cup finals after a night of high drama against Poland at Wembley.

Sir Alf Ramsey was duly removed as England manager, to be succeeded by Don Revie, supremely confident after guiding Leeds to the second league title of his reign. But to defend their domestic crown and challenge in Europe the Leeds board sprang one of the most spectacularly ill-starred appointments imaginable in Brian Clough.

He was sacked after just 44 days in charge and a week before Leeds' Champions Cup opener at home to Zurich. Assistant Maurice Lindsay took temporary charge and Leeds won 4-1 with goals from Allan Clarke (two), Peter Lorimer and Joe Jordan. The tie was subsequently won 5-3 on aggregate, and in round two Leeds thrashed Ujpest Dozsa, by 5-1 under the managership of former England full-back Jimmy Armfield.

The remainder of the Champions Cup field, sorted by a primitive seeding system, was not exactly vintage. Celtic were fading fast, the glamour of Benfica and Real Madrid was missing, and Bayern had hit a flat patch which prompted the mid-season replacement of Udo Lattek by world football's own 'flying doctor', Dettmar Cramer. Italy was not represented, champions Lazio having been suspended from Europe after a UEFA Cup dust-up with Ipswich.

Bayern came through after another East German duel. The European Supercup was not played this year: the second-round draw matching Bayern with Magdeburg rendered the new trophy redundant. At half-time in the first leg Magdeburg appeared on the brink of a major shock. They led 2-0 through an own goal from Johnny Hansen and a further strike from Jurgen Sparwasser, right on the interval.

Bayern should have been awake to Sparwasser; four months earlier he had scored the historic goal in Hamburg with which East Germany beat West Germany in their group match in the World Cup finals.

Just as Gerd Muller's nose for goal had pulled West Germany around in the World Cup, so it pulled Bayern around against Magdeburg. He scored twice in 18 minutes after the interval in a 3-2 revival win and then twice again as Bayern won 2-1 in front of a curious crowd of 33,734 in East Germany.

Barcelona believed this was to be the season in which they would lay their European Cup jinx. In vain. In their semi-final against Leeds they conceded early goals both at Elland Road and back in the Nou Camp, first to Billy Bremner, then to Peter Lorimer. Despite a numerical advantage gained by the second-leg expulsion of McQueen, they faded away 3-2 overall. Leeds' prize was a trip to the newly-rebuilt Parc des Princes to face a Bayern side who would be inspired, in surprising fashion, by Muller.

When Bayern president Wilhelm Neudecker had signed a chunky little Muller their then Yugoslav coach Tschik Cajkovski was not impressed, complaining: 'You can't expect me to put that little elephant in among my thoroughbreds!'

F.C.Bayern/Leeds
Munich   United

RIGHT: **COACH DETTMAR CRAMER WHO WAS KNOWN BY SEVERAL NICKNAMES IN GERMANY – 'NAPOLEON', 'THE PROFESSOR' AND 'FOOTBALL'S POPE'**

But Neudecker pulled rank and Cajkovski did as he was told. He never regretted it either. Muller scored a record 365 goals in 427 Bundesliga games for Bayern, his only German club, and a further 68 in 62 appearances for West Germany including the winner in the 1974 World Cup Final.

But Muller was far more than the 'scorer of little goals', as acclaimed by national manager Helmut Schon. He was also an outstanding all-round footballer with capacities for organization and vision which were rarely noted until this 1975 Champions Cup Final.

Leeds will always consider they were robbed. French referee Michel Kitabdjian rejected appeals for two penalties – one for a trip on Allan Clarke, another for hands by Franz Beckenbauer. He also ruled out a Leeds 'goal' by Peter Lorimer because Billy Bremner had been standing offside in front of keeper Sepp Maier.

The Bayern perspective was very different. Paul Breitner had been sold the previous summer to Real Madrid and replaced by Bjorn Andersson. After only four minutes, however, the Swede was fouled, kicked on the ground while awaiting treatment and had to be substituted; then Uli Hoeness was hurt, forced to limp on for the next half-hour before being replaced himself before the interval.

Coach Cramer pushed forward Klaus Wunder, substituting for Hoeness, as a lone striker, pulled Conny Torstensson deep to buttress midfield and withdrew Muller into an unaccustomed linking role.

Positioning himself fearlessly in the eye of the Leeds midfield, Muller demanded possession, held up the ball, drew colleagues into prime supporting positions and sought to spark Wunder's pressure-relieving pace up in attack. That he also struck the decisive second goal was no more nor less than he deserved.

Leeds' furious fans ripped out seats and went on a rampage which cost the club two years out of European competition.

WEDNESDAY 28 MAY 1975
PARC DES PRINCES, PARIS

BAYERN MUNICH	2
ROTH 71, MULLER 81

LEEDS UNITED	0

HT: 0-0. ATT: 48,000. REF: KITABDJIAN (FR)

BAYERN:
MAIER – B. ANDERSSON (WEISS 4), SCHWARZENBECK, BECKENBAUER*, DURNBERGER – ZOBEL, ROTH, KAPELLMANN – TORSTENSSON, G. MULLER, HOENESS (WUNDER 42). COACH: CRAMER.

LEEDS:
STEWART – REANEY, MADELEY, HUNTER, F. GRAY – BREMNER*, GILES, YORATH (E. GRAY 80) – LORIMER, A. CLARKE, JORDAN. MANAGER: ARMFIELD.

*CAPTAIN.

RENAISSANCE OF THE FRENCH GAME

The Champions Cup was invented by Frenchmen but, since Reims in the 1950s, none of their teams had made it to the final. Saint-Etienne looked as if they might end this sad state of affairs

Years had passed since French football had had anything of which to boast. The glory of the national team had faded into memories of third place at the 1958 World Cup, and the once great Reims had not merely vanished from the Champions Cup in the early 1960s, they had suffered the double humiliation of relegation and bankruptcy.

Raymond Kopa had argued his way through the closing, injury-riddled seasons of his career, and Just Fontaine – forced by leg fractures into premature retirement – had been briefly leader of the players' union and then national coach before settling for the comfort of media punditry. France had not appeared at the World Cup finals since their first-round exit from England in 1966.

Then, in the mid-1970s, came the stirrings of revival. The federation lured Stefan Kovacs from Ajax to bring a new eye to the task of national manager. And a football-mad factory boss named Roger Rocher down in provincial Saint-Etienne put his money behind the local team in a way which was, in that era, unheard of.

Saint-Etienne had collected their first league title in 1957, their second in 1964, then four in a row from 1967 to 1970. The manager was Albert Batteux, Reims' boss in the 1950s.

By the time Les Verts regained domestic primacy, in 1974, red-haired centre-back Roby Herbin had become an equally inspiring coach, and imported experience had been added in Yugoslav goalkeeper Yvan Curkovic and Argentine defender Oswaldo Piazza.

Their composure and confidence fired up impressionable young Frenchmen, such as centre-back Christian Lopez, midfield terrier Dominique Bathenay, playmaker Jean-Michel Larque and brothers Herve and Patrick Revelli in attack. In due course they would be joined by a precocious talent who needed no lessons in self- confidence: the eel-like winger Dominique Rocheteau.

In 1974–75 Sporting of Lisbon, Hajduk Split and Ruch Chorzow were turned over in dramatic style before Bayern proved too wily in the semi-finals. The next season, Les Verts went one better.

KB Kobenhavn (beaten 5–1 overall) and Rangers (4–1) provided few initial problems. But the quarter-final pairing with Dynamo Kiev was something else.

Kiev were one of Europe's class acts, high technical ability having been honed with a scientifically refined preparation programme developed by former Soviet left-winger Valeri Lobanovsky. The previous year they had won the Cup-Winners' Cup on the back of the attacking brilliance of goal-scoring left-winger Oleg Blokhin, who had duly earned the European Footballer of the Year accolade.

At 23, Blokhin was considered a Soviet Cruyff. But the biggest hurdle for Blokhin, as with all Soviet and eastern European teams in Europe, was the long, icy winter which left them ring-rusty and perpetually vulnerable against match-fit western Europeans in the quarter-finals.

The first leg against Saint-Etienne was staged, not in chilly Kiev, but in the warmer climes of Simferopol in the Crimea. That suited Kiev, who would have won by a landslide, instead of merely 2–0, had it not been for the acrobatic brilliance of Curkovic in goal.

The Stade Geoffroy-Guichard was developing a reputation as a European Cup inferno, but Kiev survived the first half of the return unscathed.

Twenty minutes into the second half, with the game still goalless, Kiev were poised to administer the coup de grâce. Blokhin slalomed off into the distance, past full-back Gerard Janvion, past Lopez, and closed in on Curkovic. He had two options: to chip the goalkeeper or square to unmarked team-mate Vladimir Onishenko. For some unfathomable reason, the European Footballer of the Year did neither: he hesitated and tried to dribble one more time around Lopez. This time Lopez was able to dispossess him and clear the ball to safety.

At this precise moment, Kiev heads went down, and Saint-Etienne stormed to a 3-0 win in extra time.

Larque scored the only goal of the two semi-final ties against PSV Eindhoven and Saint-Etienne thus became the first French club in 17 years to reach the final of the event

Frenchmen had dreamed up. Sadly, for them, it would prove a massive anti-climax.

A fading Bayern were still good enough to beat a Real Madrid side, who had beaten Derby in a storming quarter-final, in the semis.

The final was staged at Hampden where Madrid and Eintracht Frankfurt had left an explosion of memories in 1960. By contrast, Bayern against Saint-Etienne left little but a string of regrets: above all regret that Bayern, despite playing dreary, negative football, capitalized on a single long-range strike from Franz Roth.

Bayern would go to beat Brazil's Cruzeiro for the World Club Cup but the spark was missing. Less then six weeks after winning at Hampden Park, Maier, Beckenbauer, Schwarzenbeck and Hoeness were in the West German side deprived of their European national team crown by Czechoslovakia in a penalty shootout in Belgrade.

Going, going . . .

THE SHOCK OF THE NEW

Many of the top dogs in European football were being overhauled by rivals - Borussia Monchengladbach, Brugge, PSV and Torino all came good, but it was Liverpool the others had to look out for...

Further power shifts were under way. In Germany, Bayern were being overtaken by Borussia Monchengladbach, where ex-Munich coach Udo Lattek had taken over from Hennes Weisweiler, whose insistence on team above stars was leading him to disaster at Barcelona.

In Holland, Ajax and Feyenoord had been pushed aside by PSV Eindhoven, while the most effective Dutch marksman of the era was Rob Rensenbrink, who was leading the Belgian club Anderlecht to two Cup-Winners' Cup triumphs in three seasons. Yet back in Belgium domestic command had been wrenched away by Anderlecht's northern rivals Brugge under Ernst Happel.

Even at Liverpool, a change of direction had occurred. Two years earlier, in July 1974, manager Bill Shankly had suddenly retired. Speculation on the reasons varied from Shankly's own wish to make up for lost time with his family to the value of his contract. The later consensus was that 'Shanks' had grown tired; he was human after all.

At first, it was impossible to imagine Liverpool without the Scot's passionate ferocity but, just as he had organized a perpetual regeneration of the team, so he had ensured a succession system out of the famed Boot Room. Bob Paisley thus inherited a fine team including Kevin Keegan the finest English player of his generation.

Liverpool saw off Crusaders of Belfast 2-0, 5-0 in a first round which saw Benfica tumbled by Dynamo Dresden. Phil Neal (penalty) and John Toshack scored in the first leg; Keegan, David Johnson (two), Terry McDermott and Steve Heighway in the return.

In the second round, Liverpool returned from a tiring trek to Turkey to play Trabzonspor with a 1-0 defeat, but a salvo of three goals in the first 18 minutes from Heighway, Johnson and Keegan easily overcame the deficit back at Anfield. Elsewhere, conveniently, Madrid were removed from the equation by Brugge and Torino by Borussia.

Liverpool claimed a dramatic win - on the away goals rule - over Saint-Etienne in the quarter-finals, where Bayern's reign came to an end. Their defeat by Kiev freed Franz Beckenbauer to fly off and share the brief fun and games of life with New York Cosmos in the North American Soccer League.

Liverpool, however went marching on. Zurich folded up both home and away. Neal scored two goals, one a penalty, in the first leg, and hard-working Jimmy Case struck twice at Anfield. Liverpool cruised in 6-1 on aggregate to face Borussia in Rome.

RIGHT: KEVIN KEEGAN MISSED LIVERPOOL'S FIRST LEG IN SAINT-ETIENNE BUT WAS BACK TO SCORE FOR THE REDS IN THEIR FAMOUS 3-1 VICTORY AT ANFIELD WHEN 'SUPERSUB' DAVID FAIRCLOUGH STRUCK THE WINNING GOAL

The two clubs were old foes. They had met in the 1973 UEFA Cup Final when the first leg was abandoned because of torrential rain, handing then manager Shankly the chance to revise his team and tactics decisively for the replay.

Contrastingly, two of the smallest men on the pitch also boasted the two largest profiles. England's Keegan and Denmark's Allan Simonsen were both bound to become European Footballer of the Year – Simonsen in 1977, Keegan in 1978 and 1979 – but both were also developing itchy feet.

This was Keegan's last competitive appearance for Liverpool before his £500,000 transfer to Hamburg, while Simonsen would wait just a year longer before flying off to Barcelona. But, while Liverpool would replace Keegan audaciously and magnificently with Kenny Dalglish from Celtic, Borussia would never replace Simonsen. Still, these were issues for the future.

Liverpool had been riding the crest of wave which had swept them to the brink of a fabulous treble. On 14 May, they had secured their 10th league title with a goalless draw against West Ham; but a week later they lost 2–1 to Manchester United in the FA Cup Final. They had four days

in which to pick themselves up again for the European showdown in the Stadio Olimpico, which was turned into Kop-from-home by more than 30,000 Liverpool fans.

Liverpool quickly hit their stride. Before the half-hour, they had glided into the lead. Heighway, the university graduate who later became master of the Liverpool academy, opened the way to goal for midfielder McDermott.

At last Borussia came to life and levelled through Simonsen. Only the reflexes of Ray Clemence and the mental and physical resilience developed down the years defied a Borussia siege.

Then, midway through the second half, Liverpool won a corner on the left, and powerful Tommy Smith, scattering German defenders right and left, headed them back in front. Eight minutes from time Borussia's captain, Berti Vogts, tripped Keegan and the reliable Neal slotted home the penalty. Liverpool were champions of Europe.

Paisley beamed broadly and proudly at the assembled media as flashlights exploded at the post-match press conference. Watching from the back of the media scrum, dignified but largely ignored in the commotion, stood Bill Shankly.

ABOVE: **LIVERPOOL'S PHIL NEAL (2), EMLYN HUGHES (6) AND JIMMY CASE (8) PARADE THE EUROPEAN CUP BEFORE SOME OF THE REDS' 30,000 ECSTATIC SUPPORTERS**

WEDNESDAY 25 MAY 1977
OLIMPICO, ROME

LIVERPOOL 3
MCDERMOTT 27, SMITH 65, NEAL 82 PEN

B. MONCHENGLADBACH 1
SIMONSEN 51

HT: 1–0. ATT: 57,000. REF: WURTZ (FR)

LIVERPOOL:
CLEMENCE - NEAL, SMITH, E. HUGHES*, JONES - CALLAGHAN, CASE, R. KENNEDY, MCDERMOTT - KEEGAN, HEIGHWAY.
MANAGER: PAISLEY.

MONCHENGLADBACH:
KNEIB - VOGTS*, WITTKAMP, WOHLERS (HANNES 79), KLINKHAMMER - BONHOF, WIMMER (KULIK 24), STIELIKE, SCHAFER - SIMONSEN, HEYNCKES.
COACH: LATTEK.

*CAPTAIN.

A BHOY'S OWN STORY

Kenny Dalglish replaced Kevin Keegan as the star striker in Liverpool's line-up, while Juve president Gianni Agnelli promised his Number 1 the pick of the production line for services rendered

When Kenneth Mathieson Dalglish signed for Liverpool from Celtic for £440,000 in the summer of 1977, he was the perfect successor to Kevin Keegan. He had joined the Bhoys at the time of their Lisbon triumph and would manage the singular achievement of scoring 100 league goals in both Scotland and England.

He would become Scotland's record international with 102 caps as well as the only player-manager to lead a club to the English league and cup double.

He was also a comparative rarity in being brought straight into Liverpool's first team rather than schooled in the reserves according to the usual Shankly/Paisley tradition. But then, when a club boasts the crowns of both England and Europe, a slow start to the following season is not an option.

Liverpool decided to live without the World Club Cup mayhem, instead contenting themselves with thrashing Keegan and his new club Hamburg 1–1, 6–0 in the European Supercup.

Real Madrid and Feyenoord, of the European grandees, were missing from the first-round draw of the Champions Cup. The significance, in Madrid's case, was immense. For the first time since they had beaten Servette in the inaugural Champions Cup in 1955, the six-times champions had not qualified for Europe at all.

The odds on West Germany regaining ground had lengthened. In the previous two years, both Bayern Munich (as holders) and Borussia Monchengladbach (as Bundesliga champions) had competed. Now it was down 'only' to Borussia. They were among eight contenders who had retained their domestic title: the others were Liverpool, Dresden, Benfica, Jeunesse d'Esch (Luxembourg), Trabzonspor (Turkey), Omonia (Cyprus) and Brugge (Belgium).

Brugge were breaking out of the shadow of Anderlecht, though the Brussels club were dominating the Cup-Winners' Cup. Brugge had reached one European final of their own in 1976, when they lost to Liverpool in the UEFA Cup after leading the first leg 2–0 at half-time at Anfield. Now Brugge had Liverpool in their sights, with revenge the spur.

When Liverpool joined the fray it appeared that the luck of the draw was not with them. Dresden were standing in the way. Not for long. Dalglish's European Cup debut for Liverpool was marked by a 5–1 win at Anfield which included a rare goal from another newcomer in central defender Alan Hansen. In mid-season, they would be joined by a third new Scot in aggressive midfielder Graeme Souness.

Liverpool progressed 6–3 on aggregate while Brugge, 9–2 first-round winners against KPs of Finland, came through 2–1 against Panathinaikos. Brugge's English centre-forward Roger Davies, a 27-year-old 'veteran' of Derby's semi-final run in 1973, followed up his treble against the Finns with the home opener against the Greeks.

A Dalglish-less Celtic, Nantes and Red Star were other second-round losers, while interest ended at the quarter-final stage for Benfica, Ajax, Atletico Madrid and Celtic's surprise conquerors, Innsbruck. Ajax lost on penalties to Juventus, for whom Dino Zoff saved two spot-kicks. 'Tell him to come and see me and choose any car he wants,' said

RIGHT: **BOB PAISLEY WAS THE MOST SUCCESSFUL MANAGER IN LIVERPOOL'S HISTORY AFTER HE WAS ELEVATED FROM THE SHADOWS OF THE BOOT ROOM AS BILL SHANKLY'S SUCCESSOR**

the Juventus (and Fiat) owner, Gianni Agnelli. For the first time since 1960, not one eastern European club reached the last eight.

Benfica faced Liverpool in the Estadio da Luz off the back of a 46-game unbeaten run. Nene gave them a 13th-minute lead, but Liverpool proved happily at home in the rain. Goals from Jimmy Case and Emlyn Hughes punctured both Benfica's record and their confidence. Dalglish broke his European goal-scoring duck for Liverpool in the 4-1 return stroll.

Meanwhile, English referee Pat Partridge was keeping a lid on tempers in Spain, where Atletico Madrid beat Brugge 3-2 but lost 4-3 on aggregate. Seasoned Julien Cools and centre-forward Raoul Lambert scored decisive goals in the last half-hour as the Spanish revival burned itself out.

Brugge then needed extra time, punctuated by the expulsion of rugged Claudio Gentile, to edge out Juventus 2-1 in the semi-finals. Their reward was the longed-for repeat against Liverpool, who had overcome Borussia yet again: this time 4-2 on aggregate. Crucially, a muscle strain robbed Borussia of Allan Simonsen in both games. He was the competition's top scorer with five goals, and without him Borussia's attack stuttered to near standstill.

Dalglish scored Liverpool's second goal, his 29th of his rewarding first season. There was still one left in his armoury – the lone goal which brought victory at Wembley over Brugge in an undistinguished final.

Undistinguished not for any lack of ambition by Liverpool, but due largely for the cautious negativity of Brugge coach Ernst Happel. He had plotted Feyenoord's 1970 victory over Celtic, but then he had far better players than his injury-hit Belgian champions.

Liverpool's victory provided welcome consolation for English football after an otherwise depressing international season which had brought a second failure in a row to qualify for the World Cup finals.

LEFT: **FREED BY GRAEME SOUNESS'S INCISIVE PASS, KENNY DALGLISH CALMLY STEADIES HIMSELF BEFORE CHIPPING THE BALL HOME**

WEDNESDAY 10 MAY 1978
WEMBLEY, LONDON

LIVERPOOL   1
DALGLISH 64
CLUB BRUGGE   0

HT: 0-0. ATT: 92,000. REF: CORVER (HOL)

LIVERPOOL:
CLEMENCE – NEAL, THOMPSON, HANSEN, E. HUGHES* – CASE (HEIGHWAY 63), R. KENNEDY, SOUNESS, MCDERMOTT – DALGLISH, FAIRCLOUGH.
MANAGER: PAISLEY.

BRUGGE:
JENSEN – BASTIJNS*, KRIEGER, LEEKENS, MAES (VOLDERS 70) – SORENSEN, COOLS, DE CUBBER, VANDEREYCKEN, KU (SANDERS 60) – SIMOEN.
COACH: HAPPEL.

*CAPTAIN.

THE YEAR OF THE UNDERDOGS

Back in 1978, you didn't have to have money to run a successful team, even if it came in handy. Everything was possible if you had the right manager. Step forward, Brian Clough and Bob Houghton

'Old Big 'ead' was back. In January 1975, four months after being ignominiously forced out of Leeds, Brian Clough had returned to work, back in the east Midlands, at Second Division Nottingham Forest – just the other side of the M1 from Derby.

Time had offered Clough a refreshing perspective. He accepted that, in his headstrong way, he had approached the Leeds job in a way guaranteed to make ill-judged enemies. But the terms of his dismissal were gilded with long-term financial security. Clough may have been a conviction socialist, but he enjoyed the personality lifestyle.

At the end of that first half-season under Clough, Forest finished 16th out of 22 clubs; in 1976 they were eighth; in 1977, when Derby tried in vain to lure Clough back, they were promoted from third place; and in 1978 they went straight through and won not only the First Division championship but the League Cup as well.

Significantly, they finished seven points clear of Liverpool in the league and beat Liverpool 1–0 in the League Cup Final replay. Scottish left-winger John Robertson settled it with a penalty. He was among the half a dozen who shared the fast-track ride from second-division obscurity to European glory.

Success generated the money to buy even better players, such as the England goalkeeper Peter Shilton, from Stoke, and the controversial Scottish terrier, Kenny Burns, from Birmingham City. But Clough also fished successfully in non-league waters for the likes of Long Eaton's Garry Birtles, whom Clough and Taylor would turn into a million-pound England centre-forward.

UEFA's seeding system took no account of clubs with little or no European track record. Thus, in the first round, unseeded Forest were drawn against Liverpool, in Europe for the 15th successive season. Crucially, Liverpool misjudged the City Ground opener. A goal down to an early strike from Birtles, Liverpool refused to shut up shop and were chasing an equalizer when Birtles broke away and created a second for Colin Barrett. Holders' skipper Emlyn Hughes said later: 'We treated it like a league match rather than a European away match. We attacked too much.'

'Perhaps now you people will realize we are quite a good side,' Clough told the TV cameras after the goalless second leg. Complacency also cost the rest of Europe's cream dear – which assisted the Forest cause.

In the first round alone, Juventus lost to Rangers, Monaco lost to Sweden's Malmo with their English manager Bob Houghton, while Brugge lost to Wisla Krakow. In the second round Real Madrid were beaten by Grasshopper Zurich and the goals of shooting star Claudio Sulser, while Kiev Dynamo lost to Malmo and PSV Eindhoven lost to Rangers.

Forest advanced to the quarter-finals with a 7–2 aggregate destruction of Ferenc Puskas-managed AEK Athens.

RIGHT: **TREVOR FRANCIS, THE UK'S FIRST £1-MILLION FOOTBALLER, HEADS THE WINNING GOAL PAST MALMO GOALKEEPER JAN MOLLER**

They now drew Grasshoppers, for whom Sulser had scored nine goals in four games, prompting talk of an assault on the European Cup record of 14 goals set by Jose Altafini in the 1962–63 season. It was only talk and was soon stilled. Forest won 4–1, 1–1. Along the way Clough also made Birmingham City's striker Trevor Francis Britain's first £1 million footballer.

Eligibility rules forced Francis to sit out both the quarter-final and the dramatic semi-final victory over Koln, in which Forest hit back to win 1–0 in Germany after being held 3–3 at home. Not even the promise of a 40,000-Mark bonus could force the Germans back into the game and the tie.

Awaiting Forest in Munich were Houghton's Malmo with their highly-organized mixture of full-time professionals and part-time travel agents, students and firemen.

As IFK Gothenburg's new young coach, Sven-Goran Eriksson, would recall later: 'Bob and Roy Hodgson brought English organization to our game and a new way of playing. Instead of standing off and counter-attacking they pressed when the opposition had the ball. They introduced all the things I'd seen as a kid every Saturday when I watched English football on TV.'

Houghton had reached Sweden and Malmo via English non-league football and South Africa. No Swedish club had ever previously reached the semi-finals of the Champions Cup, let alone the Final. Malmo's sky blues had been assisted by the luck of the draw and the failings of the usual ruling class. But Houghton also benefited from the solidity of goalkeeper Jan Moller and experience of 1974 World Cup midfielders Bo Larsson and Staffan Tapper.

Unfortunately Larsson was unfit for the final. A knee injury suffered against Wisla would end his career. Worse followed when long-striding Tapper had to be substituted after half an hour.

No surprise then, that time Forest's dominating pressure should be properly rewarded. Just on half-time Robertson's left-wing cross was dive-headed home by Francis – who thus marked his European debut with the one touch which repaid all of his £1m fee and more.

LEFT: **IF THE CUP FITS, WEAR IT: TREVOR FRANCIS BASKS IN THE GLORY OF VICTORY**

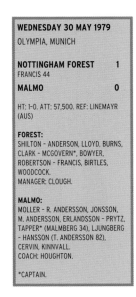

WEDNESDAY 30 MAY 1979
OLYMPIA, MUNICH

NOTTINGHAM FOREST	1
FRANCIS 44	
MALMO	0

HT: 1–0. ATT: 57,500. REF: LINEMAYR (AUS)

FOREST:
SHILTON – ANDERSON, LLOYD, BURNS, CLARK – MCGOVERN*, BOWYER, ROBERTSON – FRANCIS, BIRTLES, WOODCOCK.
MANAGER: CLOUGH.

MALMO:
MOLLER – R. ANDERSSON, JONSSON, M. ANDERSSON, ERLANDSSON – PRYTZ, TAPPER* (MALMBERG 34), LJUNGBERG – HANSSON (T. ANDERSSON 82), CERVIN, KINNVALL.
COACH: HOUGHTON.

*CAPTAIN.

1980S

THE DESCENT INTO CHAOS

Triumph and tragedy marked the 1980s, and European football's descent into hooligan chaos reached its nadir with the Heysel Stadium disaster in Brussels. Within weeks English clubs had been barred from European competition for what proved to be five years. The Hillsborough tragedy of 1989 would also contribute to major changes in the presentation and financing of top-level football. By the end of the decade, the balance of power out on the pitch had swung back towards Italy and Milan were revitalized. The club's ambitious president Silvio Berlusconi ended up making almost as many headlines as Milan's star players such as Marco Van Basten and Ruud Gullit.

RIGHT: **FLARES GO OFF AS LIVERPOOL AND ROMA PLAYERS LINE UP BEFORE THE 1984 CHAMPIONS CUP FINAL IN ROME**

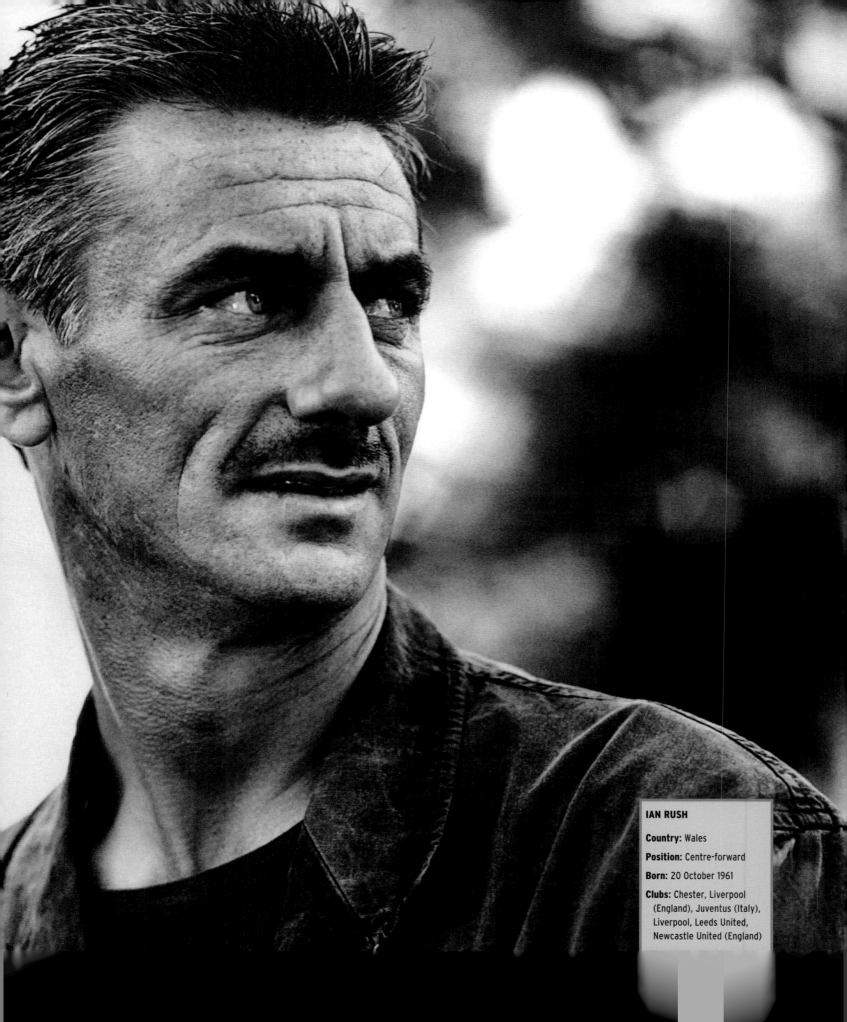

IAN RUSH

Country: Wales

Position: Centre-forward

Born: 20 October 1961

Clubs: Chester, Liverpool
(England), Juventus (Italy),
Liverpool, Leeds United,
Newcastle United (England)

IAN RUSH

Joining Liverpool, particularly when I did late in the 1979-80 season, had to be considered a dream in any footballer's language. They had twice been European champions as well as the dominant club in England for more than a decade. But the perspective from the outside can be deceptive. I have to admit that at first, on arriving from Chester, I found it all a real struggle.

The team had gone out of the European Cup in the first round twice in a row – following those back-to-back wins in 1977 and 1978 – with early knockouts by Nottingham Forest and Dinamo Tbilisi.

At the start of the 1980-81 campaign we still had many of the men who had triumphed a few years before, and as Oulu Palloseura, Aberdeen and CSKA Sofia were overcome I never had a look-in.

Then my luck turned. Bob Paisley picked me for the League Cup Final replay win over West Ham, and the boss then had me in the side for the first leg of the European semi-final against Bayern Munich. We drew 0-0 at Anfield, and I was back on the bench for the second leg in Germany. I did not get on the pitch, but we drew 1-1 thanks to an away goal from Ray Kennedy.

Before the final against Real Madrid in Paris I went off to play for Wales against England buoyed up by the fact that Bob had told me I would be in the squad. I thought he meant in the 16. Instead I was 17th man, which in those days meant that although I was on the bench I didn't get stripped.

How can I complain, looking back? That was a great Liverpool team, and we proved it by winning the cup for a third time, with Alan Kennedy hitting the late winner. But remember that I was a young kid. I wanted to play. I was happy for the club, but disappointed for myself.

I wanted to leave. I went to see Bob Paisley that summer and told him so. After that, when he sent me on as a substitute in the first round against Palloseura the next season, I honestly thought I was putting myself in the shop window. But I scored my first goal for the club in that game,

which we won 7-0 – and quickly everything changed for the better for me.

I must say that Kenny Dalglish was very good to me. He gave me the perfect piece of advice when he said: 'Don't worry about anything else – if you want to stay in the side, your job is to get goals. Then you can gradually add the other things to your play.'

You can never predict how everything will work out. David Johnson got injured, which was bad luck for him but good for me, because it meant I was in the side regularly. We beat AZ67 Alkmaar – and I scored again – then went out to CSKA Sofia.

It may sound strange as we still had so many players who had won the competition, but I felt the inexperience of newer boys like Bruce Grobbelaar, Mark Lawrenson, Ronnie

LEFT: **IAN RUSH SPENT THE 1987-88 SEASON WITH JUVENTUS**

Whelan and me in this kind of football cost us. We were all right back on home ground in the English Football League, but European football was completely different. Teams sat back and hit you on the break, and we kept getting caught out. We were not smart enough.

No matter how often it happened, we just did not seem to learn our lesson. The same thing happened again in 1982–83. We won comfortably against Dundalk and HJK Helsinki, then lost 4–3 on aggregate to Widzew Lodz in the quarter-finals.

But you cannot play all these matches in different conditions, in different countries, against different clubs and players and styles, without building up the 'knowledge'. So I felt different about our prospects when we launched our 1983–84 campaign. I felt at last we had the experience we needed to make an impact.

We beat Odense 6–0 over the two legs in the first round, then played Athletic Bilbao. They held us goalless at Anfield and thought they were through then. But we went to Spain and won 1–0. The goal was something of a collector's item. Alan Kennedy didn't have a right foot, but he crossed with that foot; I rarely scored with a header, but I headed this one in.

We were picking up momentum. In the quarter-finals we beat Benfica home and away and I scored for the 1–0 win at Anfield and again in the 4–1 win in Lisbon. Our class showed in the Stadium of Light. I still look back on that as one of our great performances in Europe.

In the semi-final there was another. We beat Dinamo Bucharest 1–0 in the match at Anfield, remembered for that infamous incident when Graeme Souness was accused of breaking the jaw of one of their players. That really stoked up the atmosphere for the return in Romania. The stadium in Bucharest that night was the most intimidating place we had ever been. But Graeme loved it! He just seemed to get bigger and better as the game went on. I scored twice and we went through to the final against Roma in their own Olympic Stadium.

Joe Fagan had taken over as manager from Bob Paisley the year before, but little had changed. He had Ronnie Moran and Roy Evans working with him as a team, and the approach to the final was typical Liverpool: keep your feet on the ground and treat it as another game.

Phil Neal gave us the lead, but even when Roberto Pruzzo equalized, we still felt we were the stronger team. We couldn't get the second goal, though, and it went to penalties. Joe said: 'Don't worry about it, you've done all you can,' and that helped us to relax.

Graeme Souness, Phil Neal and I all wanted to take the first kick, but then we saw Steve Nicol walking away from us with the ball. There was nothing we could do about it – and he missed.

Graeme and Phil were on target, and then, with the count at 2–2, it was my turn. I can tell you that was the longest walk I have ever taken in football, with 80,000 Italians whistling at me. But as I ran up, their keeper helped me by moving to the right. I saw him out of the corner of my eye, which meant it was 'just' a little matter of knocking the ball into the other corner.

Brucie then did his famous knee-shaking act on the line and Francesco Graziani shot over. Now it was down to Alan Kennedy. He had missed every one when we had practised penalties in training and, for the first time, their keeper went the right way... but the shot was perfectly placed, right in the corner, and he had no chance.

The feeling was fantastic. To go and win the European Cup in the backyard of the opposition was a tremendous feat. I don't think it will happen again.

Graeme Souness left in the summer for Sampdoria. That was a big blow because he had been a major influence, but we had more experience among us now and felt we could cope.

We started our defence by beating Lech Poznan 5–0 on aggregate. Then I got a hat-trick in the first leg against Benfica and, despite a 1–0 defeat in Lisbon, we went through. Then came FK Austria, and after a 1-1 draw in Vienna, we won 4-1. I scored twice in the first leg of the semi-final against Panathinaikos, but as I was on a booking, Joe Fagan left me out of the return in Athens to avoid any risks. We won 1-0 anyway.

Of course, the final against Juventus at the Heysel Stadium in Brussels will never be remembered for the football, but for the tragedy that cost so many lives. Until the memories were revived last spring when the clubs were drawn together in the Champions League, I am not sure many people could have told you that Michel Platini scored the winner for Juventus in Heysel from a penalty. At that stage we knew something had happened, but we really did not know what. We just wanted to get it over with. The whole match was unreal. When I joined Juventus later on, many people there told me they had felt exactly the same way.

The two clubs have had a strong bond ever since then. For example, when I was transferred back to Liverpool, all the negotiations were done by telephone, which just shows how much trust there was between the clubs and the people.

In football terms, the ban which followed the Heysel tragedy hit English football hard. Everton had won the League title in 1985, and I honestly believe they could have gone on to win the European Cup the following season... if Liverpool had not done it again, of course. I still believe we were the two best teams in Europe at the time.

LEFT: **IAN RUSH SCORED A TOTAL OF 20 GOALS FOR LIVERPOOL IN EUROPE: HIS PARTNERSHIP WITH KENNY DALGLISH MEANT THE REDS REIGNED AS EUROPE'S TOP CLUB IN THE MID-1980S**

MIGHTY MOUSE JOINS THE REVOLUTION

The varying number of foreign imports allowed in each league led to disparities between different European sides. After leaving Liverpool in 1977, Kevin Keegan was finally coming to terms with life in Hamburg

Two years of Liverpool, plus one year and possibly more of Nottingham Forest, stirred unrest across the continent. The issue, with huge irony considering what the future held in store, was foreign imports.

Real Madrid, beating Levski Sofia of Bulgaria 3–0 overall in the late summer of 1979, were permitted only two foreigners: German midfielder Uli Stielike and the black England winger Laurie Cunningham, who had sold himself to Madrid during his summer holiday on the strength of a decisive display for West Bromwich Albion against Valencia in the UEFA Cup.

Milan, barred from using foreign players altogether, fell immediately. They drew 0–0 in Porto, then lost 1–0 at home. New coach Massimo Giacomini complained: 'It's an uneven playing field. The Spanish clubs can have two foreigners from anywhere, the Germans and the Dutch have their Danes and Swedes, while the English can pick as many Scots and Irish as they like.'

Giacomini was wide of the mark in thinking that German clubs looked only to Scandinavia. Hamburg, back for the first time since their epic run to the 1961 semis, had looked both south-east and north-west. Linking defence and midfield was the Yugoslav Ivan Buljan, while the attacking sparkle was provided by England's Kevin Keegan.

'Mighty Mouse' was voted European Footballer of the Year in both 1978 and 1979 But by Christmas, the goalposts were shifting. Keegan had already decided to move on at the end of the season. He could have doubled his £120,000-a-year salary at Real Madrid or in Italy, where the borders were about to creak open, while Chelsea were English favourites. No one foresaw Keegan returning, instead, to Southampton. Ever the exemplary professional, Keegan did not allow any of this to distract him from his football as the Champions Cup reached the quarter-final stage.

RIGHT: **LAURIE CUNNINGHAM IN ACTION FOR REAL MADRID AGAINST HAMBURG IN THE VOLKSPARKSTADION. ONE OF THE FIRST BLACK PLAYERS TO REPRESENT ENGLAND AT ANY LEVEL, HE SADLY DIED IN A CAR CRASH OUTSIDE MADRID IN 1989, SHORTLY AFTER HELPING RAYO VALLECANO BACK INTO SPAIN'S TOP FLIGHT**

LEFT: **WINGER JOHN ROBERTSON IS MOBBED BY TEAM-MATES AFTER SCORING THE WINNER IN THE 19TH MINUTE**

Forest launched their defence comfortably against Osters and Arges Pitesti. But Dynamo Berlin were a different proposition. The East German police club had just embarked on a remarkable run of 10 successive league titles. Everything was tilted in their favour, from transfers to referees. They were as dominant as they were despised.

On 5 March 1980, Dynamo made headlines round Europe by beating Forest 1–0 at the City Ground in the quarter-final opener. Hans-Jurgen Riediger marked his return after a broken ankle with the 63rd-minute winner. Many assumed that Forest had been weakened by the mid-season sale of striker Tony Woodcock to Koln The appearance proved to be deceptive, however, as Forest hit back 3–1 behind the Berlin Wall with a double from Trevor Francis. Similarly, Real Madrid recovered from 2–0 down in the first leg to overcome Celtic 3–0 in the return. Hamburg missed hepatitis victim Buljan against his old club Hajduk Split, but still managed an away goals win, while Frank Arnesen and Soren Lerby scored in Ajax's 4–0 win over Strasbourg.

Lerby added another in the semi-final against Forest, but this time Ajax lost 2–1. Madrid, anticipating staging the final, thought they were home and dry when two goals from Carlos Santillana beat Hamburg in the Bernabeu. But Keegan and Co thrashed Madrid out of sight, 5–1, in the Volksparkstadion.

This time Cunningham's away goal could not save Madrid, who ended up with 10 men. Their underrated, moustachioed playmaker, Vicente del Bosque, was sent off six minutes from time.

Unsurprisingly, Madrid fans stayed away from the final in a half-empty Estadio Bernabeu despite the personal drama of the English duel between Keegan and Brian Clough, Forest's manager.

Clough and assistant Peter Taylor were away spying on Hamburg when news filtered through of Trevor Francis, scorer of two crucial goals in the semi-final defeat of Ajax, tearing an Achilles tendon in a league game against Crystal Palace. He missed the Champions' final and the European Championships.

To compound Clough's problems, the wayward Stan Bowles – a typical gamble of a signing from Queens Park Rangers – walked out on the club a week earlier. Thus Forest lined up a squad of 15 in Madrid, one short of the permitted maximum.

Hamburg had their own problems. Coach Zebec, an alcoholic, had been taken ill just before the season's end. Midfield general Jimmy Hartwig was missing with a knee injury and towering spearhead Horst Hrubesch would not even have been on the bench, nursing an ankle problem, had this not been the European Cup Final.

Keegan worked himself into the ground to little effect. Hrubesch's deputy, Jurgen Milewski, bounced off Larry Lloyd and Kenny Burns. When Hrubesch did appear, for the second half, he was so much a passenger his presence was more hindrance than help. It was all over by then, anyway. In the 19th minute John Robertson drifted in from the left and surprised keeper Rudi Kargus with a right-foot shot which scuffed in off a post.

Clough and Taylor – to polite applause from those Madrid fans who had bothered to turn out – again paraded the prize which justified their new three-year contracts.

WEDNESDAY 28 MAY 1980
BERNABEU, MADRID

NOTTINGHAM FOREST　　**1**
ROBERTSON 19

HAMBURG　　**0**

HT: 1–0. ATT: 51,000.
REF: GARRIDO (POR)

FOREST:
SHILTON – V. ANDERSON, LLOYD, BURNS, F. GRAY (GUNN 84) – MCGOVERN*, O'NEILL, BOWYER – MILLS (O'HARE 68), BIRTLES, ROBERTSON.
MANAGER: CLOUGH.

HAMBURG:
KARGUS – KALTZ, JAKOBS, HIERONYMUS (HRUBESCH 46), NOGLY* – BULJAN, MEMERING, MAGATH – KEEGAN, MILEWSKI, REIMANN.
COACH: ZEBEC.

*CAPTAIN

LOOKING TOWARDS THE FUTURE

Nottingham Forest took a busman's holiday in Japan. Meanwhile, Real Madrid began their relentless march towards the final, as mighty Liverpool set off in the same direction with a 10-goal spree

Nottingham Forest had prepared for their second Champions Cup triumph by flying off on a team holiday break to Mallorca. They followed it up with a working jaunt to Japan. The reason for this exemplified the increasing popularity of the professional game around the world.

Japan wanted to host the World Cup one day. Traditionalists in Europe and South America thought this ludicrous, but the idea had been planted years earlier by Sir Stanley Rous during his presidency of FIFA. Eventually, of course, that dream would come true: in 2002 Japan and South Korea would jointly host the World Cup and the Far East in general would be courted by Europe's major clubs.

Forest's role in the pre-history was to accept an invitation to revitalize the battle-scarred World Club Cup after Japanese sponsorship had taken it to Tokyo. An 18-hour flight – from London via Anchorage and then down to Japan – was the cost in terms of time. A 1–0 defeat by Nacional of Uruguay, the South American champions, was the result. Then came the 18-hour flight back.

Ironically, by the time Forest were playing for world domination – 11 February 1981 – their grip on the European crown had already been released. CSKA Sofia, having deposed Ajax in 1973, repeated the feat in the first round. Tzvetan Yonchev scored the lone goal in Sofia, and Rujdi Kerimov struck the lone goal at the City Ground.

Years later Forest manager Brian Clough, rejecting claims that he ruled by fear, said: 'We surprised people because we were unconventional.' So now, with Forest eliminated, it was back to convention.

Real Madrid were little changed from the side who had collapsed dramatically in the 1980 semi-finals against Hamburg. Even Yugoslav coach Vujadin Boskov had survived the fall-out.

Liverpool thrashed Oulu Palloseura of Finland then saw off Scottish champions Aberdeen and their up-and-coming young manager Alex Ferguson in the second-round.

Much later, at Manchester United, Ferguson would put Liverpool in the domestic shade. But Aberdeen did not possess such weapons back in the autumn of 1980. They lost 1–0 at home – Terry McDermott again – and 4–0 at Anfield. Perversely, Scots scored all but one of the goals: Willie Miller with an own goal, Kenny Dalglish and Alan Hansen. Phil Neal was the odd marksman out.

Liverpool were thus one of four former champions to reach

RIGHT: **LIVERPOOL'S TERRY McDERMOTT (EXTREME RIGHT OF PICTURE) SCORES AGAINST ABERDEEN AT PITTODRIE, THE ONLY GOAL OF THE GAME**

the quarter-finals. Following them into the last eight were Real Madrid, Internazionale and Bayern Munich. The Germans had thoroughly enjoyed again thrashing their old rivals from Ajax 5-1 in the Olympic stadium: Rummenigge and Dieter Hoeness, brother of aspiring general manager Uli, both struck twice. Back in Amsterdam Ajax won 'only' 2-1. The identity of the scorer of their second goal, an 18-year-old named Frank Rijkaard, went comparatively unremarked. Bayern won home and away against Banik Ostrava to earn a semi-final against Liverpool while Madrid – missing the injured Laurie Cunningham – snuffed out Moscow Spartak to draw old enemy Inter.

Liverpool, having beaten CSKA easily enough in the quarter-finals, then teetered on the brink against Bayern. Anfield saw no goals and extra time was looming in Munich when Ray Kennedy struck with eight minutes to go. Rummenigge's equalizer was too little, too late.

Simultaneously Madrid and Inter fought out their now customary war of attrition in the other semi. Santillana and Juanito struck in Madrid; sweeper Graziano Bini got one back in Milan. Madrid, not for the first time against Inter, sneaked through 2-1.

But sneaking through would not be enough against Liverpool in the final. As Bob Paisley, after becoming the first manager to win the most prestigious club competition three times, put it: 'Real Madrid may be a great club but we're the better team.'

Indeed, Liverpool's consistency across all competitions in the late 1970s and 1980s gains in appreciation the more time passes and the more players and coaches fret about overheated fixture schedules. The competitive spirit imbued by Bill Shankly and maintained by Paisley delivered commitment in league, League Cup, FA Cup and in all three European competitions.

Liverpool arrived in the Parc des Princes knowing that victory was essential for them to return to the Champions Cup. They had slipped to fifth, their lowest placing since 1965. They had lost to Everton in the fourth round of the FA Cup but made amends by winning the League Cup for the first time.

Madrid coach Boskov was undecided about Cunningham. Injury had sidelined him for half the season. Without him Madrid had reached the final and finished narrow runners-up in the Spanish league.

In the end Boskov gambled that the provocation of facing English opposition might spur Cunningham back into his form of the previous season when he staged a match-winning display against Barcelona in Camp Nou.

The gamble failed. Cunningham looked ring-rusty and a stranger to his team-mates. Nine minutes from the end Alan Kennedy chested down a throw-in, walked through a pitiful excuse for a tackle by Julio Garcia Cortes and rammed an angled winner low past goalkeeper Agustin.

LEFT: **PHIL THOMPSON LIFTS THE EUROPEAN CUP AS LIVERPOOL BECOME THE FIRST BRITISH TEAM TO WIN THE TROPHY THREE TIMES**

WEDNESDAY 27 MAY 1981
PARC DES PRINCES, PARIS

LIVERPOOL	1
A. KENNEDY 82	
REAL MADRID	0

HT: 0-0. ATT: 48,360.
REF: PALOTAI (HUN)

LIVERPOOL:
CLEMENCE - NEAL, THOMPSON*, HANSEN, A. KENNEDY - LEE, R. KENNEDY, SOUNESS, MCDERMOTT - DALGLISH (CASE 87), JOHNSON. MANAGER: PAISLEY.

REAL:
AGUSTIN - GARCIA CORTES (PINEDA 87), SABIDO, GARCIA NAVAJAS, CAMACHO* - ANGEL, DEL BOSQUE, STIELIKE - JUANITO, SANTILLANA, CUNNINGHAM. COACH: BOSKOV.

*CAPTAIN

FOOTBALL'S NEW COMMERCIALISM

More and more plans were afoot to squeeze profit out of the People's Game. But the original, simplistic seeding system resulted in early baths for some of the continent's big boys

Twenty-five years had passed since the first Champions Cup Final. Across the world it had inspired a competitive revolution which had changed the face of the game. Domestic leagues and cups were no longer the only prizes. Players, coaches and fans were excited by the cross-continental glory nights which rewarded even clubs who finished in the wake of the title winners.

The Fairs Cup, taken over by the European federation in 1971 and converted into the UEFA Cup, had been running since the mid-1950s; the Cup-Winners' Cup since 1960; the European Supercup from 1971. Japanese sponsorship cash had breathed new life into the World Club Cup. Copycat champions' cups had sprung up all over the world, from Africa to the Americas.

Concerns stirred within FIFA Haus in Zurich. The world federation's Brazilian president, Joao Havelange, had moved quickly to capitalize on the commercial value of the World Cup. Simultaneously, UEFA was developing the European Championship. But national team competitions needed two- and four-year time spans: the Champions Cup now represented the day-by-day pinnacle of international football.

Restrictions on imports and the continuing overriding value of gate receipts ahead of sponsorship and TV income also guaranteed a breadth of competition. Aston Villa proved the point, spectacularly. They ranked among football's great traditionalists. Their own William McGregor had been a driving force behind the 1888 launch of the Football League. Since then they had won the league and FA Cup seven times each.

One-time manager Tommy Docherty famously commented that Villa fans would 'turn up to watch the shirts dry'. That supporting power was significant in driving them to Champions

RIGHT: **PAUL BREITNER SLOTS HOME A PENALTY FOR BAYERN MUNICH VERSUS CSKA SOFIA**

LEFT: **STRIKER PETER WITHE KNOCKS IN THE WINNING GOAL. LATER HE USED TO ROLL UP HIS TROUSER LEG AND JOKE: 'THIS IS THE SHIN THAT WON THE EUROPEAN CUP.'**

Cup glory. It was a success achieved remarkably against a background of internal turbulence whirling around the on-and-off chairmanship of the club by travel firm millionaire Doug Ellis.

Victims in the fall-out included Ron Saunders, the manager who had shrewdly guided Villa to the 1981 league title. Saunders, outwardly dour but with a laconic sense of humour, was forced out after a contract bust-up just before the Champions Cup quarter-finals. Thus it was his erstwhile chief scout, Tony Barton, who blinked his way into the glare of publicity while steering Villa towards the ultimate European spotlight.

Valur Reykjavik (7–0), Dynamo Berlin (2–2, with an away goal), Dynamo Kiev (2–0) and Anderlecht (1–0) were brushed aside on their march to the final. Here they met a Bayern Munich side including three players who would feature in the West German squad who would be runners-up at the imminent World Cup finals in Spain.

Villa were assisted by the failures of a simplistic seeding system which 'permitted' a first-round meeting of Juventus and Celtic and a second-round match-up between Bayern and Benfica. Thus half the contingent of eight quarter-finalists were ring-rusty eastern European clubs. Only one progressed, CSKA Sofia, who maintained their jinx over the European Cup-holders by defeating Liverpool 2–1 on aggregate.

Bayern Munich then put eight goals past CSKA in the two legs of their own semi-final and were not unduly concerned to learn of Villa's own progress. They had fretted at the likely prospect of meeting Anderlecht in the Rotterdam final. Villa, they thought dismissively, presented a far simpler option.

So much for arrogance. Bayern set up camp on the Dutch coast at Sheveningen. They were already counting chickens. Barcelona had just won the Cup-winners Cup so the Supercup would pack out the Olympic stadium and television channels would be queueing for the rights auction. Then the trip to Tokyo for the World Club Cup promised another £350,000.

The Germans had heard of Aston Villa but nothing of their players. 'The cup is ours,' said defender Wolfgang Dremmler, 'anything else is too fantastic to believe.'

This was not, of course, Barton's attitude. His promotion to manager had trebled his salary and one of his first toys was a Mercedes-Benz. But that did not affect his attitude to German engineering. 'Bayern have two terrific players in Breitner and Rummenigge,' he said, 'but we have the better team.'

The odds against Villa even lengthened 10 minutes into the game when goalkeeper Jimmy Rimmer injured a shoulder and had to be substituted by Nigel Spink. 'My Mum will be pleased!' Spink was reported to have said as he quit the substitutes' bench. The 23-year-old had only ever played once before. But the challenge proved the making of both him and Villa.

In the first minutes of the second half Klaus Augenthaler and Bernd Durnberger both missed badly; Allan Evans cleared off the goal-line … and left-winger Tony Morley turned Dremmler inside out before crossing for Peter Withe to anticipate keeper Manfred Muller's lunge.

The lanky centre-forward almost fell over the ball as he applied the finishing touch from a few yards out before somehow managing to propel it over the goal-line. Withe, ironically, had once been sold by Nottingham Forest because Brian Clough did not think he was the man to spearhead an assault on the Champions Cup.

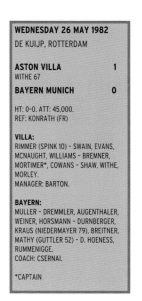

WEDNESDAY 26 MAY 1982
DE KUIJP, ROTTERDAM

ASTON VILLA   **1**
WITHE 67

BAYERN MUNICH   **0**

HT: 0-0. ATT: 45,000.
REF: KONRATH (FR)

VILLA:
RIMMER (SPINK 10) – SWAIN, EVANS, MCNAUGHT, WILLIAMS – BREMNER, MORTIMER*, COWANS – SHAW, WITHE, MORLEY.
MANAGER: BARTON.

BAYERN:
MULLER – DREMMLER, AUGENTHALER, WEINER, HORSMANN – DURNBERGER, KRAUS (NIEDERMAYER 79), BREITNER, MATHY (GUTTLER 52) – D. HOENESS, RUMMENIGGE.
COACH: CSERNAI.

*CAPTAIN

THE YEAR OF LIVING DANGEROUSLY

Hooliganism, terrorism and war were the background to a season in which the Champions Cup trophy went missing and Juventus strove hard to be the top club in Europe after Italy had won the World Cup

Both the football world and the world in general were becoming increasingly dangerous places. The lead-up to the World Cup in Spain in the summer of 1982 had been scarred abroad by the Falklands War and domestically by an ETA bomb which wrecked Madrid's main telephone exchange.

Italy had become the first European nation to win the World Cup three times, and their top scorer Paolo Rossi, a betting scandal villain turned hero, had now set his sights on winning the Champions Cup with Juventus.

Aston Villa approached their defence – against Liverpool, among others – with concern about the increasing threat of hooliganism. Their semi-final resistance against Anderlecht in Brussels the previous season had been played out against a backdrop of fan violence. A smattering of Villa-following drunks had sprawled their way across Brussels, battled with local fans and police at the Parc Astrid and then scrapped their way back into the city centre after the game. At a time when continental police and clubs claimed to have sorted out their own hooligans – and when English clubs were taking a more disciplined and responsible attitude to their own fans' travel – events in Brussels had appeared ominous.

In the event, the final in Rotterdam had gone off peacefully under the watchful gaze of extra units of Dutch riot police and the problem appeared to have been laid to rest. Nevertheless Villa had to play their opening home game in 1982–83 against Besiktas behind closed doors.

RIGHT: **JUVENTUS STRIKER ZBIGNIEW BONIEK POWERS HIS WAY PAST TONY MORLEY OF ASTON VILLA. JUVE WON 5-2 ON AGGREGATE**

Further embarrassment landed on their doorstep when the Champions Cup trophy, loaned by Villa to a Midland pub function, was stolen. Fortunately the cup, insured for £750,000, was recovered later in Sheffield. But Villa did not hang on to it for much longer before losing their grip, in a more orthodox manner, to Juventus in the quarter-finals.

Michel Platini was the man of the moment in European football. He had joined Juve after an outstanding World Cup, and took a prime role in beating Villa after creating all of France's goals in a 3–0 win over Portugal. He would go on to be Serie A's top scorer for each of his first three seasons in Turin.

Villa's exit focused attention back on the Champions Cup after a brief spell in which the Cup-Winners' Cup had stolen much of the limelight. The reason was £3 million-worth of Argentine talent named Diego Armando Maradona, who had transferred after the World Cup finals from Argentinos Juniors to Barcelona.

Maradona had struck a hat-trick against Apollon of Cyprus on his European club debut and promised to conquer the old world just as he had conquered the new. In the event, a bout of hepatitis and then a horrendous ligament injury inflicted by Andoni Goikoetxea – known ever after as the 'Butcher of Bilbao' – prevented him from fulfilling his potential in Catalonia.

Back in the Champions Cup, Hamburg edged Real Sociedad 3–2 in the semi-finals and thus qualified for a final duel in the new Athens Olympic stadium with Juventus, who had reached their second final in 10 years by defeating Widzew Lodz 4–2 on aggregate. Juventus angrily denied that their players had used the muscle-strengthening drug carnitine, which was rumoured

to have helped Italy at the World Cup. 'We would never get into that,' said coach Giovanni Trapattoni. Not that he needed to after the final. Juventus, beaten by Ajax in 1973 in Rotterdam, lost again – conceding victory this time to their German rivals and coach Ernst Happel.

At the press conference after the final he looked bored by it all. But then, Happel had seen it all before. He had played the big matches in the 1950s, guided Feyenoord to Cup glory in 1970 and pulled Hamburg together when the fans feared the failure to hang on to Kevin Keegan.

'My teams have always been successful against Italian clubs in Europe,' said Happel. 'There is no secret. Each match is different. We knew how Juventus would play and what we had to do. From the first minute until the last minute we played with discipline in all departments.'

Several of his players also exorcized demons from the previous year's World Cup Final: Manni Kaltz had his revenge over Paolo Rossi, Horst Hrubesch had the rare table-turning privilege of mugging Claudio Gentile. Both Kaltz and Hrubesch were survivors of the Hamburg team beaten by Nottingham Forest three years earlier. So was Felix Magath. He not only tied together the loose ends in midfield but scored the only goal after nine minutes.

So much for the all the natural talents of Platini and Zibi Boniek. Somewhere down the line Juventus had blundered into believing the hype. Happel shuffled away for the summer with a journalist compiling his memoirs. 'Have you got a smile out of him?' the journalist was asked.

'Oh yes,' came the reply, 'at least three times.'

WEDNESDAY 25 MAY 1983
OLYMPIC, ATHENS

HAMBURG   1
MAGATH 9

JUVENTUS   0

HT: 1–0. ATT: 73,500.
REF: RAINEA (ROM)

HAMBURG:
STEIN – KALTZ, JAKOBS, HIERONYMUS, WEHMEYER – ROLFF, GROH, MAGATH – MILEWSKI, HRUBESCH*, BASTRUP (VON HEESEN 56).
COACH: HAPPEL.

JUVENTUS:
ZOFF – SCIREA* – GENTILE, BRIO, CABRINI – BONINI, PLATINI, TARDELLI – BONIEK, ROSSI (MAROCCHINO 56), BETTEGA.
COACH: TRAPATTONI.

*CAPTAIN

NORTHERN LIGHTS SHINE AGAIN

It was all change at many leading European clubs as major personalities jumped ship or moved on to pastures new. Elsewhere, minds were turning to new ways of turning a profit from the game

Success for northern European clubs represented the triumph of 1980s pragmatism over romance. Real Madrid and Benfica, the fading old guard, had both ended up as losers in the other two European finals of 1983. In the Cup-Winners' Cup Alfredo di Stefano was the Madrid coach who had to give best to Alex Ferguson and an Aberdeen side containing no fewer than five future British club managers in Gordon Strachan, Alex McLeish, Willie Miller, Eric Black and Mark McGhee. In the UEFA Cup, Benfica, guided by the Swede Sven-Goran Eriksson, had fallen to Belgium's Anderlecht.

Elsewhere, the veteran Johan Cruyff stalked out on Ajax, after a league-and-cup double, to join rivals Feyenoord; former captain Billy McNeill parted company with Celtic after guiding them to three league championships in five years; Andrea Rizzoli, president of Milan's 1963 European champions, died at 69; UEFA's Italian president Artemio Franchi was killed in a road accident and Bob Paisley retired as manager of Liverpool after winning 13 trophies in nine years.

Joe Fagan stepped up from the Boot Room with a minimum of fuss, and his managerial debut in Europe was decisive enough: Liverpool beat OB Odense 1-0, 5-0. Ian Rush scored the lone goal which beat Bilbao – Dundee United and Roma.

The Scots emulated the 1963 achievements of neighbours Dundee in reaching the last four. They conceded only two goals to Malta's Hamrun Spartans, Standard Liege and Rapid Vienna en route to a dramatic defeat by a Roma side who had snuffed out IFK, CSKA and Dynamo Berlin. Outstanding were the Brazilian midfielder Paulo Roberto Falcao, Italian World Cup-winning right-winger Bruno Conti and Roberto Pruzzo, the free-scoring centre-forward. Pruzzo netted twice in the Stadio Olimpico where Roma picked themselves up off the floor after losing 2-0 at Tannadice.

Benfica had seen off Olympiakos in the second round 3-1 overall. One of their three goals in the Estadio da Luz was

RIGHT: **LIVERPOOL GOALKEEPER BRUCE GROBBELAAR GATHERS THE BALL SAFELY AGAINST BENFICA AS DEFENDER ALAN HANSEN STANDS BY**

scored by lanky Danish striker Michael Manniche. Foreign players were still a novelty to fans of Benfica who had ended their prohibition after the old talent mines of Angola and Mozambique had gained independence.

A quarter-final against Liverpool was the last draw Benfica coach Sven-Goran Eriksson wanted. 'I consider them the best team in Europe now,' he said, 'and possibly over the last decade. But we can't escape. So play them we will and we aren't going to be afraid of their reputation or ability.' Fine words, but that was all. Ian Rush scored in both legs. The difference was that he scored the only goal at Anfield but contributed to a magnificent 4-1 triumph in the Stadium of Light.

Liverpool's semi-final defeat of Dinamo Bucharest went a similar way: a 1-0 home win followed by a decisive 2-1 success abroad. The unstoppable Rush scored twice more. Liverpool would thus face Roma in... Rome.

For years Roma had been a byword for financial wastage. This was the club whose reward for paying a world record £250,000 for Angelo Sormani in 1963 had been one domestic cup. Eventually a more pragmatic president in Dino Viola brought in Nils Liedholm, Milan's 1958 Champions Final captain, to stabilize the ship. Roma ended a 41-year drought by winning the 1983 scudetto.

But then Liedholm and Conti fell out while schemer Falcao, his contract expiring, started collecting offers for a summer auction. Even Liedholm was no longer secure. Roma had Benfica's Eriksson primed to move in.

Travelling to Rome presented Liverpool with surprisingly few problems. All their decisive displays had been away from Anfield. Held at home by Bilbao, restricted to one goal at home by both Benfica and Dinamo Bucharest, yet still they had come through. Skipper Graeme Souness said: 'We've no worries about going to Rome. When you're under pressure it puts you on your toes.'

Falcao, latest emperor of Rome, wanderered around midfield looking barely interested; up front Francesco Graziani was hampered by age and Pruzzo by a stomach complaint.

Phil Neal struck the opener after 13 minutes with the first goal attempt worthy of the name; Pruzzo back-headed an equalizer just before the break after enormous perseverance by Conti. But when it came to penalties so Roma, confronted by the wobbly knees of Bruce Grobbelaar, lost their nerve.

Liverpool started badly with Steve Nicol shooting over the bar, but Conti and Francesco Graziani copied him from Roma's second and fourth. Alan Kennedy, the unlikely 1981 match-winner in Paris, stepped up to beat Franco Tancredi and secure Liverpool's fourth Champions Cup.

Falcao, having opted out of the penalty contest, went overnight from hero to scapegoat. Roma's fans saw him play only four more times.

LEFT: **ROMA'S FRANCESCO GRAZIANI BLAZES HIS VITAL PENALTY OVER THE BAR TO HAND THE EUROPEAN CUP TO LIVERPOOL FOR THE FOURTH TIME**

WEDNESDAY 30 MAY 1984
OLIMPICO, ROME

LIVERPOOL	1
NEAL 15	
ROMA	1
PRUZZO 38	

AFTER EXTRA TIME
LIVERPOOL WON 4-2 ON PENS
HT: 1-1. 90 MIN: 1-1. ATT: 69,693.
REF: FREDRIKSSON (SWE)

LIVERPOOL:
GROBBELAAR - NEAL, LAWRENSON, HANSEN, A. KENNEDY - WHELAN, LEE, SOUNESS*, JOHNSTON (NICOL 72) - DALGLISH (ROBINSON 94), RUSH. MANAGER: FAGAN.

ROMA:
TANCREDI - NAPPI, RIGHETTI, NELA, BONETTI - FALCAO, TONINHO CEREZO (STRUKELY 115), DI BARTOLOMEI* - CONTI, PRUZZO (CHIERICO 64), GRAZIANI. COACH: LIEDHOLM.

*CAPTAIN

DESPERATE TIMES FOR FOOTBALL

The season started off well but went downhill fast as hooliganism mired the game and a Leeds United fan came to be murdered. It all culminated in the Bradford City fire and tragedy at Heysel

The story of the Champions Cup in the 1984–85 season remains largely irrelevant. The only statistic of concern is the figure 39: the death toll among Juventus fans in the Heysel Stadium in Brussels before the final against Liverpool.

Yet term had opened amid enormous promise at both international and domestic levels. Ian Rush, with his 32 goals, had been awarded the golden boot as the leading league marksman in Europe; Diego Maradona had left Barcelona for Napoli for a world record £5million; Karl-Heinz Rummenigge had quit Bayern Munich for Internazionale; and Barcelona had gambled on a bright young English coach in Terry Venables.

Liverpool began the season slowly. They lost 1–0 to Independiente of Argentina in the World Club Cup in Tokyo and fell 2–0 to Juventus in the European Supercup amid the snows of Turin.

In the Champions Cup, however, it was a different tale. Lech Poznan, Benfica (again), FK Austria and Panathinaikos failed to disturb Liverpool's progress back to the final. Juventus matched them with victories over Ilves Tampere of Finland, Grasshopper, Sparta Prague and Bordeaux.

In the other competitions, Real Madrid won the UEFA Cup beating Videoton of Hungary and the Cup-winners Cup was picked up by Everton, from the other side of Liverpool's Stanley Park, who overcame Rapid Vienna.

But trouble was escalating: In the Cup-winners Cup, Celtic had to replay their second round tie against Rapid Vienna after a missile felled one of the Austrian players win at Celtic Park; in the UEFA Cup Internazionale's Giuseppe Bergomi was knocked to the ground by a marble thrown from the crowd during their semi-final defeat by Real in Madrid.

RIGHT: **BORDEAUX'S ALAIN GIRESSE OUTWITS MASSIMO BONINI (4) AND GAETANO SCIREA (6) OF JUVENTUS IN THE SEMI-FINAL**

On May 11, a Leeds fan died after hooligan trouble collapsed a wall after their last game of the season at Birmingham City. The same day, 53 fans died in the Valley Parade fire tragedy at Bradford. It was the worst British football disaster since 66 fans lost their lives at Ibrox Park, Glasgow, in 1971.

Eighteen days later – with football still numb – Liverpool, Juventus and their fans turned up in Brussels for the Champions Cup Final.

Pre-match coverage on television and radio might have been taken up by Liverpool's surprise appointment of Kenny Dalglish as player-manager to succeed retirement-bound Joe Fagan. Instead, the world's commentators found themselves describing deathly mayhem.

Trouble began around an hour before kick-off. Sectors Y and Z, up behind the one goal, were recipes for disaster with Juventus and Liverpool fans separated by a low chicken-wire fence and a scattering of police.

Someone threw a bottle to spark an exchange of missiles across the 20 yards dividing the two sets of fans. Then Liverpool fans charged. Juventus fans retreated both back and down the terracing, crushing those at the end against a free-standing wall overlooking a stadium exit. When the wall gave way bricks, concrete and fans cascaded down on to the ground beneath.

It was only a matter of seconds before medical help began to arrive but, for 39 fans, it was already too late.

Out in the car park, hasty tents were thrown up to shield and care for the injured and the dying. Police reinforcements circled the pitch and, one hour 28 minutes late, Liverpool kicked off.

The decision to play on remains controversial. Grisly and offensive for some, playing on kept the remaining fans in the stadium, heading off the near certainty of more violence outside the ground and averting traffic problems for the emergency services.

As for the game, Juventus won it 12 minutes into the second half. Michel Platini converted a penalty after substitute Gary Gillespie was judged to have brought down Zibi Boniek. Liverpool protested in vain that the foul had been committed outside the box.

The Belgian legal service eventually prosecuted UEFA, the Belgian federation and the stadium authorities for inadequate security and ticket distribution.

The Football Association withdrew its clubs from European competition, a decision which was ultimately overtaken when UEFA instituted its own indefinite ban with three years extra for Liverpool (reduced to one year extra on appeal).

'I don't know what's happening to football supporters,' said Fagan the next day. 'It's certainly not a sport any more. What is a game of football when that number of people are dead?'

WEDNESDAY 29 MAY 1985
HEYSEL, BRUSSELS

JUVENTUS PLATINI 57 PEN	1
LIVERPOOL	0

HT: 0-0. ATT: 60,000.
REF: DAINA (SWZ)

JUVENTUS:
TACCONI - SCIREA* - FAVERO, BRIO, CABRINI - BONINI, PLATINI, TARDELLI - BRIASCHI (PRANDELLI 84), P. ROSSI (VIGNOLA 89), BONIEK.
COACH: TRAPATTONI.

LIVERPOOL:
GROBBELAAR - NEAL*, LAWRENSON (GILLESPIE 3), HANSEN, BEGLIN - WHELAN, NICOL, WARK - DALGLISH, RUSH, WALSH (JOHNSTON 46).
MANAGER: FAGAN.

* CAPTAIN

THE HEALING PROCESS BEGINS

In the wake of Heysel, English teams were banned from European competition, leaving the way open for the other nations. And Terry Venables moved to Barcelona just as Maradona left for Naples…

Football's own fallout from Heysel was nothing compared with the human tragedy, but it was extensive.

Bert Millichip, chairman of the Football Association, answered the public mood when he unilaterally withdrew English clubs from European competition, but the haste in which he acted later drew revisionist attack. Nowhere was the European exit felt more keenly than in Liverpool. Everton's finest team in years had just won both the Cup-Winners' Cup and the league championship. They could have gone a long way in the Champions Cup in 1985–86.

Millichip and the Football Association – which ratifies all European entries – volunteered the withdrawal not merely as a statement of regret but as the only practical way to protect villages, towns and cities across the continent from the marauding violence which so often accompanied English clubs.

UEFA, under Jacques Georges, a Frenchman who rarely evinced any sympathies for the English game, accepted Millichip's gesture… and extended it for an indefinite period.

One consolation for English reporters, wishing to stay on the European trail themselves, was that they had a perfect excuse: his name was Terry Venables.

In spring 1984, Barcelona president Josep Lluis Nunez had needed a new coach. His target was Bobby Robson, then at Ipswich. Robson reigned at Portman Road, under the benign gaze of the Cobbold brewing family, much as Alf Ramsey had done 20 years earlier. Like Ramsey, Robson was bound for the England job and a knighthood. He was also a man of his word and refused to break his Ipswich contract for the Barcelona dream.

Nunez, hugely disappointed, asked Robson to recommend an alternative. Robson suggested 42-year-old Venables, then turning out a bright young team at Queen's Park Rangers in west London. It says everything about Nunez's respect for Robson that he did, indeed, gamble on a coach who was virtually unknown outside Britain.

RIGHT: **TERRY VENABLES (RIGHT) IN SEVILLE WATCHING HIS BARCELONA SIDE TAKING ON STEAUA BUCHAREST**

Venables, from Dagenham in east London, had played for England at every possible level from youth, amateur, Under-23 and B to senior level. A mainstream club career with Chelsea and Tottenham was his springboard to management. Venables was cute and sharp. His public relations skills were as high class as his innovative coaching talents. Later the media would be split in their assessment of Venables, but that was not until after the complexities of his business life – his pubs and his clubs – spilled over into the football world.

In 1984, Venables was on the way up. As soon as he secured the Barcelona job, he took Spanish lessons and, with a small scrap of paper as cue, gave his opening address to the cules (Barcelona fans, known for historical reasons as 'backsides') in Spanish. That gesture alone endeared him to the fans. Simultaneously Barcelona sold Diego Maradona on to Napoli for £5m and imported Scotland's centre-forward Steve Archibald, many of whose goals were laid on by Bernd Schuster, a headstrong German. Schuster, his career guided by a Svengali-like wife, was free to concentrate on his club career after falling out with national coach Jupp Derwall and refusing to play for West Germany.

They finished 10 points clear of runners-up Atletico Madrid in the Spanish league, losing only two of their 34 games. Already the name of Barcelona appeared to be virtually engraved on the 1986 Champions Cup.

That impression was enhanced by the charmed life which bore the Catalans to the final. They beat Sparta Prague and FC Porto on away goals, squeezed Juventus 2–1, then hit back from 3–0 down in the semi-final to beat IFK Gothenburg on penalties. Even more luckily for Venables and Barcelona, the final was to be held in Spain.

But that was where their luck ran out, against the Romanian army team of Steaua Bucharest, only the second eastern European club ever to reach the final. Stage, history and omens all pointed to Barcelona even though they had scored only nine goals en route. Steaua had put a superior 13 past Vejle, Honved, Kuusysi Lahti and Anderlecht.

Five small plane loads of Romanian fans flew in to Seville. The remainder of the 70,000 crowd were all willing on Barcelona to claim that elusive first Champions Cup. Venables had counselled long and hard against complacency but in vain. As his Romanian counterpart, Emerich Jenei, said: 'Barcelona had everything to lose, we had everything to win.'

Barcelona commanded the early possession but Steaua sweeper Miodrag Belodedici looked to have played in European finals all his life. Gradually the Romanians began to gain in confidence. Even so, it was a surprise five minutes before the end when Venables, trying to shake things up, took off Schuster. Venables thought: 'He looked tired.' Schuster disagreed. He strode into the dressing rooms without a glance at the dugout.

Thus the final turned on the worst sequence of penalties at such a level. Not until shot No 5 did anyone score, Steaua's Marius Lacatus. Gavril Balint converted their next. In the meantime keeper Helmut Ducadam saved from Alexanco, Pedraza and Alonso then, finally and decisively, from Marcos.

Hours before kick-off the wife of Barcelona captain Jose Sanchez had given birth. Ruefully, he said: 'This is both the happiest and saddest day of my life.'

WEDNESDAY 7 MAY 1986
SANCHEZ PIZJUAN, SEVILLE

STEAUA BUCHAREST	**0**
BARCELONA	**0**

AFTER EXTRA TIME
STEAUA WON 2-0 ON PENS.
HT: 0-0. 90 MIN: 0-0. ATT: 75,000.
REF: VAUTROT (FR)

STEAUA:
DUCADAM - BELODEDICI - IOVAN*, BUMBESCU, BARBULESCU - BALINT, BALAN (IORDANESCU 72), BOLONI, MAJARU - LACATUS, PITURCA (RADU 107).
COACH: JENEI.

BARCELONA:
URRUTI - GERARDO, MIGUELI, ALEXANCO*, JULIO ALBERTO - MARCOS, VICTOR, SCHUSTER (MORATALLA 85), PEDRAZA - ARCHIBALD (PICHI ALONSO 106), CARRASCO.
COACH: VENABLES.

*CAPTAIN

THE ENGLISH ARE NOT MISSED

Barcelona added Lineker and Hughes to their ranks as they mounted a further attack on the supremacy of Real Madrid. Behind closed doors, new formats were being suggested for the future of the game

The summer of 1986 belonged to Diego Maradona, who excited Napoli's Italian dreams by the manner in which he inspired Argentina's World Cup triumph in Mexico. Napoli fans took almost as much pleasure as Argentine supporters in the malicious deception of the 'Hand of God' goal against England.

But Napoli had finished only third in Serie A. Juventus were back in the Champions Cup, strengthened by Denmark's Michael Laudrup as they pursued the twin target of achieving their European dream while staying ahead of the game in Italy – and of Milan refinanced by media tycoon Silvio Berlusconi.

Meanwhile the only way in which English league stars could now pursue their European dream was by moving abroad. Thus

England's Gary Lineker – six-goal top scorer in Mexico – and Wales's Mark Hughes quit Everton and Manchester United respectively to spearhead Barcelona's domestic pursuit of Real Madrid, who were returning to the Champions Cup after two seasons of success in the UEFA Cup. Dutch coach Leo Beenhakker looked for goals to Emilio Butragueno, who had scored four for Spain against Denmark at the World Cup.

Steaua Bucharest apart, two other former champions set out in hope: Celtic and Bayern Munich. Bayern, having invested the £3-million Rummenigge fee wisely, had won the German double, pipping Werder Bremen on the last day of the league season, then beating Stuttgart 5–2 in the cup final. Their dubious

RIGHT: **THE OUTSTANDING MICHEL PLATINI OF JUVENTUS TAKES ON REAL MADRID'S CENTRAL DEFENSIVE PAIRING, MANUEL SANCHIS (5) AND JOSE SALGUERO (4)**

LEFT: **PAULO FUTRE, PORTO'S BRILLIANT YOUNG STARLET, MESMERIZES THE BAYERN DEFENCE WITH HIS CLOSE CONTROL AS HE EMBARKS ON ANOTHER INCISIVE RUN**

reward was a testing first-round start against PSV Eindhoven who had finally persuaded parent company Philips to invest in breaking the Ajax/Feyenoord stranglehold on Dutch football. Leading PSV's assault on Europe were Ruud Gullit, winger Gerald Vanenburg and Danish midfielder Frank Arnesen.

In the event, PSV did not manage even one goal over the two legs. Bayern won it in Eindhoven in the first game with strikes from Reinhold Mathy, and progressed past FK Austria and Anderlecht to a semi-final against Real Madrid. The Spanish champions, after an easy start against Young Boys Berne, had struggled to edge out Juventus and Red Star.

Behind closed doors in West Germany, UEFA leaders considered a blueprint for the future. The Champions Cup had a regular, convenient entry of 32 clubs. The favourite proposal was for eight to be seeded into groups of four clubs each. They could play each other home and away and the group winners could go on to the knockout quarter-finals.

Now everyone, giants and minnows alike, could be guaranteed three home games. The idea was circulated to the national associations for further consideration.

In the meantime, another new name was breaking into European club consciousness: FC Porto. Europe, from a Portuguese perspective, had been almost exclusively the preserve of the Lisbon giants Benfica and Sporting. Porto, from the north, were the poor relations of the so-called 'big three'. So it was a matter of both surprise and rejoicing when victories over Rabat Ajax of Malta, Viktovice and Brondby lifted them into the last four in the spring of 1987.

The final would thus pit newcomers (Porto or Kiev) against former champions (Bayern or Madrid).

Vienna's rebuilt Prater stadium was a perverse venue, its 60,000 capacity contrasting starkly with average 4,000 attendances at local league matches. But the choice was an acknowledgement of a three-year redevelopment demanded after lumps of concrete had begun falling off the old façade.

Collapsing façades summed up the failures of Kiev Dynamo and Real Madrid to reach the final. In Kiev's case, doubling up as the Soviet national team had sapped even the scientifically applied resources of their coach Valeri Lobanovsky. They lost 2-1 both home and away against Porto. Madrid's prospects were wrecked by a 4-1 defeat in a stormy first leg in away to Bayern in Munich. Madrid finished with nine men after the expulsions of Juanito and Mino.

In Vienna Bayern, as against Aston Villa in 1982, were favourites. As in 1982 they finished again with losers' medals despite scoring first through left winger Ludwig Kogl. The Germans then gave up all serious attempt to score again. They had taken single-goal final victories over Rangers in the 1967 Cup-winners Cup and over Saint-Etienne in the 1976 Champions Cup. But in the last 13 minutes that defensive shield buckled.

First Rabah Madjer cheekily back-heeled an equaliser from a short cross by Juary. Then, with nine minutes remaining,g Madjer crossed from the left to the far post, where Juary shot home. Porto's players were so delighted to see skipper Joao Pinto collect the Cup that they forgot to collect their winners' medals in their haste to run the trophy to their delirious fans.

WEDNESDAY 27 MAY 1987
PRATER, VIENNA

FC PORTO   **2**
MADJER 77, JUARY 81

BAYERN MUNICH   **1**
KOGL 25

HT: 0-1. ATT: 62,000.
REF: PONNET (BEL).

PORTO:
MLYNARCZYK - JOAO PINTO*, EDUARDO LUIS, CELSO, IGNACIO (FRASCO 66) - QUIM (JUARY 46), JAIME MAGALHAES, SOUSA, ANDRE - FUTRE, MADJER.
COACH: JORGE.

BAYERN:
PFAFF - WINKELHOEFER, NACHTWEIH, EDER, PFLUGLER - FLICK (LUNDE 82), MATTHAEUS*, BREHME - M RUMMENIGGE, D. HOENESS, KOGL.
COACH: LATTEK.

*CAPTAIN

BUSINESS AS USUAL

Real Madrid took on Napoli amid eerie silence and before a crowd of 499, which didn't stop sparks from flying. Meanwhile Partizani of Albania were expelled for having four players sent off in one game

'Now for the Champions Cup,' bawled Diego Maradona after inspiring Napoli to their first Italian league title. Tens of thousands of Neapolitans, many of whom had probably never set foot within the Stadio San Paolo, ran out into the streets singing, chanting and dancing after the 1-1 draw with Fiorentina which sealed the title. It was a poor game but, together with Internazionale's 1-0 defeat by Atalanta – former Nottingham Forest hero Trevor Francis scoring the goal – was enough to secure Napoli's title with one game to go.

As Napoli awaited the first-round draw, their domestic rivals went into the transfer market. Juventus bought Ian Rush from Liverpool to replace Michel Platini, who had retired at just 32, while Milan put their faith in the Dutch pair of Marco van Basten from Ajax and Ruud Gullit from PSV.

Napoli were novices in terms of European experience and were thus unseeded in the draw... which was UEFA's only excuse for how they came to be matched against Real Madrid. Both clubs were shocked – Madrid because they would have to face Maradona and Co without any support, the excesses of the Ultrasur against Bayern having earned Madrid a two-match closed-door order.

What should have been one of the biggest European club occasions was thus played out in front of 499 staff, officials and media in the Estadio Bernabeu, which was nevertheless surrounded by riot police with water cannon on account of unrealized fears that the Ultrasur might try to storm the gates.

RIGHT: **PSV'S RONALD KOEMAN, WHO COMBINED ELEGANCE ON THE BALL WITH A STEELY APPROACH OFF IT, BEATS THE CHALLENGE OF A BORDEAUX PLAYER**

Out on the pitch the mood was bad-tempered and the quality patchy. Madrid attacked down the wings, forcing Maradona deep to assist Italian resistance. Playmaker Michel converted a penalty in the first half and defender Miguel Tendillo bludgeoned another goal in the second. The players kicked and snapped as they left the pitch at the final whistle in an eerie silence.

Naples, for the return, was the exact opposite. Even a cacophonous 82,231 crowd, however, paying Italian record receipts of £2.2 million, could not prevent Madrid, for the 12th time, seeing off Italian opposition. Defender Giovanni Francini shot Napoli ahead on nine minutes, Careca missed an open goal on 40, and Emilio Butragueno punished him and Napoli with an equalizer three minutes later. Napoli faded under the mental pressure of needing to score three times to win the tie. Not even Maradona could generate a spark of inspiration. His solitary European club trophy would thus be the UEFA Cup, in 1989.

Madrid-Napoli was not the only tie which provided first-round heat. Partizani of Albania were expelled from European competition and banned for four years after having four players sent off in a 4-0 defeat by Benfica in Lisbon. Ironically, Partizani had been assisted to their Albanian title win by points penalties imposed on domestic rivals Dinamo, Nentori and Flamurtari for poor disciplinary records.

The remainder of the competition proceeded comparatively peacefully. Madrid believed their name was on the trophy when they beat holders Porto, then took revenge over Bayern Munich, only to slip up on away goals against PSV in the semi-finals. They took defeat badly. Michel and Hugo Sanchez were banned for nine and three matches respectively for jostling referee Bruno Galler (bans reduced on appeals to three matches and one match).

Benfica followed up the Partizani scrap by knocking out Aarhus, Anderlecht – avenging their 1983 UEFA Cup Final defeat – and Steaua in the semi-finals. They reached the final under a coach in his first year, ex-midfielder Toni.

PSV were relieved to line up with Ronald Koeman after obtaining a trimming of a three-match UEFA ban imposed for comments in a magazine interview in which he appeared to praise a team-mate for putting French playmaker Jean Tigana out of PSV's quarter-final against Bordeaux.

Fans in Stuttgart were not expecting a goal-fest. Both clubs had managed only nine goals apiece on their way to the Final. Not until the 34th minute did right winger Gerald Vanenburg produce the first shot of the game, forcing a diving save from Silvino. In the second half Koeman shot over the top from a touched free kick. Extra time came and went with nothing more to entertain the crowd and thus the final went to penalties for the second time in three years.

Koeman rammed home PSV's first and everyone followed suit in the 10-kick sequence. Thus 5-5 and so to sudden death. Anton Janssen scored before Hans Van Breukelen crowned an outstanding season by stopping Veloso's underpowered kick.

PSV coach Guus Hiddink had every reason to be satisfied. His team had already won the Dutch league and cup, now they had completed the treble. As he said: 'I don't like penalties but justice was done.' Prophetically, he also tipped Holland, replete with a PSV nucleus, to succeed in the European Championship finals a few weeks later, back in West Germany.

WEDNESDAY 25 MAY 1988
NECKAR, STUTTGART

PSV EINDHOVEN	0
BENFICA	0

AFTER EXTRA TIME
PSV WON 6-5 ON PENS.
HT: 0-0. 90 MINS: 0-0. ATT: 68,000.
REF: AGNOLIN (IT).

PSV:
VAN BREUKELEN - GERETS*, NIELSEN, R. KOEMAN, HEINTZE - VANENBURG, LERBY, VAN AERLE, LINSKENS - KIEFT, GILLHAUS (JANSSEN 107).
COACH: HIDDINK.

BENFICA:
SILVINO - VELOSO, DITO, MOZER, ALVARO - CHIQUINHO, SHEU*, ELZO, PACHECO - M. MAGNUSSON (HAJRI 112), RUI AGUAS (VALDO 56).
COACH: TONI.

*CAPTAIN

THE BENEFITS OF HORSE SENSE

Johan Cruyff returned to Barca as manager but it was in Italy that football caught a glimpse of its new money-making future as Silvio Berlusconi took over the reins at Milan and went to work on his side

Two diverse events in the summer of 1988 – quite apart from Johan Cruyff's return to Barcelona as coach and Holland's European Championship victory – appeared to be setting the agenda for the next two decades. The first was the Italian league triumph of Milan, powered by the aggressive, acquisitive Silvio Berlusconi. The second was UEFA's imposition of a limit of four foreigners per team in European competition, 'to protect the clubs, the competitions, and encourage the development of home-grown talent', as president Jacques Georges put it.

These restrictions in fact had a minimal effect, because most countries imposed even more rigorous controls. Worst affected – though not until after their return in 1990 – would be the English clubs, for whom Northern Irish, Scottish and Welsh players counted as foreigners. In any case, the whole artificial farrago would be swept away in the mid-1990s.

Berlusconi was a different story, because of who he was and because of what he represented; this was nothing more nor less than the aggressive commercialism which would swiftly revolutionize the face of European football.

A long-time Milan fan, Berlusconi had built a millionaire's empire through a media conglomeration based on regional commercial television channels.

Milan were in a sorry state when Berlusconi swooped,

RIGHT: **BRILLIANT ORANGE: MILAN'S FABULOUS DUTCH TRIUMVERATE OF RUUD GULLIT, MARCO VAN BASTEN AND FRANK RIJKAARD, WHO HELPED MAKE UP ONE OF THE GREATEST ITALIAN TEAMS EVER**

LEFT: RUUD GULLIT KNOCKS
THE BALL BEYOND STEAUA
BUCHAREST GOALKEEPER SILVIU
LUNG FOR MILAN'S THIRD GOAL

in the nick of the time. One of the European Cup's original giants had been relegated twice in quick succession – once as punishment for match-fixing – and were £20 million in debt.

Berlusconi, setting a pattern that Roman Abramovich would emulate at Chelsea, paid off the debts and provided the cash to buy Marco van Basten, the finest centre-forward of his era, from Ajax and Ruud Gullit from PSV Eindhoven for a then world-record £6 million. After Milan won the Serie A scudetto for the first time in nine years, Berlusconi financed the acquisition of a third key Dutchman in Frank Rijkaard.

Milan were favourites from the outset in the 1988–89 Champions Cup. Serious opposition was represented by Real Madrid, Werder Bremen, Red Star Belgrade and a Steaua team inspired to reach a record final by the intuitive and sharp-tempered Gheorghe Hagi.

Milan had to prove their mettle in Europe almost from the start and long before the Italian season opened. The start of Serie A was delayed until October after the conclusion of the Olympic Games. Still, even ring-rusty Milan found the initial task easy against Vitosha Sofia. Pietro Paolo Virdis, a journeyman Italian forward, and Gullit made it 2–0 in Bulgaria. Van Basten – having signed off the previous season with Holland's wonderful European title-winner against the Soviet Union – rattled home four goals in a 5–2 win back in Milan.

Berlusconi's edifice shook next time out against Red Star. The Yugoslavs took the lead in Milan, only for Virdis to level. He was then sent off in Belgrade when Milan, a goal down to a strike from Dejan Savicevic, were rescued by the fog. German referee Dieter Pauly abandoned the game after just under an hour. Next day, the teams played out another 1–1 draw, and the tie thus went to penalties. Goalkeeper Giovanni Galli saved from

both Savicevic – ironically, given his later transfer to Milan – and Mitar Mrkela before Frank Rijkaard put away the decisive kick.

It was hardly easier in the quarter-finals. Milan's tie with Bremen produced just one goal, scored from a second-leg penalty by the lethal Van Basten.

In the semi-final, Madrid, reinforced by Bernd Schuster's arrival in midfield, could not hold Van Basten either. Milan followed up their 1–1 draw in the Bernabeu with a 5–0 romp back in the Stadio Meazza at San Siro. Van Basten, naturally, was again among the scorers. Madrid had never taken a worse beating in Europe.

The Barcelona final between Milan and Steaua took place under yet another gloomy shadow. A month earlier, just after UEFA's executive had agreed to readmit English clubs to European competition in 1990, so 96 Liverpool fans were killed and 170 injured at Hillsborough before an FA Cup semi-final against Nottingham Forest.

That disaster prompted a move to all-seater stadia in international competition. The demand for massive new investment was timed perfectly to suit the multinationals and their TV marketeers. In the driving seat, of course, sat Berlusconi. He even defied a strike threat by Spanish engineers to fly in his own technicians and extra cameras to ensure 300 million television spectators around the football world could watch 'his' Milan win the Champions Cup for the third time.

Paolo Maldini duly became the first son to emulate his father, Cesare, as a European Cup-winner, while victory also enshrined Ruud Gullit and Marco Van Basten, each the scorer of two goals, as rivals to Diego Maradona for the crown of the world's greatest player. Maradona won 'only' the UEFA Cup with Napoli.

WEDNESDAY 24 MAY 1989
NOU CAMP, BARCELONA

MILAN 4
GULLIT 18, 38, VAN BASTEN 27, 46
STEAUA BUCHAREST 0

HT: 3–0. ATT: 100,000.
REF: TRITSCHLER (WG)

MILAN:
G. GALLI - TASSOTTI, COSTACURTA
(F. GALLI 74), F. BARESI*, P. MALDINI
- DONADONI, COLOMBO, RIJKAARD,
ANCELOTTI - GULLIT (VIRDIS 60),
VAN BASTEN.
COACH: SACCHI.

STEAUA:
LUNG - PETRESCU, UNGUREANU,
BUMBESCU, IOVAN - STOICA*,
MINEA, HAGI, ROTARIU (BALINT 46) -
LACATUS, PITURCA.
COACH: IORDANESCU.

*CAPTAIN

1990S

TEN YEARS THAT SHOOK FOOTBALL

The 1990s were the most turbulent years in European club history. England returned to the Champions Cup after a six-year absence, while Marseille took the trophy to France for the first time but were then kicked out for match-fixing. Real Madrid regained winners' status, but it was Manchester United who served up the most dramatic success in the cup's history. Off the pitch, the collapse of Communism in the east brought 18 more nations into UEFA with their eyes on a share of the profits generated by the commercially driven introduction of the mini-league format. Simultaneously, a little-known Belgian footballer rocked the foundations of not only the European but the world game.

RIGHT: **BARCELONA PLAY HOSTS TO MANCHESTER UNITED IN THE WORLD-FAMOUS NOU CAMP, NOVEMBER 1994**

PAOLO MALDINI

Country: Italy

Position: Left-back, central defender

Born: 26 June 1968

Club: AC Milan

PAOLO MALDINI

Maldini

I have been extremely lucky. Not only because I have won the Champions Cup five times and played in eight finals, but because, when I look back over my career, I realise how fortunate I was to play in the particular era I did.

Of course, I did not always understand this at the time. But in the 1980s and early 1990s, it was easier for young players to break through even at Serie A level. For example, I made my debut for Milan at 16 because, when a couple of players were injured, there was always the chance the coach would turn to you. Today, all the big clubs have 25 or more players in their squad – a majority of them foreigners – and that makes it tough for a youngster to get a break.

My first match was against Udinese in 1985 and, just four years later, there I was winning my first Champions League final against Steaua Bucharest. It's a game, oddly enough, about which I can recall very little – though it has assumed legendary status for many of Milan's fans because that victory launched a great new era in our history.

What I do remember is that our victory was achieved in circumstances which will probably never be repeated, given that the entire Nou Camp stadium in Barcelona was packed full of our own fans.

Nowadays, UEFA's rules and regulations would not allow one club to buy up all the tickets but that is what Milan did that night. I remember sitting on the team bus as we made our way into the ground, surrounded on all sides by Milan fans. It was like sailing in through a red-and-black sea of humanity.

Looking back, I am sure those scenes had as much of a positive effect on us as they had a negative effect on the Romanian players.

The next year, against Benfica at the Prater stadium in Vienna, was entirely different. We were sure we would beat the Portuguese again – as my father's team had done in 1963 – but we went into that game very tired. We had to summon up every last spark of energy, so it was not surprising that we struggled a bit. It was a Champions Cup

that we won much more with our heads than with our legs.

Every final, you see, is different. The third I played is proof enough. Now I can smile, thinking back about the way we played against Marseille in Munich, especially in the first half. It was incredible that we managed to lose to them. It was also a painful defeat at the time because there was no way we deserved to lose – and that is talking about only the match itself, not about other issues which emerged later.

When you are lucky enough to take home so many prizes, it sometimes happens that you do not remember exactly what you have won or how you won it. That is not to dismiss the value of each occasion, more a reflection on the relentless pace of today's football: no sooner have you taken home one medal than you are back at the beginning of the pursuit for another.

LEFT: PAOLO MALDINI CELEBRATES THE WINNING GOAL (SCORED BY KAKA) IN THE DERBY AGAINST INTERNAZIONALE IN SERIE A, FEBRUARY 2005

One exception to that rule, though, was our 1994 Champions League final win over Barcelona. The press, especially the foreign media, gave us no hope. Barcelona were certainly a good side, but we knew they had weaknesses and how to exploit them and we went for it, ruthlessly.

We did miss Franco Baresi and Alessandro Costacurta through suspensions but we had the advantage of having wrapped up the Italian League scudetto long before the final. Barcelona, by contrast, had won the Spanish title just days before the match, so they had been fighting, mentally, on two fronts.

Of course, success in any match depends on your overall, comprehensive approach and not only on your physical readiness. But I must say that at no stage – for all that they had forwards like Romario and Hristo Stoichkov – did we feel that they were a better team than us.

My memory of that night in Athens is that we played an almost perfect game. We completely stifled difficult opponents and gave them absolutely nothing.

In football you must accept that you can lose. We did it not only against Marseille but against Ajax in 1995 and, of course, Liverpool in 2005. For years, after we lost to Ajax in Vienna, I thought that perhaps that was destined to have been my last final. And then, eight years later, I had the unforgettable experience of raising the Champions Cup after we beat Juventus at Old Trafford in 2003.

People may think it strange that this match means so much to me – a final we won only in a penalty shoot-out. But there was a very special family connection. That was not only my first time as Champions Cup-winning captain but it was back in England where, 40 years earlier, Milan had won their first cup... with my father as captain.

RIGHT: **MALDINI SHOOTS FOR GOAL AGAINST REAL MADRID AT THE SAN SIRO IN 2002**

LEFT: **MALDINI BECAME THE OLDEST AS WELL AS THE QUICKEST SCORER IN A CHAMPIONS LEAGUE FINAL IN 2005 WHEN HE VOLLEYED THE BALL INTO THE NET AFTER 53 SECONDS AGAINST LIVERPOOL, BUT HE STILL FINISHED UP ON THE LOSING SIDE**

THE RISE OF THE MEDIA MOGULS

Where Italy had Berlusconi, France had Bernard Tapie, a man with a supreme talent for making and losing money. Marseille were on the up, but trouble followed every step of the way

The 1980s had produced social and political turbulence around the globe and football felt the 'trickle-down' fallout. Opportunities to access the televisual and commercial riches likely to be generated in the 1990s attracted a new breed of would-be club owners: men who saw only the potential millions and whose knowledge of the game was often disruptively scanty.

At least Milan's owner and president Silvio Berlusconi had long been a fan. In fact, he had bought the club against the advice of father Luigi, who feared 'all the bad publicity it brings its presidents'. Silvio responded that the likes of Felice Riva in the early 1960s and Felice Colombo 20 years later had lacked his business rigour.

Further afield, eastern Europe's communist rock-face had crumbled, just like the Berlin Wall, amid the aftershocks of the self-destructive reforms launched in the Soviet Union by Mikhail Gorbachev. In due course, Russia would produce its own self-made millionaires with a yearning for football club toys.

Of course the West remained far ahead. The era which raised Berlusconi in Italy produced similar men elsewhere with driving ambitions and ruthless streaks. The French media, for example, could hardly believe their good luck when France threw up its own apparent Berlusconi in Bernard Tapie.

The 'rags to riches, back to rags and back again to comparative riches' story of Tapie would one day be turned into a feature film by the director Marina Zenovich. Tapie was a small-time singer turned actor turned businessman turned asset-stripping multi-millionaire. At one stage he owned the Marseille docks and a television channel, was a socialist MP and even attained junior ministerial rank under President François Mitterrand.

RIGHT: **BERNARD TAPIE, WHO WAS RESPONSIBLE FOR REVIVING MARSEILLE'S FORTUNES AND THEN FOR CAUSING THEM TO PLUNGE DURING THE CLUB'S PERIOD OF DISGRACE**

But above all else Tapie will be remembered for his role in the most dramatic of the many rises and falls in the history of Olympique Marseille – because this was the stage on which he finally over-reached himself.

In 1986 Tapie bought control on a whim, following a suggestion made during a dinner at the Soviet Embassy by the wife of mayor Gaston Defferre. He splashed out on outstanding players, including Uruguayan Enzo Francescoli, Germany's Rudi Voller and Klaus Allofs, France's own Jean Tigana, Manuel Amoros and Jean-Pierre Papin and England's Chris Waddle. The former Tottenham winger became the fourth-most-expensive player in the world when he signed for £4.25 million.

Five times in a row from 1989 Marseille won the French league title. Tapie, who never hesitated to breach the privacy of the dressing room to issue a reprimand or a call to arms, demanded the lion's share of the credit.

But winning leagues and cups in France was not enough. Tapie envisaged jousting with Berlusconi on the international stage. Their weapons were going to be their football clubs.

Marseille's initial salvo fell short. Milan progressed towards the 1990 final by disposing of Finland's HJK Helsinki in the first round by 5–0 overall and of John Toshack's Real Madrid 2–1 in the second round. But, lacking the injured Ruud Gullit for almost all the season, they needed extra time against both Belgium's Mechelen in the quarter-finals and Bayern Munich in the semi-finals. That secured a second successive final appearance, this time against Benfica.

The Portuguese club's presence in Vienna infuriated Tapie, because it was achieved at the expense of Marseille in the after a blatant handball went unpunished by Belgian referee Marcel Van Langenhove.

Hence Vata Garcia's 'illegal' goal ensured a rare repeat of a final. As in 1963, Benfica lost again to Milan who had needed victory to return to the Champions Cup the next season. Diego Maradona's Napoli had snatched the Serie A scudetto from them through a victory at Atalanta awarded to them amid controversy by the league disciplinary committee.

A coin had apparently floored Napoli's Brazilian midfielder Alemao; years later it emerged that Alemao was told by Napoli physios to stay down to achieve just that cynical end.

Milan also needed to win to justify Berlusconi's self-appointed stance as the would-be revolutionary leader who was promoting a self-selected, self-perpetuating 'European Television League.' The TV spectacle from the Prater was hardly enthralling. Milan won, deservedly, but thanks only to the class of Marco Van Basten and a winning strike from fellow Dutchman Frank Rijkaard midway through the second half.

Naturally, Europe's sports headlines the next morning were devoted to the extended reign of Milan and their big-money superstars. No such publicity was granted to the simultaneous transfer of a journeyman Belgian pro from FC Liege to French second division Dunkerque.

But, in time, Jean-Marc Bosman would prove more influential than all of Milan's superstars put together.

WEDNESDAY 23 MAY 1990
PRATER, VIENNA

MILAN	**1**
RIJKAARD 67	
BENFICA	**0**

HT: 0–0. ATT: 58,000. REF: KOHL (AUS)

MILAN:
G. GALLI - TASSOTTI, COSTACURTA, F. BARESI*, MALDINI - ANCELOTTI (MASSARO 67), COLOMBO (F. GALLI 89), RIJKAARD, EVANI - VAN BASTEN, GULLIT.
COACH: SACCHI.

BENFICA:
SILVINO - JOSE CARLOS, RICARDO, SAMUEL, ALDAIR - THERN, VITOR PANEIRA (VATA 78), JAIME PACHECO* (CESAR BRITO 59), VALDO - HERNANI, M. MAGNUSSON.
COACH: ERIKSSON.

*CAPTAIN

DAWN OF THE BOSMAN ERA

In Belgium, a footballing nobody's transfer passed virtually unnoticed but was later to have a seismic effect on the game worldwide. Diego Maradona scored his only European Cup goals

Jean-Marc Bosman's transfer from Liege to Dunkerque was one event among many in the soccer summer of 1990. Above all, Germany – 'West' for the last time before football caught up with reunification – won the World Cup in Italy against Diego Maradona's grumpy Argentina.

England fell to the Germans in the semi-finals after a penalty shoot-out but gained international consolation: UEFA, pushed by new president Lennart Johansson, agreed to readmit English clubs to European competition. In fact, English champions Liverpool's extra season of banishment meant they were still barred from the Champions Cup, which thus went ahead again without English representation. But Manchester United would make amends by not only entering but winning the Cup-Winners' Cup.

As for Bosman, he was bitterly upset when his Belgian club Liege refused to ratify his transfer, since Dunkerque were unable to come up with the necessary paltry fee of around £4,000. Bosman was out of contract with Liege, but was frozen out of the game by the anachronistic Belgian regulations. Liege cut his wages by 60 per cent.

A local court ruled that Bosman was free to join Dunkerque, but the Belgian federation, fearing the wider consequences of its loss of authority, appealed. Ironically, such an impasse simply could not have arisen under the more sophisticated rules of Belgium's neighbours.

Out on the pitch, Diego Maradona scored his first – and last – two Champions Cup goals in Napoli's 3–0 first-leg defeat of Hungary's Ujpest. His team-mate Alemao, who had helped them trick their way to the Italian title, scored one of Napoli's brace in the return.

Marseille opened up with a 5-1, 0-0 defeat of Dinamo Tirana. Jean-Pierre Papin scored a first-leg hat-trick supported by strikes from Philippe Vercruysse and a tempestuous new signing named Eric Cantona. On the bench sat none other than Franz Beckenbauer, West Germany's World Cup-winning manager of a few months earlier.

FINALE COPPA DEI CAMPIONI

STELLA ROSSA — OLYMPIQUE MARSIGLIA

BARI · 29 MAGGIO '91

RIGHT: **CHRIS WADDLE, THEN THE WORLD'S FOURTH-MOST EXPENSIVE PLAYER, IS MOBBED BY THE MEDIA AFTER HIS GOAL FOR MARSEILLE HAD KNOCKED OUT THE HOLDERS MILAN**

Tapie had met Beckenbauer after buying a controlling stake in adidas, with which 'Der Kaiser' had long-time promotional links. From there it was a short step to the Stade Velodrome. Beckenbauer said, 'Tapie is a dynamic personality who knows exactly what he wants.' Later he changed his mind.

As for the Italians, Napoli drew 0-0 home and away against Moscow Spartak and thus went to a shoot-out. 'El Diego' put away his kick, but Marco Baroni missed and Napoli lost 5-3. Maradona lasted only another two months at Naples before quitting Italian football under a dope-test cloud.

Holders Milan, awarded a first-round bye, opened up with a narrow win over Brugge. Coach Arrigo Sacchi fretted over a goalless draw at home before Milan won 1-0 in Belgium despite having Marco van Basten sent off.

That red card and ensuing suspension proved crucial against Marseille in the quarter-finals. Milan, misfiring badly in the Dutchman's absence, could only draw 1-1 at home, Ruud Gullit and Papin matching strikes. In the return, Chris Waddle scored on 75 minutes and Milan appeared to be heading out. Then, with two minutes remaining, referee Bo Karlsson awarded a free-kick and Marseille fans, thinking the match was over, overflowed on to the pitch. As the players waited for police to clear away the fans, so one of the floodlights failed.

Milan's players, fearing for their safety, walked off and subsequently refused Karlsson's instruction to return to complete the game. Karlsson counted down to the 90 minutes, declared the match abandoned and Marseille the winners. Milan, blaming Marseille incompetence over both floodlights and security, vainly demanded a replay. Marseille thus progressed to a semi-final against Moscow Spartak, which they won 3-1, 2-1.

The other semi matched Red Star against Bayern Munich. It proved a disastrous tie for Bayern's Klaus Augenthaler. Bayern lost 2-1 at home but were 2-1 ahead in the return in Belgrade, and heading for extra time, when the luckless sweeper put through his own goal in the last minute. Red Star went on to the final, Bayern merely went home.

Red Star were only the third eastern European club to reach a final after Partizan in 1966 and Steaua in 1986 and 1989. They played against the backdrop of increasing domestic tension and in the sure knowledge that the exit door beckoned midfielders Robert Prosinecki and Sinisa Mihajlovic, plus forwards Dejan Savicevic and Darko Pancev.

Beckenbauer, a fish out of water in Marseille, had been replaced by veteran coach Raymond Goethals. This was Goethals's second stint, having earlier taken Marseille to the semi-finals in 1989. With his trademark white, wide-belted coat and permanent cigarette dangling from a corner of his mouth, Goethals looked the archetypal French football coach: except that he was Belgian.

Both he and Red Star coach Ljubko Petrovic used midfielders to protect their defence rather than support attack. Hardly surprisingly, that produced a 0-0 draw and the fourth penalty shootout in a final. Red Star won it 5-3 and Waddle thus suffered his second shootout defeat in Italy inside 12 months after England's Turin failure against West Germany in the World Cup.

On the other side of the coin Red Star's sweeper Miodrag Belodedici, previously with Steaua, became the first player to make Cup-winning appearances with two different clubs (Jimmy Rimmer was an unused substitute for Manchester United in 1968 and a starter for Aston Villa in 1982).

TOP LEFT: **RUUD GULLIT ATTEMPTS TO CALL HIS MILAN TEAM-MATES OFF THE PITCH AT MARSEILLE'S VELODROME STADIUM**

ABOVE: **RED STAR CELEBRATE BEFORE THE INEVITABLE BREAK-UP OF THEIR SIDE AFTER THE BIG EUROPEAN CLUBS MOVED IN FOR THEIR STARS**

WEDNESDAY 29 MAY 1991
SAN NICOLA, BARI

RED STAR BELGRADE	**0**
MARSEILLE	**0**

AFTER EXTRA TIME
RED STAR WON 5-3 ON PENS.
HT: 0-0. 90 MIN: 0-0. ATT: 58,000.
REF: LANESE (IT)

RED STAR:
STOJANOVIC* - JUGOVIC, BELODEDICI, NAJDOVSKI, MAROVIC - SABANADZOVIC, MIHAJLOVIC, PROSINECKI, BINIC - SAVICEVIC (DODIC 84), PANCEV.
COACH: PETROVIC.

MARSEILLE:
OLMETA - AMOROS, BOLI, MOZER, DI MECO (STOJKOVIC 112) - GERMAIN, CASONI, FOURNIER (VERCRUYSSE 75) - WADDLE, PAPIN*, PELE.
COACH: GOETHALS.

*CAPTAIN

FOOTBALL DANCES TO TV'S TUNE

After much political toing and froing, the Champions Cup now had a format to suit it to the brave new world of televised football. Johan Cruyff was back driving Barcelona to success as coach

In the late 1970s Liverpool had fronted up a proposal to turn the initial rounds of the Champions Cup into a mini-league system. In the late 1980s, far more threateningly, Milan president Silvio Berlusconi had produced his own blueprint for a European Television League.

A balancing act had to be achieved. UEFA needed the big clubs, but the big clubs also needed the European federation, which legitimized their presence within the football family. The players likewise needed to remain within that family to participate in the World Cup and European Championship.

UEFA thus moved diplomatically forwards by deciding to replace the quarter-final and semi-final rounds with a group structure comprising two mini-leagues of four clubs each, playing each other home and away and with the winners heading direct into the Wembley final – the Empire Stadium's selection being another welcome-back gesture towards English football.

What UEFA did not recognize, however, was the pace of political change driven by the European Union. President Lennart Johansson and long-serving general secretary Gerd Aigner even swam against the tide by restricting clubs to a maximum of four non-national players (players not qualified to play for the club's national association). UEFA said it wanted to protect grass-roots development, but an instant anomaly was the effect on returning English clubs, who found that their Scots, Welsh and Irish players were suddenly 'foreigners'.

UEFA's attitude to the law was disgracefully expressed in a decision to prohibit Belgium from hosting European finals after its appeal court rejected UEFA's appeal against a suspended jail term imposed on former general secretary Hans Bangerter; he had been charged as UEFA's representative responsible for the Heysel disaster. The European federation was clinging firmly to the arrogant mantra dictated by former president Jacques Georges: 'We are a Swiss-based organization and the laws of the European Community are nothing to do with us.'

Other people thought differently. Jean-Marc Bosman had seen his action against the Belgian football authorities referred to the European Court of Justice in Luxembourg. Belgian courts considered that, in the light of European law, they lacked juridical competence. As Bosman, increasingly

impoverished by his legal battle, set up a temporary home in the garage adjoining his parents' home, the rich and famous played on. For him, a decision was still some way away.

Red Star defended their crown with a transfer-torn team; the only other previous winners in the draw were PSV Eindhoven and Benfica; Marseille were there again, while Barcelona returned for the first time in six years.

Barca's coach now was Johan Cruyff. Ironically, he would prove far more successful at the Nou Camp as manager than

RIGHT: **WEARING ARSENAL'S UNUSUAL OLD SECOND STRIP, KEVIN CAMPBELL HOLDS OFF AN AUSTRIA VIENNA DEFENDER AS ALAN SMITH SCORES FOR THE HOME SIDE AT HIGHBURY**

he had been as a player. He remained, however, as innovative as ever. He was the first coach to use a TV monitor in his dug-out, and he believed in using the full length and breadth of the pitch. The technical virtuosity of his Spanish players, mixed with hand-picked imports, allowed Barcelona to circulate the ball with a speed, control and accuracy which had their opponents chasing shadows. Versatility was also a Cruyff watchword. England's Gary Lineker, in Cruyff's early days, had been pushed away to the right wing. To English fans it looked bizarre. But that was how Barcelona had won the 1989 Cup-Winners' Cup, so Cruyff could point to results.

Success came at a heavy price. Chain-smoker Cruyff had needed emergency heart surgery during the 1990–91 season and was still convalescing while assistant and former winger Charly Rexach took the team on to the league title. Now was surely the time to end that Champions Cup jinx.

Barca opened up by defeating Hansa Rostock, last champions of the now-defunct East Germany. Cruyff was back in the dug-out to see his team, inspired in attack by the hot-tempered Hristo Stoichkov and two-goal Michael Laudrup, win 3–0 at home and lose by an inconsequential 1–0 away. It nearly went wrong in the second round, however. Barcelona won 2–0 at home to Germany's Kaiserslautern with two goals from future sports director Txiki Beguiristain, but they were losing 3–0 in Germany, heading into stoppage time, before Jose Bakero popped up with the tie-turning last-kick away goal.

Barcelona were accompanied into Group B by Dynamo Kiev, by a Sparta Prague side who had surprisingly ousted Marseille, and by a Benfica outfit who had not only outwitted but even ultimately outrun Arsenal. Barcelona topped the group ahead of Sparta with a game to spare.

Group A matched Sampdoria, Red Star, Anderlecht and Panathinaikos. Sampdoria set the pattern by defeating Red Star 2–0 on the opening match day. They never looked back and ended two points clear of the fading holders.

With instability increasing in the Balkans, Red Star had been forced by UEFA to play their home matches in Hungary and Bulgaria. Their sole consolation for a collapsing season was a World Club Cup victory over Chile's Colo-Colo.

BELOW: **JOHAN CRUYFF, THE BARCA MANAGER, PREACHES WHAT HE PRACTISED AS THE OUTSTANDING PLAYER OF HIS GENERATION**

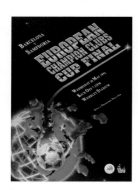

ABOVE: **WITH NINE MINUTES OF EXTRA TIME REMAINING, RONALD KOEMAN BLASTS HOME BARCA'S WINNER FROM OUTSIDE THE BOX**

FAR RIGHT: **KOEMAN AND HIS TEAM-MATES, IN ORANGE, EMBARK ON A BOUT OF JOYOUS CELEBRATION**

HISTORY REPEATS ITSELF FOR BARCA

Barcelona coach Johan Cruyff did not pull any punches after his ghostbusters finally laid the hoodoo of those Champions Cup Final defeats in 1961 and 1986.

'It's been a great night,' he said deep in the bowels of Wembley Stadium, 'because it's been such a long time coming. Winning the cup as a player was very special, but winning it as a coach is fantastic as well. Ronald Koeman is a coach's dream: he can create a goal out of nothing at any time of the game.' In fact only nine minutes remained of extra time when Koeman

thundered home the winner from a tapped free-kick.

Sampdoria kept their own feelings to themselves. Their players and coach Vujadin Boskov, a loser also with Real Madrid in 1991, skipped the post-match press conferences. The Brazilian perception of Toninho Cerezo in midfield and the lethal understanding of 'twins' Roberto Mancini and Gianluca Vialli up in attack had proved insufficient.

This was history repeating itself. Four years earlier Barcelona had beaten Sampdoria in the final of the Cup-

Winners' Cup. But then the Genoa club financed by oil tycoon Paolo Mantovani had been on the up. Defeat at Wembley was the end of an era. Sampdoria had finished sixth in Serie A and the ambitious Vialli would head off within weeks for Juventus.

Not that Barcelona cared. They had choreographed the greatest moment in their history down to the finest detail. Just before the decisive free-kick, Cruyff had been preparing to bring on Miguel Angel Nadal in midfield for the tiring youngster, Josep Guardiola. When the kick was whistled, Cruyff held Nadal back. As soon as the ball flew beyond Gianluca Pagliuca, Cruyff sent on not Nadal but Jose Ramon Alexanko. Thus the veteran club captain was there in place to lead his team up the 39 steps and collect the prize that mattered most. Not only that, but Barcelona, forced to play the game in orange, had brought their 'real' maroon-and-blue shirts for their players to wear as they collected their medals.

Barcelona thus became only the second Spanish club to win the Champions Cup (after Real Madrid) and the third club (after Juventus and Ajax) to have collected all three main European club trophies at one time or another. Koeman not only collected the official man of the match award but became the third player (after Jimmy Rimmer and Miodrag Belodedici) to win the Champions Cup with different clubs, having been a winner in 1988 with PSV Eindhoven.

Of course, Cruyff also joined the history-makers as the second cup-winning captain-cum-coach (after Real Madrid's Miguel Munoz) and only the third cup-winning player-turned-coach (after Munoz and Italian Giovanni Trapattoni).

Koeman, goalkeeper Andoni Zubizarreta, Michael Laudrup and Hristo Stoichkov thus secured their place in Barcelona's player pantheon alongside old heroes such as Ladislav Kubala, Luiz Suarez, Sandor Kocsis and Co. They were still celebrating long after Sampdoria had slunk away, their players throwing their shirts to their fans more in tantrum than tribute.

WEDNESDAY 20 MAY 1992
WEMBLEY, LONDON

BARCELONA 1
KOEMAN 111

SAMPDORIA 0

AFTER EXTRA TIME
HT: 0-0. 90 MIN: 0-0. ATT: 70,827.
REF: SCHMIDHUBER (GER)

BARCELONA:
ZUBIZARRETA* - NANDO, R. KOEMAN, JUAN CARLOS, FERRER - GUARDIOLA (ALEXANKO 113), BAKERO - EUSEBIO, M. LAUDRUP, STOICHKOV - SALINAS (GOIKOETXEA 64).
COACH: CRUYFF.

SAMPDORIA:
PAGLIUCA - MANNINI, PARI, VIERCHOWOD, LANNA - LOMBARDO, KATANEC, TONINHO CEREZO, BONETTI (INVERNIZZI 72) - VIALLI (BUSO 100), MANCINI*.
COACH: BOSKOV.

*CAPTAIN

THE FOOTBALL MONEY-GO-ROUND

Some called it 'a break with tradition', others 'a betrayal', but a new format for the Champions Cup arrived shaped by the wishes of TV broadcasters and Silvio Berlusconi's vision for the future

KNOCK-OUT STAGE

In the autumn of 1991 UEFA had summoned an extraordinary congress at which the 35-strong membership granted it full control of all television and commercial rights to the new mini-league system. The experiment was now formalized in the officially branded UEFA Champions League – note, no apostrophe – and a young, Lucerne-based marketing company named TEAM was contracted to package it and sell it.

TEAM could trace its history back to the Brazilian Joao Havelange's victory over Sir Stanley Rous in the 1974 FIFA presidential elections. Votes for Havelange, from Africa in particular, were swung by Horst Dassler, the influential adidas director. Dassler's reward was to be granted commercial control of the World Cup, first in partnership with English sport's super salesman Patrick Nally and then in his own right, from 1982 onwards, through Dassler's specialist company ISL. Bosses of ISL were Dassler's former aide Klaus Hempel and Jurgen Lenz. After Dassler's premature death in 1987, Hempel

RIGHT: **JOSEP GUARDIOLA OF BARCELONA REACHES THE BALL JUST AHEAD OF CSKA MOSCOW'S DIMITRI KORSAKOV**

FAR RIGHT: **ERIC CANTONA IN HIS DAYS AS A LEEDS PLAYER GETS THE BETTER OF STUTTGART'S UWE SCHNEIDER**

and Lenz were ousted by the rest of the family. They set up a new office around the corner in Lucerne, used their top-level contacts to perfect effect and thus won for their new agency – TEAM – the most lucrative ongoing contract in football's commercial history.

It was with TEAM's guidance that UEFA set up the Champions League parameters: a small pool of multinational sponsors were signed up and guaranteed match broadcast exposure on every Champions League programme worldwide. In each country exclusive rights were sold, virtually at auction, to one single broadcaster.

That, in the United Kingdom, was initially ITV. Later, after pressure from the European commission, single-broadcasting restrictions were varied. Not that this reduced the value of the TV contracts, because cable and satellite channels were by then falling over themselves to buy into the action.

The commercial complexity applied only to the league stage which made up, initially, the second half of the season. The first half was taken up with the opening knock-out rounds. In 1992–93 that spelled failure for, among others, holders Barcelona at the hands of CSKA Moscow, and Leeds United at the hands of Scotland's Rangers.

Leeds, last winners of the Football League championship ahead of the launch of the Premier League, had only just scrambled through the first round. UEFA had amended its foreign players rule in the face of continuing pressure from the European commission.

Now clubs could field a maximum of five foreign-born players, but at least two must have lived in the club's country of origin for at least five years. The so-called 'three and two' rule would haunt Stuttgart coach Christoph Daum for years after.

In the first round Stuttgart beat Leeds 3–0 at home and thought they had progressed on the away-goals rule after losing 'only' 4–1 at Elland Road. However, Daum had miscounted in introducing foreign substitute Jovica Simanic for the last eight minutes. Leeds protested, UEFA ordered a single-leg replay in neutral Barcelona, and goals from Gordon Strachan and substitute Carl Shutt – on in place of the ineffective Eric Cantona – brought a 2–1 win.

It was Leeds's last hurrah. In the second round, they lost 2–1 both away and home to Rangers. Top-scoring Ally McCoist struck decisively both at Ibrox Park and at Elland Road.

GROUP STAGE

Bernard Tapie's European ambition was burning stronger than ever. When Marseille slithered out against Red Star Belgrade in the second round the previous season, Tapie had stormed into

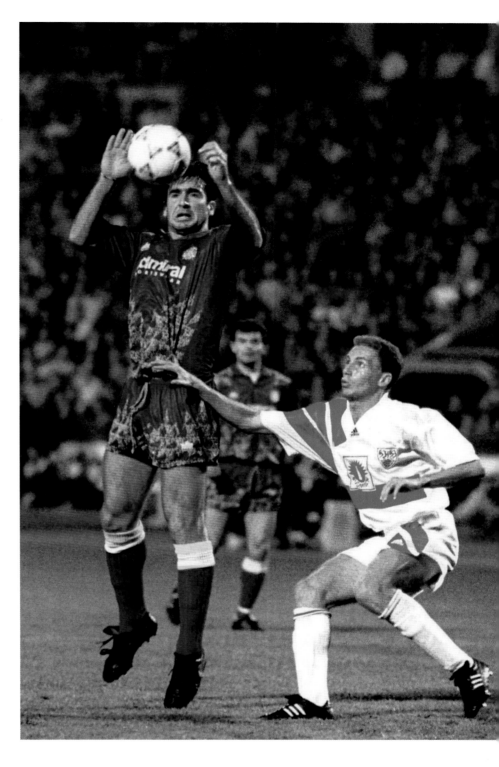

the dressing room afterwards promising the most explosive clear-out in the history of even this most turbulent club.

Wherever Marseille went they were pursued by scandal, controversy and worse. In 1991, Tapie had been suspended for a year by the French football authorities for 'injuring sporting morale' with his furious tirades at referees; his players, led by star striker Jean-Pierre Papin, had threatened to strike in support of 'BT'.

SILVIO BERLUSCONI

In the autumn of 1991, Milan's president Silvio Berlusconi, interviewed by this author for World Soccer magazine, set out a vision for the future of European club football which becomes more prescient with every season that passes.

'Gradually the concept of the national team will become less and less important. It is the clubs with which fans associate. A European championship for clubs is inevitable. The new format is a step in the right direction, but only a step.

'The European cups, as they have been organized, have become a historical anachronism. It's economic nonsense that a club such as Milan might be eliminated in the first round. A European cup that lasts the whole season is what Europe wants.

'After all, Europe wanted an economic community with monetary union and a customs union. It's inevitable it should want a football union too. And the clubs will lead the way – each playing around 80 games a season.

'In my six years as president I have never seen our best team play – except in my head. Someone is always injured or ill or suspended. So we need many quality players and the players themselves accept this.

'Milan are my laboratory for the future. We have to reach an audience beyond the stadium. That means television, the theatre of the global village.

'Football is currently ignoring part of its support. First are the fans in the stadium, but that means only 50,000 or 60,000. Then there are the fans who watch bits and pieces of soccer on the state channels. But the third audience, which we are not yet reaching, is to be found through pay-TV. Through cable and satellite you must be able to reach the committed fan who wants to watch our games.

'Milan must be a part of that. We would like to be the best, of course. But at the highest level winning or losing is often a matter of luck. What is important is that we are among the main actors in this theatre.'

Amid all the controversy they had strode on to win the league title, and might have won the double as well. But then Marseille were drawn against Bastia in the semi-finals of the French cup. It was the biggest match in Corsica for more than 20 years, and Bastia put up a massive temporary stand to more than double the 8,500 capacity of the old Furiani stadium.

Tragically, around 15 minutes before the scheduled kick-off, the new stand started to collapse. Fans plunged more than 60 feet into a tangle of seats and scaffolding.

Players, including Marseille's Englishman Trevor Steven, ran to help the rescuers. Amazingly, only 14 people were killed, although more than a thousand were hurt.

The French federation decided to abandon the cup.

Marseille were not to blame, of course. Rather the incident exemplified the passion and allure which attached to Tapie's team. Living up to that pressure was by no means always easy for the players; they were forever under the spotlight. However, they progressed unbeaten through their Group One campaign, winning three and drawing three of their six matches on the way to topping the table and reaching the final.

Rangers finished one point adrift, to their frustration and disbelief. Succeeding years proved this narrow failure to have been perhaps the most costly in the Light Blues' long and proud history.

Milan, as expected, topped Group Two by following up on an intimidating opening display which saw Marco van Basten score all their goals in a 4-0 thrashing of IFK Gothenburg.

ABOVE: **MARCO VAN BASTEN SCORES THE THIRD GOAL FOR MILAN IN THEIR 4-0 ANNIHILATION OF GOTHENBURG**

MARSEILLE WIN BATTLE BUT LOSE WAR

Marseille's delight in becoming the first French club to win the Champions Cup lasted only days. Even on the night of the final in Munich, whispers told of a gathering storm to dwarf anything else in the club's history.

The story of the match is simple. Coach Fabio Capello had steered Milan through a record sequence of 58 unbeaten league matches and victories in all six Champions League ties on the road to Munich. He was thus the man who got it right for the best part of two years but wrong on the night which mattered.

Milan had their best team out, including £13-million, world-record signing Gianluigi Lentini in midfield. In attack, Capello gambled on Marco van Basten at centre-forward. He had scored six goals in the Champions League and 13 in 15 Serie A matches, but was struggling to overcome recurring ankle trouble. All this meant only a place on the substitutes' bench for the former Marseille favourite, Jean-Pierre Papin.

Milan had the class but Marseille the commitment. Two minutes before half-time Basile Boli powered through a crowded penalty box to head home Abedi Pele's corner for the only goal. An hour later Bernard Tapie was joining his players on their lap of honour.

In truth it was a lap of dishonour. Six days earlier, back in France, Marseille had beaten struggling Valenciennes 1–0 to secure the league once more and clear their heads for Munich. But at half-time in Valenciennes the home club had protested to the referee that Marseille had tried to bribe three of their players – forward Christophe Robert, Argentine World Cup-winner Jorge Burruchaga and midfielder Jacques Glassmann – successfully in two cases.

RIGHT: **AS MARCEL DESAILLY AND CHRIS WADDLE QUEUE UP FOR THEIR SHARE OF THE GLORY, MIDFIELDER FRANCK SAUZEE HOLDS ON TO THE TROPHY**

Offizielles Programmheft
**38. FINALE
UM DEN POKAL
DER EUROPÄISCHEN
MEISTERVEREINE**
DM 2.50

OLYMPIQUE MARSEILLE – AC MAILAND
Mittwoch, 26. Mai 1993 · 20.15 Uhr

WEDNESDAY 26 MAY 1993
OLYMPIA, MUNICH

MARSEILLE 1
BOLI 43

MILAN 0

HT: 1-0. ATT: 64,400. REF:
ROTHLISBERGER (SWZ)

MARSEILLE:
BARTHEZ - ANGLOMA (DURAND 64),
BOLI, DESAILLY, EYDELIE - SAUZEE,
DESCHAMPS*, DI MECO - BOKSIC,
VOELLER (THOMAS 78), PELE.
COACH: GOETHALS.

MILAN:
S. ROSSI - TASSOTTI, COSTACURTA,
F. BARESI*, P. MALDINI - DONADONI
(PAPIN 56), ALBERTINI, RIJKAARD,
LENTINI - VAN BASTEN (ERANIO 85),
MASSARO.
COACH: CAPELLO.

*CAPTAIN

Later it emerged that before the game Robert's wife had been handed £30,000 in cash at the Marseille team hotel by defender Jean-Jacques Eydelie. She had then buried it in her mother's garden. When Robert tried to draw his team-mates into the scandal, Glassmann blew the whistle. Nine days after Marseille's Munich triumph, the French league called in the public prosecutor.

In time it emerged that Marseille had fixed far, far more than just the infamous match with Valenciennes. Tapie's lieutenants had siphoned off cash into various anonymous bank accounts in Switzerland and Liechtenstein. With the help of a small army of agents, this cash was used to swing transfer deals and influence referees.

Tapie eventually – though not until 1997 – went to jail for match-fixing. Eydelie, Burruchaga, Robert and Marseille general manager Jean-Pierre Bernes all received indefinite bans.

Marseille were stripped of their 1993 league title and relegated as punishment. They had to sell all their best players to stay afloat financially and were barred from the following season's Champions Cup after being initially drawn against AEK Athens.

Glassmann was rewarded with FIFA's fair play award but, such being the perversity of the French game, was jeered wherever he played. Many fans blamed him for destroying the Marseille dream, and also for breaking an unwritten code of loyalty. Glassmann was not the only innocent victim. Van Basten aggravated his ankle injury in Milan's losing cause in Munich. He never played again.

As for Tapie, a decade later he returned to his beloved Marseille... as general manager.

ABOVE: **PURSUED BY RUDI VOLLER, BASILE BOLI RACES TOWARDS THE MARSEILLE FANS AFTER SCORING PAST GOALKEEPER SEBASTIANO ROSSI**

THE GREAT DASH FOR CASH

As football's brave new world began to offer greater financial rewards, Arsene Wenger's Monaco replaced disgraced Marseille and gave several of Europe's bigger clubs a run for their money

KNOCK-OUT STAGE

Manchester United, in 1993, had become the first winners of the new FA Premier League. The top division of the historic Football League, increasingly frustrated at having to share so much of their income with the lower-division minnows, had connived with the Football Association to break away. Negotiations had taken around 18 months and the timing was perfect. Manchester United had led the restructuring race to the Stock Exchange in 1991 and had been best placed to take commercial advantage of both the Premier League power

RIGHT: MANCHESTER UNITED'S ERIC CANTONA IS SENT OFF AGAINST GALATASARAY IN THE INTIMIDATING ATMOSPHERE OF THE ALI SAMI YEN STADIUM

game and, very soon, the BSkyB satellite buy-out of the competition's TV rights.

Over the next decade, hundreds of clubs around the world sent inquiry teams to Old Trafford to wonder at the Megastore and English football's financial miracle. Even officials from Germany, Italy and Spain pondered whether similar restructuring was the answer. In fact, the English game had moved only to copy the continental system by which the leagues operated as direct subsidiaries of the national association. The brilliance of the Premier League revolution was in the branding and marketing.

In the autumn of 1993, of course, the jury remained out on whether the Premier League's dash for (comparative) self-

control would work. Similarly, the credibility of the Champions League and/or Cup was on the line. It was not only the Marseille scandal. Georgian club Dinamo Tbilisi, previous winners of the Cup-Winners' Cup, were expelled from the competition and fined after trying to bribe the referee of their preliminary-round home leg against Northern Ireland's Linfield.

The scope of the competition had been extended as political and military events in eastern Europe brought more new nations into the UEFA fold. Thus 20 clubs competed in the preliminary round and were joined by a further 22 clubs in the first round. Two knock-out rounds followed, with the surviving eight clubs entering the two-group Champions League. Beyond that UEFA had decided to reintroduce semi-finals to reduce the number of dead matches towards the end of the group stage. Thus the group-winners would play off against the 'opposite' runners-up in single-match semi-finals. The group-winners were deemed to deserve home advantage.

British interest did not reach that far. Rangers, anxious to make up for their near-miss in 1993, lost on away goals to Levsky Sofia in the first round. Manchester United, having finally cracked the domestic title challenge after 26 impatient years in the wilderness, fell by the same sword, but in the second round and against Galatasaray of Turkey.

Manager Alex Ferguson was a frustrated man. United had led 2–0 within 13 minutes of the kick-off in the first leg at Old Trafford, with a third-minute strike from inspirational skipper Bryan Robson and an own goal by Hakan Sukur. But the Turks hit back fearlessly through Arif Erdem and Swiss international Kubilay Turkyilmaz (two). Only a late equalizer from Eric Cantona saved United's pride and unbeaten home European record.

A goalless draw in the intimidating atmosphere of the Ali Sami Yen stadium in Istanbul sent United out on the away-goals rule. Galatasaray went on into the group stages. They would not win a match, as it turned out, but they celebrated all the way to the bank.

ABOVE: **ONE OF THE MOST FEARSOME SIGHTS IN FOOTBALL, RANGERS' DUNCAN FERGUSON LEAPS ABOVE LEVSKI SOFIA'S ALEXANDER MARKOV TO PUT A HEADER IN ON GOAL**

1993-94

GROUP STAGE

The most surprised entrants into the group stage were Monaco. They had finished third in France the previous season behind Marseille and Paris Saint-Germain and had expected to be playing European football in the UEFA Cup.

Then Marseille were expelled from the Champions League and Monaco, because they had yet to open their UEFA Cup campaign, were propelled up among the nouveaux riches.

At least they had the players for it, headed by Jurgen Klinsmann, the West German World Cup-winning striker. Klinsmann enjoyed talented support from Belgian playmaker Enzo Scifo and future French World Cup-winners in Lilian Thuram, Manu Petit and Youri Djorkaeff. Bringing the best

out of them was an up-and-coming young coach from Alsace named Arsene Wenger.

First-round opponents AEK Athens were initially reluctant to play Monaco. They had been drawn originally against Marseille and pleaded to UEFA in vain for a walkover into the second round. They never got there. Monaco beat them 2-1 overall and then former holders Steaua Bucharest 4-2 to reach the group stage.

Here they were matched in Group A with Moscow Spartak, Galatasaray and favourites Barcelona, still under the command of Johan Cruyff. The decisive matches saw Barcelona beat Monaco both home and away. Txiki Beguiristain scored both goals in Barca's 2-0 win in the Nou Camp, and Hristo Stoichkov

Five minutes before half-time Costacurta was sent off for tripping Klinsmann. He was not the only Milan player who would miss the final. Captain and sweeper Franco Baresi was shown a yellow card and, because it was his third of the campaign, he too was automatically condemned to missing Milan's seventh appearance in the final.

Despite their handicap, Milan dominated the second half. Demetrio Albertini scored with a superb long-range shot after a free-kick, and Daniele Massaro volleyed a magnificent third after a defence-splitting, cross-field pass from Christian Panucci.

As Milan coach Fabio Capello said: 'It was an extraordinary performance to win such an important game so decisively with only 10 men.'

In the other semi-final, Barcelona had to wait only 10 minutes before the path to the final opened up before them. That was how long it took for Stoichkov to open the scoring against Porto from close range after an attack organized by Romario and raiding left-back Sergi. The same three players were involved in the second goal after 35 minutes. The Brazilian striker found Sergi in space on the left and once more the lethal Stoichkov pounced in front of goal. Porto lost all hope of recovery when captain Joao Pinto was sent off on the hour. Dutchman Ronald Koeman scored Barcelona's third goal in the 72nd minute – unusually for him from open play. Later Sergi said: 'This was probably our best game of the season.'

BELOW: **PORTO'S BULGARIAN STRIKER EMIL KOSTADINOV TAKES ON TOUGH-TACKLING RONALD KOEMAN OF BARCELONA**

scored the winner in the Stade Louis II. Outclassed, Spartak and Galatasaray managed a meagre one win and seven goals between them.

Like Barcelona, Milan came through Group B unbeaten, a point ahead of FC Porto. That produced a semi-final line-up of Milan at home to Monaco and Barcelona at home to the Portuguese.

Milan won comfortably by 3–0, despite playing more than half the match with only 10 men after the first-half expulsion of central defender Alessandro Costacurta. They took the lead after 14 minutes when Monaco failed to mark up at a left-wing corner from Zvonimir Boban. French international Marcel Desailly rose to head past 'keeper Jean-Luc Ettori.

MIGHTY MILAN

In the words of the clichéd old football report, Milan kicked off with a rush... and were soon out of sight against a Barcelona side who had been many neutrals' favourites. After all, Barcelona boasted the one-touch, perpetual motion style instilled by Johan Cruyff, while Milan had selection problems. Suspension had cost them central defenders Alessandro Costacurta and Franco Baresi, while the requirements of UEFA's restrictions on foreigners left Romania centre-forward Florin Raducioiu and Denmark forward Brian Laudrup in the stand.

Barcelona's attack was spearheaded by a fearsome partnership in Bulgaria's Hristo Stoichkov and the Brazilian Romario, who was about to inspire his country's record fourth World Cup triumph in the United States. However, they saw very little of the ball. Instead, Milan took the game by the scruff of the neck, with Frenchman Marcel Desailly providing the power and Yugoslav Dejan Savicevic all the skill and inspiration. Desailly, signed the previous autumn from Marseille, thus became the first man to win the Champions Cup with two different clubs in successive seasons.

Ironically, coach Fabio Capello had considered Savicevic, the former Red Star man, a talented luxury who lacked the temperament either to sit patiently in the stand or to slot comfortably into the team pattern on the odd occasions when injuries demanded his services. The exiled Slav had been saved only – and repeatedly – by a one-man fan club comprising Silvio Berlusconi. But that was nothing in power terms. Milan's president had by now used his football springboard to become prime minister. Shamelessly he had adopted the fans' chant of 'Forza Italia' as his party's name.

No one doubted his Midas touch, least of all Milan fans. Now Savicevic scored one goal and was involved in creating the other three. Christian Panucci also had a ninth-minute 'goal' disallowed by English referee Philip Don for offside. Don had been appointed at short notice after death threats to the original referee, Dutchman John Blankenstein. Given the presence of his compatriot Johan Cruyff on the Barcelona bench, Blankenstein's appointment by UEFA had always been unwise.

Five years earlier Milan had also won the Champions Cup Final 4–0. But Steaua had offered mere token resistance. This was very different. Barcelona were on top of their game, but Milan were simply on a different footballing planet. Cruyff sat impassively back on the Barca bench, apparently resigned to the fact that Milan were in unstoppable mood. Goalkeeper Andoni Zubizarreta would later become the Catalan scapegoat but, in fairness, while the Basque icon may not have been at his

best, he was exposed by his defence's inability to withstand Milan's skill and pace.

Milan had threatened already through Panucci, Massaro and Desailly before Savicevic glided around Miguel Angel Nadal and chipped to the far post for Massaro to open the scoring.

LEFT: **THE VICTORIOUS MILAN
SIDE CELEBRATE IN THE
OLYMPIC STADIUM, IN ATHENS**

WEDNESDAY 18 MAY 1994
OLYMPIC, ATHENS

MILAN   **4**
MASSARO 22, 45, SAVICEVIC 47,
DESAILLY 59

BARCELONA   **0**

HT: 2-0. ATT: 70,000. REF: DON (ENG)

MILAN:
S. ROSSI – TASSOTTI*, F. GALLI,
P. MALDINI (NAVA 84), PANUCCI –
DONADONI, DESAILLY, ALBERTINI,
BOBAN – SAVICEVIC, MASSARO.
COACH: CAPELLO.

BARCELONA:
ZUBIZARRETA* – FERRER, R. KOEMAN,
NADAL, SERGI (QUIQUE 73) –
GUARDIOLA – BEGUIRISTAIN (EUSEBIO
51), AMOR, BAKERO, STOICHKOV
– ROMARIO.
COACH: CRUYFF.

*CAPTAIN

Then Savicevic and the Croat, Zvonimir Boban, combined with Panucci and Roberto Donadoni to build a second for Massaro on half-time.

Two minutes after the interval Savicevic himself scored after dancing past Nadal. He hit the post on 58 minutes, Barcelona failed to clear and Demetrio Albertini put in Desailly for goal number four. Six minutes from time the irrepressible Savicevic again hit an upright.

As the shattered Zubizarreta said, 'Milan played to 100 per cent of their potential – perfect.'

RESCHEDULING THE FIXTURES

Everything was being done to ensure the progress of the top dogs to produce viewing figures for the television companies. Meanwhile, a young Ajax side went into battle with all the confidence of youth

GROUP STAGE

This was the watershed season when a cup competition was converted into the foundation stone for the long-awaited European superleague envisaged by Milan owner Silvio Berlusconi. Stability had been the key to success down the years for domestic competitions, but the Champions League was bucking the rules.

Now four groups of four teams played in the first half of the season after a preliminary knock-out round. In the spring, competition stepped back into knock-out mode in line with the Cup-Winners' Cup and the UEFA Cup. One short-lived by-product was that champion clubs outside the top 24 nations were removed from the Champions League set-up altogether and dumped into the expanded dustbin of the UEFA Cup.

The pace of expansion owed much to television pressure. Competing clubs were guaranteed the income from three home matches on top of set appearance money and bonuses per point. But UEFA benefited the most. The lucrative exclusive TV and sponsorship deals provided an annual income from which all the junior competitions plus various development agencies could be funded.

TV channels gained the virtual security of an ongoing national interest through the legitimate fixing of entry procedures. The UEFA coefficient (a ranking based on a computation of match results over the preceding five years) was used to seed top-nation clubs direct into the mini-leagues.

UEFA also cleared Wednesday nights for the Champions League. Tuesday became the designated night for the UEFA Cup, with Thursday for the Cup-Winners' Cup. Later, after the 1999 scrapping of the Cup-Winners' Cup, the UEFA Cup switched to Thursdays, with the expanded Champions League taking over Tuesdays.

RIGHT: **HRISTO STOICHKOV CELEBRATES ONE OF HIS TWO STRIKES FOR BARCELONA AGAINST MANCHESTER UNITED IN THE NOU CAMP**

FAR RIGHT: **GEORGE WEAH GIVES OLIVER KAHN 'THE EYES' AS HE PLACES THE BALL BEYOND THE BAYERN GOALKEEPER**

However, results out on the pitch showed that not all the self-obsessed giants of the European club game were as good as they thought.

In Group A, IFK Gothenburg were surprise winners ahead of the 1994 finalists Barcelona, with Manchester United the most notable of failures. They finished level on points with Barcelona but failed in the head-to-head contest against the Spanish champions. Johan Cruyff's men drew 2-2 at Old Trafford, then thrashed United 4-0 at home with one superb goal from Romario and two equally adept from Hristo Stoichkov. United fretted over the import restrictions which cost them the presence of Danish goalkeeper Peter Schmeichel between the sticks and the four-game suspension which barred French inspiration Eric Cantona.

In Group B, Paris Saint-Germain were the only team to end the mini-league stage with a 100 per cent record. Bayern Munich, with Lothar Matthaeus reverting from sweeper to midfield, followed them thanks to a decisive 4-1 win over Dynamo Kiev on the last match day. French striker Jean-Pierre Papin, completely fit – albeit just briefly – scored twice.

Group C saw Benfica and Hajduk Split qualify. Hajduk were one of three quarter-finalists to progress all the way through from the preliminary round. Argentina's Claudio Caniggia starred for Benfica, scoring twice in a crucial 3-1 win over Anderlecht. He also missed a penalty.

In Group D, Ajax Amsterdam dominated the keynote confrontation with holders Milan. The Dutch champions won both home and away to establish themselves as cup favourites. Milan squeezed through courtesy of a 1-0 victory over Casino Salzburg in Vienna on the last match day. The clubs had finished level on points, and Milan, like Barcelona, qualified on head-to-head results.

The first Italo-Austrian duel had proved stormy. Salzburg goalkeeper Otto Konrad was struck on the head by a bottle in the Stadio Meazza. Konrad played on after treatment but was later substituted after Milan went 2-0 ahead. Konrad spent the night in hospital after Salzburg, without him, lost 3-0.

KNOCK-OUT STAGE

The fixture pressure developed by the Champions League forced cuts in many leagues' winter break. But three of the eight 1995 quarter-finalists were still hampered: Hajduk Split, IFK and rivals Bayern Munchen.

The Swedes wandered around Europe playing friendlies to regain fitness after their close-season. Their confidence was strengthened when Lothar Matthaeus fell awkwardly during one of Bayern's own friendlies and was ruled out for the season. Hajduk used the winter break to contract several new players, but Barcelona were weakened by homesick Romario's exit to Flamengo of Rio de Janeiro, while Milan 'lost' veteran Dutchman Ruud Gullit back to Sampdoria.

Thus it was not one of Milan's foreign superstars who made all the difference against Benfica but home-grown Italian Marco Simone. He scored twice in a 12-minute spell midway through the second half of the first leg. Milan might even have won the goalless return against Benfica had not both Simone and Zvonimir Boban been foiled by the posts.

Ajax, with an average age of 23 despite the presence of 32-year-old Frank Rijkaard, had no problems with Hajduk. They drew 0-0 away and won 3-0 at home. Two-goal defender Frank de Boer outscored his attacking twin Ronald for once.

The normal pattern of draw away, win at home was upset in Munich and Gothenburg. Bayern were held 0-0 by IFK in the Olympic stadium, and their prospects in the return dipped further after 22 minutes when goalkeeper Sven Scheuer was sent off. Their Italian coach Giovanni Trapattoni pulled out all the tactical stops and Bayern seized a two-goal lead through Alex Zickler and Christian Nerlinger. The eventual 2-2 draw secured qualification on the away-goals rule.

Finally, the 'tie of the round' saw Barcelona held 1-1 in the Nou Camp by a goal from George Weah, the newly crowned African Footballer of the Year. Back in Paris, it seemed as if the fates were with Barcelona. PSG hit the posts five times, and just after the break Barcelona snatched the lead through Jose Bakero. Catalan hopes faded in the closing 18 minutes, however, when Paris gained overdue reward for their near-misses through Rai and Vincent Guerin. Paris were through to their third consecutive European semi-final; Barcelona, beaten in the Champions Cup Final the previous year, had this time fallen two rounds short.

In the semi-finals, Ajax and Bayern had old scores to settle. Memories of the great old days of Cruyff, Keizer and Krol came flooding back. Not so much in the goalless first leg in Munich but rather in the return in Amsterdam, when Ajax secured their place in the final with a runaway 5-2 victory. One goal for Jari Litmanen, another for the Nigerian Finidi George and a third

for Ronald de Boer, provided Ajax with a 3-1 interval lead. Only one brief incident in the second half worried the Dutch: that was when defender Danny Blind handled in the penalty box. Hungarian referee Sandor Puhl, to Dutch relief, awarded a

yellow card rather than a red and not only did Ajax qualify for the final – so did their skipper.

The other semi-final possessed an intriguing element in Milan's thinly disguised admiration for PSG's attacking leader, Weah. In the event, he never got a look in as Zvonimir Boban stole away in the last minute to convert a cross from Dejan Savicevic. The former Red Star man was Milan's hero in the return, scoring both Milan's goals in a 2–0 victory.

LEFT: **FORMER RED STAR MIDFIELDER ZVONIMIR BOBAN (9) CELEBRATES HIS 91ST MINUTE STRIKE AGAINST PARIS ST-GERMAIN WITH MARCEL DESAILLY AND FRANCO BARESI: MILAN WON 2–0**

FRANK RETURNS TO HAUNT OLD FRIENDS

Triumph in Vienna was, with hindsight, Ajax's last hurrah. The financial landslip prompted by the Champions League would see the Amsterdam club's much-admired development system turn into a nursery, not so much for them as for richer neighbours in Spain, Italy and England.

Within little more than two years, their entire winning team – apart from retirement-bound Frank Rijkaard – had been lured abroad. In the meantime they left a proud legacy in the form of players, none more promising than 18-year-old substitute Patrick Kluivert, whose late winner earned the Dutch a fourth Champions Cup.

Rijkaard's contribution was a perfect farewell to international football. The 32-year-old midfielder had scored Milan's winner in the 1990 final against Portugese side Benfica in the same Viennese stadium. This time Rijkaard, who had already announced his end-of-season retirement, created the decisive goal. Rijkaard said later: 'I feel sorry for my Italian friends, but sometimes football is like that.'

Kluivert was not the only 18-year-old substitute who tormented Milan in the climactic last few minutes of the 1994–95 UEFA Champions League campaign. He had entered soon after the Nigerian, Nkankwo Kanu, had joined the action to disturb Milan's defensive control. The plan was for their young legs to wear down the Italian club's elder statesmen.

Van Gaal explained: 'Milan were more experienced than us. That's why I put two 18-year-old boys on the field in the second half and they won it for us.'

Milan, with only one player aged under 25 and missing the injured Dejan Savicevic, came close to a goal only in the 44th minute, when Marco Simone's volley was fisted away by goalkeeper Edwin van der Sar.

Victory for Ajax avenged their defeat by Milan in the 1969 final and guaranteed them the honour of being top seeds, as holders, the following season. For Milan, defeat prevented them equalling Real Madrid's record of six wins in European football's most prestigious club event. Having lost their domestic league title to Juventus, Silvio Berlusconi's irritated giants were not destined to return for several years.

RIGHT: **FRANK RIJKAARD IN ACTION AGAINST HIS FORMER CLUB, MILAN. RIJKAARD'S 32 YEARS RAISED THE AVERAGE AGE OF HIS TEAM TO 23, WHICH SHOWS HOW YOUTHFUL THE OTHERS WERE**

Back in Holland, the city of Amsterdam erupted into a jubilant mass of red and white as thousands of fans poured into the city centre to celebrate. They danced on tram stop shelters, waving red banners and scarves. Some wore T-shirts emblazoned 'Louis for president' – referring to Ajax coach Louis van Gaal.

Having beaten the Italian side twice at the group stage, Ajax thus boasted a hat-trick of victories against Milan over the season. As Italian coach Fabio Capello said, 'Any team who can beat the holders three times in one season deserve to win the cup.'

UEFA and its sponsors could not have been happier. A survey by the marketing managers from TEAM revealed that 3.64 billion viewers across Europe had watched its Champions League broadcasts. That represented a staggering 61 per cent increase (1.4 billion viewers) in a year.

Back in Belgium, however, Jean-Marc Bosman barely noticed. He was focused solely on the imminent trial of his case before the European Court of Justice in Luxembourg. UEFA's hierarchy remained unconcerned. After all, what did European law matter to the newly enriched European football federation?

WEDNESDAY 24 MAY 1995
ERNST-HAPPEL-STADION, VIENNA

AJAX 1
KLUIVERT 83
MILAN 0

HT: 0-0. ATT: 49,500.
REF: CRACIUNESCU (ROM).

AJAX:
VAN DER SAR – REIZIGER, BLIND*, F. DE BOER – R. DE BOER, SEEDORF (KANU 52), RIJKAARD, DAVIDS – GEORGE, LITMANEN (KLUIVERT 65), OVERMARS.
COACH: VAN GAAL.

MILAN:
S. ROSSI – PANUCCI, COSTACURTA, F. BARESI*, P. MALDINI – DONADONI, ALBERTINI, DESAILLY, BOBAN (LENTINI 83) – SIMONE, MASSARO (ERANIO 89).
COACH: CAPELLO.

*CAPTAIN

ABOVE: **ON THE EVE OF HIS RETIREMENT AS A PLAYER, FRANK RIJKAARD FINDS THAT A SHINY PIECE OF SILVERWARE IS INFINITELY PREFERABLE TO THE USUAL GOLD WATCH**

LEFT: **MANAGER LOUIS VAN GAAL HOLDS UP THE CHAMPIONS CUP SEIZED BY HIS TALENTED YOUNG AJAX SIDE AS THE CROWD GOES CRAZY AND PHOTOGRAPHERS SNAP AWAY FOR TOMORROW'S BACK PAGES**

BOSMAN MOVES THE GOAL-POSTS

The Bosman ruling went further than anyone had expected and opened up a fabulous new world of wealth to top-flight footballers. But Dynamo Kiev were expelled for a scandal involving fur coats

GROUP STAGE

The European Court published its judgement on 15 December 1995, and it was an historic victory for Jean-Marc Bosman against his club Liege. The Court went even further than Bosman had expected. Not only did it rule that all European Union professionals could move fee-free between member states on the expiry of their contracts, but it also ruled illegal, as a consequence, all regulations restricting the employment of EU citizen footballers within other member states.

Bosman's victory opened up a fabulously wealthy new

RIGHT: **JUVENTUS STRIKER GIANLUCA VIALLI ATTEMPTS TO SHOW BORUSSIA DORTMUND DEFENDER JURGEN KOHLER A CLEAN PAIR OF HEELS**

world for his fellow professionals, but in winning it he lost everything. Fighting the European and Belgian authorities cost him his home, two marriages, his playing career and the prospect of any further employment within the game.

Although in addition to winning the case advocate Jean-Louis Dupont won Bosman a million euros in compensation, much of that went in legal fees even before the Belgian taxman demanded a cut.

Like Jacques Glassman, the whistle-blower who brought down Marseille, Bosman became persona non grata within the football family because he stood up for what he believed to be right. His supporters included FIFpro, the international players' union to which the English Professional

Footballers' Association is affiliated. But, with the exception of contributions from the Dutch national squad and a few individuals in gratitude for the service he had done his fellow professionals, Bosman received no financial recognition.

FIFpro duly organized a benefit match, but even that was tainted because various federations scandalously refused permission for its staging within their territories.

The Bosman ruling was published just after the completion of the Champions League group stage, which featured a preliminary knock-out round, followed by four groups of four clubs. Domestic champions seeded 25 and below had been hived off into the UEFA Cup.

Dynamo Kiev were one of eight clubs 'promoted' from the preliminaries. They were then expelled from Group A after their opening 1–0 home win over Panathinaikos. It came to light that the Spanish referee Antonio Lopez Nieto and his assistants were offered expensive fur coats by Kiev's directors on the eve of the match. Danish club Aalborg, Kiev's qualifying victims, took over their Group A slot. Kiev were banned for three seasons, although the ban was later commuted.

Group A saw Panathinaikos and Nantes reach the quarter-finals, with FC Porto surprisingly edged out, while the only club with a 100 per cent record proved to be Moscow Spartak

LEFT: **WITH HIS DAZZLING RUNS AND INCH-PERFECT FREE-KICKS, ALESSANDRO DEL PIERO WAS THE OUTSTANDING PLAYER IN THE JUVENTUS SIDE WHICH REACHED THE FINAL IN 1996. HE WAS THE PERFECT REPLACEMENT FOR ROBERTO BAGGIO**

in Group B. They invested their Champions League cash wisely in bringing home internationals such as striker Sergei Yuran, midfielder Vasili Kulkov and goalkeeper Stanislav Cherchesov. But English champions Blackburn Rovers, for all steel magnate Jack Walker's millions, proved a disappointment. A misjudgement by England goalkeeper Tim Flowers presented Yuran with the only goal of their home opener against the Russians. From that point, Spartak never looked back and Blackburn never looked like qualifying. Legia Warsaw finished runners-up.

Juventus topped Group C. The pre-season sale of Italy's 1994 World Cup hero Roberto Baggio to Milan was compensated by the emergence of Alex del Piero. He inspired the early victories which lifted Juve into the last eight ahead of Dortmund with two match days remaining.

Ajax began their title defence in Group D as they ended 1994–95 – with a 1–0 win. This time Real Madrid were the victims of Marc Overmars's 14th-minute goal. The Dutch champions thus shot straight to the top of the table and never lost command of a group in which Madrid finished runners-up Teenage striker Raul Gonzalez became the youngest player to score a Champions League hat-trick in Real's 6–1 thrashing of Ferencvaros.

KNOCK-OUT STAGE

Lennart Johansson announced that he had been left quite unimpressed by the Bosman judgement. 'Nothing has changed,' he said. 'We cannot allow the law to interfere with our game.' That was rich coming from the president of a European federation whose legal, commercial and marketing expertise

TOP: **NANTES' NICOLAS OUEDEC PUMPS THE BALL UPFIELD AGAINST SPARTAK MOSCOW**

had nailed into financial submission the continent's most powerful sponsors and broadcasters.

In fact, Johansson could not have been more wrong. Sitting on its Swiss sidelines, UEFA had ignored the reality that its clubs had to abide by the laws of other lands. Its restrictions still worked for Switzerland, but were illegal throughout the rest of western Europe. Within weeks the European Union federations had lifted controls on EU players and, going beyond Bosman, had extended the principle of no-fee transfers on expiry of contracts to national as well as international transfers.

The remainder of the Champions League season was governed by UEFA's outmoded regulations, but only by gentlemen's agreement. Behind the scenes, feverish activity was under way as the giants planned how to invest their Champions League cash in the best players western Europe now had to offer. On the pitch, the group winners did not have everything their own way in the quarter-finals. Panathinaikos, Juventus and Ajax all progressed, but Spartak fell to French champions Nantes. The first leg in France saw Japhet N'Doram and Nicolas Ouedec provide a 2–0 victory over a ring-rusty Russian team who were further weakened by the sales of 'keeper Stanislav Cherchesov, skipper Viktor Onopko, midfielder Vasili Kulkov and striker Sergei Yuran to Austria, Spain and England. The Russians quickly levelled the aggregate score in Moscow, but eventually lost 4–2 overall.

There were no such problems for Ajax against Borussia Dortmund. The tie was virtually decided by the first leg in Germany and a goal in each half from Edgar Davids and Patrick Kluivert.

Dortmund's hopes of a second-leg surprise were wrecked when skipper and sweeper Matthias Sammer was sent off. Ajax won the return by 1–0 with a goal from teenager Kiki Musampa.

A clash of outsiders matched Legia Warsaw against Panathinaikos. The first leg, in icy Warsaw, was dominated by Polish goalkeeper Jozef Wandzik – playing against his fellow-countrymen.

His saves secured a goalless draw for Panathinaikos, who won 3–0 back in Athens, where two goals fell to another Polish export in striker Krzysztof Warzycha.

The outstanding quarter-final saw Real Madrid and Juventus renew a 34-year rivalry. Madrid had been disturbed by the coaching replacement of Jorge Valdano by Arsenio Iglesias. But he had brief cause to celebrate after Raul's first-half goal brought victory in the Bernabeu. Outstanding for Madrid was Denmark's Michael Laudrup, once of Juventus. But his inside knowledge proved of no avail in Turin: Juve won 2–0 and 2–1 overall.

The semi-finals, with a pre-ordained draw, matched Ajax

against Panathinaikos and Juventus against Nantes. Ajax suffered a major setback when they marked their last European tie in the old Olympic stadium with a 1–0 defeat to an 87th-minute goal from the prolific Warzycha.

But Ajax coach Louis van Gaal was being prophetic rather than arrogant when he warned: 'We are not beaten yet.' Within four minutes of the kick-off in Athens, Jari Litmanen silenced 75,000 noisy Greek fans by levelling the aggregate score. He struck again 13 minutes from the end and Panathinaikos, throwing caution to the wind, were punished further on the break by Nordin Wooter.

Juventus won their home leg against Nantes by 2–0 with second-half goals from captain Gianluca Vialli and Vladimir Jugovic. Vialli's goal, surprisingly, was his first European goal of the season, but he followed up with another in France as Juve went through 4–3 on aggregate.

BELOW: **LENNART JOHANSSON WAS UNIMPRESSED BY THE BOSMAN RULING: 'NOTHING HAS CHANGED' WAS HIS RESPONSE, WHICH WAS SIMPLY FLYING IN THE FACE OF FACTS**

JUVENTUS CELEBRATE BELATED GLORY

When Juventus won the Champions League they celebrated as if it had been for the first time. Their previous victory, in 1985, had been in the shadow of the Heysel disaster. As chief executive and former striker Roberto Bettega said, 'This is for real. We could never celebrate winning in 1985. We have waited a long time for this.'

But even the achievement of squeezing past outgoing holders Ajax on penalties would prove to be tarnished glory. Four years later, outspoken comments about the muscle-bound nature of various Juve players by Zdenek Zeman, an Italian-based Czech coach, turned out to be their undoing. Zeman's comments prompted a criminal investigation by a Turin public prosecutor, Raffaele Guariniello, himself ironically a Juve fan.

Guariniello had long been concerned about rumours of doping in Italian football. Zeman's comments gave him the excuse to home in on Juventus.

An inquiry team removed more than one hundred medicines and potions from the club's premises and this ultimately – in November 2004 – led to a suspended jail sentence for club doctor Riccardo Agricola for 'sporting fraud' between 1994 and 1998.

In the spring of 2005, Dick Pound, head of the World Anti Doping Agency, demanded that Juventus be stripped of the titles they had won in those years which included three Serie A titles, one Italian cup, one World Club Cup, one European Supercup and... this 1996 Champions' crown. Victory, even if claimed only by virtue of a shoot-out, was deserved on the day. Juventus out-shot Ajax by 13–6 and outdid them on corners 10–6. Afterwards, coach Marcello Lippi hailed the way his players – intriguingly, with hindsight – had maintained the pace of their game throughout the 120 minutes.

Juventus could have won it early on. First Alex del Piero needed just a little too long in front of goal, then Fabrizio Ravanelli, the grey-haired 'Silver Fox', fired hastily high and wide. Finally Ajax 'keeper Edwin van der Sar and Frank de Boer allowed Ravanelli to steal the ball from between them and shoot home from the narrowest of angles.

One goal was less than Juve deserved but they allowed Ajax

RIGHT: (L TO R) **GIANLUCA VIALLI, MICHAEL REIZIGER, PATRICK KLUIVERT AND MORENO TORRICELLI ARE INVOLVED IN BALLETIC ACTION**

FAR RIGHT: **SKIPPER GIANLUCA VIALLI WITH THE TROPHY. BEHIND HIM IS GOALSCORER FABRIZIO RAVANELLI**

to equalize four minutes before half-time. De Boer, making up for his blunder, surprised Angelo Peruzzi with a free-kick and, when the ball was pushed out to Jari Litmanen, the Finn scored to become the competition's top marksman with nine goals. Gianluca Vialli hit the bar and was foiled brilliantly on three occasions by Van der Sar as Ajax survived into extra time.

Surviving penalties, however, turned out to be beyond them. Juve succeeded in Rome where Olimpico hosts Roma had failed against Liverpool in 1984. Ajax coach Louis van Gaal was disappointed but not surprised. He said, 'You can tell, at the start of the penalties, who is going to win. When you have only a few players volunteering, then you know you have lost.'

WEDNESDAY 22 MAY 1996
OLIMPICO, ROME

JUVENTUS   1
RAVANELLI 12

AJAX   1
LITMANEN 40

AFTER EXTRA TIME
JUVENTUS WON 4-2 ON PENS.
HT: 1-1. 90 MIN: 1-1. ATT: 70,000.
REF: DIAZ VEGA (SP)

JUVENTUS:
PERUZZI - TORRICELLI, FERRARA, VIERCHOWOD, PESSOTTO - CONTE (JUGOVIC 43), PAULO SOUSA (DI LIVIO 56), DESCHAMPS - RAVANELLI (PADOVANO 76), VIALLI*, DEL PIERO. COACH: LIPPI.

AJAX:
VAN DER SAR - SILOOY, BLIND*, F. DE BOER (SCHOLTEN 67), BOGARDE - R. DE BOER (WOOTER 91), LITMANEN, DAVIDS - GEORGE, KANU, MUSAMPA (KLUIVERT 46). COACH: VAN GAAL.

*CAPTAIN

NEW FACES IN THE DRESSING ROOM

It was all change at the summit of European football as the old restrictions on nationality disappeared. Rosenborg of Norway defeated Milan and Zinedine Zidane became a Juventus player

GROUP STAGE

Squad statistics tell the tale of the instant effect of Bosman. Juventus had played out 1995-96 with four foreigners but now boasted six, including new star Zinedine Zidane. Borussia Dortmund increased their import quota from six to 10, Milan from six to eight and Manchester United from three to seven (discounting the UK and Irish contingents). Over subsequent seasons the foreigner count exploded, also handing national

RIGHT: **AJAX'S NIGERIAN FORWARD TIJANI BABANGIDA (LEFT) AGAINST AUXERRE**

coaches a convenient excuse for disappointments in World Cups and European Championships.

Simultaneously, the élite clubs moved towards a joint strategy vis-à-vis UEFA and the Champions League. This would eventually lead to the creation of G-14, with its secretariat in Brussels, because the clubs at least recognized the central significance of the European Union to world football.

Perversely, the 1996–97 group stages saw the end of the Milan era. Their dreams of winning the cup for a record-equalling sixth time were blown away in unlikely fashion on the last match-day of Group A, when the Norwegians of Rosenborg Trondheim went to the Stadio Meazza needing nothing less than victory … and achieved it by 2–1. FC Porto won the group.

Rosenborg were a prime example of everything which was both good and bad about the Champions League. Having once reached the group stages, they used the income to buy their domestic rivals' top players, thus simultaneously strengthening their own domestic position while undermining their opponents.

The Norwegians had no need of a place in the semis or the final to balance their budget, as did the Italians, Spanish and English. Merely taking part was enough. By 2005 they had capitalized on that financial trick so effectively that they had carried off the Norwegian league title 13 years in a row.

That victory over Milan remained the high point of their exploits. Milan had just reappointed Arrigo Sacchi as coach, after his resignation as Italy boss the previous Sunday, and needed only one point. But they fell behind to Harald Brattbakk after 29 minutes and lost to a 69th-minute winner from Vegard Heggem. In between, French striker Christophe Dugarry equalized on the stroke of half-time.

Milan's astonishing collapse deprived the competition of an all-Italian quarter-final against the newly crowned world club champions Juventus. Silvio Berlusconi, Milan's millionaire owner, described the defeat as 'the lowest point in our luck and in the league since I have been at Milan'.

While Milan were sinking, European pedigree was being roused elsewhere on the continent. Ajax, bidding to reach their third consecutive final but needing an away win from their last Group A tie to qualify, rose to the challenge and beat Grasshopper 1–0 in Zurich. Patrick Kluivert's goal kept alive the Dutch champions' remarkable record of not having lost an away tie for three seasons. Ajax thus finished second behind Auxerre, who clinched their quarter-final place with a 2–1 win over Rangers in France.

In Group C, Manchester United, third before their last group game, defeated Rapid Vienna 2–0 in Austria and had Juventus

to thank for snuffing out Fenerbahce's quarter-final hopes by the same score in Turin. Ryan Giggs and Eric Cantona scored for United, whose fans spent as much time listening out for the score from Turin as watching their own side's level-headed performance in sub-zero temperatures.

Atletico Madrid beat Widzew Lodz 1–0 in their final fixture to win Group B ahead of Dortmund, who finished runners-up after winning their final match 4–3 against the faded glories of Steaua Bucharest.

KNOCK-OUT STAGE

Nigeria had struck a major blow for African football in 1996 by winning the Olympic Games football gold in Sydney. The legacy of confidence invested in their players quickly made itself felt across the European game. No one felt it more strongly than Ajax Amsterdam and Atletico in the Champions League quarter-finals.

Ajax, Juventus, Manchester United and Borussia Dortmund were favourites heading into the last eight and justified their status by progressing. But Ajax very nearly did not make it.

ABOVE: **PAUL GASCOIGNE OF RANGERS HITS THE TURF AFTER A CHALLENGE FROM BERNARD DIOMEDE OF AUXERRE**

BELOW: **JEAN-MARC BOSMAN WRAPS HIMSELF IN THE FLAG OF THE EUROPEAN COMMUNITY AFTER THE JUDGE RULED IN HIS FAVOUR AND SIMULTANEOUSLY TRANSFORMED THE ENTIRE WORLD OF FOOTBALL**

RIGHT: **ALESSIO TACCHINARDI OF JUVENTUS BEATS AJAX'S LEAPING RONALD DE BOER TO THE BALL**

It took Nigerian forward Tijani Babangida to score one minute from the end of extra time to set the seal on a 4–3 aggregate victory over luckless Atletico.

Holders Juventus reached the last four by beating Rosenborg 2–0 in the second, home leg and 3–1 overall. French midfielder Zinedine Zidane had led the way by taking inadvertent advantage of a blunder by Rosenborg 'keeper Jorn Jamtfall in the 29th minute. Jamtfall's clearance struck the surprised Juventus playmaker and rebounded into the net. It was one of Zidane's luckiest goals, but he had deserved a change of international fortune.

The previous summer Zidane's colourless performances for France at Euro 96 in England had rung alarm bells in Turin. Happily, Zidane's lethargy was due merely to the combined effects of a car accident shortly before the finals and an extra-long season. His previous club, Bordeaux, had played the

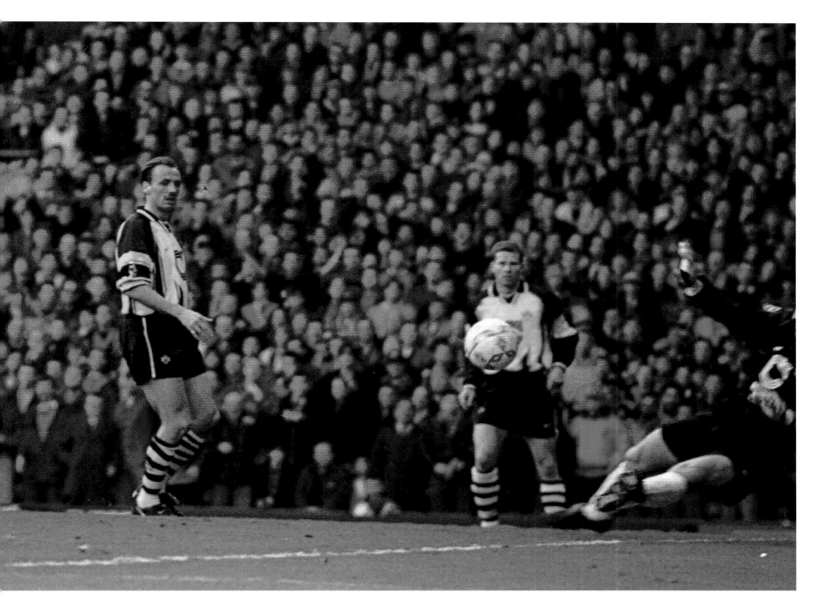

summertime Intertoto Cup in 1995 and then gone all the way through to the following year's UEFA Cup Final.

Manchester United became the first English semi-finalists for 12 years when they beat FC Porto 4–0 at home and forced a 0–0 draw away. United withstood a barrage of early pressure from the Portuguese champions, unaware of problems outside the ground where 20 fans were injured after clashes with police amid security chaos.

In the other quarter-final, Borussia Dortmund beat Auxerre 4–1 on aggregate in a duel between two of Europe's most venerable coaches in German Ottmar Hitzfeld and Frenchman Guy Roux.

The semi-final repeat between Juventus and Ajax generated none of the nail-biting tension of the 1996 final. First-half goals from Nicola Amoruso and the giant Christian Vieri earned a 2–1 win for Juve in Amsterdam, and they ran away 4–1 with the second leg. A 70,000 crowd in the Delle Alpi saw veteran Attilio Lombardo head in a corner in the 34th minute and then set up Vieri in the 36th. Mario Melchiot replied for the Dutch with 15 minutes to go before Amoruso and Zidane struck twice more for Juve in quick succession.

The other tie saw Borussia Dortmund achieve the rare feat of winning both home and away against Manchester United. An own goal from Gary Pallister provided the first victory in Dortmund, a strike from Lars Ricken the second at Old Trafford. With veteran Jurgen Kohler in brilliant form at the heart of the defence and goalkeeper Stefan Klos making stunning stops from Andy Cole and substitute Ryan Giggs, the Germans survived relentless pressure. 'Losing the goal so early in the game was a bit of a handicap, but we could have overcome that if we had taken any of the chances,' said United's manager Alex Ferguson, before adding: 'Next season we will be back.'

ABOVE: **OLE-GUNNAR SOLSKJAER PUTS THE BALL IN THE BACK OF THE NET FOR MANCHESTER UNITED AGAINST BORUSSIA DORTMUND, BUT THE GOAL IS RULED OUT BY THE REFEREE**

DORTMUND UPSET THE OLD LADY

The sight of Portuguese midfielder Paulo Sousa hobbling around the Olympic stadium's athletics track in triumph said everything about Borussia Dortmund's surprise dethroning of holders Juventus.

Dortmund had been outsiders from the moment the two clubs emerged from their semi-finals, and the fact that the final was in the back yard of fierce domestic rivals Bayern was expected to be of little assistance. Juventus were clear favourites and Dortmund were there to make up the numbers.

But Dortmund coach Ottmar Hitzfeld, due to retire

'upstairs' after the final by his own choice, had other ideas. So did back-to-fitness Matthias Sammer in the heart of defence; so did Dortmund's two former Juventus midfielders Sousa and German Andreas Moller.

Sousa did not want only victory: he wanted revenge. Juve had transfer-listed him at the end of the previous season while he was still convalescing from a knee injury. Dortmund had taken the gamble and Sousa wanted to repay both clubs in contrasting ways. In the closing minutes of the final he had to be carried off, nursing a badly bruised leg. But not even a

RIGHT: **KARLHEINZ RIEDLE RUNS PAST THE POST IN CELEBRATION AFTER SCORING FOR DORTMUND AGAINST**

fracture would have prevented him limping back out for the presentations and the opportunity to celebrate a Juventus defeat just a year after he had been celebrating their victory.

Dortmund's success enhanced German domination of European football. The national team were European champions, Schalke had just won the UEFA Cup – also against Italian opposition in Internazionale – and Sammer was the reigning European Footballer of the Year.

History was against Dortmund. Juve had beaten them in the 1993 UEFA Cup Final, the 1995 UEFA Cup semi-final and on aggregate in a previous Champions League tie. But they possessed an inner knowledge of the Italian team's organization, not only through Moller and Sousa but through two more Juve old boys in defenders Stefan Reuter and Jurgen Kohler.

Dortmund took the lead with their first shot after 29 minutes. Juve failed to clear Moller's corner, Scot Paul Lambert centred and Karlheinz Riedle chested down before shooting home. Four minutes later, Riedle rose unmarked to head home another Moller corner. Central defenders Ciro Ferrara and Paulo Montero stood and stared at each other in recrimination while Riedle skipped away, ecstatic. On the day before the final he had told his team-mates of his dream that he would score twice. Dortmund held their advantage to half-time despite a spirited Juventus fightback. Zinedine Zidane shot against a post and Christian Vieri had a 'goal' disallowed for handball.

Lippi rang the changes at half-time to bring the barely fit Alex del Piero into the action. The switch paid off when Del Piero's close-range shot climaxed a move engineered by Croatia striker Alen Boksic.

Six minutes later, however, Hitzfeld countered with a match-winning substitution of his own. Lars Ricken had been on the pitch only 16 seconds when he pursued a slide-rule pass from Moller and lobbed out-of-position 'keeper Angelo Peruzzi from 30 yards.

Peruzzi had missed the previous day's training session to fly home and visit his wife and new baby daughter. Doubtless he wished he had stayed there.

WEDNESDAY 28 MAY 1997
OLYMPIA, MUNICH

BORUSSIA DORTMUND   3
RIEDLE 29, 34, RICKEN 71

JUVENTUS   1
DEL PIERO 64

HT: 2-0. ATT: 65,000. REF: PUHL (HUN)

DORTMUND:
KLOS – REUTER, KOHLER, SAMMER*, KREE – HEINRICH, LAMBERT, PAULO SOUSA, MOLLER (ZORC 88) – RIEDLE, CHAPUISAT (RICKEN 70).
COACH: HITZFELD.

JUVENTUS:
PERUZZI – PORRINI (DEL PIERO 46), FERRARA, MONTERO, IULIANO – DI LIVIO, DESCHAMPS, ZIDANE, JUGOVIC – VIERI (AMORUSO 73), BOKSIC (TACCHINARDI 87).
COACH: LIPPI.

*CAPTAIN

LEFT: **THE OUTSTANDING ANDREAS MOLLER IN HIS TEAM'S MOMENT OF TRIUMPH**

THE TRIUMPH OF PRAGMATISM

The Champions League rules continued to be adapted to suit all interested parties as the European Cup grew away from its roots. In Madrid, fans found another way of moving the goalposts

GROUP STAGE

Champions League? Not from 1997 onwards. The trophy with which revived Real Madrid flew home at the season's end had been turned into a hybrid by UEFA's controversial expansion to admit runners-up from the nations ranked as Europe's top eight. That meant expanding the first round proper from four to six groups, with the group winners plus the two runners-up with the best records reaching the quarter-finals.

To do that UEFA had to attract the support of the minnow nations. It achieved this by recalling the downgraded champions from the UEFA Cup and putting them into the Champions League preliminary stages. Bringing runners-up into the Champions Cup was not new. Several of the launch clubs in 1955–56 had not been champions because the competition had been organized, initially, by invitation.

Then Real Madrid's subsequent domination persuaded UEFA to allow the Spanish runners-up to enter in 1956–57 (Bilbao), 1957–58 (Sevilla) and 1958–59 (Atletico Madrid).

The runners-up who kicked off a new era in the second qualifying round for the 1997–98 Champions League were Barcelona (Spain), Newcastle United (England), Feyenoord (Holland), Bayer Leverkusen (Germany), Paris Saint-Germain (France), Parma (Italy), Sporting (Portugal) and Besiktas (Turkey). The one anomaly was the presence in the preliminary draw of both Turkish champions Galatasaray and runners-up Besiktas. UEFA's eight top-seeded countries had all been promised two Champions League places, but the award of a direct seeding to holders Dortmund meant pushing Turkey back in the pecking order. Happily both Galatasaray and Besiktas won through to the group stage.

RIGHT: **DAVOR SUKER OF REAL MADRID SCORES AGAINST ROSENBORG FROM CLOSE RANGE**

Intriguingly, only one of the domestic runners-up progressed to the quarter-finals: Germany's Leverkusen.

In effect the groups were decided over two match-days. Borussia Dortmund, Manchester United, Dynamo Kiev and Bayern Munich had a comparatively easy ride – all four sewing up their own group leadership with one game to play and a fortnight remaining. But that still left an abundance of drama for the sixth and last match day.

Juventus had a close call in Group B. They qualified as one of the two group runners-up with best records because, while they were beating group winners Manchester United 1–0, Rosenborg Trondheim could only draw 2–2 with Olympiakos in Group D. Juventus owed their win to a late goal from Filippo Inzaghi. However, it would not have been enough if Predrag Djordjevic had not scored two minutes from time to salvage a 2–2 draw for Olympiakos and thus eliminate Rosenborg.

Had the Norwegians held on for a 2–1 victory, they would have gone through to the quarter-finals with 13 points as one of the two best second-place teams.

Instead, they finished with 11 and went out. Juventus went through with 12 points, and Leverkusen got in with 13 as the other 'best runners-up' (the deciding factors being points scored, mutual results, goal difference and goals scored).

Juve hero Inzaghi said: 'I didn't realize we had qualified until I saw my team-mates jumping up and down on the touchlines. This must be the most important goal of my career.'

Real Madrid waited until the last matchday to win Group D, which they did by thrashing FC Porto 4–0. Croatia's Davor Suker scored twice, with the other two coming from Fernando Hierro and Brazilian left-back Roberto Carlos. Leverkusen and Monaco, in Group F, played out a 2–2 draw which was good enough to see both through.

BELOW: **MANCHESTER UNITED'S TEDDY SHERINGHAM GETS HOT UNDER THE COLLAR AGAINST JUVENTUS**

KNOCK-OUT STAGE

Germany had three sides in the quarter-finals: Leverkusen, holders Borussia Dortmund and Bayern Munich. Yet, remarkably, within six months all the talk would be about a German crisis after the national team collapsed in the World Cup quarter-finals in France.

Leverkusen were now out of their depth. Real Madrid proved it by beating them 4-1 on aggregate. The margin would

have been greater but for Leverkusen goalkeeper Dirk Heinen in the second leg in Spain. He pulled off two superb first-half saves from Raul but had no answer when French international Christian Karembeu scored four minutes into the second half.

Karembeu had only just joined Madrid after a long battle to quit Sampdoria, but was proving worth the wait since he had also scored Madrid's goal in the first leg. New striking hero Fernando Morientes and veteran defender Fernando Hierro (penalty) extended the lead.

Dortmund needed an extra-time goal from Swiss veteran Stephane Chapuisat to lift them into the semi-finals at the expense of Bayern. His goal, after 109 minutes, was the only one either side managed in the two legs.

Juventus slipped through eventually against Dynamo Kiev but, again, did not make life easy for themselves. Held 1–1 at home, Juve had to go and win 4–1 in the Ukraine capital for a 5–2 aggregate success.

Pippo Inzaghi scored a hat-trick. As coach Marcello Lippi commented: 'When this team have to rise to the occasion, they always manage it.'

Completing the semi-final line-up were Monaco at the expense of Manchester United. After forcing a 0–0 draw in the principality, United fell behind at Old Trafford to an early strike by David Trezeguet. Ultimately, they went out on the away-goals rule despite a second-half effort from Norway striker Ole-Gunnar Solskjaer. Manager Alex Ferguson complained that Monaco 'only had one shot and that was the goal'.

Monaco coach Jean Tigana said: 'The highest point in my career as a player was when France beat Brazil in the 1986 World Cup in Mexico. This is the highest point as a coach.' It was also the end of road for Tigana, as Monaco then fell 6–4 on aggregate to Juventus in the semi-finals. Juventus dominated the first leg to win 4–1 thanks to a hat-trick, including two penalties, from Del Piero and a late goal from Zinedine Zidane. A 3–2 defeat in Monte Carlo changed nothing.

Chaos theory turned into reality in the other semi-final, between Real Madrid and Dortmund, after probably the most embarrassing incident in the Estadio Bernabeu's history. Minutes before kick-off a group of notorious Ultrasur supporters brought down the ball-catch netting behind one of the goals. One post fell on to the goal frame, smashing the cross-bar and uprooting the frame. Dutch referee Mario van der Ende took both teams off the pitch and the kick-off was delayed by 45 minutes. No spare goal could be found in the Bernabeu, so groundstaff had to break into Madrid's training ground three miles away for a replacement.

When the match did get under way, goals from Fernando Morientes and Christian Karembeu earned Madrid a 2–0 win, but they also collected a massive fine from UEFA for their security failures. By comparison, the second leg was a tame goalless draw, so Madrid's overall victory set up what Juve coach Marcello Lippi described as 'the dream final'.

LEFT: **FABIEN BARTHEZ EMBRACES HIS TEAM-MATES AFTER MONACO'S 1-0 VICTORY AT OLD TRAFFORD, TO WHERE HE WOULD RETURN IN 2000 AS MANCHESTER UNITED'S 'KEEPER**

REAL GO BACK WHERE THEY BELONG

'This,' said Alfredo Di Stefano, 'is what European cup finals should be all about.' While Juventus coach Marcello Lippi had called it 'the dream final', the occasion would turn out, of course, to be a delight for the one team and a nightmare for the other.

The match-up in Amsterdam's Arena was a throwback to another era, when Europe's Latin aristocrats ruled the football world, buying the best players and paying them the biggest wages, building – and filling – the largest stadia in Europe, and lifting the game into a new dimension.

Not all the commercial and professional millions in play could equate to the value of the tradition represented by the two clubs. Hence Marca, the Spanish sports daily, had left its entire front page blank white the morning after Madrid had qualified for their first Champions Cup Final since 1981; hence Italy's Gazzetta dello Sport cleared six pages to recount the events of Juve's semi-final triumph and look towards the final.

Closer to the big day, trouble set in when Dutch air traffic controllers refused to accept charter flights bringing not only Spanish and Italian fans but even the Juventus team. UEFA gave the Dutch federation 24 hours to sort it out, and eventually the government declared a temporary lifting of flight restrictions to avert a potentially embarrassing public relations disaster.

In goal there appeared little to choose between the happily secure Angelo Peruzzi and Madrid's grumpy German, Bodo Illgner.

In defence, Juve missed the solidity of the injured Ciro Ferrara, while illness denied Madrid the services of Aitor Karanka. Compensation for Juve had been in the progress of Mark Iuliano, whereas Madrid leaned even more heavily on the aggressive leadership of Fernando Hierro.

Juventus possessed both skill and direction in midfield through the contrasting French duo of Didier Deschamps and

RIGHT: **FERNANDO MORIENTES COULDN'T LOOK MORE DELIGHTED IF HE TRIED**

Zinedine Zidane, but Madrid had been galvanized by the mid-term arrival of Christian Karembeu alongside the perceptive Fernando Redondo.

In attack, Pippo Inzaghi had wiped away Juve's concerns over the sale of Christian Vieri to Atletico Madrid. For Madrid, Fernando Morientes had made such rapid progress that Davor Suker was no longer first-choice partner for the trickily naughty Pedrag Mijatovic.

As in 1997, Juventus were favourites. As in 1997, they ended up with losers' medals. A technically engrossing game played at remarkable pace saw the Italians seize early control, only for Madrid – with ex-Ajax man Clarence Seedorf tireless in midfield and Hierro a tower of strength – to 'think' their way back into the match.

Madrid had lost form so badly in the Spanish league that they had finished outside the top two places which would have guaranteed a Champions League return the following season. It was almost unthinkable for the aristocrats from the Spanish capital. Juventus, crowned Italian champions once again, did not have that worry.

Yet, in the second half, Madrid cast off the pressure and began to play their football. In the 66th minute, Yugoslav striker Mijatovic seized on a loose ball on the edge of the six-yard box, stepped wide of Peruzzi and clipped the ball home. It was the only goal.

After 32 years Real Madrid, original champions of Europe, were back where they knew they always belonged. Two later days Jupp Heynckes, their German coach, was sacked.

LEFT: **ZINEDINE ZIDANE SEES HIS SHOT BLOCKED BY REAL MADRID DUO FERNANDO HIERRO AND CHRISTIAN PANUCCI**

WEDNESDAY 20 MAY 1998
ARENA, AMSTERDAM

REAL MADRID	1
MIJATOVIC 66	
JUVENTUS	0

HT: 0-0. ATT: 50,000. REF: KRUG (GER)

MADRID:
ILLGNER – PANUCCI, HIERRO, SANCHIS*, ROBERTO CARLOS – KAREMBEU, REDONDO, SEEDORF – RAUL (AMAVISCA 90), MIJATOVIC (SUKER 89), MORIENTES (JAIME 81). COACH: HEYNCKES.

JUVENTUS:
PERUZZI* – TORRICELLI, IULIANO, MONTERO, PESSOTTO (FONSECA 71) – DI LIVIO (TACCHINARDI 46), DESCHAMPS (CONTE 77), DAVIDS, ZIDANE – INZAGHI, DEL PIERO. COACH: LIPPI.

*CAPTAIN

PIONEERS MARCH BACK TO THE FRONT

Threatened with a breakaway league, UEFA offered more prize money and managed to persuade Europe's top clubs to keep things in the family. On the pitch, Manchester United were at their peak

GROUP STAGE

The brave new commercial and televisual world depended heavily on traditional 'names' to sell the products – whether cars, tyres or satellite dishes.

Conveniently, then, the age of the Champions League had been dominated by Milan, Ajax, Juventus, Borussia Dortmund and Real Madrid – all original European pioneers. It was appropriate that in 1999 Manchester United joined them on the podium after defeating Bayern Munich 2-1 in one of the most dramatic of finals.

Such an explosive ending was a fitting climax to a tumultuous year which started with UEFA's representative Lennart Johansson being trounced by Sepp Blatter in FIFA's presidential election on the eve of a World Cup won in some style by the French hosts.

Zinedine Zidane scored two goals in the concluding victory

RIGHT: **INTER MILAN GOALKEEPER GIANLUCA PAGLIUCA TIPS THE BALL OVER THE BAR AGAINST REAL MADRID AT THE BERNABEU**

FAR RIGHT: **SERGIY REBROV SCORES FOR DYNAMO KIEV AGAINST ARSENAL AT HIGHBURY**

over Brazil to wipe the floor with critics of his displays in Juve's cup final defeats by Dortmund and Madrid.

Behind the scenes, UEFA was working flat-out to keep the big clubs on board. Media Partners, a Milan-based marketing agency working with the blessing of Silvio Berlusconi, had generated proposals for a breakaway superleague. To be played in midweek with no promotion or relegation, the ties would be screened worldwide on sponsored pay-per-view.

This time, at least, UEFA saw the danger signs. Johansson and chief executive Gerd Aigner knew the clubs preferred the convenience of remaining within the family, but recognized the economic realities and the danger to their own competitions and income. Also, UEFA would not be thanked by the rest of the game for allowing a handful of greedy clubs to carve up the structure of world football.

Halfway through the new season's group stage, UEFA

brokered a peace deal with the 12 rebel clubs (Ajax, Barcelona, Bayern Munich, Borussia Dortmund, Internazionale, Juventus, Liverpool, Manchester United, Marseille, Milan, Porto and Real Madrid). Adriano Galliani, Berlusconi's right-hand man at Milan and future president of the Italian league, said, 'The clubs have affirmed their wish to work with UEFA. We must make concessions but so must UEFA.'

The clubs agreed to let UEFA control the purse strings, while the European federation responded with a sharp increase in the clubs' income share via match fees and points bonuses. Winning the Champions League had been worth £8 million to Real Madrid in 1998. Four years later, Madrid would earn double the money for winning the same prize.

Two of the 12, Manchester United and Bayern Munich, had been drawn together in Group D. The Germans finished with their noses in front, pipping United by one point. Even so, United progressed to the quarter-finals courtesy of the complex qualifying system: the winner of each of the six groups went through to the last eight, plus the two runners-up with the best records. At least United were in good company in qualifying via the back door. So did holders Real Madrid from Group C, which was won by old rivals Internazionale.

Olympiakos Piraeus qualified as winners of Group A, along with Juventus from Group B – though the Italians were not sure of reaching the quarter-finals until after the final whistle of their last group match. UEFA undertook a detailed study of the rules and regulations before confirming that Juve placed ahead of Turkey's Galatasaray and Norway's Rosenborg. All three clubs had finished on eight points.

There were no such problems in Groups E and F for Dynamo Kiev and Kaiserslautern. The attacking power of Kiev's young strikers Andriy Shevchenko and Sergiy Rebrov lifted them three points clear of Lens and Arsenal, while Kaiserslautern finished five points clear of Benfica.

KNOCK-OUT STAGE

A flurry of drama marked the quarter-finals which saw the new improved Manchester United march on and holders Real Madrid tumble out.

United were proving unstoppable in all directions. They were on their way to winning the English league and FA Cup double with a team perfectly balanced between youth and experience, home-grown players and imports.

Peter Schmeichel was arguably the best goalkeeper in the world, organizing his defence with a ferocity which Roy Keane matched with his leadership in midfield. David Beckham was emerging as a major personality on the right of midfield, his crossing talents superbly complemented by the pace and skill of Ryan Giggs on the left.

Opponents' efforts to defend the flanks left gaps in the centre which were ruthlessly exploited by strikers Dwight Yorke and Andy Cole. Few clubs had the supporting luxury of quality forwards such as England's Teddy Sheringham and the Norwegian Ole-Gunnar Solskjaer to bring off the substitutes' bench. Yorke had cost £12 million from Aston Villa the previous autumn and was in the midst of a golden thread of form which brought him 52 goals in 89 starts over four years for United.

Two of the most important of those goals earned United a 2–0 home win over Internazionale in the quarter-finals which the Italians could not overturn back in Milan.

Madrid shot themselves in the foot ahead of their tie against Kiev Dynamo by replacing Dutch coach Guus Hiddink. Hiddink had guided Holland to the World Cup semi-finals the previous year and then steered Madrid to victory in the World Club Cup. But the internal politics of the Bernabeu dressing room proved too much and he was abruptly 'thanked' with a short-lived replacement by John Toshack. The tie with Kiev was a personal triumph for Andriy Shevchenko, who scored in the 1–1 draw in Spain and both goals in the Ukrainians' 2–0 home win.

RIGHT: **REAL MADRID'S GUTI GOES FLYING AFTER A CHALLENGE FROM DYNAMO KIEV'S VLADYSLAV VASCHUK**

Juventus squeaked through against Olympiakos, an 85th-minute away goal from Antonio Conte in the second leg handing them the away-goals advantage. As for the all-German clash, Bayern had fewer problems than they feared seeing off Kaiserslautern – winning 2-0 at home and by a masterful 4-0 away. Nerves got the better of Kaiserslautern in front of their own fans; they never recovered after the eighth-minute expulsion of their Hungarian central defender, Janos Hrutka.

United appeared to be on their way out after being held 1-1 by Juventus at Old Trafford in the first leg of the semi-final. But manager Alex Ferguson said he was confident that United would score in Turin. Not only did they score but they secured a sensational 3-2 win after Juventus had seized an early 2-0 lead with goals from Filippo Inzaghi. United's goals were scored by Keane, Cole and Yorke. Keane's satisfaction at playing the game of his life was marred by a second yellow card which would bar him from leading United out in the final.

'After that performance I can say only that Manchester deserve to win the cup itself,' said Juventus coach Carlo Ancelotti, generous in defeat.

Bayern, of course, had other ideas after beating Kiev 3-3, 1-0. The Germans had goalkeeper Oliver Kahn to thank for a string of superb saves in the second leg in Munich. He held Shevchenko and Co at bay just long enough for Mario Basler to snatch a breakaway goal for Bayern at the other end. After that 36th-minute strike, Kiev faded and Bayern strode into the final.

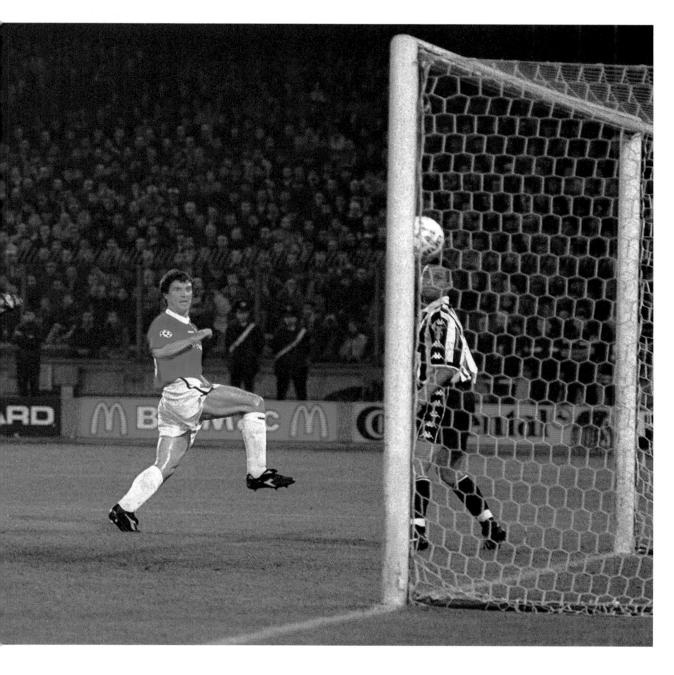

LEFT: **ROY KEANE (SECOND RIGHT) SCORES AGAINST JUVE IN THE SEMI-FINAL BUT A SECOND YELLOW CARD KEPT HIM OUT OF THE FINAL**

MANCHESTER UNITED PULL OFF A MIRACLE

'You know, this would have been Sir Matt Busby's 90th birthday today. Well, perhaps he was up there kicking a lot for us tonight,' said manager Alex Ferguson, basking in the barely credible euphoria of United's final glory.

The climax of the world's greatest international club competition had never seen anything like it as United won with two stoppage-time goals. United's achievement of the treble of UEFA Champions League, domestic league and FA Cup – emulating the feats of Celtic, Ajax and PSV Eindhoven – was matched by the amazing concluding drama.

Just as United and their fans – and even manager Ferguson – could barely believe it, neither could Bayern. In the moments which followed referee Pierluigi Collina's final whistle Ferguson looked almost as dazed and shell-shocked as Bayern boss Ottmar Hitzfeld. The difference was that Hitzfeld continued to look shell-shocked as the cup presentation took place.

Ferguson quickly emerged from his stupor. 'I didn't like most of the match,' he said, 'but the most important thing it showed was that you can never deny our people's spirit and will to win. That's what did it for us. In the closing minutes I had been preparing myself mentally for defeat – thinking that maybe it wasn't our year and I would need to keep my dignity. Then, well... at the final whistle I was just stunned. I didn't say anything to the players. I just hugged and kissed them – slavered all over them. It was the greatest moment of my life.'

Both finalists were below strength. United missed suspended skipper Roy Keane, plus Paul Scholes from midfield, while Bayern lacked injured top scorer Giovane Elber and French World Cup-winning left-back Bixente Lizarazu. Ferguson adjusted by moving David Beckham inside from the wing and switching Ryan Giggs from left to right.

United were the more nervy in the opening exchanges, especially goalkeeper Peter Schmeichel in his last game for the club. A couple of fluffed clearances encouraged Bayern, who went ahead in the sixth minute. Mario Basler's low, curling

RIGHT: **IN HIS REGULATION CLUB SUIT, MANAGER ALEX FERGUSON ACKNOWLEDGES UNITED'S AMAZING TURNAROUND WITH A BIG SMILE AND TWO CLENCHED FISTS**

free-kick eluded Schmeichel after Ronny Johnsen had tripped Carsten Jancker.

As time ticked on down, so United threw on substitute strikers Teddy Sheringham and Ole-Gunnar Solskjaer and left gaps at the back in an increasingly desperate pursuit of an equalizer. Bayern nearly capitalized. Substitute Mehmet Scholl hit a post on 79 minutes, and then Carsten Jancker's overhead effort struck the bar. Bayern were still leading 1–0 when fourth official Fiorenzo Treossi held up the illuminated board signalling three minutes of added time.

The numbers stood out red for danger, but Bayern failed to notice. In the last minute of the 90, United forced a corner. Schmeichel charged upfield, exacerbating the penalty box chaos. Stefan Effenberg hooked out the loose ball, Giggs drilled it back in and Sheringham turned the equalizer inside Oliver Kahn's right-hand post.

It seemed, agonizingly for the Germans, that United had won a last-minute reprieve. It was going to extra time. But worse was to come for Bayern's distraught defenders. United forced Sami Kuffour into conceding another corner. Beckham curled it in, Sheringham headed on and Solskjaer stabbed the ball up into the roof of the net.

Bedlam erupted all around the ground. For the second time in their history, Manchester United were kings of Europe – and the treble turned Alex Ferguson into a knight to remember.

LEFT: **IT'S NOT OVER UNTIL IT'S OVER: OLE-GUNNAR SOLSKJAER EMPHASIZES THIS ANCIENT TRUTH WITH HIS LAST-MINUTE GOAL AS MANCHESTER UNITED COMPLETE ONE OF FOOTBALL'S MOST AMAZING COMEBACKS**

WEDNESDAY 26 MAY 1999
NOU CAMP, BARCELONA

MANCHESTER UNITED   **2**
SHERINGHAM 90, SOLSKJAER 90
BAYERN MUNICH   **1**
BASLER 6

HT: 0-1. ATT: 90,000.
REF: COLLINA (IT)

UNITED:
SCHMEICHEL* - G. NEVILLE, STAM, JOHNSEN, IRWIN - GIGGS, BECKHAM, BUTT, BLOMQVIST (SHERINGHAM 66) - YORKE, COLE (SOLSKJAER 80).
MANAGER: FERGUSON.

BAYERN:
KAHN* - BABBEL, MATTHAEUS (FINK 80), KUFFOUR, LINKE - BASLER (SALIHAMIDZIC 89), JEREMIES, EFFENBERG, TARNAT - JANCKER, ZICKLER (SCHOLL 71).
COACH: HITZFELD.

* CAPTAIN

2000S

NO LONGER THE PEOPLE'S GAME?

The new millennium saw the advent of a brave, if less romantic, new order within European football. The Bosman ruling had ushered in commercial conformity along with set dates for international competitions and even fixed pan-European transfer deadlines. Money now ruled more than ever before. The 'Galactico' scale of Real Madrid's achievements in the Champions League was trumped by the billionaire potential of Chelsea's new Russian owner, Roman Abramovich. But the trophy-winning efforts of Porto in the Champions League and Greece in the European Championship proved that even the best-paid plans of football's ruling class could not guarantee results on the pitch.

RIGHT: **AC MILAN VERSUS JUVENTUS AT 'THE THEATRE OF DREAMS', AKA OLD TRAFFORD, IN THE 2003 FINAL**

theatre of football

ZINEDINE ZIDANE

Country: France

Position: Midfielder

Born: 23 June 1972

Clubs: Cannes, Bordeaux
(France), Juventus (Italy),
Real Madrid (Spain)

ZINEDINE ZIDANE

I was aware of the European Cup when I was growing up, but not from a really, really young age. I think the first European Cup final I remember clearly, my first sense of the trophy being different from the other games, was the Heysel tragedy final of 1985, with Michel Platini playing for Juventus against Liverpool.

Obviously, that was not a pleasant final to have as your first genuine memory of the European Cup, but it does remain the earliest I can recall. You see, whatever Platini did for Juventus had a huge impact on everyone in France. He was a fantastic player.

Not that I was a Juventus fan – I supported Olympique de Marseille. I used to go regularly to watch them play at the Stade Velodrome in the 1990s. I remember Chris Waddle, Jean-Pierre Papin and Basile Boli. I liked Waddle, but my hero was always Enzo Francescoli, the Uruguayan. He was amazing – I named my son after him. He remains my idol, one of the all-time greats, and the player who most inspired me. I consider myself fortunate to have met him since.

I did not attend either of Olympique's two European finals, 1991 or 1993, but I remember watching them with

LEFT: **ZINEDINE ZIDANE SUCCEEDED LUIS FIGO AS THE WORLD'S MOST EXPENSIVE PLAYER WHEN HE WENT FROM JUVENTUS TO REAL MADRID FOR £45 MILLION IN 2001. HE WAS FIFA WORLD PLAYER OF THE YEAR IN 1998, 2000 AND 2003**

friends; a whole load of us gathered round the television. I did go to a lot of their home games, though. I think you enjoy the matches more from the stands than on the pitch. I certainly did. That is not to say I do not enjoy playing, of course. Football is still more a hobby than a job for me. I have always seen it like that and I am proud of being a footballer. But I remember watching games from the stands in Marseille so fondly. It is a great stadium with a unique atmosphere.

When they finally won the European Cup, Marseille was an incredible place to be, the party atmosphere was indescribable. It's a very special city, one that loves football. People have told me it's like Liverpool, and I can

understand that; Marseille is a tough city, a port which has its problems but also one that has a soul, a real sense of community and identity. The place went crazy in 1993: a French team winning the European cup, a team that was not from a capital city – and against Milan, of all people.

I had to wait for my own debut in the European Cup until I was at Juventus. They had won it the season before, in 1996, and we reached the final again, but lost to Borussia Dortmund, which was so disappointing. Then the next year we lost to Real Madrid. Thank goodness I was part of the France team who won the World Cup a few weeks later! But honestly, I went into that World Cup final thinking: 'Oh, dear, here we go again.' I had to win that one, because I'd lost three finals in a row: a UEFA Cup Final with Bordeaux against Bayern Munich in 1996, then the Champions finals against Borussia in 1997 and Madrid in 1998. I was starting to think I would never win anything, so it was vital to win the World Cup.

Not that winning the World Cup diminishes the importance of the European Cup, and it certainly did not spoil my appetite. I still wanted to win it one day – perhaps more than most because of those lost finals. Luckily, I was able to win it in my first season with Madrid.

I went to Spain because I wanted to try something new. I was feeling a little tired of Italy. It was difficult playing there, much harder than it is in Spain for players like me, and Real Madrid were the perfect opportunity. People have asked me about the napkin story from Monte Carlo and, yes, it is true that, during a meal, the Real Madrid president Florentino Perez passed a napkin down to me asking if I wanted to play for Madrid. But, no, he did not write the message in English: it was me who wrote in English: 'Yes.' I don't really know why. His message to me was in French, I think, maybe Spanish. I can't remember exactly, but it wasn't in English!

The expectation at Real Madrid is probably greater than anywhere else – although the pressure at Juventus was pretty intense. At Madrid, I started enjoying my football again, because the attitude to the game in Spain is different. Also, I found that the style of play suited me better. There are complications playing for Real Madrid, but you know about that when you sign for them. You expect that intensity. Real Madrid are the biggest club there is, from a huge capital city, with lots of fans and loads of attention from all the media.

All the more so in the European Cup. To be honest, I try to approach all matches and competitions in the same way, but you feel something different about Madrid when it comes to the European Cup. It's a sense that this is 'Madrid's competition'.

I'm glad to say that finally, with Madrid, I won the trophy, against Bayer Leverkusen in Glasgow. People talk about my winning volley, but nine times out of ten that would have flown into the crowd.

I was lucky: I caught it just right, quickly and cleanly, but I had to strike it like that because the ball came down from so high. I'm not saying it was a bad cross from Roberto Carlos, though. As it turned out it was quite the opposite: the perfect cross. After all, it ended up a goal, didn't it?

I could not sleep that night, and I admit I watched the goal a few times on video. That was the perfect image of what Real Madrid is all about: the club which always has to win.

LEFT: **ZIDANE'S WONDERFUL VOLLEY WHICH WON REAL THEIR RECORD NINTH EUROPEAN CUP AT HAMPDEN PARK, GLASGOW, AGAINST BAYER LEVERKUSEN**

GETTING THE BALANCE RIGHT

The format of the competition continued to evolve, although it wasn't totally successful to judge by the number of dull games. Still, Real Madrid versus Manchester United was a cracker...

GROUP STAGE

UEFA's approach to the Champions League was Olympian. But instead of Citius, Altius, Fortius – swifter, higher, stronger – the European federation's motto would have read: bigger, longer, richer.

The major clubs were demanding a permanent right of access. Their cause, to bend and expand the qualification formula, was supported by television channels from the Big Five (England, France, Germany, Italy and Spain) which needed the guaranteed presence of 'their' clubs to justify their enormous outlay.

Thus the Champions League expanded again in 1999–2000. Now it comprised a weirder concoction than ever, with two qualifying rounds, a first group phase of eight groups of four teams, then a second phase of four groups of four teams ... before the knock-out stages.

This prompted a rethink about the other two European cup competitions. Admitting non-champions into the Champions League lowered the quality of the UEFA Cup, whose credibility was further compromised by the decision to relegate into it the third-placed clubs from the first-round groups of the Champions League. The Cup-Winners' Cup had been wound up altogether after Lazio's 1999 victory over Mallorca. Domestic cup-winners were added to the flotsam and jetsam of the UEFA Cup.

The first group stage of the revamped Champions League, as critics had feared, produced dull matches with too great a disparity between the likes of Manchester United, Barcelona, Lazio and Real Madrid and minnows such as Slovenia's Maribor and Austria's Sturm Graz.

Not that the giants had matters all their own way. The qualifying rounds had removed the reviving CSKA Moscow,

RIGHT: **BAYERN MUNICH'S PAULO SERGIO HEADS HOME HIS SIDE'S FOURTH GOAL AGAINST REAL MADRID**

Dinamo Tbilisi, the fast-rising French champions Lyon, Partizan Belgrade and Rapid Vienna. Joining those embarrassed failures were former UEFA and Cup-Winners' Cup holders Parma. They were dispatched by a Rangers team under Dutch coach Dick Advocaat who, courtesy of Bosman, saw only one Scot start both legs: midfielder Barry Ferguson.

Further Italian depression followed in the first group stage. Although Fiorentina and Lazio, coached by the Swede Sven-Goran Eriksson (formerly of IFK, Benfica and Roma), advanced, Milan blundered by losing their last Group H game 3–2 to Galatasaray. Milan thus finished bottom of the table and dropped out of Europe altogether, while the Turks were third.

Galatasaray's fine team, featuring home-grown centre-forward Hakan Sukur, Romanian playmaker Gica Hagi and Brazil's 1994 World Cup-winning goalkeeper Claudio Taffarel, slipped down into the UEFA Cup. Their consolation was going on to win it – on penalties in Copenhagen – against fellow Champions League exiles Arsenal.

Lazio, Barcelona, Valencia and Sparta Prague all topped their groups undefeated, while one defeat apiece was the acceptable return for other winners such as Rosenborg, Real Madrid, Chelsea and holders Manchester United.

Barcelona remained undefeated in the second group stage as well, while United again lost just the once by 2–0 in Florence against Fiorentina, whose goals came from the Argentinian duo Gabriel Batistuta and Abel Balbo. Valencia followed United through.

A Spanish trio in the quarter-finals was completed by Real Madrid, who finished second to Bayern Munich in Group C and pipped Dynamo Kiev – with whom they finished level on points – by courtesy of their superior head-to-head record. The veteran Ukrainian coach Valeriy Lobanovskiy was furious because Kiev had the better goal difference.

KNOCK-OUT STAGE

Real Madrid and Manchester United, the two venerable 'old boys' among the last eight, set the competition alight with their quarter-final.

Madrid had proved so erratic in the Spanish league that they had sacked coach John Toshack in mid-season and then suspended the £23-million French striker Nicolas Anelka when he dared question the tactical preferences of caretaker Vicente del Bosque, a runner-up as a player against Liverpool in 1981, whose avuncular manner was deceptive (so deceptive that it would ultimately cost him his job, though not for several more highly successful years).

Madrid were held goalless at home by United in the first leg, and raced into a 3–0 lead after 52 minutes of a sensational

BELOW: **IN MURKY CONDITIONS CREATED BY FLARES THROWN ON TO THE SAN SIRO PITCH BY FANS, CHELSEA'S ALBERT FERRER SWINGS OVER A CROSS DESPITE THE ATTENTIONS OF MILAN'S ANDRIY SHEVCHENKO**

return at Old Trafford. United skipper Roy Keane scored an own goal and Raul added two more. Fernando Redondo was the colossus in midfield who helped snap United's grip on the cup. David Beckham and Paul Scholes (penalty) struck late on, but this time around substitutes Teddy Sheringham and Ole-Gunnar Solskjaer could not fashion a repeat of the miracle of Barcelona.

Madrid's heroes included centre-back Ivan Campo, who would later star with nearby Bolton, and the England winger Steve McManaman, who had run down his Liverpool contract so that he could join Madrid on a free transfer.

The other ties saw Bayern Munich squeeze out FC Porto, Valencia thrash prospective Italian champions Lazio – winning 5–2 in Spain with a highly memorable hat-trick from midfield tyro Gerard – and Barcelona needing extra time to get the better of Chelsea in a topsy-turvy thriller.

Barcelona and Chelsea met in even more controversial circumstances.

Victory over United fired Madrid's confidence against Bayern Munich, their old nemesis, in the semi-finals. Anelka, who had forced his way out of Arsenal controversially the previous summer to join Madrid, had now made his peace with Del Bosque. The coach duly restored him to the attack and the Frenchman expressed his thanks by scoring both home and away in the 3-2 overall defeat of the Germans.

Barcelona were favourites to beat Valencia in the other semi-final. But Valencia's Argentine coach Hector Cuper had other ideas. Cuper had been appointed by Valencia on the strength of taking Mallorca to the Cup-Winners' Cup Final the previous season. He built hard-working, compact teams, but Valencia also benefited from the skilful leavening provided by the likes of Gaizka Mendieta in midfield and Argentine forwards in winger Christian 'Kily' Gonzalez and striker Claudio Lopez, nicknamed The Louse.

Mendieta was outstanding against Barcelona, scoring in both legs which Valencia won, with surprising ease, 4-1, 2-1. He not only dispatched Barcelona but also fatally undermined Barcelona's long-serving president Josep Lluis Nunez and their former Ajax coach, Louis van Gaal.

BELOW: **BARCELONA'S RIVALDO AND AMEDEO CARBONI OF VALENCIA TUSSLE FOR THE BALL**

Chelsea won 3-1 at Stamford Bridge, then lost 5-1 in Barcelona after extra time. The nail-biting drama in the Nou Camp included a potentially crucial penalty miss by Brazilian World Player of the Year Rivaldo.

The referee responsible both for awarding that spot-kick, and for sending off Chelsea's Nigerian left-back Celestine Babayaro eight minutes into extra time, was Sweden's Anders Frisk – who one day would again be officiating when

REAL USE LOCAL KNOWLEDGE TO WIN

Champions Cup history was made in the magnificent Stade de France, with two clubs from the same country contesting the final for the first time. Madrid were favourites to foreigners, while debutants Valencia were favoured by a majority of Spaniards. But Madrid, the men in black, knew them too well.

Manchester United were being lauded as the richest club in Europe, but football grandeur was still about more than money, and Madrid moved way out into a class all their own as they won La Octava – their eighth Champions Cup.

Madrid had made a habit of drawing the best out of their old retainers. Alfredo di Stefano and Ferenc Puskas were winning European cups deep into their 30s; team-mate Luis Molowny became the backroom master par excellence, emerging every now and then as caretaker to win one trophy or another; now his mantle had fallen on the modest Vicente del Bosque.

Both teams quickly fell into a pattern of play possible only between teams who knew each other well, although

even half-chances were few and far between in the opening exchanges. Steve McManaman busily covered the length and breadth of the pitch in attack and very nearly gained a reward on the half-hour when a deflected cross from Fernando Morientes ricocheted off his shin and forced a sharp reflex save from Jose Santiago Canizares.

Morientes was playing only because of injury to Brazil winger Savio, but he was a perpetual, lurking danger and, six minutes before half-time, he headed the opening goal from a short right-wing cross by right-back Michel Salgado, son-in-law of president Lorenzo Sanz.

Valencia pressed strongly in the minutes before the interval but failed to pull the goal back, and this proved decisive as the second half drew on. The more they threw men forward, the more they were at the mercy of the pace of Nicolas Anelka, Raul and McManaman on the break.

Two goals in a five-minute spell midway through the second half killed them off. First Valencia only half-cleared a long throw from Brazilian left-back Roberto Carlos and

McManaman volleyed Madrid's second. Then, five minutes later, with Valencia encamped in the Madrid penalty box, the ball was hammered clear and Raul ran unchallenged from half-way before rounding Canizares and sliding in goal number three. It was a breathtaking slalom which reminded old-timers of how Puskas had run similarly from half-way to score against Benfica in the 1962 final. Then, of course, Madrid lost. This time, as Raul had said, 'Losing has not crossed my mind. I have thought only of winning, winning and winning'.

Three goals ahead, Madrid could afford the sentimental gesture of bringing on 35-year-old club captain Manuel Sanchis to lift the trophy for the second time in three years on the night he equalled Paco Gento's record of 97 European appearances. Placards around the Stade de France proclaimed the message: 'Welcome Home!' They referred to the final's return to its first host city (although the inaugural final in 1956 had been played in the old Parc des Princes). Real Madrid fans screamed much the same thing when their heroes paraded the trophy back in the Spanish capital's Cibeles square.

LEFT: **AITOR KARANKA (LEFT) EMBRACES FERNANDO MORIENTES AFTER THE STRIKER GRABBED THE FIRST GOAL FOR REAL MADRID**

FAR LEFT: **CHRISTIAN KAREMBEU AND NICOLAS ANELKA BRAVE THE CELEBRATORY DOWNPOUR TO CLING ON TO THE CUP**

WEDNESDAY 24 MAY 2000
STADE DE FRANCE, SAINT-DENIS

REAL MADRID	**3**
MORIENTES 39, MCMANAMAN 67, RAUL 75	
VALENCIA	**0**

HT: 1-0. ATT: 78,000.
REF: BRASCHI (IT)

MADRID:
CASILLAS - MICHEL SALGADO (HIERRO 84), IVAN CAMPO, KARANKA, ROBERTO CARLOS - RAUL*, REDONDO, IVAN HELGUERA, MCMANAMAN - ANELKA (SANCHIS 79), MORIENTES (SAVIO 71). COACH: DEL BOSQUE.

VALENCIA:
CANIZARES - ANGLOMA, PELLEGRINO, DJUKIC, GERARDO (ILIE 68) - MENDIETA*, FARINOS, GERARD, KILY GONZALEZ - ANGULO, CLAUDIO LOPEZ. COACH: CUPER.

*CAPTAIN

FIGO'S HOMAGE FROM CATALONIA

Florentino Perez became president of Real Madrid and signed Luis Figo from Barcelona as English and Spanish clubs dominated the competition. Ominously, Bayern Munich were still in the hunt...

GROUP STAGE

France had lit up European football in the summer of 2000 by winning the European Championship with a golden goal against Italy in Rotterdam. But as the tournament reached its climax, a remarkable battle was being waged simultaneously off the pitch.

Defeated hero of the semi-finals had been the Portuguese winger-turned-playmaker Luis Figo. Although a last-kick golden goal penalty by Zinedine Zidane brought France victory over Portugal, Barcelona's Figo was the outstanding player. Admiring fans of co-hosts Holland and Belgium were not the only observers who thought so. Their opinion was shared by a Spanish millionaire property developer.

Florentino Perez had grown increasingly concerned at what he saw as profligate management of Real Madrid by president Lorenzo Sanz. In the summer of 2000, and despite Madrid's Champions Cup triumph, Perez not only challenged Sanz in the club's presidential election but beat him. His trump

card was the promise to sign Figo from... Barcelona. Perez kept his word, as did Figo, although the transfer made him a figure of hate throughout Catalonia. Missiles were hurled at him on his annual returns to the Nou Camp, including, on one occasion, a pig's head.

Even more remarkably, Perez wiped out Madrid's astronomical £350-million debt by selling land around the Estadio Bernabeu after the city council – at his persuasive behest – reclassified it for development. Not that this did Madrid a lot of good on the pitch in 2000–01, even if they began well enough. They topped their table in the first group stage, as did Arsenal, Valencia, Sturm Graz, Bayern Munich, Anderlecht, Milan and Deportivo La Coruna.

The presence at the top table of 'Super Depor' was further evidence of the benefits generated by a combination of the Bosman ruling and a television explosion in western Europe. Depor had always been a modest yo-yo club, sliding up and down between Spain's top divisions. Suddenly, they had the money to invest – wisely and successfully – in a solid squad in which Spanish pride was mixed with Brazilian technique and Argentine know-how. Depor, agreed the experts, were one of Europe's outstanding teams in the full sense of the word.

First-round failures included most notably Juventus – who did not even secure the consolation of a UEFA Cup slot – and Barcelona. Other former winners who failed to advance included PSV Eindhoven and Hamburg. Portugal's Sporting Clube were the sole team not to register a victory. Only three teams managed to complete their programme undefeated: Valencia, Manchester United and Deportivo.

English and Spanish clubs dominated the second group stage, with both nations providing three quarter-finalists. Bayern Munich and Turkey's Galatasaray were the interlopers to the party organized by Arsenal, Leeds United and Manchester United from England and Madrid, Deportivo and Valencia from Spain.

Leeds were back for the first time in almost a decade. They had been runners-up to Milan in Group H in the first stage and runners-up to Madrid in Group D in the second round. Qualification for the quarter-finals was secured by a concluding 3–3 draw against a Lazio side depressed by the knowledge that

RIGHT: **THE LEAST POPULAR MAN IN CATALONIA, LUIS FIGO IN ACTION AGAINST LAZIO**

coach Sven-Goran Eriksson had already agreed to quit and make history as England's first foreign manager.

Peter Ridsdale, the Leeds chairman, had made available every penny he could raise in building a team intended to be a permanent, self-financing presence in the Champions League. 'Living the dream,' he called it, never for a moment envisaging the nightmare to come.

KNOCK-OUT STAGE

Racist abuse of players had long been a sorry vocal feature of football crowds. But it had also long been tolerated by directors, officials and players. From the early 1970s English league matches had been marked by the 'monkey chants' and fruit missiles aimed at a rapidly increasing number of black players, initially of immigrant West Indian background.

BELOW: **JUVENTUS STAR EDGAR 'THE PIT BULL' DAVIDS AND DEPORTIVO LA CORUNA'S CESAR SAMPAIO BATTLE FOR POSSESSION**

The issue had been highlighted by the game's successful attraction of a wealthier audience following the creation of all-seater stadia. Simultaneously, television producers realized that the technology which was bringing all the action and all the noise into the nation's homes was picking up the bad with the good.

The English players' union, the Professional Footballers' Association, was among the initial leaders in a number of anti-racism campaigns.

Progress was slow but at least it was progress of a sort, and it drew attention to the problem. The reality – that education was needed throughout Europe – was thrown into ever sharper focus.

Ajax Amsterdam had threatened to pull out of European competition after one racist-fuelled visit to the Hungarian capital Budapest to play Ferencvaros. Arsenal then fell foul of the most high-profile racist chanting incident yet noted in the Champions League in the 2000–01 quarter-finals.

Drawn against Valencia, manager Arsene Wenger's men hit back in the first leg at Highbury from 1–0 down to win 2–1 with second-half strikes from Thierry Henry and Ray Parlour. They then lost 1–0 in Mestalla to a 76th-minute goal from Valencia's Norway striker John Carew and were eliminated by the away goal conceded at Highbury.

Bitterness at such a narrow defeat was exacerbated by the racist abuse aimed at Arsenal defenders Ashley Cole and

Lauren, skipper Patrick Vieira and forwards Henry, Sylvain Wiltord and substitute Nwankwo Kanu. At one stage the game was interrupted as Carew – himself black – tried to calm the fans, but all to no avail.

Valencia were fined £9,250 by UEFA, which was a derisory fistful of small change to the club, as Vieira pointed out. UEFA, demonstrating a breathtaking ignorance of the issue, then disgracefully fined Vieira £2,300 for daring to criticize the sum.

Arsenal were not the only English losers. Manchester United went out in the quarter-final for the second year in succession. This season, as in the previous one, their conquerors would go on to win the competition. Bayern Munich coach Ottmar

Hitzfeld had the satisfaction of getting the better of his old friend and rival Sir Alex Ferguson both at Old Trafford (1–0) and in Munich's increasingly outdated Olympiastadion (2–1). Holders Real Madrid lost 3–2 in Turkey against Galatasaray but enjoyed a comfortable 3–0 ride back at the Bernabeu courtesy of two more goals from Raul. However, Spanish champions-elect Deportivo left themselves too much to do against Leeds and came up just short – losing 3–2 on aggregate after a 3–0 loss at Elland Road.

In the semi-finals, Bayern avenged their defeat of the previous year by winning home and away to dethrone Madrid, while Valencia reached a second straight final after holding Leeds goalless at Elland Road and running out easy 3–0 winners at the Mestalla, where Alan Smith was shown an academic red card in the last minute.

Leeds manager David O'Leary, positive in defeat, praised the season-long progress achieved by his 'babies'. In football terms, as it turned out, his team would never grow up. In little more than a year O'Leary himself would be gone, and even the £30-million sale of defender Rio Ferdinand to Manchester United could not bring Leeds out of the financial tail-spin plunging them towards relegation and the verge of bankruptcy.

LEFT: **ZINEDINE ZIDANE, REAL'S WORLD RECORD SUMMER SIGNING**

FAR LEFT: **LEEDS UNITED'S RIO FERDINAND AND NIGEL MARTYN CAN NOT BELIEVE THE REFEREE IS ALLOWING JUAN SANCHEZ'S STRIKE TO STAND DURING THEIR 3–0 SEMI-FINAL SECOND LEG LOSS IN VALENCIA**

BECKENBAUER STILL HAS MIDAS TOUCH

Franz Beckenbauer was back. By now Bayern Munich's former sweeper, skipper and coach was club president, and his Midas touch continued to work as Bayern defeated Valencia in a penalty shoot-out.

Not that the 46th European Cup final will be remembered for its quality. Until golden goal extra time neither goalkeeper was ever seriously tested from open play.

Italian observers, pondering their own clubs' European failures, were left even more perplexed and depressed by the inability of Juventus and the rest to make a stronger impression.

Valencia duly created an unwanted piece of history as the first club to lose two successive finals. But it could have been different. The Spaniards, battle-hardened for the final by their 2000 defeat at the hands of Real Madrid, set off in style, scoring in the second minute. Norway striker John Carew rounded Ghanaian defender Sami Kuffour out on the left, and Swedish defender Patrik Andersson handled the ball after falling in the

RIGHT: **MAN OF THE MATCH OLIVER KAHN STOPS SLOVENE FORWARD ZLATKO ZAHOVIC'S PENALTY IN THE SHOOT-OUT**

ensuing goalmouth scramble. Valencia skipper Gaizka Mendieta fired low past goalkeeper Oliver Kahn's right hand.

The explosive pace was maintained, and four minutes later Bayern were awarded a penalty of their own after Jocelyn Angloma tripped Stefan Effenberg in full flight. However Mehmet Scholl's kick ricocheted over the bar off the legs of 'keeper Jose Santiago Canizares and Valencia survived.

Six minutes into the second half, Bayern were awarded a second penalty. This time it was skipper Effenberg who took the responsibility. He made no mistake and the teams were back on level terms. Neither side could find a winning goal, either during the rest of normal time or in the extra 30 minutes, which meant the agony and ecstasy of the shoot-out.

It all came down to the ultimate gladiatorial drama between goalkeepers Kahn and Canizares.

Up in the VIP box among kings and prime ministers, Pele, Michel Platini and Jorge Valdano looked on, hypnotized, as Kahn saved victoriously from Zlatko Zahovic, Amedeo Carboni and Mauricio Pellegrino.

Victory rounded off a magnificent four days for Bayern, who had retained their German domestic championship the previous weekend. UEFA also breathed a corporate sigh of relief that the Champions League had been won by a club who were, indeed, formal champions back home.

Bayern thus carried off the cup for the fourth time in what was their eighth final. No wonder that their players, after the lap of honour, did not want to leave the pitch.

Valencia coach Hector Cuper admitted that he could not watch the penalties. Not so Beckenbauer, who said: 'You have to be lucky to win in a shoot-out, but I think this team deserved it. Kahn has been fantastic in the Champions League. He is the main reason we won.'

LEFT: **OUTSTANDING SKIPPER STEFAN EFFENBERG – OR 'EFFING STEFFENBERG' AS ONE ENGLISH PLAYER MEMORABLY CALLED HIM – HOLDS UP THE TROPHY FOR ALL TO SEE**

WEDNESDAY 23 MAY 2001
GIUSEPPE MEAZZA, MILAN

BAYERN MUNICH   1
EFFENBERG 50 PEN

VALENCIA   1
MENDIETA 2 PEN

AFTER EXTRA TIME
BAYERN WON 5-4 ON PENS.
HT: 0-1. 90 MIN: 1-1. ATT: 70,000.
REF: JOL (HOL)

BAYERN:
KAHN – SAGNOL (JANCKER 46), KUFFOUR, P. ANDERSSON, LIZARAZU – SCHOLL (PAULO SERGIO 108), EFFENBERG*, HARGREAVES, LINKE – SALIHAMIDZIC, ELBER (ZICKLER 100). COACH: HITZFELD.

VALENCIA:
CANIZARES – ANGLOMA, AYALA (DJUKIC 90), PELLEGRINO, CARBONI – MENDIETA, SANCHEZ (ZAHOVIC 67), AIMAR (ALBELDA 46), BARAJA, KILY GONZALEZ – CAREW. COACH: CUPER.

*CAPTAIN

REAL MADRID GO GALACTIC

Real Madrid had a formidable line-up featuring some of the world's most expensive talent. It seemed Sir Alex Ferguson had a major appointment with destiny but he wasn't happy with David Beckham

GROUP STAGE

The events of 9/11 cast their pall over the Champions League. The opening Tuesday night of the 2001-02 campaign was the very day of the terrorist attacks on New York and Washington. UEFA, characteristically slow to respond to the real world, ordered Tuesday's matches to go ahead before bowing to outraged sentiment and postponing the Wednesday schedule.

Appeals against the results of the first games, however, were rejected. Borussia Dortmund's Matthias Sammer was one of several coaches who claimed that news of the events had upset their players – leading, in Borussia's case, to a 2-2 draw away to Dynamo Kiev.

'We had to force ourselves to go out for the match,' said Sammer, 'because of the tragedy in America. It's no surprise we played really badly.'

Real Madrid, when they did join the action, signalled their intentions for their centenary season by emerging as 2-1 winners from a testing opener away to Roma. It was only the third time Madrid had won in Italy and, ironically, they did so in the absence of Zinedine Zidane. Their world record £45-million signing had been ruled out by a suspension held over from his days with Juventus.

Luis Figo, Zidane's predecessor as the world's costliest player, moved into the Frenchman's playmaking role and not only scored one goal but also created the other for Guti. Madrid, revelling in their new 'Galacticos' nickname, duly

RIGHT: **FINNISH MIDFIELDER JARI LITMANEN SCORES FROM THE PENALTY SPOT FOR LIVERPOOL AGAINST ROMA**

became the first team to reach the second round.

They were accompanied by group runners-up Roma and, from the other groups, Liverpool and Boavista, Panathinaikos and Arsenal, Nantes and Galatasaray, Juventus and Porto, Barcelona and Bayer Leverkusen, Deportivo La Coruna and Manchester United, plus holders Bayern Munich and Sparta Prague.

Third-place finishes and consolation places in the UEFA Cup were the lot of Lokomotiv Moscow, Borussia Dortmund, PSV Eindhoven, Celtic, Lyon, Lille and Feyenoord, the UEFA Cup's ultimate victors.

Among those eliminated were Lazio. The Italians, who replaced coach Dino Zoff with Alberto Zaccheroni in mid-campaign, paid a heavy price for the summer sales of stars such as Juan Veron and Pavel Nedved and the depressing form of strikers Hernan Crespo and Claudio Lopez. In eight Serie A outings and six Champions League games, the Argentines managed two goals between them.

English media excitement grew in the second stage. While old rivals Manchester United and Bayern Munich qualified

from Group A, Barcelona and Liverpool progressed from Group B thanks to Roma's collapse. The Italians had led the group with two matches remaining after a superb 3–0 win over Barcelona through goals from Emerson, Vincenzo Montella and Damiano Tommasi, but then slipped up against both Galatasaray and Liverpool.

In Group C, Real Madrid became the first certain qualifiers with two matches to spare after winning 2–1 away to FC Porto in Portugal thanks to early strikes from Santiago Solari and Ivan Helguera. Panathinaikos followed.

Group D ended in bad-tempered confusion with Leverkusen and Deportivo qualifying at the expense of Arsenal and Juventus. UEFA's decision to use head-to-head results before goal difference to separate teams level on points was the cause of English and Italian last-day depression. Deportivo, already sure of qualifying through that system, put out a weakened team at home to Leverkusen and lost. It effectively eliminated Arsenal, who had beaten Leverkusen 4–1 only a few weeks earlier. The Gunners finished third in the group, with Juve bottom.

KNOCK-OUT STAGE

Sir Alex Ferguson, in the eyes of the media, was on something akin to a divine mission. He had decided that this would be his last season as manager of Manchester United and, by friendly accident, the Champions League Final was to be staged at Hampden Park, in his home city of Glasgow.

ABOVE: **BAYER LEVERKUSEN'S BRAZILIAN DEFENDER LUCIO STRETCHES IN A BID TO BLOCK ARSENAL STRIKER THIERRY HENRY'S SHOT**

The plans for Ferguson's retirement – specifically, into what role at United, if any, he would be moving – had yet to be settled. But United's chief executive Peter Kenyon had been so convinced of the need to find a new manager that he had reached an informal agreement with Sven-Goran Eriksson.

Whispers that United were poised to steal England's manager were circulating freely in the game, while confirmations and denials were notable by their absence. United's players, however, remained unaffected.

In the previous nine years under Ferguson they had won seven league championships and three FA Cups – including three doubles – in addition to that magnificent 1999 Champions League triumph.

United had strengthened their attack with the forceful Dutchman Ruud van Nistelrooy, who fed greedily on the wing assists from David Beckham and Ryan Giggs.

But concern was increasing over the rising tension in Ferguson's relationship with Beckham, whose pop star cult status had been enhanced by his marriage to 'Posh' Victoria Adams of the Spice Girls.

Out on the pitch, the tension weighed only on opposing defenders. United were drawn against Deportivo in the quarter-finals. They won 2–0 in north-west Spain, with goals from Beckham and Van Nistelrooy, and 3–2 back at Old Trafford.

Depor had defenders Lionel Scaloni and Aldo Duscher sent off – Duscher for inflicting the injury which would deprive Beckham of full fitness at the World Cup finals that summer. The injured Manchester United superstar became the object of constant media speculation in his home country: would he/ wouldn't he be available to captain Sven-Goran Eriksson's promising side in the summer and the broken metatarsal bone in his foot seemed to take a veritable eternity to heal.

RIGHT: **WITH SAMI HYYPIA GROUNDED, LUCIO BEATS JERZY DUDEK TO SCORE FOR BAYER LEVERKUSEN AGAINST LIVERPOOL**

The semi-finals matched United, without the injured Beckham, against the unfashionable Bayer Leverkusen.

Coach Klaus Toppmoller had welded an effective unit out of disparate elements, which included penalty-taking goalkeeper Hans-Jorg Butt, Brazilians in central defender Lucio and playmaker Ze Roberto, injury-prone sweeper Jens Nowotny and attacking midfielder Michael Ballack.

Ballack had scored twice as the Germans beat Liverpool 4–3 on aggregate in the quarter-finals, and he struck his sixth of the campaign in helping end Ferguson's dream. Bayer edged United on the away goals rule: drawing 2–2 at Old Trafford, then 1–1 at the BayArena. In both matches United had led 1–0 and, in both matches, it was Oliver Neuville who grabbed the decisive equalizer. Ferguson, denied his dream departure, decided to stay on as manager after all; Eriksson stuck with England.

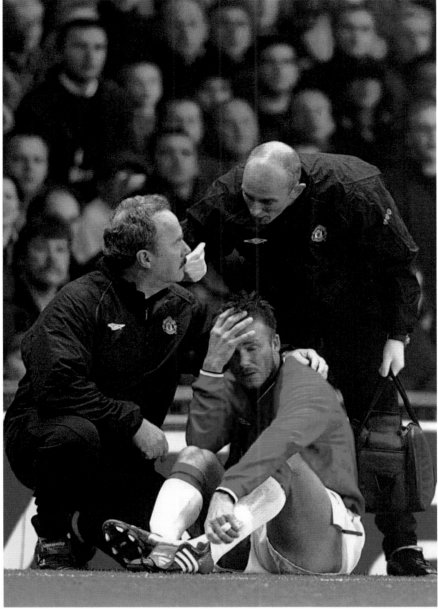

In the other half of the draw, Madrid had proved unstoppable. They took revenge over Bayern Munich for the previous season's defeat and then faced old Spanish enemies Barcelona in the semis.

For the Spanish media it was the Tie of the Century. Madrid had beaten Barcelona in the 1960 semis but had been eliminated – for the first time in the European Cup's history – by the Catalans the following autumn. On top of that, it was 20 years since Madrid had won in the Nou Camp, where the first leg was to be staged.

So much for history. Zinedine Zidane and Steve McManaman scored the second-half goals which provided Madrid with a 2–0 success. A 1–1 draw back in the Estadio Bernabeu saw them return to Hampden on a 3–1 aggregate.

ABOVE: **DAVID BECKHAM LOOKS DISTRAUGHT AFTER THE CHALLENGE FROM DEPORTIVO'S ALDO DUSCHER WHICH THREATENED TO PUT HIM OUT OF THAT SUMMER'S WORLD CUP FINALS**

REAL CLINCH CUP FOR THE NINTH TIME

Destiny decided it: not only did Real Madrid's world-record signing Zinedine Zidane score a magnificent winning goal, but victory was saved by a home-grown substitute 'keeper in Iker Casillas, who accomplished a remarkable triple-save sequence four minutes into extra time.

Between them, they secured Madrid's record-extending ninth European Cup as a glittering climax to their centenary season. Coincidentally, Zidane also walked away with his first winner's medal.

Hampden had seen Madrid first lay claim to legendary status back in 1960 with the 7–3 trouncing of Eintracht Frankfurt. Now once again the victims were German.

Everything seemed to conspire against Bayer Leverkusen, right down to the suspension which denied them the creative services of Ze Roberto and the ligament injury which sidelined skipper and defensive anchor Jens Nowotny.

Madrid's toughest opposition was not, perhaps, Leverkusen but the weight of expectation created by the realization that this was their last chance of a trophy in their centenary season. They had finished third in the league and runners-up in the Spanish cup, and a further failure would have been a grievous 'reward' for all those world-record millions invested in Zidane and Luis Figo, not to mention Raul's golden handcuffs.

Oddly, Leverkusen confronted a similar nightmare after finishing runners-up in the German league and runners-up in their own cup. For them, too, the treble had been there, and they too had let it slip, piece by painful piece.

Leverkusen's bid to become the fourth German winners appeared lost when Raul struck in Madrid's first serious attack in the ninth minute. Roberto Carlos, preparing a throw-in, spotted Raul drifting behind the Leverkusen defence and popped the ball into his stride. Raul claimed his 34th Champions League goal by pushing the ball ever so gently past Hans-Jorg Butt's left hand.

In 1960, Frankfurt had scored first and Madrid had saved the day by snapping back. Now history was turned on its head as Leverkusen squared within five minutes. Bernd Schneider curled in a free-kick from the left and Lucio rocketed into the penalty box to rise above the Madrid defence and head the equalizer.

Leverkusen, who had been aggressively chasing shadows in midfield in the early minutes, now found new confidence and direction. But it was Madrid who struck next with the class expected of the world's number one footballer.

Zidane had coasted quietly around Hampden until the 44th minute. Then Santiago Solari sliced a gap on the left, Roberto Carlos swung in a looping cross and Zidane uncoiled

RIGHT: **HAMPDEN PARK HAS SELDOM SEEN A BETTER GOAL THAN ZINEDINE ZIDANE'S EXPLOSIVE VOLLEY**

FAR RIGHT: **REAL'S PLAYERS FULLY ENJOY THEIR NINTH EUROPEAN CUP WIN**

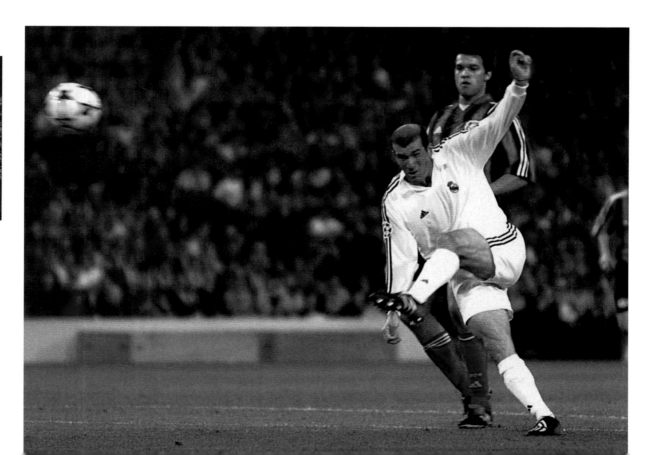

WEDNESDAY 15 MAY 2002
HAMPDEN PARK, GLASGOW

REAL MADRID 2
RAUL 9, ZIDANE 45

BAYER LEVERKUSEN 1
LUCIO 14

HT: 2-1. ATT: 52,000. REF: MEIER (SWZ)

MADRID:
CESAR (CASILLAS 68) - MICHEL SALGADO, HIERRRO*, IVAN HELGUERA, ROBERTO CARLOS - FIGO (MCMANAMAN 61), MAKELELE (FLAVIO CONCEICAO 73), ZIDANE, SOLARI - RAUL, MORIENTES. COACH: DEL BOSQUE.

LEVERKUSEN:
BUTT - ZIVKOVIC, LUCIO (BABIC 90), PLACENTE - SCHNEIDER, SEBESCEN (KIRSTEN 65), RAMELOW*, BALLACK - NEUVILLE, BASTURK, BRDARIC (BERBATOV 38). COACH: TOPPMOELLER.

*CAPTAIN

just outside the penalty box to explode a left-foot volley high beyond Butt's right hand. It was a goal to grace the greatest of occasions and would have honoured any one of the Madrid greats who had gone before.

The longer the match went on, the more physical it became. Injury-hobbled Luis Figo was substituted by Steve McManaman, and goalkeeper Cesar, injured in falling under pressure, had to be replaced by Casillas.

Swiss referee Urs Meier then signalled seven minutes of additional time, which proved sensational. First goalkeeper Butt joined the Leverkusen attack at a free-kick, only to glance his header inches wide, then Casillas produced that stunning hat-trick of last-ditch stops from Yildiray Basturk, Ulf Kirsten and Schneider.

No wonder that it was Casillas, rather than Zidane, that the Madrid reserves hoisted shoulder-high at the final whistle.

LIKE FATHER, LIKE SON

As Italian sides made a comeback, Paolo Maldini made history by following his father as the captain of a European Cup-winning side. Once more Real Madrid versus Manchester United was a classic

GROUP STAGE

Statistics reigned supreme amid Milan's resurgence to claim their fifth Champions Cup. Skipper Paolo Maldini finished the tournament not only emulating father Cesare – winning captain in neutral England back in 1963 – but with a European club record 123 appearances.

Along the way he had overtaken Barcelona and former Ajax defender Frank de Boer, who was left on 121. Also surpassed was Maldini's compatriot, the former Internazionale defender Giuseppe Bergomi, who played a grand total of 117 European club games between 1980 and 1999.

The first group stage saw Arsenal and Borussia Dortmund qualify from Group A with a game to spare. Arsenal secured progress despite losing twice in a row, by 2–1 to home to

Auxerre – an unhappy 53rd birthday for manager Arsene Wenger – then 2-1 in Dortmund despite Thierry Henry's free-kick. Dortmund's Czech playmaker Tomas Rosicky scored from a deflected free-kick of his own and a controversial penalty awarded against 'keeper David Seaman.

Group B saw Valencia qualify on the back of a 1-0 win in Liverpool. That left Gerard Houllier's men needing a win in Basel on the last match day. A topsy-turvy tie saw them fight back to 3-3 from 3-0 down but Michael Owen's equalizer was not enough. Liverpool ended third, one point behind Christian Gross's Swiss champions.

Holders Real Madrid qualified from Group C despite going off the boil. First they dropped a 2-0 lead at home to AEK Athens – AEK coach Dusan Bajevic described the 2-2 draw as a 'historic' result – then they lost 1-0 in the Bernabeu to Roma. Francesco Totti scored the decisive goal. Victory delighted Roma coach Fabio Capello, who had laid the foundations of this Madrid side five years earlier.

The Italian revival was maintained in Group D by Internazionale despite a surprise home defeat by Lyon, and in Group E by Juventus despite a 1-0 defeat away to Sir Bobby Robson's Newcastle United. Manchester United booked their place in the second stage from Group F after a mere four match days, followed by the 2002 runners-up Bayer Leverkusen. Their German rivals Bayern Munich were embarrassed to finish bottom of Group G without a win in six games. 'FC Hollywood' and coach Ottmar Hitzfeld were savaged by the media after losing home and away to group-winners Milan.

Barcelona, in Group H, were the only club to win all six games and came close to a repeat in the second phase. Only a goalless away draw against runners-up Inter spoiled a record which made a nonsense of erratic domestic form which saw coach Louis van Gaal replaced by Radomir Antic.

Inter shattered Newcastle's dreams by winning 4-1 at St James's Park. Newcastle had to play most of the match with 10 men after Craig Bellamy's early expulsion for throwing a punch at Marco Materazzi. Bellamy had already missed three first-phase matches through suspension for a TV-spotted head-butt against Dynamo Kiev.

Leverkusen responded to finishing bottom of the group by sacking coach Klaus Toppmoller, their hero eight months

BELOW: **CHRISTIAN GROSS'S FC BASEL WALK OFF THE OLD TRAFFORD PITCH AFTER LOSING 3-1 TO MANCHESTER UNITED**

earlier. Arsenal snatched initial leadership of Group B by winning 3–1 in Rome with a hat-trick from Henry but ultimately had to give best to Ajax and Roma.

Milan and Real Madrid led the way from Group C, followed by Manchester United and Juventus from Group D. United floored Juve twice in a week, winning 2–1 at Old Trafford and then 3–0 in Turin, where Juve shamed Italian clubs' reputation for disciplined defending. The Old Lady of Turin still squeezed through a statistical minefield after they, Basel and Deportivo all finished on seven points.

KNOCK-OUT STAGE

Three years earlier Manchester United and Real Madrid, meeting in the quarter-finals, had provided the tie of the round. Now they repeated the explosive magic, although this time neither went on to ultimate glory.

Madrid had added Ronaldo, Brazil's nine-goal World Cup-winning leader the previous summer, to their 'Galactico' squad. He failed to score in the first leg in Spain, which Madrid won 3–1, but struck a memorable hat-trick inside the first hour

at Old Trafford. When coach Vicente del Bosque substituted him, the Old Trafford crowd – who included an obscure young Russian businessman named Roman Abramovich – rose for a sporting standing ovation.

But the drama was not over. At the time Madrid led 3–2 with United having replied through Ruud van Nistelrooy's 14th goal of the European campaign and an own goal off defender Ivan Helguera.

Around the time Ronaldo went off, United manager Sir Alex Ferguson brought on David Beckham, who had been relegated to the deep-freeze of the substitutes' bench by a breakdown in the relationship between manager and player. Tangled emotions must have gone through both men's minds as Beckham struck twice to salve United's pride with a 4–3 victory, but a 6–5 aggregate defeat.

Elsewhere, another embattled coach was winning his important battle. Milan's Carlo Ancelotti, sacked two years earlier by Juventus, had not always been at one with owner/prime minister Silvio Berlusconi and executive Adriano Galliani over tactics and selection.

ABOVE RIGHT: **RONALDO IS CONGRATULATED BY ZINEDINE ZIDANE AND CLAUDE MAKELELE AFTER COMPLETING HIS HAT-TRICK AT OLD TRAFFORD**

FAR RIGHT: **ANDRIY SHEVCHENKO BLASTS A GOAL AGAINST INTER MILAN IN A RARE LOCAL DERBY THROWN UP BY THE CHAMPIONS LEAGUE DRAW**

But the man who had been Milan's midfield anchor when they won the cup in 1989 and 1990 under Arrigo Sacchi masterminded a 0–0, 3–2 win over Ajax which lifted the Italians into their first semi-final in eight years.

They were joined by neighbours Internazionale, who beat Valencia on away goals. Juventus provided Italy with a third semi-finalist by outlasting Barcelona.

After a 1–1 draw in Turin, Juventus resisted magnificently in the Nou Camp, despite the 79th-minute expulsion by English referee Graham Poll of midfielder Edgar Davids, the so-called 'Pit Bull'. Once more, the score was 1–1 at 90 minutes, but Barcelona struggled to keep up the pace in extra time and substitute Marcelo Zalayeta struck Juve's winner with six minutes remaining.

One of the semi-finals – as with the infamous quarter-final of April 2005 – paired Milan with neighbours Inter. This 'Euro-derby' was more cautious than classic.

Although the San Siro stadium is home to both clubs, Milan were nominally home in the goalless opener and thus won through courtesy of the away-goals rule after a 1–1 draw in the return. Andriy Shevchenko scored in first-half stoppage time. Inter levelled only shortly before the end through Nigerian substitute Obafemi Martins.

Juventus came through against Real Madrid in the other semi-final to set up the first all-Italian final. Czech playmaker Pavel Nedved was outstanding in the first leg, won 2–1 by Real in Madrid, and even better in the return, which Juve turned around 3–1. Unfortunately, Nedved also collected his second yellow card of the competition, and celebrations of his decisive third goal were muted by the knowledge that he would miss the final.

Madrid, for whom Juve old boy Zinedine Zidane struck a last-minute consolation goal, appeared to lack conviction right from the start. They badly missed the leadership of talismanic nine-goal Raul, ruled out of the tie by appendicitis.

Final 2003

MILAN STAY COOL AS JUVE CRACK UP

ABOVE: **ANDRIY SHEVCHENKO SENDS GIANLUIGI BUFFON THE WRONG WAY IN THE PENALTY SHOOT-OUT AND MILAN ARE HOME AND DRY**

It was nerve which decided the 2003 final after 120 minutes and a penalty shoot-out. Milan, shored up by veteran know-how, held theirs; Juventus, five of whose multi-millionaires refused point blank to take a spot-kick, lost theirs – and with it the first all-Italian final.

Unique places in European football were thus secured by Paolo Maldini and Clarence Seedorf. Skipper Maldini followed in the footsteps of 'Papa Cesare', who had raised the first of Milan's five cups 40 years earlier in England.

Dutch midfielder Seedorf became the first man to win the prize with three different clubs after his triumphs with Ajax in 1995 and Real Madrid in 1998. The fact that he missed one of the penalties was forgotten in the happy aftermath.

Juventus, significantly, were lacking Czech playmaker Pavel Nedved through suspension, while Milan had everyone available after veteran defender Alessandro Costacurta passed a late fitness test. Milan also possessed, in Carlo Ancelotti, a coach with recent and invaluable insight into the Juve psyche.

Rivera' or the 'new Baggio'. But his creative contribution was fitful and his shooting poor.

Milan thought they had the lead after only eight minutes. Pippo Inzaghi crossed from the left and Shevchenko fired low past Gianluigi Buffon. Unfortunately, Manuel Rui Costa's supporting momentum had seen him run in front of Buffon and into an offside position.

Juventus made a tactical switch at half-time, rearranging their midfield with the replacement of Mauro Camoranesi by Antonio Conte. The veteran substitute nearly made a decisive impact within a minute, heading against the Milan crossbar from Del Piero's cross, and Milan were thankful to concede 'only' a corner.

At the other end Maldini, diving, headed wide a right-wing free-kick by Andrea Pirlo. That was on the hour and was the last significant chance as both teams shadow-boxed their way to 'silver goal' extra time.

This was a short-lived experiment by UEFA, intended to provide a less extreme alternative to golden goal sudden death which had turned out to be less than totally successful. Now teams entering extra time played the full first 15 minutes of it whether or not a goal was scored. If the scores were level at that stage, they then played the full second 15 minutes. This was meant to dispel overcautious play.

A week earlier an FC Porto team under Jose Mourinho, coaching's rising star, had come through that same test to beat Celtic and win the UEFA Cup. In the event the International Board declared the system illegal the following spring.

Milan and Juve duly failed to produce a goal of any shade or colour and stumbled to a shoot-out. Juve first had problems finding enough willing shooters, and then David Trezeguet, Marcelo Zalayeta and Paolo Montero all misfired.

After the game, Juve coach Marcello Lippi summed up, with masterful understatement: 'When four or five players refuse to take a penalty, it's difficult.'

WEDNESDAY 28 MAY 2003
OLD TRAFFORD, MANCHESTER

MILAN 0
JUVENTUS 0

AFTER EXTRA TIME
MILAN WON 3-2 ON PENS.
HT: 0-0. ATT: 63,215. REF: MERK (GER)

MILAN:
DIDA – NESTA, COSTACURTA (ROQUE JUNIOR 66), MALDINI*, KALADZE – GATTUSO, PIRLO (SERGINHO 71), RUI COSTA (AMBROSINI 87), SEEDORF – SHEVCHENKO, F. INZAGHI. COACH: ANCELOTTI.

JUVENTUS:
BUFFON – THURAM, FERRARA, PAULO MONTERO, TUDOR (BIRINDELLI 42) – CAMORANESI (CONTE 46), TACCHINARDI, DAVIDS (ZALAYETA 65), ZAMBROTTA – DEL PIERO*, TREZEGUET. COACH: LIPPI.

*CAPTAIN

He sent out Milan to seize the initiative from the start. They failed to score but at least they took so much out of Juve's legs that, even when Milan had been reduced to 10 effective men in extra time with Roque Junior a passenger, Juve lacked the energy to capitalize.

The match was a classic only in chessboard terms. Few chances were created, although Milan's Ukrainian striker Andriy Shevchenko was man of the match. He rounded off a mixed season by climaxing a performance of pace and physical commitment by converting the decisive penalty.

Nedved's absence offered Alex del Piero an opportunity to express the skills which once earned him labels as the 'new

LEFT: **FOLLOWING IN HIS FATHER'S FOOTSTEPS TO WIN THE EUROPEAN CUP, SKIPPER PAOLO MALDINI EMBRACES CESARE MALDINI**

FOOTBALL'S RUSSIAN REVOLUTION

Just when football had developed prudent housekeeping habits, along came Roman Abramovich to buy Chelsea and take transfer fees sky high. Meanwhile, Jose Mourinho's Porto were on a roll

GROUP STAGE

Just when it seemed as if football was getting a grip on its chaotic finances, with UEFA laying down an accountancy standard, along came Roman Abramovich to blast financial logic out of the water.

Chelsea had qualified for the Champions League by finishing fourth in the Premiership under the leadership off the pitch of the irascible Ken Bates and the guidance on it of the idiosyncratic Italian Claudio Ranieri. Then, on 26 June 2003, came the 'Russian Revolution' sparked by a 37-year-old son of Saratov, a southern Russian city on the banks of the Volga.

Initially, it was whispered that Abramovich had bought

RIGHT: **HENRIK LARSSON DEMONSTRATES THE THIN LINE BETWEEN SUCCESS AND FAILURE BY HEADING JUST WIDE OF OLIVER KAHN'S GOAL DURING THE CELTIC V BAYERN MUNICH GAME AT CELTIC PARK**

Chelsea by accident, having spotted Stamford Bridge only on the drive back to Heathrow after a visit to Tottenham. He was painted as a man who had thrown millions at the club on an instant, ignorant whim. But inquiries into the murky world of post-communist Russia revealed a businessman who courted Europe's most influential politicians and power-brokers and never acted on the spur of the moment.

Orphaned before the age of three, brought up by uncles, schooled in the ruthless, fast-changing world of the collapsing communist empire, Abramovich had amassed a fortune which sent him straight to the top of the Sunday Times Rich List.

For a matter of small change, some £140 million, he bought the west London club and immediately paid off its crippling debts. Then, over the next 15 months, he splashed out £210

million on some of Europe's finest footballers.

Nor did he spend only on players. Within months he had lured Peter Kenyon from Manchester United as chief executive and was pursuing England manager Sven-Goran Eriksson, whose guidance was obvious behind a number of the signings.

Ranieri, as the Italian himself acknowledged, was a 'dead man walking'. But 'the Tinkerman' – initially a derisory label, but one he liked – scampered endearingly down his cul-de-sac. Chelsea beat Zilina of Slovakia 2–0, 3–0 in the qualifying round, then topped group G ahead of Sparta Prague, conceding only three goals in their six games.

UEFA had changed formats again. President Lennart Johansson, alarmed by European players' evident fatigue at the 2002 World Cup, had enforced a revisionist switch. This saw the second group stage replaced by a knock-out round. The G-14 elite was opposed to the plan on financial grounds, but, for once, the greater good prevailed.

ABOVE: **ROMAN ABRAMOVICH AT THE STADE LOUIS II STADIUM BEFORE CHELSEA'S SEMI-FINAL FIRST LEG WITH MONACO. WATCHING IN THE BACKGROUND IS FORMER CHAIRMAN KEN BATES**

Group A saw French champions Lyon surprisingly finish ahead of Bayern Munich, who overtook Celtic on the last match day by defeating Anderlecht 1–0 with a penalty from their new Dutch spearhead Roy Makaay.

Arsenal recovered from the shock of an opening 3–0 beating at Highbury by Internazionale to top Group B. Arsene Wenger's men came back from the dead after taking just one point from their first three games. Thierry Henry struck twice in their 5–1 revenge triumph away to Inter.

Even more remarkable was the progress of Monaco in Group C on the back of an 8–3 thrashing of Deportivo La Coruna. Before the match Depor goalkeeper Jose Molina had told coach Jabo Irureta that he was feeling a little unwell but was OK to play.

By half-time, when Molina was substituted, Depor were 5–2 down. Monaco's reserve striker, the Croat Dado Prso, built himself an international reputation overnight with four goals. Remarkably, Depor still managed to qualify for the second round as group runners-up.

Juventus, seeking amends for the Old Trafford penalties fiasco, topped Group D ahead of Real Sociedad, joined by Manchester United and Stuttgart (Group E), Real Madrid and Porto (Group F) plus Milan and, surprisingly, Celta Vigo (Group H).

Madrid, having plundered Manchester United for David Beckham and coach Carlos Queiroz, strolled easily onwards. They won 3–1 away to Porto and patronizingly gave some of the youngsters a run-out for the concluding group game against the Portuguese runners-up. It ended 1–1, but Porto coach Jose Mourinho would have the last laugh.

KNOCK-OUT STAGE

Monaco were also to have a laugh at Madrid's expense. Coach Didier Deschamps had seen his plans for the season thrown into confusion by serious injury the previous summer to their top-scoring striker Shabani Nonda. In a panic, and just before the 31 August transfer deadline, Monaco went to Real Madrid to arrange the one-season loan of Fernando Morientes.

The Spanish World Cup centre-forward had been relegated to the subs' bench in Madrid by Ronaldo. Ironically, despite having missed the eight-goal thrashing of Deportivo, he would still emerge as the tournament's nine-goal leading marksman. One of those nine goals was the crucial away strike which pulled Monaco back to 'only' 2–1 down away to Lokomotiv Moscow in the Russian capital in the first leg of their second-round knock-out tie.

French football took further pride in Lyon's defeat of Real Sociedad. Surprisingly, to outsiders, Monaco's progress was not universally welcomed in France. Domestic rivals such as Marseille, Paris Saint-Germain and even Lyon resented the way Monaco used the principality's tax-haven status to attract the likes of Morientes, who were beyond the others' reach because of high 'mainland' tax rates.

Deschamps snapped back: 'If we weren't successful in Europe the French ranking would drop and these other clubs wouldn't have so many European places available. They're jealous.'

In the quarter-finals Monaco, with right-winger Ludovic Giuly hampered by injury, were drawn against a Real Madrid buoyed by victory over Bayern Munich. Deschamps's fears that this was a step too far appeared well-founded when Madrid led 4–1 in Spain with nine minutes to go. Then up stepped the exiled Morientes with another priceless late goal, this time against his own club.

The return became French football legend. Raul extended Madrid's overall lead and Giuly's equalizer in first-half stoppage time appeared of minimal importance. But, as Giuly walked off at half-time, Zinedine Zidane muttered: 'Haven't you worked it out – we're absolutely shattered.' Morientes headed Monaco's second shortly after the restart. Giuly flicked home a second. At 5–5 on aggregate, Monaco had triumphed courtesy of the away-goals rule.

'Now we don't need to fear anyone,' said Giuly. Not even Chelsea, who had seen off Arsenal – suffering their usual Champions League stage fright – in the quarter-finals. In the first leg Monaco hit back from 1–0 down at home, despite having Alekos Zikos sent off, to beat west London's big spenders 3–1.

Chelsea manager Claudio Ranieri was blamed for misjudging his use of substitutes and, unbelievably, back at Stamford Bridge he repeated the mistake.

Chelsea went 2–0 up, only to concede a controversial and morale-sapping goal to Ibarra on half-time. Morientes, roaming freely around Stamford Bridge, drove in a superb equalizer for the 2–2 draw.

Monaco, against all the odds, had forged their way through to a final joust with another bunch of outsiders from Porto.

The second-round tie against Manchester United could hardly have begun worse for Porto coach Jose Mourinho. For the home leg striker Derlei was injured, while midfield anchor Costinha was suspended, and United went ahead on 14 minutes through Quinton Fortune.

But United had problems of their own, with Rio Ferdinand ruled out by an eight-month ban for failing to take a dope test. South African Benni McCarthy capitalized with a volley in the 29th minute and a header in the 78th. United suffered further when skipper Roy Keane was sent off for treading on keeper Vitor Baia.

After 32 minutes at Old Trafford, Paul Scholes put United level on aggregate and ahead on away goals, but it was not enough. In the last minute, Costinha disobeyed orders not to drift forward and scored from close range after Tim Howard only parried McCarthy's free-kick.

Mourinho jigged in delight down the Old Trafford touchline and Porto duly danced past Lyon in the quarter-finals and Deportivo in the semis.

BELOW: **TIM HOWARD CANNOT HOLD BENNI MCCARTHY'S FREE-KICK AND PORTO'S COSTINHA PUTS THE REBOUND BEYOND HIS REACH. MANCHESTER UNITED ARE OUT**

MOURINHO OUTSWIMS HIS FELLOW SHARKS

The previous year, after Porto's UEFA Cup Final victory, coach Jose Mourinho had been asked about rumours that he was planning to move on. He responded that he had worked hard at Porto, wanted to see how far he could go in the Champions League, and would then consider his options.

Reaching the Champions' final had not been among his calculations back then. He had said: 'We can do quite well but we cannot expect to live with the sharks.' Yet now Mourinho was about to become a shark himself: before the final in the heart of the Ruhr, it was an open secret that he would be replacing Claudio Ranieri at Chelsea.

That was the quirk about this final. Monaco and Porto were not approaching it as empire-builders. Quite the reverse. Both were about to sell off the family silver.

Porto were to lose playmaker Deco to Barcelona, while defenders Paulo Ferreira and Ricardo Carvalho would follow Mourinho to west London. As for Monaco, Dado Prso was joining Rangers, loanee Luis Ibarra was heading back to Porto, Fernando Morientes was returning to the Real Madrid auction room, Edouard Cisse and Jerome Rothen were off to Paris

Saint-Germain, and Ludovic Giuly would join Barcelona.

Porto started favourites, if only on account of the UEFA Cup-winning experience. Only one French club had emerged victorious from five previous tilts at the crown, and even that success – Marseille's in 1993 – had been tarnished by charges of corruption.

Deschamps had been the captain who raised the cup for Marseille that day. But he had added a 'legitimate' victory with Juventus three years later and thus now stood one match from becoming the youngest winning coach: at 35 he was 10 months younger than Real Madrid's Jose Villalonga in 1956.

The first half saw little goalmouth action. Porto used their anchor Costinha to stifle Fernando Morientes, while Monaco lost luckless Giuly to injury after a mere 22 minutes. At one stage, Monaco – spurred on by Rothen down the left – began to take the upper hand. Yet it was Porto who opened the scoring against the run of play through Carlos Alberto.

Given Monaco's attacking failure, Deschamps should have made changes at half-time. Instead he persisted for more than a quarter of an hour with the team whose touch and

RIGHT: **PORTO'S DECO PICKS HIS SPOT FOR THE SECOND GOAL AGAINST MONACO**

confidence faded a little further every time they fell victim to Porto's disciplined offside trap. Thus Monaco were eventually punished twice by substitute Dmitri Alenitchev on the break. First he helped set up Deco for goal number two, then he strode clear himself to thump home Derlei's assist.

Porto were not pretty, and much of their passing was below their own deft standard. Yet their second Champions Cup – 17 years after the first – meant that they had at last emulated the achievement of Benfica, twice victorious more than 40 years earlier.

When it came time to celebrate, however, Mourinho had vanished into the crowd. He had bigger sharks to fry.

LEFT: **PORTO'S COLOURFUL SUPPORTERS IN FULL FORCE**

BELOW: **AS HIS PORTO PLAYERS CELEBRATE, THE BROODING FIGURE OF JOSE MOURINHO STANDS FRESHLY BEMEDALLED IN THE BACKGROUND**

WEDNESDAY 26 MAY 2004
AUFSCHALKE, GELSENKIRCHEN

FC PORTO   3
CARLOS ALBERTO 39, DECO 71, ALENITCHEV 75

MONACO   0

HT: 1-0. ATT: 53,053.
REF: MILTON NIELSEN (DEN)

PORTO:
VITOR BAIA* - PAULO FERREIRA, RICARDO CARVALHO, JORGE COSTA, NUNO VALENTE - COSTINHA - PEDRO MENDES, DECO (PEDRO EMANUEL 85), MANICHE - DERLEI (MCCARTHY 79), CARLOS ALBERTO (ALENITCHEV 60). COACH: MOURINHO.

MONACO:
ROMA - IBARRA, RODRIGUEZ, GIVET (SQUILLACI 72), EVRA - CISSE (NONDA 64), BERNARDI, ZIKOS, ROTHEN - GIULY* (PRSO 68), MORIENTES. COACH: DESCHAMPS.

*CAPTAIN

REDS SNEAK UP ON THE INSIDE RAIL

Football has changed over the years but it has never been able to banish controversy. There was more than ever this term as unfancied Liverpool went from zeroes to heroes in a very short space of time

GROUP STAGE

The term which climaxed with Liverpool winning one of the most sensational of finals began just like the initial campaign back in 1955.

Many basic elements remained the same as they had been when the competition started. The destiny of the grand silver cup was still contested between two teams of 11 players. The goals separating victory from defeat were still approved in an instant by a lone referee.

But much else had changed.

Sharp eyesight was demanded to interpret the flickering black-and-white images recorded by primitive TV coverage of the first final. Now more than two dozen cameras claim almost every angle in colour.

In 1955, the players wore only numbers and, occasionally, club badges on their shirts. There were no sportswear logos, no shirt adverts, no subliminal assortment of stripes and swirls. Beyond that, there were neither high-tech footballs nor boots fashioned to swerve the ball in and around the goalmouth. Nor were there all-seater stadia, while protection against the elements was minimal for spectators.

The referee wore only black. No trendy colours. No further assistance beyond his two linesmen. Life was simpler. There were no extra complications from the away-goals rule or penalty shootouts. Nor did you need a fourth official to check the substitutes; there was no need, there were no substitutes.

As Alfredo Di Stefano observed: 'Today's footballers only appear to play more than us; it's not true when you consider

RIGHT: **PHILLIP COCU CELEBRATES AFTER SCORING FOR PSV AGAINST MILAN IN THE SEMI-FINAL. MILAN HIT BACK IMMEDIATELY THROUGH AMBROSINI TO TAKE THE WIND OUT OF THE DUTCH CLUB'S SAILS**

today's substitutions and rotation. We used to play the full 90 minutes of every game – even if we were injured.'

Attitudes quickly changed with the worldwide spread of professionalism. In the 1950s, football was still in touch with its sporting roots. Di Stefano again: 'We never celebrated a goal like today's players. We had too much respect for our opponents.'

There were no tabloid storms about footballers' failure as role models. The age of the angry young man lacked anyone to compare with the scowling youth of a Wayne Rooney or Antonio Cassano. England captain Billy Wright marrying Joy Beverley was a world away from the wedded life of the Beckhams.

The money had changed. Di Stefano, Paco Gento and Jose Maria Zarraga each collected a £1,250 bonus in 1960 for having won all five European Cups with Real Madrid. While English footballers were nailed to a £20 weekly maximum wage, it seemed astronomical. Yet Michael Owen, on joining Madrid from Liverpool in the summer of 2004, turned over as much every couple of hours.

Still a dozen of the 1950s pioneers were among the 32 clubs contesting the 2004–05 groups. Six 'old boys' were among the 16 who progressed: Madrid despite the short, turbulent coaching reigns of Jose Camacho and Mariano Garcia Remon, Juventus, Manchester United, Milan, Barcelona and holders Porto – who sacked new Italian coach Gigi Del Neri before the season had even begun for 'poor timekeeping'.

Accompanying them were old faces in new places. Liverpool demanded a major rebuilding job of Rafa Benitez (ex-Valencia); Leverkusen and Bayern Munich had been shaken up by former Cup-winning players in Klaus Augenthaler and Felix Magath; PSV Eindhoven had gone back to the future with successful 1988 coach Guus Hiddink; Internazionale leaned on Roberto Mancini (ex-Sampdoria); Chelsea powered in greedy pursuit of everything in sight under the self-proclaimed 'special one', Jose Mourinho. Stability was a rare boast for Didier Deschamps (Monaco), Thomas Schaaf (Werder Bremen) and Paul Le Guen (Lyon) – and Le Guen quit as soon as Lyon, the next May, had secured their fourth successive French league title.

Qualifying failures included CSKA Moscow. They finished third in Chelsea's group, the draw having raised eyebrows since the Brazilian-sprinkled Muscovites were sponsored by the Sibneft oil corporation owned by... Roman Abramovich. Ironically, it was CSKA who went on to European glory, winning the UEFA Cup into which they had been relegated by Chelsea and Porto.

And Liverpool? They sneaked through thanks to a magnificent goal from Steven Gerrard, three minutes from the end of their concluding group game against Olympiakos.

BELOW: **LIVERPOOL AND JUVENTUS PLAYERS OBSERVE ONE MINUTE'S SILENCE AT ANFIELD IN MEMORY OF THE HEYSEL STADIUM VICTIMS**

KNOCK-OUT STAGE

A frown flitted across the face of Sepp Blatter. The setting was a country house hotel in South Wales and the date was Saturday, 26 February 2005. The annual meeting of the law-making International Board had just approved experiments with goal-line technology.

The FIFA president believed in the universality of the game: that it should be played under the same conditions from World Cup Final to pub league. Now the one body on which England still commanded a decisive say in the worldwide game had defiantly opened the door to technological assistance.

Anders Frisk might have wished for video support at half-time in Barcelona. Chelsea's 2-1 defeat in a second-round first leg was followed by claims that home coach Frank Rijkaard had breached the sanctity of the referee's dressing room at half-time and thus influenced the subsequent expulsion of striker Didier Drogba.

Chelsea manager Jose Mourinho had refused to attend the obligatory post-match press conference. His behaviour and subsequent comments earned a two-match touchline ban. But the intimidatory atmosphere assisted Chelsea to a 4-2 turnaround win at Stamford Bridge.

Controversy was nothing new for Frisk. He had abandoned a group match in Rome after being struck by a missile following his sending-off of Philippe Mexes. But this time the consequences were extreme. His telephones, email and home were inundated with threats to himself and his family.

Frisk's response was immediate retirement, a dramatic gesture consistent with his theatrical style of refereeing.

Of course, the Champions League coped without him. Arsenal, crucially below par in Munich, slipped out 3-2 on aggregate to Bayern. Real Madrid, lacking in conviction under a third coach in Brazilian Wanderley Luxemburgo, lost in extra time to Juventus. Michael Owen's rise in stature could not compensate for the fading of Luis Figo.

Liverpool won home and away against Bayer Leverkusen; PSV saw off Monaco; Milan edged stuttering Manchester United; Inter saw off Porto and Lyon thrashed Werder Bremen 3-0 away and 7-2 in France, where Sylvain Wiltord scored a hat-trick.

In the quarter-finals, the Arsenal discard scored his sixth goal of the campaign to earn a shootout against PSV, but here Lyon came unstuck.

Bayern, meanwhile, were no match for a second English challenge. Frank Lampard scored two superb goals at Stamford Bridge and Chelsea flowed on despite losing 3-2 in the last European tie to be played in Munich's iconic Olympiastadion. Milan repeated their 2003 win over Inter to the fury of their neighbours' fans. The second leg had to be abandoned by German referee Markus Merk after a firework-flecked hail of missiles – one felling Milan goalkeeper Dida – halted play 16 minutes from time.

Further Italian losers were Juventus. For the first time in the 20 years since Heysel they had been drawn against Liverpool. A highly charged emotional occasion at Anfield, when an unforgiving band of Juve fans turned their backs on a memorial gesture, ended in a 2-1 home win. Surprisingly, that sufficed back in goalless Turin.

Liverpool thus flew home knowing Chelsea came next.

Europe was consumed by a tie which far overshadowed Milan's scrappy scuttling of PSV.

Mourinho and Chelsea were heading for the club's first league title in 50 years, but Liverpool had learned vital lessons from their earlier defeat by Mourinho's men in the League Cup final. Assisted by injuries which denied Chelsea the starting commitment of wingers Arjen Robben and Damien Duff, Liverpool emerged goalless from Stamford Bridge. Back at Anfield, manager Rafa Benitez ordered another cautious start. His perverse reward was a disputed fourth-minute goal for Luis Garcia which – backed by the defensive inspiration of Jamie Carragher – proved decisive.

Chelsea claimed William Gallas had hooked the ball back into play before it crossed the line but Slovak referee Lubos Michels would have none of it.

Tens of millions of viewers quickly realised that even slow-motion TV replays could not resolve the mystery of the ball crossing the line or not. Blatter must have smiled, back then.

LIVERPOOL'S AMAZING COMEBACK

Liverpool made more money out of the 2004–05 Champions League than Milan. Their share of UEFA's pot added up to £20.5 million, while Milan coined 'only' £17.5 million. But victory in Istanbul, as it turned out, was not about the money but the glory.

The momentous recovery which sent a fifth European Cup into a permanent place of honour at Anfield ensured this final a legendary slot in not only the European Cup but international and club football in general.

Three billion TV viewers in 200 countries were transfixed by Liverpool's record-beating comeback from 3–0 down at half-time. Even captain Steve Gerrard, man-of-the-match scorer of Liverpool's first goal and fouled for the penalty which led to their equalizer, appeared in a trance afterwards.

He said: 'Milan deserved to be three-up at half-time. There were some heads down in the dressing room at the interval and I was afraid it was going to be tears at 90 minutes. But the manager made some changes and put a bit of belief back into the players. The important thing was to get a bit of respect back for the fans.'

Tactically, the days of the WM formation, of catenaccio and 4–2–4 had long gone. Both teams began with sophisticated variations of 4–4–2. But whereas Milan, initially, had the right men to express themselves perfectly on that stage Liverpool did not. Milan began with their 'gala' line-up, while Benitez gambled on the fragile fitness of Australian Harry Kewell to assist Milan Baros up front. The ploy meant leaving a chasm in midfield for which Liverpool were duly punished.

After just 53 seconds Kaka was fouled by Djimi Traore and Andrea Pirlo's right-wing free kick was hooked home by skipper Paolo Maldini. Ironically, his records in becoming both the fastest scorer in a Champions' Final and the oldest, at 36, would be forgotten in defeat.

The injured Kewell was substituted by midfielder Vladimir Smicer to little effect. Andriy Shevchenko was wrongly judged offside as he 'scored' on 29 minutes but it hardly mattered as Kaka twice helped set up Chelsea loanee Hernan Crespo in the seven minutes before half-time.

What happened next is hotly disputed by the separate camps. Traore claimed that the celebratory sounds coming from the Milan players at the break inspired Liverpool's revival; Benitez said switching to three at the back was crucial; others saw the injury to full-back Steve Finnan which prompted Didi Hamann's arrival in central midfield as decisive.

The sum total, at least, contributed to Liverpool pulling level after what Milan coach Carlo Ancelotti later described as 'six inexplicable minutes of madness'.

Gerrard headed the first from John Arne Riise's left-wing cross; Smicer thundered the second off goalkeeper Dida's hands; and Xabi Alonso stabbed home a rebound after Dida parried his initial penalty following Gattuso's trip on Gerrard.

Milan could have regained all that lost ground three

RIGHT: **STEVEN GERRARD SETS LIVERPOOL ON THE COMEBACK TRAIL AS HE HEADS HOME JOHN ARNE RIISE'S CROSS**

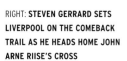

minutes from the end of extra time. But Jerzy Dudek made a remarkable double save from Shevchenko before the Polish goalkeeper defied the Ukrainian again, to permanent effect, in the shoot-out.

Liverpool were not the only winners. UEFA, having generated £30 million in the first year of the Champions League, was now collected around £1.5 billion: big business.

For Gabriel Hanot, editor of L'Equipe and founding father of the competition, of course, sporting merit had been all that mattered... and so it was on the night in Istanbul.

LEFT: **AFTER HIS CLOWNISH ANTICS IN THE SHOOT-OUT, JERZY DUDEK STOPS ANDRIY SHEVCHENKO'S POORLY STRUCK PENALTY TO BRING A FIFTH EUROPEAN CUP TO LIVERPOOL**

BELOW: **STEVEN GERRARD HOLDS UP THE EUROPEAN CUP, A SCENE WHICH NOT EVEN LIVERPOOL'S MOST ARDENT FANS COULD HAVE ENVISAGED WHEN THEIR SIDE WERE 3-0 DOWN**

WEDNESDAY 25 MAY 2005
THE ATATURK STADIUM, ISTANBUL

LIVERPOOL   **3**
(GERRARD 53, SMICER 55, ALONSO 59)

MILAN   **3**
(MALDINI 53SEC, CRESPO 38, 43)

3-2 ON PENALTIES AFTER EXTRA TIME
HT: 0-3. 90MIN: 3-3. ATT: 69,000
REF: MEJUTO GONZALEZ (SP)

LIVERPOOL:
DUDEK - FINNAN (HAMANN 46), CARRAGHER, HYYPIA, TRAORE - LUIS GARCIA, GERRARD*, ALONSO, RIISE - BAROS (CISSE 83), KEWELL (SMICER 22). MANAGER: BENITEZ

MILAN:
DIDA - CAFU, NESTA, STAM, MALDINI* - KAKA, PIRLO, GATTUSO (RUI COSTA 111), SEEDORF (SERGINHO 83) - CRESPO (TOMASSON 83), SHEVCHENKO. MANAGER: ANCELOTTI

PENALTIES (MILAN FIRST): SERGINHO OVER 0-0, HAMANN 0-1; PIRLO SAVED 0-1, CISSE 0-2; TOMASSON 1-2, RIISE SAVED 1-2; KAKA 2-2, SMICER 2-3; SHEVCHENKO SAVED 2-3.

*CAPTAIN

BARÇA DO A EUROPEAN DOUBLE

Arsenal defeated an unlikely list of fancied sides to reach their first Champions League final, against Barcelona, while holders Liverpool were forced to work their way through mid-summer pre-qualifying

GROUP STAGE

Valdebibas sits on the northward-spreading fringe of Madrid, near Barajas airport. There, in May, 2006 – 50 years after the first European Cup Final – Real Madrid played Reims once more.

This anniversary celebration marked the official opening of the Estadio Alfredo Di Stefano, which is as far as fans may progress inside Madrid's new sports city. The great man, recovered from heart surgery, was guest of honour. Old foe-turned-team-mate, Raymond Kopa, sent apologies from a retirement home in Corsica after surgery of his own.

Eight days later, Paris was host – as it had been in 1956 – to the real thing between Barcelona and Arsenal. In 1956, the venue was the old Parc des Princes; now it was the Stade de France, officially within Saint-Denis, but 'Paris' in football parlance.

The Madrid re-run was history on display, with all the club's trophies from the Di Stefano era being brought under guard from the Bernabeu and displayed in front of the main stand.

But Paris was also a history lesson between Barcelona, historic under-achievers in Europe, against Arsenal, whose legend had been honoured by the copying of the club's name worldwide.

RIGHT: **LIVERPOOL SKIPPER STEVEN GERRARD ESCAPES THE ATTENTIONS OF CHELSEA'S NEW GHANAIAN MIDFIELDER MICHAEL ESSIEN IN THE GROUP G TIE BETWEEN THE CUP HOLDERS AND THE PREMIERSHIP CHAMPIONS AT ANFIELD**

Two Frenchmen were looking further ahead. The one week saw Zinedine Zidane playing his last game in Madrid before heading for the World Cup and retirement; the next week saw Thierry Henry pondering whether to leave Arsenal for Barcelona. Thus history repeated itself again: in 1956 the see-sawing Frenchman had been Kopa, balanced between Reims and Madrid.

At least in 1956 the holders returned automatically the next season to defend their crown. This time, initially, that same opportunity was denied to Liverpool, despite the drama of their recovery to beat Milan in Istanbul. UEFA, in redrafting the rules for the Champions League, had omitted the right of defence. Liverpool, in finishing fifth in the Premiership, had failed to guarantee automatic re-entry to the competition. The Football Association and Premier League had to lobby hard before UEFA acquiesced with bad grace, obliging Liverpool to begin their defence of the trophy in the first qualifying round.

Hence, on 12 July – a mere 48 days after partying in Istanbul – manager Rafael Benitez and Co found themselves heading back to square one. The draw had been kind: Liverpool faced only the short trip to see off TNS of Wales, before despatching Kaunas of Lithuania and then CSKA Sofia to regain entry to the group stages and a renewal of their rivalry with Chelsea.

Both meetings in Group G, at Anfield and then Stamford Bridge, ended goalless, but the return was hardly peaceable after a clumsy tackle by Chelsea's new Ghanaian, Michael Essien, on Dietmar Hamann. Liverpool's veteran German said it was the worst tackle he had ever suffered, and the incident sparked a touchline spat between Benitez and his Chelsea counterpart, Jose Mourinho – who later accused the Liverpool bench of 'crying' throughout the game.

By then, both clubs had made sure of qualifying with a game to spare – as had Juventus and Bayern Munich, Arsenal and Ajax, Barcelona, Lyon and Real Madrid plus Internazionale.

This was fortunate for Madrid, whose hasty dismissal of Brazilian coach Wanderley Luxemburgo after less than a year was rewarded with a pride-pricking 2-1 defeat in their last group match by bottom club Olympiakos Piraeus. Rosenborg Trondheim, whose 13-year league-championship-winning reign in Norway had just come to an end, finished third and claimed the consolation of a UEFA Cup fade-out.

Milan had to wait until the last matchday before topping Group E, while Rangers scraped out of Group H after drawing 1-1 with Internazionale, and Artmedia Bratislava simultaneously failed to beat Porto. Peter Lovenkrands's goal kept manager Alex McLeish in his job for the rest of the season.

Artmedia were already popular with Rangers: in the third qualifying round, they had eliminated 'old firm' rivals Celtic. Artmedia won the first leg in Bratislava 5-0, the worst

possible start for new Celtic manager Gordon Strachan.

He would have the last laugh, however. Celtic went on to win the Scottish league, while Hearts – revived by a Lithuanian transplant from banker Vladimir Romanov – ultimately pipped Rangers to the second Champions League slot.

The one blow to English pride was Manchester United's failure to progress for the first time in 11 years. A 2-1 defeat away to Benfica on the last matchday – despite an early lead provided by Paul Scholes – was a worrying introduction to European football for Malcolm Glazer and his sons, United's much-derided new American owners.

Goals from Geovanni and Beto left United bottom of the group, so they missed even the consolation of a place in the UEFA Cup. Those goals also provided United with a depressing return to the city in which George Best had risen to world fame back in 1965. The Northern Irishman, who had just died at the age of 59, after a long battle against illnesses brought on by the lifestyle he enjoyed in his earlier days, would not have recognized this United.

BELOW: **CRISTIANO RONALDO HOLDS HIS HEAD IN FRUSTRATION AS EVERYTHING GOES WRONG FOR MANCHESTER UNITED EN ROUTE TO THE 2-1 DEFEAT BY BENFICA IN LISBON WHICH KNOCKED THEM OUT OF THE CHAMPIONS LEAGUE**

KNOCK-OUT STAGE

No-one had any doubts that when Roman Abramovich bought Chelsea and their debts, his ambitions stretched way beyond winning merely the League Cup and the Premiership. Jose Mourinho and £200m-worth of players had achieved those targets in the Portuguese coach's initial season. Next step up was the Champions League.

Semi-finals defeats by Monaco in 2004 and by Liverpool in 2005 had established Chelsea's European potential. Mourinho appeared supremely confident in the fact.

Chelsea had already left Manchester United and Arsenal trailing in the Premiership title race, and Mourinho had blithely expressed a lack of concern over whether Chelsea finished first or second in their first-round group, because he assessed all the potential opponents as top quality.

Finishing second, on the 'wrong' side of the seeded second round draw, proved to be a costly misjudgement by Mourinho. After UEFA's assortment of plastic lottery balls had been spun around the goldfish bowls, Chelsea found themselves being drawn once more – as in the previous season's quarter-final – to face Barcelona.

But this was not the same, fragile Barcelona of 2004-05, when they were a team concentrating most intently on winning their first Spanish league title for six years. This was a more mature team, strengthened by the addition of a remarkable Argentine teenager.

Lionel Messi was such a talented kid that Barcelona brought him to Spain aged 13. In the summer of 2005 he had captained Argentina to victory in the World Youth Cup in Holland. An eligibility dispute had restricted his appearances for Barcelona in the first half of the Spanish season, and thus he now had something to prove.

Barcelona also had something to prove in general. They felt they had been 'psyched out' of it by Chelsea in the row over referee Anders Frisk the previous season. Coach Frank Rijkaard was quietly determined that they would not fall into the same trap twice – and they did not.

Barcelona won 2-1 at Stamford Bridge, where Chelsea's left-back Asier Del Horno nonsensically left Norwegian referee Terje Hauge with no option but to show him the red card for ignoring the ball and blundering through on Messi.

The Catalans could have won more easily. Messi hit the bar and John Terry – who had earlier put though his own goal – twice cleared off the line before Samuel Eto'o struck a late winner.

A 1-1 draw back in Barcelona, where Mourinho was still taunted as 'the translator' after his initial spells there under Bobby Robson and Louis Van Gaal, was not enough as Chelsea paid the price for overconfidence. One trophy – the Premiership again – was all Abramovich would have to show for his investment.

Chelsea would have considered it poor consolation that the holders Liverpool, who had headed them by one point in the group, also succumbed – to a surprising 3-0 aggregate defeat by Benfica.

Barcelona went on to reach the final by defeating Benfica and Milan and, in the process, establishing themselves as Europe's form team. In terms of quality, Arsenal, after

RIGHT: **SKIPPER THIERRY HENRY CELEBRATES AFTER SCORING ARSENAL'S SECOND GOAL IN THE 2-0 VICTORY OVER JUVENTUS IN THE QUARTER-FINAL. IT WAS ALSO ONE OF THE GUNNERS' LAST HOME MATCHES AT HIGHBURY**

overcoming both the surprise pre-season sale of captain Patrick Vieira to Juventus and then a string of injuries, were not far behind. They proved the point by defeating imploding Real Madrid, bad-tempered Juventus and then the disciplined newcomers Villarreal.

Oddly, Villarreal were the most awkward of the three. Madrid and Juventus went out complacently to play their own football and proved vulnerable to Cesc Fabregas's work ethic in midfield and Thierry Henry's electric pace in attack.

Only against Villarreal, who paid pragmatically close-marking attention, did Arsenal struggle.

Argentine playmaker Juan Roman Riquelme, outstanding throughout the Champions' campaign, should have taken the tie into extra time with a last-minute penalty in front of the 'Yellow Submarine's' own supporters. But Arsenal goalkeeper Jens Lehmann dived left to save, propelling himself into the number-one slot with World Cup hosts Germany and launching the Gunners into their first Champions' final.

ABOVE: **FRENCH RIGHT WINGER LUDOVIC GIULY ANTICIPATES KAKHA KALADZE'S TACKLE TO STRIKE BARCELONA'S CRUCIAL GOAL AWAY TO MILAN IN THE SPANISH CHAMPIONS' SEMI-FINAL TRIUMPH IN THE STADIO MEAZZA**

LEFT: **JENS LEHMANN IS ARSENAL'S PENALTY HERO AFTER DIVING TO SAVE JUAN ROMAN RIQUELME'S LAST-MINUTE PENALTY AND THUS SECURE THE 1-0 AGGREGATE VICTORY OVER VILLARREAL WHICH SENT THEM INTO THE FINAL**

BARÇA VANQUISH VALIANT ARSENAL

'Ronaldinho v. Thierry Henry' was the billing for the final, overshadowing the team contest between two great European under-achievers. Barcelona had won the Champions' crown just once, while Arsenal had never previously progressed beyond the quarter-finals.

Barcelona were acknowledged as the finest footballing side in Europe, just ahead of Arsenal – once manager Arsene Wenger had begun to guide his squad beyond a lengthy injury crisis. The Catalans' ultimate victory was thus logical in perspective but controversial in nature, and short of the footballing style and craft for which the neutrals longed.

At least the final contained a built-in consolation prize. Both teams were assured of a return ticket for next season, Barcelona as champions of Spain and Arsenal through a fourth-place finish secured on the last day of the season through Thierry Henry's hat-trick against Wigan.

Neither side had lost any of their 12 matches on the road to the city with dual connections. Ronaldinho, current World and European Footballer of the Year, had spent two seasons with Paris Saint-Germain, while Henry had been born and brought up in the capital. An additional twist of intrigue was the possibility of Henry leading Arsenal for the last time before switching sides.

Coaches Frank Rijkaard and Arsene Wenger caused few ripples with their line-ups. Arsenal preferred the experience of revived Sol Campbell to Swiss youngster Philippe Senderos in defence, while Ashley Cole had regained his fitness just in time to play at left-back.

The absences of Campbell and Cole earlier in the season had prompted a critical storm when Wenger picked a first-ever Premiership squad without a single Englishman for a 5-1 win over Crystal Palace in February. Wenger had been caught off guard by the fuss, protesting: 'When I pick my team I look at players, not passports.'

Barcelona had Rafael Marquez fit to take his place in the heart of defence, the first Mexican to appear in a Champions' final. But both he and skipper Carles Puyol were caught asleep in the second minute when Henry skipped in front of them to reach a low short cross from Emmanuel Eboue, and was foiled only by the alert Victor Valdes. The ball bounced away for a corner, and Valdes was immediately in superb action again, this time beating away Henry's powerful angled drive.

If Arsenal had started with Jose Antonio Reyes or Robin Van Persie, or even the retiring veteran Dennis Bergkamp to partner Henry in attack, they might have pressed home that early advantage decisively. Instead, foregoing a second striker for the sake of five men strung cautiously across midfield, they lacked the essential weaponry.

Barcelona's initial tactics were doubtless a delight to Wenger. Ronaldinho sat far up front like an orthodox centre-forward, which simplified Arsenal's task of controlling him. Ludovic Giuly played wide right and Samuel Eto'o wide left.

RIGHT: **JENS LEHMANN IS CAST IN THE ROLE OF SCAPEGOAT AS HE IS SENT OFF BY REFEREE TERJE HAUGE FOR BRINGING DOWN BARCELONA STRIKER SAMUEL ETO'O IN THE OPENING STAGES OF THE FINAL**

The first time the Cameroonian moved into the centre proved disastrous for Arsenal. The Cameroon striker exchanged passes with Ronaldinho and was arrowing towards goal when fast-advancing keeper Jens Lehmann sent him tumbling. Referee Terje Hauge immediately blew for the foul – infuriating Barcelona, since Giuly had whipped the loose ball into the net.

Hauge disallowed the goal, awarded Barcelona a free kick on the edge of the penalty box and sent off Lehmann. It was not how the German had wanted his final Arsenal appearance to end.

Wenger and Rijkaard agreed later that the offence deserved a red card, but Wenger would have preferred a delay on the whistle. That way Arsenal would have conceded the goal in the likelihood that Lehmann would have been shown 'only' a yellow card and they would have retained 11 men. Robert Pires was sacrificed for replacement keeper Manuel Almunia As it was, the sending-off killed the game for which the purists had hoped.

Barcelona, it seemed, now needed only play their football and – maybe not sooner, but surely later – the goals would come. Arsenal's panic was evidenced by the manner in which the rattled Eboue took out Gio van Bronckhorst at the knee.

Ironically, it was Arsenal who took the lead. More perversely, the goal stemmed from a dive by Eboue, which gained an undeserved free kick at the expense of Barcelona captain Puyol. Henry floated in a perfect, fading free kick and Campbell headed gloriously home. 'I was sure there was a goal in this match for Sol,' said Wenger, 'because Barcelona are poor in the air at defending set pieces.'

Barcelona's bemused team went in at half-time haunted by their previous disaster finals: the luckless 3–2 defeat by Benfica in 1961, the penalty shocker against Steaua in 1985 and the humiliation by Milan in 1994.

Fate then teased them again. When Ronaldinho sliced Arsenal open and Eto'o turned Campbell, the striker saw Almunia's despairing right hand deflect the ball against a post. At the other end, Henry wasted a clear run-in on goal and Barcelona punished him conclusively.

First, Henrik Larsson touched a through-ball delicately to the left and Eto'o darted in to beat Almunia on the near post, as Arsenal appealed in vain for offside. If the goal was illegal, it only balanced out the Gunners' own in the first half. The record sequence of ten clean sheets had thus ended five minutes short of the thousand.

Almost immediately, it was all over. Juliano Belletti charged forward from right-back, Larsson turned the ball brilliantly back into his path and the Brazilian rocketed an angled shot through Almunia.

Andreas Iniesta, on as a second half substitute, had brought new zest to Barcelona's midfield, Larsson had laid on both goals while and Belletti struck the winner. Arsenal had been sunk by the subs.

WEDNESDAY MAY 17 2006
STADE DE FRANCE, PARIS

BARCELONA 2
(ETO'O 76, BELLETTI 80)

ARSENAL 1
(CAMPBELL 36)

HT: 0-1. ATT: 85,000
REF: HAUGE (NOR)

BARCELONA:
VALDES - OLEGUER (BELLETTI 70), MARQUEZ, PUYOL*, VAN BRONCK-HORST - VAN BOMMEL (LARSSON 60), EDMILSON (INIESTA 46), DECO - GIULY, RONALDINHO, ETO'O.
COACH: RIJKAARD

ARSENAL:
LEHMANN - EBOUE, TOURE, CAMPBELL, COLE - HLEB (REYES 84), FABREGAS (FLAMINI 73), GILBERTO SILVA, PIRES (ALMUNIA 19), LJUNGBERG - HENRY*.
MANAGER: WENGER
SENT OFF: LEHMANN (18)

*CAPTAIN

SEVEN-UP MILAN MAKE THE MOST OF THEIR ESCAPE

Italy's World Cup win should have provided their clubs with a perfect launch-pad into the Champions League. But a match-fixing scandal cast a long shadow that stretched all the way to the final itself

GROUP STAGE

At kick-off the giants were all lined up, bar one, either in the qualifying rounds of waiting in the groups. But this was a campaign whose launch was overshadowed by the worst corruption scandal in the history of even the credibility-challenged Italian game.

Incredibly, the increasingly tawdry revelations had shared football space in the Italian media by the national team's remarkable and contradictory triumph at the World Cup finals in Germany.

Azzurri manager Marcello Lippi had used the daily diet of disgust over the ongoing corruption trial back home to build a siege mentality which brought his team grittily beyond Ghana, the United States and Czech Republic in the first round, then past Australia, Ukraine and hosts Germany – magnificently in extra-time – to reach the final in Berlin.

Even here, against France, controversy reigned. In the dying minutes of extra-time French playmaker Zinedine Zidane marked – and marred – the last match of a magnificent career by earning a red card for head-butting Italy's

RIGHT: **FABIO CANNAVARO BRINGS INTO THE CHAMPIONS LEAGUE THE ACROBATIC CONFIDENCE WHICH HELPED PERSUADE REAL MADRID TO SIGN ITALY'S WORLD CUP-WINNING SKIPPER**

whispering centre-back Marco Materazzi. Italy prevailed in the penalty shootout and carried home the World Cup, albeit to domestic chaos.

Juventus, Milan, Lazio and Fiorentina had all by now been convicted of match-fixing through the wielding of fear and favours within the corridors of power. The major strategist had been Juve's general manager, Luciano Moggi. Ironically his plotting was revealed by taps of his mobile phones that had been obtained by investigators of the earlier inquiry into doping allegations.

Juventus were punished with relegation to Serie B (for the first time in their history) and were stripped of their 2005 and 2006 league titles; after appeals Milan, Lazio and Fiorentina all suffered points penalties. Fortunately, Milan's ultimate punishment of 30 points pushed them down from second place to 'merely' third ... that kept them alive in the Champions League, albeit in the qualifiers rather than the groups. Not that owner Silvio Berlusconi minded too much. Italy's former Prime Minister was relieved to stay in the competition at all.

Spain's giants appeared to benefit the most from the fall-out of 'Moggiopoli,' as the scandal was labelled. Juve's superstars refused to countenance a season in Serie B. Thus World Cup-winning captain and centre-back Fabio Cannavaro joined Real Madrid (and subsequently collected World and European footballer of the year prizes), while Lilian Thuram and Gianluca Zambrotta headed for Barcelona.

Spain's contingent thus expected to dominate the Champions League ahead of the English and weakened Italians; wrongly, as it turned out.

Qualifying was pedestrian. Dinamo Zagreb and Fenerbahce, with nine goals apiece over two legs, and Kiev Dynamo with eight enjoyed themselves respectively against Lithuania's Ekranas, the Faroes' B36 and Latvia's Metalurgs. Maris Verpakovskis put sentiment aside in scoring one of Kiev's goals against his original club.

Temporary consolation for Lithuania was in seeing Scotland's Heart of Midlothian defeat of Bosnia's Siroki Brijeg 3-0 overall. Hearts had been bought out in January 2005 by Lithuanian businessman Vladimir Romanov, but his idiosyncratic influence on not only transfer strategy but team selection had not only wrought a procession of baffled managers but undermined team spirit.

Then, to Romanov's fury, Hearts missed out on group entry after collapsing both home and away against AEK Athens in the third qualifying round. Further headline-grabbing failure was suffered by Ajax against FC Kobenhavn. A late own goal by their Belgian defender Thomas Vermaelen sent the four-times former champions spiralling down into the UEFA Cup.

No problems for any other members of the elite. Yet only England could look to a full surviving complement of four clubs. Arsenal trounced Dinamo Zagreb 5-1 and Liverpool beat Maccabi Haifa 3-2 to enter the group stage and join Chelsea and Manchester United. Spain and Italy saw Osasuna and Chievo Verona slide out against Hamburg and Levski. Almost unnoticed, Milan edged out Red Star Belgrade.

The seeding system, favourably manufactured to suit the top clubs, produced tediously predictable outcomes to the groups. Indeed, the comfort zone open to those clubs who qualified with two games to go helped fuel Frenchman Michel Platini's campaign for the presidency of UEFA.

In January 2007 Platini succeeded in ousting the long-serving Swede Lennart Johansson, partly on votes gathered from middle-ranking nations attracted by his proposal to cut back on the four-club Champions' access afforded to England, Italy and Spain.

Events in the groups - with runaway qualifications for Liverpool and PSV Eindhoven, Lyon and Real Madrid, Arsenal and Porto, Bayern and Internazionale, Valencia and Roma - justified Platini's distress at the competition's loss of passion and drama.

Serious uncertainty enlivened only three groups. A last-round moment of magic from Ronaldinho saw Barcelona edge out Werder Bremen to follow Chelsea through from Group A. Manchester United helped pull through Celtic - who were losing 3-1 at Kobenhavn - by defeating Benfica at the death in Group F. And, in Group H, Lille progressed at the last gasp by winning away to, and qualifying with ... Milan, aided by AEK Athens, who needed two late goals to draw 2-2 away to Anderlecht.

BELOW LEFT: **HEARTS OWNER VLADIMIR ROMANOV WAS DISAPPOINTED TO SEE THE EDINBURGH CLUB FALL IN THE QUALIFIERS**

BELOW RIGHT: **CHELSEA OWNER ROMAN ABRAMOVICH HAD TO ACCEPT YET ANOTHER EUROPEAN DEFEAT AT THE HANDS OF LIVERPOOL**

KNOCK-OUT STAGE

Roman Abramovich's investment in Chelsea, by now estimated at around £500 million to meet both debts and transfer fees, had been repaid by 'Special One' Jose Mourinho with two Premiership titles and one League Cup (with a second just around the spring corner). But no observer of the Chelsea phenomenon ever doubted that the Russian oligarch's football ambitions stretched out internationally.

Abramovich had been captivated by the dramatic intensity of the Champions League after attending a titanic Old Trafford duel between Manchester United and Real Madrid. Once the Premier League had been subjugated it was time to push on and, to that end, he procured two major individual talents with Europe in mind.

The one was Ukraine striker Andriy Shevchenko, whom Abramovich had long been seeking to lure from Milan; the second was Michael Ballack, Germany's World Cup captain, from Bayern Munich. The British record outlay of £31 million for Shevchenko was balanced by the acquisition of Ballack on a contract-expired free transfer; albeit Ballack's massively increased pay packet rocketed him from nowhere to fourth place in world football's rich list.

Amid his hectic jetset lifestyle, however, Abramovich may have missed out on the lesson of Real Madrid where the Galactico strategy had exploded beneath its millionaire architect, Florentino Perez.

Similarly, adjustment problems for Ballack and Shevchenko in particular, plus the first injury crises of Mourinho's Stamford Bridge reig,n ultimately undermined both Chelsea's Premiership title defence and Champions League bid.

The presence in the second round of four Premier League clubs raised the intriguing prospect of all-English final to match the Spanish and Italian affairs of 2000 and 2003. But, in terms of likely winners, Chelsea ranked far ahead of Manchester United, Arsenal and Liverpool.

The other three were all undergoing ownership changes of their own as American entrepreneurs awoke to the potential riches of the Premier League. United had been bought out, amid fan fury, by Malcolm Glazer, Liverpool were about to fall to Tom Hicks and George Gillett, while Arsenal's corporate life would be complicated by the predatory interests of Stan Kroenke.

Not that this distracted the players. Only Arsenal fell short of the semi-finals, losing surprisingly in the second round to PSV Eindhoven, whose tie-winning hero was Brazilian defender Alex in whom Chelsea – ironically – owned a part-interest.

In the closing stages of the second leg Arsenal manager Arsene Wenger gambled on the substitute's introduction of barely-fit Thierry Henry. Not only was Henry still struggling out from his World Cup hangover, but he aggravated latent injuries to such an extent that he missed the rest of the season.

Within 10 days, Arsenal's European exit against PSV was partnered by FA Cup failure against Blackburn and a 2-1 upset by Chelsea in the League Cup Final in Cardiff. No wonder Wenger later adjudged this his 'worst season' in England.

English media confidence in the Premiership takeover of the Champions League had reduced the continental contenders to mere bit players. To be fair, this was an impression the varied talents from France, Germany, Italy, Portugal and Spain did little to counter.

Chelsea saw off Mourinho's old club Porto and then Valencia to achieve a semi-final date with a Liverpool side who had outmanoeuvred holders Barcelona with surprising ease and then PSV.

On the other side of the draw Sir Alex Ferguson's Red Devils beat Lille minimally and then Roma magnificently; a goal down from the away leg, United manufactured one of the most outstanding performances of Ferguson's 20-year reign to win the return 7-1. Surprisingly, it was the first time United had overcome a first-leg deficit in Europe in 23 years. Captain Ryan Giggs, the only starting survivor from the 1999 Champions League triumph, created four of the goals.

The only blot on the knockout round was the outbreak of hooliganism both on and off the pitches. French and Italian police waded in provocatively and indiscriminately on Manchester United fans in Lens (for the Lille first leg) and Rome while Valencia's second-round win over Internazionale

RIGHT: **BAYERN MUNICH'S DUTCH STRIKER ROY MAKAAY CELEBRATES HIS RECORD-BREAKING OPENING GOAL AGAINST REAL MADRID, AT 10 SECONDS THE FASTEST IN CHAMPIONS LEAGUE HISTORY**

ended in a mass brawl among the players. Valencia's David Navarro was suspended for eight months (with two suspended) for running 40 metres from the substitutes' bench to deliver a nose-breaking punch on Inter's Nicolas Burdisso.

Italy's ability to stage trouble-free football was already in question. Weeks earlier, domestic football had been suspended for a fortnight by sports officials and politicians after the killing of a policeman at a Sicilian derby between Catania and Palermo.

Almost unnoticed, the magic of Kaka edged Milan past Celtic before the goals of Clarence Seedorf and Pippo Inzaghi in Munich sank a fading Bayern. The Germans had earlier beaten Real Madrid with the help of a tournament record goal in 10 seconds from Ray Makaay but their cracks had been laid bare

by the subsequent sacking of coach Felix Magath and recall of veteran Ottmar Hitzfeld.

When Milan lost 3-2 at Old Trafford in the first leg of the semi-finals, English fans could still dream of an all-Premiership final; premature calls were made for UEFA to consider switching the venue from Athens to the new, almost-open Wembley. But Kaka's brilliance inspired Milan to win 3-0 back in the Stadio Meazza and even then the margin was generous to United.

Milan had thus reached their 11th Champions Cup final, but only one of the previous 10 was ever mentioned in the build-up: the 2005 defeat against Liverpool in Istanbul. The reason was simple: Liverpool boss Rafa Benitez had out-manoeuvred Jose Mourinho and the Abramovich millions again. Once more, Liverpool would be going head to head with ... Milan.

ABOVE: **BRAZILIAN FORWARD KAKA FIRES MILAN TOWARDS A SEMI-FINAL SECOND LEG, REVIVAL VICTORY OVER MANCHESTER UNITED**

LEFT: **LIVERPOOL GOALKEEPER PEPE REINA SAVES, FROM GEREMI, WHAT PROVED CHELSEA'S LAST PENALTY IN THE ANFIELD SEMI-FINAL SHOOTOUT**

REVENGE IS SWEET

Milan's players celebrated their defeat of Liverpool in Athens' Olympic Stadium for a seventh Champions' triumph as if nothing untoward had happened. No match-fixing scandal, no points deductions, no appeals, no pressures behind the scenes, no friendly media, etc.

Of course, no blame for that farrago attached to two-goal hero Pippo Inzaghi or coach Carlo Ancelotti who ignored the 'expert' advice of former players and coaches and started the 33-year-old up front rather than Alberto Gilardino. Veteran captain Paolo Maldini thus climaxed his season by collecting his own fifth Champions Cup.

Ancelotti said later, with considerable sense and responsibility considering the dressing-room delirium, that Milan's victory did not wipe out what had happened but might help create an improved new image of Italian football. His city was certainly Europe's football capital now with derby rivals Internazionale also the champions of Italy.

The irony was that Milan had better deserved to win two years earlier in Istanbul courtesy of the breathtaking style and cutting edge of their football that night. This time it was Liverpool who caught the twist in the tale and a final between two teams playing below their capacity and marred by some disappointing individual performances.

Carlo Ancelotti, now twice a winner as Milan's coach in addition to having been twice a winner as a Milan player, said: 'This has been the greatest victory we've ever had – especially after all the stories last November about someone coming in to replace me! The game was like our season. We started slowly but grew in confidence as it went on.'

The game compared hardly at all with the Istanbul drama of 2005. Then Milan had dominated the first 45 minutes; in Athens they were second best. In Istanbul, Liverpool were caught unprepared; in Athens it was Milan who 'read' it wrongly. In Istanbul Milan went in three-up and deserved it; in Athens they went in one-up and did not.

As is common in the modern game, both finalists flooded midfield and thus stifled not only their opponents' attack but also limited their own. The two most glaring misses were both committed by Liverpool players: Jermaine Pennant, in the first half, and captain Steven Gerrard, of all people, in the second. Had either of the chances been taken, the story of this final – played against a backdrop of crowd control chaos – would have been different.

Milan had allowed Pennant an ocean of space out on right, with Marek Jankulovski receiving no back-up whatsoever from left-side partner Clarence Seedorf; too often Seedorf was found missing when Liverpool swept the ball wide.

Jankulovski was at fault as early as the ninth minute when Pennant caught him in possession, exchanged passes with Dirk Kuyt and should have done better than scuff his shot against the flailing keeper, Dida. As Liverpool's bad luck had it, no one was around to convert the loose ball.

RIGHT: MILAN TAKE THE LEAD IN THE FINAL AS FILIPPO INZAGHI'S DEFLECTION WRONG-FOOTS LIVERPOOL GOALKEEPER PEPE REINA

Liverpool had made the sharper start and were in the ascendancy when Milan went ahead against the run of play just before the interval. Kaka's close control on the turn provoked a trip from Xabi Alonso and Andrea Pirlo's free-kick beyond the wall ricocheted into the net off Inzaghi's forearm.

Gerrard should have levelled in the 62nd minute after a rare mistake by Gennaro Gattuso but Liverpool's captain, having drawn Dida, concentrated on placement more than power and the Brazilian goalkeeper stuck out both hands to save as he dived.

Not until 13 minutes from time – too late – did Liverpool manager Rafa Benitez bring on the gangling Peter Crouch. Later Benitez justified the delay by saying that taking off holding midfielder Javier Mascherano would always have meant handing Milan potentially fatal extra space.

He was right. By the time Kuyt headed home after a left-wing corner, Milan were already a decisive two goals ahead: again Inzaghi was the man, this time ghosting on to Kaka's superb through ball and stepping wide of Reina to slip the ball delicately inside the far post.

Gerrard said later: 'We always knew this game would be decided on small details and a bit of luck and Milan got that.'

He was both right and wrong ... Milan's being let off lightly after a match-fixing conviction could hardly be described as a 'small detail'. Not when they ended the season with the Champions League cup in their hands.

WEDNESDAY 23 MAY 2007
OLYMPIC STADIUM SPIROS LOUIS, ATHENS

MILAN	**2**
(INZAGHI 44, 82)	

LIVERPOOL	**1**
(KUYT 89)	

HT: 1-0. ATT: 85,000
REF: FANDEL (GER)

MILAN:
DIDA - ODDO, NESTA, MALDINI*, JANKULOVSKI (KALADZE 78) - GATTUSO, PIRLO, AMBROSINI, SEEDORF (FAVALLI 90) - KAKA - INZAGHI (GILARDINO 87)
COACH: ANCELOTTI

LIVERPOOL:
REINA - FINNAN (ARBELOA 87), CARRAGHER, AGGER, RIISE - PENNANT, MASCHERANO (CROUCH 77), ALONSO, ZENDEN (KEWELL 58) - GERRARD* - KUYT
MANAGER: BENITEZ

UNITED MARK ANNIVERSARIES WITH GLORY

Manchester United commemorated 50 years since the Munich air crash and the 40th anniversary of their first European crown by winning their third European Champions trophy.

The draw for the group stages took place in the shadow of the death of Sevilla defender Antonio Puerta. The midfielder had died after suffering a series of cardiac arrests during a game against Getafe at the start of the Spanish league season. In the event, his team-mates honoured his memory by defeating AEK Athens in the third qualifying round which promoted them into the mini-league stage and into Group H.

Here, surprisingly, they finished ahead of Arsenal – to the irritation of Gunners' manager Arsene Wenger. Arsenal had the best goal difference in the group of 14-4 (+10), but lost their chance of topping the table on going down to a 3-1 defeat in Spain in their penultimate match, despite taking an early lead through Eduardo, their Brazilian-born Croatia international centre-forward.

Liverpool also progressed as runners-up – behind Porto in Group A – but fellow Premier Leaguers, Chelsea and Manchester United both signalled their Cup-winning determination by ending up as winners of Groups B and F respectively.

Chelsea's achievement, with the stage's best defensive record of two goals conceded in six games, was the more remarkable since they parted company dramatically in early autumn with manager Jose Mourinho. The self-styled 'Special One' had arrived at Stamford Bridge in the summer of 2004 with every intention of repeating his achievements at Porto, which had seen league title success followed up by European glory in both in the UEFA Cup and then the Champions League.

With Chelsea, empowered by the seemingly bottomless pockets of Russian owner Roman Abramovich, Mourinho had

RIGHT: **CELTIC'S SCOTT McDONALD CELEBRATES HIS LATE WINNER AGAINST MILAN WITH MASSIMO DONATI (18) AT PARKHEAD WHILE MILAN SKIPPER MASSIMO AMBROSINI LOOKS ON DISCONSOLATELY**

believed he could skip the UEFA Cup halfway house and drive straight on from Premier League title to Champions League. However his plans were hindered by Abramovich's own predilection for taking a hand in affairs and one of those was the signing of veteran Ukraine star Andriy Shevchenko.

The ex-Milan centre-forward was past his best when he was brought into Chelsea. The Blues had duly finished runners-up to Manchester United, albeit six points adrift, and Mourinho appeared to be growing ever more gloomy amid speculation that he was being pressured to alter his hold-and-hit tactical model for something more entertainingly expressive.

Chelsea lost on penalties to Manchester United in the curtain-raising Community Shield but then opened the campaign by establishing a record of 64 consecutive home league games unbeaten. But a defeat at Aston Villa was followed by a goalless draw at home to Blackburn and then a disappointing 1-1 home draw against the gritty Norwegians of Rosenborg Trondheim in the Champions League.

Two days later and Mourinho was gone, his managerial role being taken over by Israeli Avram Grant who, with the ear of Abramovich, had arrived at Chelsea in the previous July in the role of director of football. Several players complained later that Grant's methods were behind the times, but this may have owed more to upset at Mourinho's abrupt departure. Even so Chelsea won their Champions League group unbeaten – including a 4-0 win away to Rosenborg.

Unlike England, of course, Scotland could not boast four entries into the groups, but they did enjoy the rarity of a double presence. Celtic ended up second behind Milan after enjoying a famous home win over the defending European champions. Rangers went into their final game needed a win or draw at home to Olympique Lyonnais, but ended with a 3-0 defeat and relegation to the UEFA Cup. Lyon took second place behind unbeaten Barcelona.

Internazionale and Real Madrid were the other group winners, but Madrid then fell in the second round for the fourth successive season – this time to AS Roma, who surprised most experts with a 2-1 second leg win in the Estadio Bernabeu. Madrid's erratic Portuguese defender Pepe was sent off for two bookings, and goals from Rodrigo Taddei and Mirko Vucinic put the game beyond the Galacticos' reach.

Madrid's consolation was to go on to win the Spanish league with an eight-point advantage over the so-called 'Yellow Submarine' from Villarreal, with Barcelona and Atletico Madrid far distant in third and fourth places. The champions had the title sewn up with three games to spare but the championship was, of course, merely a minimum requirement for German coach Bernd Schuster whose relationship with the influential

local media was falling apart game by game, press conference by press conference.

Back in the Champions League one of the most thrilling ties of the second round saw Turkey's Fenerbahce and Sevilla end up 5-5 on aggregate. Having been pegged back twice in their home leg before taking a slender lead, Fenerbahce recovered from two goals down in the return to force penalties. The Turkish side then held their nerve to prevail 3-2. A shootout also saw Germany's Schalke see off former European champions Porto. Schalke feared a single-goal home win with a strike from Kevin Kuranyi would be insufficient, but it was not until four minutes from time back in Portugal that Argentinian forward Lisandro levelled the aggregate for the Dragons. Unfortunately for him, the striker's luck vanished in the shootout when he missed Porto's last kick and Schalke went through 4-1 on penalties.

Schalke, one of the great clubs of inter-war football in Germany, had never lived up to their historical reputation in the European competitions. In 2006, they had signed a lucrative sponsorship deal with the Russian energy giant Gazprom, which included naming rights to the remarkable new Arena AufSchalke

ABOVE: **DESPRESSION FOR KAKA (LEFT) AND DELIGHT FOR CESC FABREGAS AND ALEXANDER HLEB AS ARSENAL WIN IN MILAN**

at Gelsenkirchen. This, they hoped – in vain as it turned out – would lead to greater things on the grandest stage.

Arsenal and Chelsea left themselves with all the work to do in the second leg, achieving 0-0 draws in first legs against Milan and Olympiakos respectively. Arsenal responded magnificently to the challenge, with late goals in the Stadio Meazza from Cesc Fabregas and Emmanuel Adebayor. Chelsea, meanwhile, again gave away nothing in defence and saw off the Greeks with second-leg goals from Michael Ballack, Frank Lampard and Salomon Kalou.

Cristiano Ronaldo continued to dominate Manchester United's season. He struck the decisive second-leg goal against

Lyon in the second round, and then the first of United's three overall against Roma in the quarter-finals. Roma complained in vain about the Portugal winger's showboating style.

With four English survivors, it was no surprise that the quarter-finals threw up an all-English tie. Arsenal found their heroics against Milan had earned a duel with Liverpool, who had seen off a nervy Internazionale, reduced by the expulsions of first Marco Materazzi in the first leg and Nicolas Burdisso in the return.

Now fortune smiled on Liverpool again with a 5-3 aggregate victory which saw them escape a penalty claim in the first leg, then edge into the last four thanks to a generously-awarded

RIGHT: **PAUL SCHOLES RIFLES THE MANCHESTER UNITED GOAL WHICH BEATS BARCELONA AND SENDS THEM THROUGH TO THE FINAL**

spot-kick of their own. Arsenal had just pulled level at 2-2, and held the away goals edge, until Steven Gerrard rammed his kick home to turn the tie inside out again.

Liverpool were thus confronted – yet again – with a Chelsea side, who had recovered from their first defeat of the campaign to overturn Fenerbahce on aggregate thanks to goals from Ballack and Lampard.

Barcelona took the other semi-final place after dispatching a spirited Celtic in the second round and Schalke in the quarters. However, crucially, they were missing the attacking inspiration of both Leonel Messi and Thierry Henry at home in the first leg against Manchester United. They were fortunate even to escape with a goalless draw after Cristiano Ronaldo missed a penalty. Thus a single strike from veteran midfielder Paul Scholes was sufficient, in the return, to lift United into their third final.

In fact, Barcelona were undergoing a season of transition. Henry's arrival spelled the imminent summer exit of Ronaldinho, and he was joined on the way out of Camp Nou by veteran French defender Lilian Thuram and Italian wing-back Gianluca Zambrotta. The upheaval cleared the way for the replacement of coach Frank Rijkaard with Pep Guardiola, and the launch of perhaps the greatest era in the club's history, but all that was yet to come.

The other semi-final saw Grant manage to succeed where Mourinho had failed twice, by beating Liverpool in a Champions League semi-final. A disastrous Jon Arne Riise own-goal late in the first leg handed Chelsea the advantage.

Defiant Liverpool forced extra time in the second leg. But a penalty conversion from England midfielder Lampard – playing only days after the death of his mother – and a further strike from Didier Drogba sent Chelsea to their first-ever Champions final.

LEFT: **AN EMOTIONAL GOAL FOR CHELSEA'S FRANK LAMPARD AGAINST LIVERPOOL, SIX DAYS AFTER THE DEATH OF HIS MOTHER**

UNITED WIN FROM RUSSIA WITH PENALTIES

If two English clubs were ever bound to confront one another in the UEFA Champions League final, then Manchester United and Chelsea were probably the two bound most closely into the history of the competition.

All the way back in 1955, when *L'Equipe*'s senior editors were dreaming up the competition which changed the face of club football for ever, Chelsea were English champions for the first time in their history. They had been invited to compete in the inaugural season of the European Champion Clubs' Cup, but were pressured, by the Football League, into withdrawing for fear of fixture complications. Under the experienced management of Ted Drake, and with an attack powerfully led by skipper Roy Bentley, Chelsea might have made an impression. But that is speculation.

United succeeded Chelsea as English champions in 1956, and they, too, were invited to compete. The Football League also ordered United to stay out of the competition, but manager Matt Busby refused, driving United to the subsequent Kiplingesque meetings with triumph and disaster.

The 2008 final was awarded to Moscow for the first time. The Soviet Union had been consigned to the history books for almost two decades and Russia appeared to be opening up to the West. Vladimir Putin was the President, and he understood the value of sport as a fast-track route in creating an international narrative.

Not that the Moscow being hosts was without its problems. The Russian authorities did not understand the determination of thousands of English fans to travel to Moscow. UEFA's warnings about Russia's need to streamline its antiquated visa system fell on deaf ears until it was almost too late. With whispers abounding that the final might have to be postponed and/or switched, the government came up with the face-saving device of accepting a match ticket as a visa. The ticket-as-visa system was in effect for the Sochi 2014 Winter Olympic Games and will be used at the 2018 FIFA World Cup.

The match was a characteristic match-up: Chelsea's focused discipline against United's outgoing swagger. Exemplifying United's positive approach, above all, was the mercurial Cristiano Ronaldo. In 2003, upon his arrival from Sporting of Libson for £12m, his theatrical mannerisms had frustrated many of the faithful at Old Trafford. He would never beat a defender once if he could beat him twice or three times.

ABOVE: **CRISTIANO RONALDO HEADS MANCHESTER UNITED IN FRONT AGAINST CHELSEA IN MOSCOW**

The fans were not always amused by these antics. Nor, ever, was his manager Sir Alex Ferguson.

But Ronaldo, still only 23 in 2008, soon learned how to adjust his roving right-wing game to the pacy demands of both Premier League and Champions League. This would prove the finest of his United seasons before his world record £80m switch to Real Madrid a year later. Ronaldo scored 42 goals in all competitions in 2007–08, and was subsequently crowned European Footballer of the Year and FIFA World Player of the Year. Not that it was all plain sailing on a chilly spring night in Moscow's Luzhniki Stadium. In fact, it was anything but plain sailing.

This was only the third time that clubs from the same country had contested the final, after Real Madrid had beaten Valencia in 1990 and Milan overcame Juventus in a 2003 penalty shoot-out. It was hardly surprising that domestic rivalry added to the nerve-shredding tension evident on the pitch.

Ferguson had sought to match Chelsea's midfield strength by fielding Owen Hargreaves, Paul Scholes and Michael Carrick in United's engine room, with Ronaldo their outlet on the left wing and Wayne Rooney and Argentinian firebrand Carlos Tevez as strikers. Chelsea, with a five-man midfield, looked to the relentlessly bullish attacking leadership of their Ivory Coast talisman Didier Drogba.

All that caution meant few clear scoring opportunities. Ronaldo capitalised on virtually the first one of the game when he headed United in front from a right-wing Wes Brown cross after 26 minutes. Twice keeper Petr Cech saved Chelsea from falling further behind before they levelled through Frank Lampard just before half-time.

Chelsea, encouraged, came out on the front foot for the second half. They also came closest to a goal but Drogba's 25-metre drive, in the 78th minute, struck a post. It remained level after 90 minutes. An increasingly fractious extra time exploded when Czech referee Lubos Michel sent off Drogba for slapping United defender Nemanja Vidic in the 116th minute.

Drogba's loss of self-control was crucial because he was not there for the penalty shootout. Still, Chelsea gained the advantage when Ronaldo's kick was saved by Cech, and captain John Terry took the last kick of the Blues' five with the trophy as their prize if he scored. Unluckily, he slipped in the act of shooting, and the ball ricocheted wide off a post. In sudden death, after Ryan Giggs had converted his attempt, Edwin Van der Sar saved from Nicolas Anelka – and Manchester United were European champions for a third time.

WEDNESDAY 21 MAY 2008
LUZHNIKI STADIUM, MOSCOW

MANCHESTER UNITED   1
RONALDO 26

CHELSEA   1
LAMPARD 45

AFTER EXTRA TIME
MANCHESTER UNITED WON 6-5 ON
PENS.
HT: 1-1. 90MIN: 1-1. ATT: 67,310
REF: MICHEL (CZ)

MANCHESTER UNITED:
VAN DER SAR - BROWN (ANDERSON
120), FERDINAND*, VIDIC, EVRA -
HARGREAVES, SCHOLES (GIGGS 87),
CARRICK, RONALDO - ROONEY (NANI
101), TEVEZ. COACH: FERGUSON.

CHELSEA:
CECH - ESSIEN, CARVALHO, TERRY*,
A COLE - MAKELELE (BELLETTI 120)
- J COLE (ANELKA 99), BALLACK,
LAMPARD, MALOUDA (KALOU 92) -
DROGBA. COACH: GRANT.

*CAPTAIN

RED CARD: DROGBA (116)

LEFT: **UNITED GOALKEEPER EDWIN VAN DER SAR TAKES THE CREDIT AFTER JOHN TERRY'S PENALTY MISS, EVEN THOUGH THE CHELSEA SKIPPER LOST HIS FOOTING AS HE STRUCK THE BALL AND THE EFFORT STRUCK A POST**

BARCELONA RULE THE WORLD

No club had ever come anywhere near Barcelona's achievements in 2009: champions of Spain, then champions of Europe, then champions of the world.

Along the way the *Blaugrana* also won the Spanish cup, the Spanish Supercopa and the UEFA Supercup to make it a unique six out of six inside the 12 calendar months. Even more remarkable, the 2008-09 season – in which they won the first three of those trophies – was coach Josep 'Pep' Guardiola's first in charge at senior level.

Guardiola, now 37, had made his name as the midfield fulcrum in Johan Cruyff's Barcelona 'Dream Team' of the early 1990s. The former club captain was a surprise but popular appointment with the fans because he was a local, Catalan, boy and had played 11 years for the club. An Olympic Games football gold medallist, in Barcelona in 1992, he wound down his career with Brescia and Roma in Italy, then in Qatar and Mexico before returning home in 2007 to join the coaching staff.

One year later, in the summer of 2008, despite lacking any top-flight managerial experience, Guardiola was appointed first-team coach in succession to Frank Rijkaard with instant and astonishing success.

A significant change had also been effected at the head of the European federation. In the spring of 2007, long-serving president Lennart Johansson of Sweden was ousted by Michel Platini. Johansson had overseen the transformation of the European Cup into the gold-encrusted Champions League. But, after 17 years, he had made the mistake of wanting to cling to power a little too long.

Platini, with his pedigree as captain and record marksman for France, and subsequent 1998 World Cup co-chairman, brought the impetus of fresh ideas from a stint working

RIGHT: **DIMITAR BERBATOV SCORES ONE OF HIS TWO GOALS IN MANCHESTER UNITED'S 3-0 WIN OVER CELTIC IN GROUP E**

alongside Sepp Blatter at FIFA. One of Platini's concerns was to break up the rich men's club cartel dominating the Champions League. Initially, he spoke of returning to a knockout system but then the financial facts of life were explained. Hence Platini reorganised the qualifying system in favour of clubs from Europe's more modest leagues. This was not merely a Frenchman's egalitarian ideal it was also a vote-winner.

This 2008–09 season was the first with the amended qualifying system in effect. Hence the group stages featured several new faces: Denmark's Aalborg, Cyprus's Anorthosis Famagusta, Romania's CFR Cluj and BATE Barisov from Belarus. All but Aalborg finished bottom of their groups, with BATE failing even to record a single win.

However, the newcomers did provide immediate shock value when Cluj, who had risen from the Romanian third division to Europe's top table in just six seasons, kicked off Group A with a stunning 2-1 away win at eventual table-toppers Roma. They also held Chelsea 0-0 at home, but then lost their remaining four games to finish bottom.

Elsewhere the group stage provided its largely accustomed predictability. Group B saw Internazionale, now coached by Jose Mourinho, open with a 2-0 win in Greece against

Panathinaikos. Veteran forward Roberto Mancini scored the opening goal, unaware that only a few seasons later he would back in the competition as a manager with Manchester City and then Galatasaray. The Greeks and Italians went through, with Germany's Werder Bremen third and Anorthosis, bottom despite a goalless draw in Bremen and 3-1 home win over Panathinaikos.

In Group C, Guardiola's first season as a Champions League coach brought top spot and a broad hint of what was to come with 18 goals in six games. Leo Messi, aged only 21, scored the two goals which beat Shakhtar in Donetsk, one each home and away against Basel and another in a 5-2 thrashing of Sporting in Lisbon. The one game he was allowed to miss was the last, a 3-2 home defeat by Shakhtar which had no effect on Barcelona's progress.

Liverpool, under Rafa Benitez, and Atletico Madrid cruised through from Group D. Both were unbeaten, as were the reigning cup-holders Manchester United in Group E, despite all the hyperbole generated around their 'Battles of Britain' with Celtic. In the event, two goals from Dimitar Berbatov propelled United to a decisive 3-0 win at home and a late equaliser from Ryan Giggs in Glasgow denied Celtic even the consolation of a narrow home win.

The remainder of the group stage was processional: Bayern Munich (unbeaten) and Lyon from Group F, Porto and Arsenal from Group G, plus Juventus and Real Madrid in Group H, all advanced to the second round. Madrid now had a distinct 'made in the Netherlands' look about them, with Rafael Van der Vaart in midfield, Arjen Robben on the wing and Ruud Van Nistelrooy in attack.

TOP: BAYERN MUNICH'S LUKAS
PODOLSKI OPENS THE SCORING
AGAINST SPORTING CLUBE DE
PORTUGAL OF LISBON IN THE
SECOND LEG OF THE ROUND OF
16 IN MUNICH

Not that this guaranteed plain sailing. One day before Madrid's final group fixture – a 3-0 home win over Zenit St Petersburg – Bernd Schuster quit as coach. Angered by the manner of the previous weekend's 4-3 home defeat by Sevilla, Schuster had little option after telling the media that his team had no chance of beating Barcelona in the forthcoming El Clasico derby. He was replaced by Juande Ramos. For what it was worth, Schuster was proved right as Madrid lost 2-0 in Camp Nou, with Samuel Eto'o and Messi scoring in the last seven minutes.

Back in the Champions League the following spring, the back story to the second round was 'reunion time'. The powers of Italy and England came face to face, with Juventus coach Claudio Ranieri heading back to his former club Chelsea, while Jose Mourinho and Sir Alex Ferguson were rivals once more as Inter were drawn against Manchester United; a third tie saw Roma matched against Arsenal.

The outcome was decisive: England 3, Italy 0. Chelsea, who began the knockout stages with a new manager for the second season in a row after Guus Hiddink had replaced Luiz Felipe

Scolari, edged Juventus thanks to a 1-0 first leg win; Arsenal and Roma both won 1-0 at home but, in the penalty shoot-out, Max Tonetto missed Roma's eighth spot-kick; Manchester United clinched their quarter-final place with a 2-0 home win on goals from Nemanja Vidic and Cristiano Ronaldo.

Madrid performed their by now customary disappearing act in the round of 16, thrashed 4-0 in their second leg at Liverpool. Neighbours Atletico also fell, to Porto. Spanish pride was eased by Barcelona and Villarreal, who saw off Lyon and Panathanaikos, respectively. The most humiliating exit was that of Sporting Clube who collapsed 12-1 on aggregate to Bayern Munich.

Thierry Henry, now of Barcelona, scored three times in the Catalans' defeat of Lyon, while Messi made the difference in the quarter-final against Bayern. He scored twice in the 4-0 first leg win, making the second leg (a 1-1 draw) a mere formality.

Yet another – almost inevitable – reunion brought Liverpool back up against Chelsea. Liverpool went 1-0 up through Fernando Torres after barely five minutes before Chelsea took what looked a commanding 3-1 lead into the second leg. The tie was far from over, however. Liverpool hit back to lead 2-0 at Stamford Bridge before second-half goals from Didier Drogba, Alex and Frank Lampard (two) saw Chelsea through despite even later goals from Lucas and Dirk Kuyt.

Arsenal obtained the all-important away goal in their first leg at Villarreal before completing a comfortable 3-0 win in the home return. Manchester United had a little more work to do after conceding two away goals in a 2-2 home draw with Porto. Returning home to Portugal, Ronaldo proved United's hero once more. He contributed the tie's winner with what even he described at the time as 'the best goal I have scored', a stunning 40-yard drive from Anderson's lay-off – it later received the Ferenc Puskas Award as FIFA's goal of the year.

Chelsea thus approached their semi-final with Barcelona full of confidence – and ended it in a fury. After a goalless first leg in Barcelona, Chelsea took an early lead back at Stamford Bridge through Michael Essien. Despite having various penalty appeals turned down, they seemed set to progress after

Barcelona's Eric Abidal was sent off on 66 minutes for bundling over Nicolas Anelka.

The Blues' command was such that, when Barcelona equalised three minutes into stoppage time, it was with their first attempt on target. Norwegian referee Tom Henning Ovrebo further infuriated Chelsea when he turned down another penalty appeal after Keita appeared to block Michael Ballack's strike with his arm. Ballack was booked for his complaints – and Drogba, who had been substituted before the equaliser – was banned for his tirade at both referee and TV cameras after the final whistle.

The other semi-final between Arsenal and Manchester United was – by comparison – far calmer. United won the home leg thanks to a John O'Shea goal, and raced to a 3-0 aggregate lead after just 11 minutes of the return at the Emirates Stadium, through Park Ji-sung and Ronaldo. Van Persie's late penalty was little consolation for Arsenal, especially after Ronaldo scored his second goal, United's third, of the evening.

BELOW: **CRISTIANO RONALDO SEES THE FINAL WITHIN REACH AFTER SCORING MANCHESTER UNITED'S SECOND GOAL, 11 MINUTES INTO THE SECOND LEG OF THEIR SEMI-FINAL AWAY TO ARSENAL**

BRILLIANT BARCELONA DOUBLE UP FOR GUARDIOLA

The final in Rome between two champions renowned for their flowing football promised to be a match made in heaven – not merely the holders against the favourites but, more simplistically, Lionel Messi v Cristiano Ronaldo. In the event Barcelona, and their little Argentinian, ran the show virtually from start to finish.

Messi had been born in Rosario but arrived in Barcelona at 13, with his family, encouraged by Barcelona's provision of growth hormone treatment. He first made international headlines in leading Argentina to World Youth Cup victory in 2005, then gained even more admirers with a Maradona-type solo goal back in Spain against Getafe. In 2008, he led Argentina to gold medal success at the Beijing Olympics and followed up in 2009 by helping inspire Barcelona's six-out-of-six success sequence.

Not surprisingly he would be voted both European Footballer of the Year and FIFA World Player of the Year.

Barcelona's club motto describes them as 'more than a club', and they also proved more of a team than the outgoing holders Manchester United to clinch a third European crown, after 1992 and 2006. It could have been so different if United had not been missed the solidity of injured Darren Fletcher in midfield or if they had taken the lead in the second minute, when Victor Valdes could not hold a powerful Ronaldo free kick and Barcelona were fortunate to clear for a corner.

The Portugal striker, playing centre-forward, twice more frightened Valdes inside the first nine minutes with shots which flew narrowly wide. But Barcelona then took over and took the lead. United were caught out by the Catalans' tactic of using Samuel Eto'o wide on the right with Messi pulled into a central striking role. Andres Iniesta burst through the centre, Eto'o cut in from the right, turned the surprised Patrice Evra and rammed home an angled, close-range shot which floored Edwin Van der Sar – and United.

Ryan Giggs fired a free kick over the bar and Ronaldo was just wide with a low drive, but Barcelona had found their feet and were not to be knocked over. Messi ran at United and shot over the bar, before Xavi produced an excellent free kick which skimmed just wide.

By now, however, Messi, for all Ronaldo's fireworks, was having the best of the issue, serving as a link on the coherent inter-passing with which Barcelona were so often bypassing United's midfield.

United manager Sir Alex Ferguson sent on Carlos Tevez at the start of the second half as a substitute for the ineffective Anderson, but without effect. Instead United had to thank the reflexes of Van der Sar from keeping them in touch: the Dutchman dived brilliantly to his left to keep out a goal-bound curling free kick from Xavi.

As time ran on, so United upped the desperation stakes by bringing on Dimitar Berbatov for Park Ji-sung, only for Barcelona to respond, almost arrogantly, by running down to the other end so Messi could head home Xavi's curling right-wing cross. Incredibly, in the heart of United's defence, the little Argentina striker was unmarked.

Ferguson conceded later that his team had fallen below their usual high standards and that Barcelona had deserved to win. He said: 'The first goal gave them the opportunity to keep possession which they do very well. We didn't deal with it well enough. That was the story of the game, really. There were disappointing performances which some individuals will know themselves.

'It's difficult to put your finger on every part of the game. At the start, we did very well, but then we lost a goal and it was a bad goal to lose. If you look at our best performances, they have been when we have defended well. But this time our defending was shoddy, particularly on that first goal.

'The way Barcelona kept possession, with Messi dropping back into midfield, made it difficult for us to get the better of them. When we did get the ball we didn't do well enough

RIGHT: **LIONEL MESSI, THE SMALLEST PLAYER ON THE PITCH, IS UNCHALLENGED AS HE HEADS BARCELONA'S DECISIVE SECOND GOAL TO CLINCH THE CUP**

WEDNESDAY 27 MAY 2009
STADIO OLIMPICO, ROME

BARCELONA 2
ETO'O 10, MESSI 70

MANCHESTER UNITED 0

HT: 1-0. ATT: 62,467
REF: BUSACCA (SWZ)

BARCELONA:
VALDES - PUYOL*, YAYA TOURE,
PIQUE, SYLVINHO - XAVI, BUSQUETS,
INIESTA (PEDRO 90) - ETO'O, MESSI,
HENRY (KEITA 72).
COACH: GUARDIOLA.

MANCHESTER UNITED:
VAN DER SAR - O'SHEA, FERDINAND,
VIDIC, EVRA - ANDERSON (TEVEZ 46),
CARRICK, GIGGS* (SCHOLES 75) - PARK
(BERBATOV 66), RONALDO, ROONEY.
MANAGER: FERGUSON.

*CAPTAIN

LEFT: **LIONEL MESSI AND ANDRES INIESTA (WITH THIERRY HENRY BEHIND HIM) PARADE THE CUP FOR BARCELONA'S FANS AFTER BEATING UNITED**

with it. Normally we are better than that. We missed Darren Fletcher but they were missing some players, too.'

Ronaldo described defeat as one of the biggest disappointments of his career while England forward Wayne Rooney conceded that Barcelona had been clearly the better team. He said: 'Barcelona not only scored two good goals but, unfortunately for us, they came at good times. They are a brilliant team. If you don't take your chances against them, they will punish you and that is what happened.'

Victory at the end of his first season as a senior coach was a thrill and delight for Guardiola. As he said: 'Perhaps I should retire now. I can't win anything else. I'm very happy, very excited for the team. We're aware we've done something magnificent. You enjoy it at the time but, with time, you enjoy it even more.

'This is the best season in the history of Barcelona. Maybe we are not the best team in history, but winning the three titles – Spanish league and cup and Champions League – has made us very happy indeed.

'We are fortunate to have the legacy of the work of Johan Cruyff and Charly Rexach and now we have to be worthy of it. We have worked hard for many, many hours this season and now many people are wonderfully happy: that is our reward.'

Guardiola said he had been surprised at the way Ronaldo had been left to attack his defence virtually single-handed in the opening minutes. He acknowledged that Eto'o's early strike had been crucial in changing the balance of the game. Taking the lead allowed Barcelona to play their favoured tiki-taka possession football and drain the life and energy out of United.

The hallmark of Guardiola the coach was already evident, as he maintained the attacking traditions he learned as a player under Cruyff in the early 1990s, and won the European Champions Cup in 1992.

He said: 'We defended very well considering we had the best team in the world as our opponents. We were never cowards. We wanted to be able to say that, whatever happened, we went out and played our game and the players did a great job.'

Guardiola praised Messi as 'the best player in the world', yet dedicated victory – in Italy – to Milan's veteran Paolo Maldini, who was just about to wind up his multi-rewarded career.

'Maldini is, for me, the best European player of the last 20 years, certainly for all those of us who are used to playing out of defence,' said Guardiola. 'He's been a role model for all of us.'

Very soon Guardiola would be a world footballing role model in his own right.

2010S

TALENT REAPS ITS DUE REWARD

Spanish football stood proud, head and shoulders above the rest of Europe in the club competition in the second decade of the 21st century. Spain had won the 2010 World Cup, sandwiched between a European Championship double and the clubs took the appropriate cue. Barcelona (twice) and Real Madrid won three of the first six of the era's Champions League finals while Atletico Madrid and Sevilla won the Europa League twice apiece. For all the worldwide popularity of the English Premier League, the glory game was being monopolized by Barcelona and Madrid and, on an individual level, by Lionel Messi and Cristiano Ronaldo.

RIGHT: **SERGIO RAMOS HEADS REAL MADRID'S EQUALIZER AGAINST ATLETICO MAADRID IN THE 2014 FINAL IN LISBON**

LIONEL MESSI

Country: Argentina

Position: Forward

Born: 24 June 1987

Club: Barcelona

LIONEL MESSI

I can remember playing football for as long as I remember anything. I can recall when I was very little, maybe three or four years old, playing in my neighbourhood at home in Rosario. It's in my mind: a picture of myself with the ball at my feet at a very young age. I always had the same style of play. Even then. The same as now. I never worried about other players kicking me or trying to kick me.

When I came to Barcelona I was still very young. Hardly 13. It was a time of mixed emotions. I was happy to be living in Barcelona and experiencing so many new things. On the other hand, at that age it was hard to be so far away from all the people I knew. I had to start again and discover new team-mates, new friends. Also I could not play at first because of injury and because there were problems with the paperwork because of my age.

That was the hardest part, because I never had any problems because of my height. I was used to it. I had always been the smallest kid, at school and in whatever team I played for. It was nothing unusual to me. Also, I always had the will to carry on training and working and playing, chasing my dream. Then I was lucky with the way the coaches changed among the youth teams at Barcelona because, after Tito Vilanova

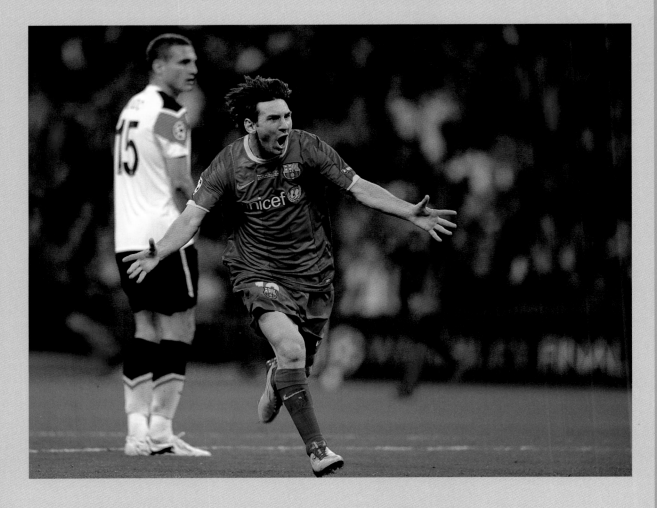

OPPOSITE: **MESSI POSES FOR A PORTRAIT PRIOR TO THE FIFA BALLON D'OR GALA 2014 AT THE PARK HYATT HOTEL ON 12 JANUARY 2015 IN ZURICH, SWITZERLAND**

LEFT: **MESSI CELEBRATES AFTER SCORING AGAINST MANCHESTER UNITED DURING THE 2008 CHAMPIONS LEAGUE FINAL AT WEMBLEY STADIUM, LONDON**

was appointed to the juniors, I began to play more often and after that my entire career changed.

In those days it was not the same system you see Barcelona teams playing now. Back then we played with only one striker and I played just behind him, with two wingers out wide. But for me the position was not an issue. I always played with the same style. But I did learn an enormous amount about the game because, even as junior players, we worked a lot with the ball and on tactics. Back in Argentina I had never been used to anything like that. Over there it was lots of running and not much more.

Eventually I played my first game for the Barcelona senior team in our traditional pre-season match, the Joan Gamper Trophy, named after the founder of our club. I was only 16 and I was told later that Fabio Capello described me as "a little devil". It was incredible that someone who had won so much as a coach and player should say that.

Then I had a tough moment with a permit problem when I thought I was about to make my league debut. I did not understand it at all. I wanted to play, I had the chance to step up into the first team and someone would not let me. Fortunately it was resolved quite quickly. Then I was lucky enough that senior players like Deco and Ronaldinho took me under their wing. I will be grateful to them for that for my whole life and to Thiago Motta and Sylvinho.

RIGHT: MESSI SCORES HIS SECOND GOAL DURING THE CHAMPIONS LEAGUE SEMI-FINAL FIRST-LEG MATCH BETWEEN REAL MADRID AND BARCELONA AT MADRID'S ESTADIO SANTIAGO BERNABEU ON 27 APRIL 2011

I do not really know what happened to the team after that. We lost the Spanish league in 2006–07 to Real Madrid, because they had a better head-to-head record against us, and a year later we lost a Champions League semi-final against Manchester United. If those seasons did nothing else they served as a lesson for us – and for me – to try to make sure these disappontments never happened again. I think what has happened since has shown we learned that lesson quite well. [In Messi's time, Barcelona have won two FIFA Club World Cups, four UEFA Champions Leagues, two UEFA Supecups, seven Spanish leagues, three cups and six Supercups.]

The talk of some sort of personal rivalry between Cristiano Ronaldo and myself is misleading. It has never existed. It has been just something invented by the media. We both want to achieve the most we can for our clubs. It has never been a case of Messi v Ronaldo.

Whatever we have won, I am still the most critical person of myself and my game. I never think about changing my style, win or lose. Sometimes I drop deeper to come into contact with the ball more and try to start up the moves from further back, combining with the midfielders. But it always depends on the game. If the ball comes to me, I always try to do what I think is the best way to head towards the opposition's goal. From there it all comes naturally.

When we lose, like anyone else, I do get wound up and that is a good thing because we all want to win, even in training. That means our hunger for success never drops. I know when I have done well and when I have done badly. I don't need anyone to tell me.

I have been fortunate, of course, in my team-mates. Xavi, for example, is a great player. He never loses the ball, he has great vision and reads the game, he controls the rhythm and pace. Andres Iniesta is similar. Maybe he scores more goals because he gets into the penalty area more, but they're similar. Andres has great vision too, and when he is on form the team revolves round him. But when both he and Xavi have been on the pitch it has been hard for the other team to get the ball.

Of course, even with the best team-mates this is football and you cannot always win. Look at Argentina in the 2014 World Cup final against Germany. You move on after even a defeat like that, but what is true is that it will be something all our players will regret for the rest of our lives, thinking about the chances we did not take that day.

As for what comes next: I can say only that I still try to improve every day. If people want to compare me with players like Pele and Maradona, footballers who were greats and are still talked about today long after they have retired, then that is flattering. But I do not think about that. I think about improving all the time and, at the end of my career, I may think about what I did. Then let people judge, if they wish.

LEFT: **MESSI LEAVES JUVENTUS'S ANDREA PIRLO IN HIS WAKE DURING THE 2015 CHAMPIONS LEAGUE FINAL IN BERLIN**

MOURINHO'S INTERNAZIONALE FAMILY TRIUMPH

When the original European Champions Cup was launched in the mid-1950s, it was all about the players. Now, such had been the developments over half a century, it was a lot more about the coaches.

Some facets had not changed. Spanish club football was dominant. In the 1950s it had been Real Madrid – Di Stefano, Kopa, Puskas, etc. – now it was Barcelona, with the mesmeric new standards set by Lionel Messi, Xavi, Andres Iniesta and their team-mates.

Reflecting the change of direction in media focus, however, the 2009–10 club competition season ended in a much more prosaic confrontation of manner and styles between Jose Mourinho and his one-time mentor Louis Van Gaal.

Mourinho believed he had revived Internazionale of Milan by developing a family atmosphere. As he said: 'If you want to win then you need a particular spirit and you need to be able to build your team and the team must work together.

This is the pride I feel in looking now at Inter – a magnificent family of footballers who have worked endlessly to achieve all they have – from the groundsman to the players out on the pitch.'

Inter and Barcelona found themselves in Group F, alongside Rubin Kazan of Russia and Dynamo Kyiv from Ukraine. It was a homecoming of sorts for Mourinho. He had been translator-turned-assistant at Camp Nou to first Sir Bobby Robson and then Van Gaal, before returning home to launch his own stellar head coaching career on the benches of Europe.

The clubs opened up with a goalless draw in the Stadio Meazza, but Barcelona won the return 2-0. That was Inter's

RIGHT: **DIRK KUYT'S PERFECT TIMING EARNS LIVERPOOL'S OPENING GOAL AGAINST DEBRECEN AT ANFIELD**

sole defeat, while Barcelona were upset 2-1 by outsiders Rubin Kazan. Those were their only slips. Barcelona topped the group with Inter as runners-up.

Only two clubs survived the group stage unbeaten: Bordeaux in Group A (ahead of Bayern Munich) and Chelsea in Group D (ahead of Porto). Three nations boasted progress for a trio of their clubs: England cheered on Arsenal and Manchester United as well as Chelsea, but waved goodbye to Liverpool; Spain lost Atletico Madrid but saw Barcelona, Real Madrid and Sevilla progress; while Inter, Milan and Fiorentina carried the Italian banner forward, despite the surprise exit of Juventus. All three exiting teams dropped into the UEFA Cup

One sour note was not revealed until years later. Hungarian club Debrecen finished bottom of Group E, behind Fiorentina, Lyon and Liverpool, losing all six games and conceding 19 goals. Later suspicious betting patterns led to match-fixing concerns over both their 1-0 defeat by Liverpool and 4-3 home loss to Fiorentina.

In both matches, heavy betting had apparently been laid on Debrecen's Montenegrin goalkeeper Vukasin Poleksic conceding three or more goals. There was never any suggestion that either Liverpool or Fiorentina – or any of their officials or players – either knew of any alleged fix or were in any way party to it. However Poleksic would be suspended for two years for failing to report a match-fixing approach. He appealed against the ban, but it was rejected by the Court of Arbitration for Sport.

In the knockout stage, the headline tie of the second round saw the return of Mourinho to Chelsea. Inter appeared to be heading out after winning only 2-1 at home and thus following the Italian exit path trodden by Milan, against Manchester United and Fiorentina, against Bayern Munich.

Instead, Mourinho's men demonstrated enormous resilience to win 1-0 at Stamford Bridge to reach the quarter-finals. Their goal was scored late by Samuel Eto'o who, years later, would spend a year at Chelsea, albeit largely on the substitutes' bench. Chelsea's campaign ended in further misery when Didier Drogba was sent off in the 87th minute for a crude stamp on Thiago Motta.

Mourinho, who had never lost a home Premier League game during his time as Chelsea manager, was thrilled, saying: 'It's a great moment for the team, a great moment for Inter, for all the players who, year after year, had problems overcoming this barrier of the last 16, and now they have done it. This qualification for the quarter-finals was earned not with luck, but with merit, thanks to a team which was perfect.'

Elsewhere in the round of 16, Bordeaux edged Olympiacos Piraeus 3-1 on aggregate, while CSKA Moscow won 2-1 away to Sevilla, who had held them to 1-1 draw in Russia. Japan midfielder Keisuke Honda struck the tie-winning free kick 10 minutes after the interval. Surprised goalkeeper Andres Palop was badly at fault.

There were no such slip-ups for Barcelona, who cruised into the last eight for a third successive season by drawing 1-1 in Stuttgart and then crushing the Germans 4-0 at Camp Nou. Lionel Messi was the second-leg inspiration. The FIFA World Player of the Year scored twice and helped lay on another for Pedro before Bojan Krkic clipped the final goal beyond veteran keeper Jens Lehmann. With Real Madrid, surprisingly, going out to Olympique Lyonnais, Barcelona thus became Spain's only survivors.

Coach Pep Guardiola was a happy man, saying: 'Only Manchester United have managed to get to the quarters the following season as reigning champions before, so I want to congratulate my team for that. Being among the eight best again and being able to compete with them fills us with excitement.'

Stuttgart coach Christian Gross could only hold up his hands in admiration. 'Barcelona are the best team in the world,' he conceded. 'As for Messi, people are right to make comparisons with Diego Maradona.'

ABOVE: **JOSE MOURINHO IS THE CENTRE OF MEDIA ATTENTION ON HIS RETURN TO BARCELONA WITH INTER**

ABOVE: LEO MESSI DELICATELY
LIFTS THE BALL OVER ARSENAL
GOALKEEPER MANUEL ALMUNIA
TO COMPLETE HIS HAT-TRICK
AT CAMP NOU IN THE QUARTER-
FINAL RETURN

Arsenal manager Arsene Wenger was similarly effusive after the quarter-finals. Barcelona held the Gunners 2-2 in north London – a double from Zlatan Ibrahimovic was pegged back by Theo Walcott and former Barcelona junior Cesc Fabregas – but they suffered the early shock of an Arsenal goal from Nicklas Bendtner at Camp Nou. Arsenal's travelling fans were celebrating for only three minutes. Messi not only equalised, but also went on to score all of Barcelona's goals in a 4-1 triumph.

'He is best player in the world by a distance,' said Wenger. 'You can stop him so that he is not always in the game. But the problem is that when he is in the game he is always dangerous, and when he goes on a run he is unstoppable. He is the only player who can change direction at such a pace. So congratulations to Barcelona: they are better than us.'

In the other quarter-finals, Bordeaux bettered Lyon in an all-French encounter, while Inter won 1-0 home and away to CSKA Moscow. Gabriel Milito scored in Milan, Wesley Sneijder in Russia. Finally, Manchester United allowed Bayern Munich to 'steal' victory on away goals in front of their own fans at Old Trafford.

Bayern won 2-1 in Munich but only by scoring two late goals after United had led for 75 minutes with a second-minute strike from Wayne Rooney. Back in Manchester, United were even quicker off the mark as goals from Darron Gibson and Nani (two) put them 3-0 head inside 41 minutes.

It should have been all over. But, two minutes later, Ivica Olic pulled a goal back. Ten minutes after the interval, United right-back Rafael was sent off and Bayern, duly encouraged, struck a magnificent – and decisive – second away goal through Arjen Robben.

For once coach Guardiola was 'thrown' by events beyond his control. The team went on a 600-mile, nine-hour bus journey to Milan for the first leg. Stops at service stations, so the players could stretch their legs, delighted autograph hunters. Guardiola sought to play down any likely effect, saying: 'Going by road means we do not have the desired recovery time, but there are many teams in the Spanish third division who travel 16 or 17 hours by coach every week. They manage. So will we.'

In fact, they did not, despite taking an early counter-attacking lead through Pedro. Sneijder levelled and, in the second half, right-back Maicon and a close-range header from Milito edged Inter to a 3-1 win. It was the first time Barcelona had conceded as many as three goals in a game that season. 'I suppose I will be blamed in Spain for the volcano,' said Mourinho. Not that he minded.

Back in Barcelona Inter, now cleared to fly, hit one setback after another. First Goran Pandev was injured in the warm-up, then former Barcelona midfielder Thiago Motta was sent off inside the first half-hour for pushing a hand into the face of Sergi Busquets.

Inter appeared to be there for the taking, but Barcelona had reckoned without Mourinho's meticulous attention to defensive detail. Barcelona grew ever more desperate: Guardiola replaced Ibrahimovic with Krkic; then ordered Gerard Pique forward as an extra centre-forward. He scored with six minutes remaining, but it was too little, too late.

'This is the best defeat of my life,' crowed Mourinho. 'It is a shame I couldn't play. I would have been awful on the pitch but I would have shed blood, just as my players did.'

BELOW: ARJEN ROBBEN SCORED THE DECISIVE AWAY GOAL WHICH TIPPED THE QUARTER-FINAL BALANCE FOR BAYERN AGAINST UNITED IN MANCHESTER

As rueful United goalkeeper Edwin Van der Sar said: 'No German team are ever beaten until they are in the team bus on the way to the airport.'

This was the point at which a surprise intervention erupted, literally, from Iceland. The explosion of the Eyjafjallajökull volcano, which had been grumbling away since late March, roared into the northern skies on 15 April and blasted so much ash into the atmosphere that European air travel was disrupted for six weeks.

UEFA, with four clubs from western Europe in the semi-finals, decided that they should make alternative travel plans. This was no problem for Bayern Munich, who won 1-0 at home to Lyon and then 3-0 back in neighbouring France, where Olic scored a hat-trick. But Barcelona were severely inconvenienced before their confrontation with Internazionale.

MOURINHO MASTERS MUNICH IN MADRID

Jose Mourinho, ever since he strutted onto the international stage with Porto in winning the UEFA Cup in 2003, had exerted a magnetising effect on the media, rarely more so than in taking charge of Internazionale for the last time before staying on in Madrid to take on the next challenge of his remarkable career, turning Real's limitless silver into silverware.

The facts were simple as Louis Van Gaal's Bayern Munich, newly recrowned as champions of Germany, and Mourinho's Iner jousted in Madrid's Estadio Bernabeu for the title relinquished by Barcelona.

Ultimately Bayern missed out on what would have been a fifth European crown, and first since 2001, while Inter finally landed their third, but first since 1965. Van Gaal thus failed to repeat his 1995 success with Ajax, while his one-time Barcelona pupil Mourinho celebrated a repeat of his own 2004 victory with Porto.

Inter's achievement was a demonstration of not only the power of destiny but also of dynasty. In 1964 and 1965, Inter's players had celebrated along with their president Angelo Moratti; now a new generation celebrated with another president Moratti – Massimo, Angelo's son.

Bayern had marginally the better of the opening exchanges. They forced the first corner after 13 minutes and though Inter's Brazilian keeper Julio Cesar was not troubled in clearing his lines, it was an early indication that Bayern would show the more obvious aggressive intent.

Four minutes later, an angled free kick from Arjen Robben forced a second corner. Unfortunately for Bayern, the advancing Martin Demichelis mistimed his header and the opportunity was gone once more.

Robben had an even better chance himself in the 27th minute after Ivica Olic and Thomas Muller had bundled their way through the front of the penalty box. However the Dutchman, perhaps surprised at the gift, scooped the ball harmlessly over the bar.

The miss proved costly when Gabriel Milito scored his fifth goal in 11 Champions League outings. Julio Cesar thumped a long clearance downfield, Milito moved the ball to his left for Wesley Sneijder – outstanding again as he had been all season – and he deftly completed the one-two. Milito stepped into the penalty area, coolly and deliberately delayed his shot until keeper Jorg Butt had committed himself and then placed the ball wide of the advancing goalkeeper into the net.

Both teams could have scored within minutes of the start of the second half. First Bayern's Thomas Muller was put clear

RIGHT: **CENTRE FORWARD DIEGO MILITO OPENS THE SCORING FOR INTER AGAINST BAYERN IN THE ESTADIO BERNABEU**

by Hamit Altintop, but he was foiled by Julio Cesar. Then, at the other end, a clever shot from Goran Pandev, after a Milito break down the left wing, was acrobatically turned over the bar by Butt.

The strategy and tactics of both teams were clear. Inter were denied the raiding power of Maicon down the right by Bayern's use of Hamit Altintop wide on the left of their midfield. But Altintop's very presence in that role illustrated the fact that Bayern were themselves missing the skill and creativity on that wing of the suspended Franck Ribery.

The Germans, therefore, looked regularly to Robben who, as the game proceeded, so continued to tease the life out of Cristian Chivu that Mourinho was forced to switch skipper Javier Zanetti to left-back instead.

At the other end, Milito was having much the better of his duel with Daniel Van Buyten and, as time went on, so Pandev found more and more space to threaten danger along with Samuel Eto'o, on his way to matching Clarence Seedorf's record third winner's medal, all with different clubs.

The game slipped decisively beyond Bayern's reach in the 70th minute. Munich were exposed too far forward and Eto'o slipped a delightful pass through a tiny gap on the left before Milito once again got the better of Van Buyten and scored his second goal.

Cue black and blue fireworks.

Mourinho, afterwards, was reticent to make any reference to his Real Madrid future. But clearly, after leading Inter to the treble of Champions League plus Italian league and cup, no further challenge remained for him in Milan, or in the Italian football maelstrom he so disliked.

Van Gaal did not suffer defeat particularly graciously. He pointed to an unpunished penalty-box handball by Maicon and opined that Bayern had played the finer – 'more difficult' – football but Inter had stolen the Cup on the counter-attack.

Not that Mourinho minded. He was already looking far ahead into dreamland, talking about grand slams – about the unique possibility of being a managerial league champion in England, in Italy and – he expected – in Spain.

ABOVE: **INTER'S PLAYERS ENJOY THE THRILL OF LIFTING THE CUP FOR THE FIRST TIME IN 45 YEARS**

SATURDAY 26 MAY
ESTADIO BERNABEU, MADRID

INTERNAZIONALE 2
MILITO 34, 70
BAYERN MUNICH 0

HT: 1-0. ATT: 73,170
REF: WEBB (ENGLAND)

INTERNAZIONALE:
JULIO CESAR – MAICON, LUCIO, SAMUEL, CHIVU (STANKOVIC 68) – ZANETTI*, CAMBIASSO – ETO'O, SNEIJDER, PANDEV (MUNTARI 79) – MILITO (MATERAZZI 90).
COACH: MOURINHO.

BAYERN MUNICH:
BUTT – LAHM, VAN BUYTEN, DEMICHELIS, BADSTUBER – ROBBEN, SCHWEINSTEIGER, VAN BOMMEL*, HAMIT ALTINTOP (KLOSE 63) – MULLER, OLIC (GOMEZ 74).
COACH: VAN GAAL.

*CAPTAIN

BARCA JOIN THE EUROPEAN ELITE

Barcelona joined Ajax Amsterdam and Bayern Munich on four European triumphs after an outstanding exhibition of creative football provided a 3-1 victory over Manchester United at Wembley.

The exhaustive command which the Champions League holds over European club football was evident right from the outset, one day less than a full 11 months before Barcelona would carry off the trophy. The long and winding road had begun all the way back on 29 June 2010, when Santa Coloma of Andorra lost 3-0 at home to Birkirkara of Malta. That was just a month and a half after Internazionale had beaten Bayern Munich in the previous season's final and halfway through the 2010 World Cup finals in South Africa.

The early rounds went largely with form though Scotland's Celtic, European champions back in 1967, were surprised to be knocked out by Portugal's Sporting Braga in the third qualifying round. Tottenham Hotspur – back among the elite for the first time since their defeat by Benfica in the 1962 semi-finals – recovered from going 3-0 down in the first 28 minutes of the first leg playoff round away to Young Boys

in Bern. They lost the match 3-2, but won 4-0 – Gareth Bale created all four goals – at White Hart Lane to reach the group stage. There was no such luck for more former European winners in Kiev Dynamo; they fell short of the group stage in losing to Ajax.

Tottenham maintained their momentum in Group A, which also featured defending champions Inter. The Italians, briefly in the managerial charge of Rafa Benitez, had lost to Atletico de Madrid in the European Supercup and were not the team they had been under Jose Mourinho, now Real Madrid's coach. As if to underline the point, Inter conceded a dramatic hat-trick to Bale, but still won 4-3 win in the Stadio Meazza.

Thus Harry Redknapp's Tottenham surprisingly finished top of the group, and the 21-year-old Welshman Bale was suddenly catapulted up into superstar status, alongside the established grandees of not only the English Premier

RIGHT: **INTER'S JAVIER ZANETTI ARRIVES JUST TOO LATE TO PREVENT GARETH BALE FIRING HIS SECOND GOAL FOR TOTTENHAM IN THE STADIO MEAZZA**

League but also the whole of Europe. He had made his name as a teenaged left-back, another protege of Southampton's vaunted academy and Spurs signed him for £7,000 in 2007. However, it took almost three years before Redknapp gave Bale his freedom to rove from a nominal left-wing role.

Europe now learned about his brilliance. Bale scored against Twente Enschede in the second game of the group stage and had just been voted Welsh Player of the Year when he struck the first, thrilling hat-trick of his career against Inter in Milan. The fact that Spurs, had playing most of the match with 10 men after a red card for keeper Heurelho Gomes, went virtually unnoticed amid the fuss.

In the return at White Hart Lane, all the old memories of Tottenham's glory, glory days were whipped up as Bale made goals for Peter Crouch and Roman Pavlyuchenko in a 3-1 win.

Germany's Schalke 04 topped Group B courtesy of the inspiration provided by Champions League record marksman Raul, winding down in style after a distinguished career with Real Madrid.

Manchester United and Barcelona topped groups C and D without conceding a goal, though it was significant that United scored only seven goals in their six games while Barcelona ran up 14. Bayern Munich, Chelsea, Real Madrid and

Shakhtar Donetsk topped the remaining four groups. Among the third-place finishers in the groups, Ajax and Benfica were former champions relegated to the Europa League along with Braga whose minus-six goal difference in Group H hardly suggested they would go on, as they did, to reach the Europa League Final.

Slovakia's Zilina, in Group F, and Serbia's Partizan Belgrade – Group G – became only the 11th and 12th teams in Champions League history to lose all six group matches. Partizan's poor performance – losing home and away to Shakhtar Donetsk, Arsenal and Braga – underlined the problems suffered by clubs in what had once been Yugoslavia. No longer were the likes of Partizan able to hold their players at home. Now they were constrained, by financial pressures, to sell not only their best senior players but also their most promising youngsters.

Only one team from the former Soviet Union reached the knock-out stage: Shakhtar Donetsk from Ukraine. But they were not typical; the top club in the mining region of the Donbass Basin, in the east of the country, was bankrolled by a billionaire, Rinat Akhmetov.

Shakhtar had become, in 2009, the second Ukraine club to win a European trophy when they landed the UEFA Cup with a team built around high-class Brazilian imports, astutely coached by Romanian Mircea Lucescu and captained by Croatia's Darijo Srna. Their home was the superb black-glass Donbass Arena, at the foot of an imposing war memorial. It would serve as one of the Ukraine venues when it was – with Poland – joint host of the 2012 UEFA European Championship finals. At this point in football and political time, Shakhtar had everything to play for.

The second round draw paired them with Italy's Roma. They had not won the Italian championship since 2001 – illustrating how the Champions League format favoured below-elite clubs in the major countries. But they were also undergoing a major transformation, as they were negotiating a takeover by an American investment group, headed by Thomas DiBenedetto.

The takeover provided little help for them. In the first leg, in the Stadio Olimpico, Roma briefly led, through an own goal from Romanian Razvan Rat, but Shakhtar levelled immediately through Jadson and went on to win 3-2. Despite their lack of match practice, because of the winter break, Shakhtar won the return 3-0 and reached the quarter-finals for the first time in their history.

Milan were another Italian team to exit at the second round stage. Tottenham beat them 1-0 at the Stadio Meazza – to a goal from England centre-forward Peter Crouch – and they had to settle for a goalless draw at White Hart Lane. Tottenham took pride in carrying north London interest into the last eight after Arsenal fell to Barcelona. Two late goals from Robin Van Persie and Andrei Arshavin had given the Gunners a 2-1 comeback win at home and, with 20 minutes remaining in Camp Nou, they were on terms at 1-1. But then Xavi and Messi scored twice in three minutes and it was all over.

Chelsea won away at FC Kobenhavn with a brace from Nicolas Anelka to progress 2-0 on aggregate, while Schalke's adventure continued, 4-2 overall against Valencia. They thus became the last German team standing, because although Bayern won 1-0 away to

Inter, with a last-minute goal from Germany striker Mario Gomez, they lost 3-2 at home and went out on the away goals rule.

Real Madrid completed the quarter-final line-up with a personal triumph for Karim Benzema. Born and raised in Lyon, Benzema returned to the club who 'made' him, and scored Madrid's equaliser in the opening 1-1 draw at the Stade Gerland. He then welcomed his old team-mates back to Spain and scored again in a 3-0 win. Jose Mourinho, it appeared, was closing in on that third Champions League title.

Goals rained across Europe in the quarter-finals: Madrid dismissed Spurs 4-0 in Madrid, with two from the future Tottenham centre-forward Emmanuel Adebayor; Schalke, remarkably, won

RIGHT: **SHAKHTAR DONETSK'S BRAZILIAN MIDFIELDER JADSON SCORES AGAINST ROMA IN THE FIRST LEG OF THE ROUND OF 16 IN THE ITALIAN CAPITAL**

5-2 away to Inter with two goals from Brazilian Edu; and Barcelona rattled Shakhtar 5-1. The only tight encounter, not surprisingly, was the 2008 final repeat between Chelsea and Manchester United. Wayne Rooney struck after 24 minutes at Stamford Bridge and Chelsea never recovered. United won 2-1 back at Old Trafford.

Their company in the last four had no trouble finishing their quarter-final jobs with legendary strikers on the mark. Barcelona won 1-0 in Donetsk (Messi), Schalke won 2-1 at home to Inter (Raul the first) and Madrid won 1-0 at Tottenham (Cristiano Ronaldo).

In the last four, at last, Schalke's adventure came to an end. Ralf Rangnick's players had surprised themselves by reaching the seming al progressing so far but, against United, it was as if they had suddenly woken up to reality. Overwhelmed by the occasion they lost 2-0 at home then 4-1 at Old Trafford. United were safely into their third final in four years.

As for free-scoring Barcelona, they reached Wembley by outscuffling old domestic 'enemy' Real Madrid in a bad-tempered tie which saw Mourinho's magic desert him. His defensive tactics betrayed Madrid's heritage and a first-leg tantrum earned him a touchline ban for the return.

Not that it mattered. Although Cristiano Ronaldo had outscored Messi in the Spanish league, the Argentinian had the last laugh in Europe. His two goals secured Barcelona a 2-0 victory in Madrid, which made the 1-1 draw in the second leg academic.

ABOVE: JAVIER 'CHICHARITO' HERNANDEZ SCORES MANCHESTER UNITED'S FIRST GOAL IN THEIR QUARTER-FINAL SECOND LEG AGAINST CHELSEA

BARCELONA'S ENGLISH LOVE AFFAIR GOES ON

Barcelona love the English connection when it comes to European club football's grandest occasion. They won their first Cup against Italy's Sampdoria at the old Wembley and had then claimed their second and third cups against English opposition comprising Arsenal in 2006 and Manchester United in 2009.

That win in Rome in 2009 had seen Barcelona beat United more easily in the end than the 2-0 scoreline suggested, squaring the finals tally between the clubs since United had beaten the Catalans in the 1991 Cup-winners Cup Final. Significantly, however, the way Barcelona had played in Rome did not satisfy coach Pep Guardiola. He wanted better: back at Wembley – the rebuilt version – he got his wish.

United had overcome a contract wrangle with star striker Wayne Rooney before claiming their record 19th League title. They entered the final at full strength, and with the emotional interest of goalkeeper Edwin Van der Sar, playing in his final match before retirement. Speculation also reigned that a United victory would prompt veteran manager Sir Alex Ferguson to call it a day, too. That rumour never had a chance to become fact.

Barcelona, champions of Spain for the 21st time, flew to London early for fear of being caught out by yet another Icelandic volcano cloud. Once there, they had to leave short-of-fitness

Carles Puyol on the substitutes' bench; the veteran captain's place in the centre of defence went to Javier Mascherano.

Usually a defensive midfielder, Mascherano took time to settle and, in those opening 10 minutes, United probably lost whatever chance they had of a victory against the odds. Twice they had Barcelona keeper Victor Valdes panicking, but United's early goal would not come. Essentially, the game was over once Barcelona began to put together their inter-passing triangles and headed for a sensational possession percentage of 68 per cent.

Lionel Messi, by now a well-established World Player of the Year, was at the heart of the creative action. If United had planned on different men picking him up in different zones of the pitch, then Messi was too quick for them all. Very early, United had reason to be grateful for the defensive resolve of Rio Ferdinand and Nemanja Vidic but even they were soon being pulled out of position.

The inevitable breakthrough was created by Barcelona skipper Xavi, darting directly at United's central defence, before releasing a perfect angle pass to the right for the unmarked Pedro to shot decisively low and wide of Van der Sar's left hand.

Of course, United, under Ferguson, never admitted to 'concession'. Rooney struck a magnificent equaliser out of nowhere as he capitalised on a high-speed return pass from Ryan Giggs in the 34th minute. But it was no more than a gesture of defiance before defeat was imposed by fine second-half strikes from Messi – inevitably – and David Villa.

It was Messi's 12th goal of the campaign – for the fourth season in a row he was overall top scorer – and his 53rd goal in all competitions. Victory was no more than Barcelona deserved against a United side in which Antonio Valencia was badly off the pace, new Mexican hero Javier Hernandez was cut adrift up front and 37-year-old Giggs was perpetually bypassed by Barcelona's tika-taka delicacy in midfield.

All that remained was for Barcelona to ring the substitutions and give Eric Abidal – having recovered remarkably quickly from a cancer tumour – the climactic glory of raising the cup.

Barcelona coach Pep Guardiola was delighted with not only the result, but also the manner in which it had been achieved: 'Far better than in 2009,' he said. United manager Sir Alex Ferguson appeared almost relieved that the margin of defeat had not been more emphatic.

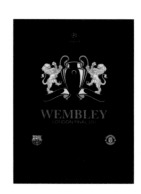

RIGHT: **MANCHESTER UNITED MANAGER SIR ALEX FERGUSON (LEFT) AND HIS ASSISTANT MIKE PHELAN ARE LOSERS FOR ONCE AT WEMBLEY**

Both clubs had won their first champions' crown in the old Wembley – Barcelona with Guardiola in their lineup in 1992 – but on this occasion the omens had suited the Spanish champions. Not that European federation UEFA would have had a problem whichever way the goals went.

No matter the outcome on the pitch Michel Platini's governing body could point proudly to an event which was watched around the world by around 250 million people and generated Đ369m to the clubs and countries involved, a rise of five percent on the previous season.

Barcelona ended the campaign an estimated Đ126m the richer, while United were minimally consoled by Đ73m. But the greatest value – an intangible one – was that afforded to Messi. Here was the greatest player of his generation, still only 23, with a magnificent temperament which saw him suffer the kicks and hacks, yet get up smartly, dust himself down and slice away at opposing defences all over again.

'He is the player who makes the difference,' said playmaker Xavi. 'He is a phenomenon for the team: he scores goals, plays the final ball, comes into midfield to help create superiority and understands the game.'

Guardiola had an appropriate last word. 'Messi,' he said, 'is unique, a one-off, the best player I have ever seen and probably the best I will ever see.'

SATURDAY 28 MAY
WEMBLEY

BARCELONA 3
PEDRO 27, MESSI 54, VILLA 69
MANCHESTER UNITED 1
ROONEY 34

HT: 1-1. ATT: 87, 695
REF: KASSAI (HUNGARY)

BARCELONA:
VALDES - DANI ALVES (PUYOL 88), MASCHERANO, PIQUE, ABIDAL – XAVI*, BUSQUETS, INIESTA - VILLA (KEITA 85), MESSI, PEDRO (AFELLAY 90). COACH: GUARDIOLA

MANCHESTER UNITED:
VAN DER SAR - FABIO DA SILVA (NANI 68), FERDINAND, VIDIC*, EVRA - VALENCIA, CARRICK (SCHOLES 77), GIGGS, PARK - ROONEY, HERNANDEZ. MANAGER: FERGUSON

*CAPTAIN

ABRAMOVICH'S DREAM REALISED

Bayern Munich had not won European club football's greatest prize for a decade. When UEFA awarded the final to their own Allianz Arena, they believed the finger of destiny was pointing at them. In the end Chelsea had other, dramatic different, ideas.

The season had begun with international football in administrative turmoil. World federation FIFA had been wracked by allegations of corruption which would rip through its Executive Committee and forced its President Sepp Blatter to launch a governance reform project.

In Europe, UEFA president Michel Platini had grown ever more concerned about the number of clubs failing to pay their players, pay transfer fees, pay their taxes and then collapse into bankruptcy. Thus the European federation launched financial fair play. Entry to its lucrative club competitions would be barred or restricted to clubs who could not balance their books.

Karl-Heinz Rummenigge, one-time Champions Cup-winning star and now Bayern's chief executive, was delighted, saying: 'It's as if we have been sitting in a tunnel and now, at last, we can see some light. At Bayern we have worked with this sort of model for 13 or 14 years and have always stayed in profit. We do not need a Roman Abramovich, a Silvio Berlusconi or some

sheikh to reach into his own pocket to cover the losses at the end of the year.'

Barcelona kicked off the action on the pitch by defeating a weakened Porto, winners of the 2011 Europa League in the UEFA Supercup in Monaco. Porto showed significant changes from the team which had beaten Braga in Dublin the previous May. Vitor Pereira had succeeded Chelsea-bound Andre Villas Boas as coach, while striker Radamel Falcao had been sold to Atletico de Madrid for £40m. The Colombian had feasted on a European competition record of 17 goals the previous season and was badly missed.

Leo Messi directed Barca's 2-0 victory over Porto. He scored the Catalans' first goal and created the second for Cesc Fabregas, newly-returned from Arsenal. A week earlier Barcelona had beaten Real Madrid to land the Spanish Supercup. They were again the team to be beaten.

The draw for the Champions League group stage saw the two extremes of financial fair play come face to face as

RIGHT: **CARLOS TEVEZ (THIRD LEFT) SHOWS NO INTEREST IN LEAVING THE SUBSTITUTES' BENCH FOR MANCHESTER CITY IN THEIR 2-0 AWAY DEFEAT AGAINST BAYERN IN MUNICH**

LEFT: **APOEL'S CONSTANTINOS CHARALAMBIDES STEPS OVER A TACKLE FROM PORTO'S FERNANDINHO IN THEIR GROUP G TIE IN CYPRUS**

self-righteous Bayern were drawn against high-spending, Abu Dhabi-owned Manchester City in Group A.

Highlights among the steadily-increasing number of rematches included Manchester United v Benfica in Group C – a repeat of the 1968 final – Chelsea's Juan Mata facing the Valencia club he had just left, in Group E, and Milan confronting Barcelona in Group H, a repeat of the classic 1994 final showdown.

Less happily, Trabzonspor were parachuted into the competition barely 24 hours before the draw after Fenerbahce were cut, controversially, by their own Turkish federation over a match-fixing scandal.

From an English perspective, Manchester City's arrival on the Champions League stage, with their galaxy of expensive superstars under Italian manager Roberto Mancini, generated the greatest expectation. But trouble erupted in their first game against Bayern in Munich.

Bayern, a mere third in the Bundesliga the previous season, had needed to beat Zurich in the play-off round to reach the group stage. But they were completely superior to City. Bayern won 2-0, and the pain of defeat for City was exacerbated by the refusal of Carlos Tevez to obey Mancini's orders and take to the pitch as a second-half substitute.

The Argentinian had already irritated Mancini with an attempt to force a transfer away the club. After the game Mancini stormed: 'It was a bad situation, to refuse to go in to help the team: I cannot accept this ... He is finished, he is finished.'

Finished, at least, for six months. Tevez, punished by the club, stormed off home to Argentina and did not return until after a springtime rapprochement. He was just in time to help City win the Premier League by a whisker and put a smile back on Mancini's face.

The same week brought contrasting fortunes for another Argentinian. Messi, in scoring twice in a 5-0 win over BATE Borisov, became Barcelona's joint all-time top-scoring foreigner with 192 goals, equalling the mark achieved by their Hungarian hero of the 1950s, Ladislav Kubala.

Barcelona went on to head Group H with five wins and one draw, 20 goals for and a mere four against. For good measure they also jetted off to Tokyo to crush Santos in the FIFA Club World Cup Final. Messi scored twice, his 28th and 29th goals of the season in all competitions. Those goals took his personal tally to nine in the 11 finals Barcelona had reached since Pep Guardiola's accession as coach in 2008.

Back in Europe, the completion of the group stage saw Bayern and Napoli progress from Group A with Manchester City following up a declaration of a record £194m loss by finishing 'only' third. Similarly embarrassed were neighbours Manchester United in Group C. Manager Sir Alex Ferguson's celebrations of 25 years at Old Trafford were dimmed by relegation into the Europa League, behind Benfica and Basel. Ajax were the other former European champions thus despatched, behind Real Madrid and Olympique Lyonnais in Group D.

ABOVE: **LIONEL MESSI SCORES ONE OF HIS FIVE GOALS IN BARCELONA'S 7-1 SECOND ROUND ROUT OF BAYER LEVERKUSEN**

English 'honour' was maintained by Chelsea and Arsenal, who both lost only once in topping Groups E and F, respectively, while Milan and Inter carried the Serie A banner forward. The greatest surprise was the sight of APOEL Nicosia winning Group G, ahead of Zenit St Petersburg, Porto and Shakhtar Donetsk. APOEL's success delighted Platini as evidence of the value of his strategy in easing group access for Europe's minnows.

Of course, APOEL were also the opponents all the others wanted to draw in the knockout stage. Lyon drew the Cypriots, but complacency betrayed them, as APOEL, superbly organised

by Serb coach Ivan Jovanovic, lost only 1-0 in France and won by the same margin at home, despite having midfielder Gustavo Manduca sent off in extra time. They then won 4-3 on penalties, after keeper Dionisios Chiotis saved the last French club's final two spot kicks, from Alexandre Lacazette and Michel Bastos.

This was not the only tight tie: Chelsea needed extra time to beat Napoli 5-4 on aggregate; Internazionale advanced on the away goals rule against Marseille; while Benfica and Milan edged Zenit and Arsenal, respectively, both 4-3. Goals flew in elsewhere. Barcelona put 10 past Bayer Leverkusen – Messi scoring five in a 7-1 home win – Bayern thumped seven against Basel and Real Madrid five against CSKA Moscow.

Madrid's reward was to be matched with APOEL. Coach Jose Mourinho did not make Lyon's mistake. Hence Madrid cantered through, 3-0 in Cyprus and 5-2 in the Estadio Bernabeu. Karim Benzema struck twice in the first leg, while Cristiano Ronaldo grabbed a double in the return. Bayern won 2-0 home and away against Marseille, and Messi scored two more in Barcelona's 0-0 and 3-1 despatch of Milan.

Chelsea, in the throes of another management crisis, narrowly overcame Benfica. The Blues won 1-0 in Lisbon, through Salomon Kalou, and 2-1 at home through a Frank Lampard penalty and Raul Meireles. They did so with a new manager in charge. Villas-Boas had paid the price for falling out with the dressing room after only eight months. Former fans' favourite Roberto Di Matteo stepped in as interim first-team coach to the season's end.

The near-impossible demands on a Chelsea manager were underscored by a club statement on the Villas-Boas sacking which acknowledged a necessary step even though 'the club is still competing in the latter stages of the UEFA Champions League and the FA Cup, as well as challenging for a top-four spot in the Premier League'.

Luck of the semi-final draw saw Barcelona and Real Madrid kept apart. The Spanish media salivated at the prospect of an El Clasico to beat them all in the final. It never happened. Madrid thought they were nearly there after losing 2-1 away

to Bayern, but could only manage to win by the same score at home. Then, in a disastrous penalty shootout, Ronaldo, Kaka and defender Sergio Ramos all failed from the spot.

Barcelona, similarly, had celebrated losing only to Didier Drogba's single goal at Stamford Bridge. They had reckoned without the unifying force which Di Matteo had wrought within his squad as Chelsea went on to achieve one of the greatest achievements in their history. In the Camp Nou cauldron, and despite the first-half sending-off of skipper John Terry, Chelsea snatched a 2-2 draw which fired them to the final in Munich.

Barcelona besieged the Londoners' goal from the start and deservedly took the lead through Sergio Busquets. Two minutes later Terry was sent off for kneeing Alexis Sanchez from behind and Barcelona capitalised by surging further ahead through Andres Iniesta. That was as close as they came before Ramires, with a superb chip on the run, pulled back a crucial away goal in first-half stoppage time.

The second half saw Messi smash the crossbar with a penalty, and later hit a post, but Chelsea somehow held out so Fernando Torres could come off the bench for a late solo goal which wrapped up the aggregate victory. With that one strike the Spaniard repaid much of the £50m he had cost the Blues in January the previous year from Liverpool.

For Barcelona, a season which had started in triumph was ending in torment. The previous weekend they had lost hope of retaining the Spanish league title after losing 2-1 at home to Real Madrid.

LEFT: **CHELSEA CAPTAIN JOHN TERRY IS SHOCKED TO BE SENT OFF IN THE SECOND LEG OF THE SEMI-FINAL AGAINST BARCELONA AT THE CAMP NOU**

CHELSEA HOLD THEIR NERVE

Chelsea, in defying a two-hour barrage from Bayern in their Munich stronghold, seized their first Champions League to fulfil a dream which had prompted Russian oligarch Roman Abramovich to buy the club back in 2003.

The Londoners, pipped on penalties in Moscow by Manchester United two years earlier, appeared doomed so many times. First Thomas Muller headed Bayern in front in the 83rd minute, only for Didier Drogba, five minutes later, to head a magnificent equaliser.

Then in extra time Chelsea conceded a penalty, only for Petr Cech to save from former Blue Arjen Robben. Lastly Juan Mata missed the Blues' first kick in the shootout, only for them to recover from 3-1 behind to win it 4-3.

Bayern had only themselves to blame. They created just about all the half-chances in a tight game, staged in a context which was all in their favour: they were playing in their own Allianz Arena while Chelsea were seriously weakened by the suspension of John Terry, a legacy from their semi-final victory over Barcelona.

Yet they knew success. Roberto Di Matteo's men had already claimed the FA Cup. Bayern, by contrast, ended up empty-handed in every direction. Borussia Dortmund had outstripped them in the Bundesliga and crushed them 5-2 in the German cup final. Thus they ended term as runners-up three times over, the same fate suffered by another Bundesliga club, Bayer Leverkusen, in 2002.

Chelsea should have competed in the very first European Champions Cup, back in 1955–56. They had been invited – along with the likes of Real Madrid, Milan, Reims, etc. – but declined, under orders from the Football League. It would be 45 years before they first played in Europe's elite competition, and they were still waiting for their first championship.

Bayern accepted the responsibility of setting the tempo in their own fortress: Franck Ribery had a shot deflected for

RIGHT: **CHELSEA CELEBRATE THEIR MOST INCREDIBLE VICTORY, ON PENALTIES AGAINST BAYERN IN MUNICH**

a corner, an angled shot from Robben ricocheted off keeper's Petr Cech's shins and against a post, then Mario Gomez lofted high over the crossbar from 12 metres. For a player who had rammed home 26 Bundesliga goals it was a terrible miss.

Bayern did have the ball in Chelsea's net seven minutes after half-time. Muller was again the creative force, this time breaking down the left. Robben's shot ricocheted off Ashley Cole to Ribery. He shot into the goal, but the effort was, correctly, ruled offside.

Cole was having a storming game. Minutes later he came to the rescue of his central defenders yet again, flinging himself in the path of another effort from Robben. Still there was no let-up. Ribery had a deflected cross pushed over the bar by Cech and then Muller dragged a shot wide after a sweeping move downfield involving Bastien Schweinsteiger, Robben and Ribery. Eventually Muller, in the 83rd minute, made no mistake with a close-range header after Ribery sailed in another cross from the left.

Bayern pulled off the tiring Muller and sent on defender Daniel Van Buyten to secure the game, the final and the cup

... all in vain. Chelsea charged forward, forced a right-wing corner and the relentless Drogba headed home Mata's kick magnificently at the near post. It was the only corner Chelsea won all night compared with 20 for Bayern.

Extra time brought a brief role reversal. Initially Chelsea seized the attacking initiative, but then Ribery escaped and Drogba, chasing back, caught the back of his ankles. Robben drove the penalty low and hard to Cech's left, but the goalkeeper produced a fine save.

Weeks earlier, Robben had missed the penalty which effectively handed the German league title to Borussia Dortmund; now he had missed the penalty which helped hand the Champions League to Chelsea.

Bayern fans were even teased in the 10th shootout in the history of European Champions finals, when Mata saw Chelsea's first kick saved by Manuel Neuer. But then Cech saved Ivica Olic's fourth Bayern penalty before Schweinsteiger – the shootout winner in the semi-final against Real Madrid – hit a post.

Thus Drogba, after having already scored his ninth goal in his nine finals with Chelsea, was presented with the chance to make history. Neuer went to his left; the Ivorian drove the ball to his left, so Chelsea were kings of Europe for the first time.

Drogba said later: 'Considering the way we turned things around against Napoli and Barcelona – I think we are great champions and deserve to be champions. In 2008, when we lost on penalties to Manchester United, it was very painful for the players, the club and fans. Today we managed to change it around.

'It was an amazing game, a crazy game. We gave everything. I don't know if we have enough energy to party!'

ABOVE: **DIDIER DROGBA SENDS BAYERN GOALKEEPER MANUEL NEUER THE WRONG WAY WITH HIS CHAMPIONS LEAGUE-WINNING PENALTY**

SATURDAY 19 MAY
ALLIANZ ARENA

BAYERN MUNICH 1
MULLER 83
CHELSEA 1
DROGBA 88

AFTER EXTRA TIME
CHELSEA WON 4-3 ON PENS
HT: 0-0. 90 MIN: 1-1. ATT: 62,500
REF: PROENCA (PORTUGAL)

BAYERN:
NEUER – LAHM*, BOATENG, TYMOSHCHUK, CONTENTO – SCHWEINSTEIGER, KROOS – ROBBEN, MULLER (VAN BUYTEN 85), RIBERY (OLIC 97) – GOMEZ.
COACH: HEYNCKES

CHELSEA:
CECH – BOSINGWA, CAHILL, DAVID LUIZ, COLE – MIKEL – KALOU (TORRES 84), MATA, LAMPARD*, BERTRAND (MALOUDA 73) – DROGBA.
MANAGER: DI MATTEO

*CAPTAIN

DEUTSCHLAND ÜBER ALLES

Wembley hosted the Champions League Final as the showpiece climax to the 150th anniversary celebrations of The Football Association. So it was ironic that two German teams showed up to enjoy the occasion.

Not that the Champions League campaign had begun promisingly for the Bundesliga. Although Bayern Munich, Borussia Dortmund and Schalke were seeded direct into the group stage, Borussia Monchengladbach were knocked out in the play-off round by Dynamo Kiev. It was a second disappointment for the German game in a matter of months after the national team's semi-final failure against Italy in the Euro 2012 semi-finals.

The European Championship finals in Poland and Ukraine had launched a busy summer of international football which was carried on, in August, by the Olympic Games tournaments during London 2012. Of course, as soon as the International Olympic Committee had swept out of town so normal football service was reserved.

Chelsea's presence, as holders, in the Champions League groups was depressing news for another London club, Tottenham Hostpur. Chelsea had finished sixth in the Premier League but, as holders, claimed England's fourth Champions League spot, forcing fourth-placed Spurs to drop into the Europa League.

Spurs' fans resentment was fuelled further by the sight of Chelsea being carved up 4-1 by Atletico de Madrid in the UEFA Supercup in Monte Carlo. Radamel Falcao scored a first-half hat-trick. Chelsea owner Roman Abramovich was not amused. This was not what he expected after covering annual losses of £67.7m with a string of new sponsorship deals and the purchases of Belgian winger Eden Hazard and Brazil midfielder Oscar.

More disappointment was to come. Chelsea had been drawn in Champions League Group E, with Juventus, Shakhtar Donetsk and Denmark's minnows Nordsjælland. They may have been minnows in this exalted company but it was another satisfying progression to suit UEFA president Michel Platini. Chelsea launched their defence disappointingly with a 2-2 home draw against Juventus, won easily in Denmark but then lost 2-1 away to Shakhtar. Two weeks later Chelsea reversed the result, but only by winning 3-2 against the club from eastern Ukraine.

Those two goals by Shakhtar's Willian – later sold to Chelsea – proved fatal. When the two clubs finished the group level

on 10 points, behind Juventus, the head-to-head results rule came into play and Shakhar carried on into the knockout stage – effectively on away goals – while the Blues were relegated to the Europa League. That method of settling group places was thus once again exposed as an unfair nonsense: Chelsea had a two-goal better goal difference in the group and outscored Shakhtar 16 to 12. Roberto Di Matteo, caretaker manager hero in Munich the previous season, had already paid with his job – thanklessly sacked after the earlier, condemnatory 3-0 defeat by Juventus.

Chelsea were not England's only group failures. Manchester City had been drawn in a so-called 'group of death', alongside former European champions Real Madrid and Ajax Amsterdam, plus Germany's fast-reviving Borussia Dortmund. Madrid had plenty to prove to their fans after a stuttering start to the

RIGHT: BRAZILIAN FORWARD WILLIAN SCORES FOR SHAKHTAR DONETSK AGAINST DANISH OUTSIDERS NORDSJAELLAND IN COPENHAGEN

Spanish league season, while City's ambition was to improve on the previous campaign, when they had been relegated into the Europa League. They came within one minute of opening with a draw in Madrid but a misjudgement by keeper Joe Hart gifted a Real winner to Cristiano Ronaldo. It was the beginning of the end already for Roberto Mancini's team. They were held 1-1 at home by Dortmund then lost 3-1 in Amsterdam. Halfway through Group D and they were already heading down and out.

Arsenal and Manchester United kept the Premier League flag flying, though Arsenal paid a costly penalty for a sloppy 2-0 home defeat in mid-Group B by Schalke. The Gunners finished runners-up, two points adrift of the Ruhr club and were thus in the 'wrong' half of the second round draw, playing the round-of-16 leg first. United, in Group H, lost their last two games by single goals, away to Galatasaray and home to CFR Cluj of Romania. However, by then, they were already certain to finish top of the group, inspiring speculation that manager Sir Alex Ferguson, once again, had targeted a cup-winning display at Wembley in May as an appropriate stage for a glorious exit.

Spain, hoping for one of their clubs to follow up on the national team's European Championship triumph, progressed all four clubs. Chilean coach Manuel Pellegrini's Malaga and Barcelona were group winners, accompanied by Real Madrid and Valencia as runners-up.

Bayern Munich, keeping faith with veteran coach Jupp Heynckes in the attempt to make amends for the previous season's home horror, topped Group F. Yet they did so only by edging Valencia on the mutual results rule after both finished on 13 points. The match which mattered was the November return in Spain when Bayern levelled through Thomas Muller eight minutes from time. Muller did not know it at the time but this proved one of the most important goals of his career because it would push Bayern top of the group and meant that they drew Arsenal in the second round.

By now Bayern were hitting their stride. In February, shortly after the resumption of the Bundesliga, they won 3-1 in north London, with goals from Toni Kroos, Muller and Mario Mandzukic, then thrashed Werder Bremen 6-1 to fly 18 points clear of Dortmund at the top of the Bundesliga. It was an appropriate way to celebrate Heynckes's 1,000th game as a player and coach.

Bayern slipped up in the second leg against Arsenal, losing 2-0 at home (Olivier Giroud and Laurent Koscielny – the latter in the 86th minute – getting the visitors' goals), but advanced on the away goals rule. Munich's reaction was smash nine goals past Hamburg in the Bundesliga. Peruvian veteran Claudio Pizarro, the Bundesliga's all-time top foreign scorer, scored four of the nine goals, but even that was not enough

to earn him a starting place when Juventus came calling in the quarter-finals.

Second round drop-outs, along with Arsenal, had included former champions Porto, Milan and Celtic, as well as Shakhtar Donetsk, Schalke and Valencia. Further past title-holders to bow out were Manchester United. Real Madrid spoiled Ferguson's dream in cruel fashion. United, with an early goal from Danny Welbeck, claimed a 1-1 opening draw in Spain. They were even gifted the lead by a Sergio Ramos own goal at Old Trafford before two goals in three minutes from Luka Modric and United 'old boy' Cristiano Ronaldo turned both the game and the tie on its head. Weeks later Ferguson announced his end-of-season retirement.

Both Barcelona and Madrid marched on through the quarter-finals. Ronaldo scored three of Madrid's goals in a 5-2 aggregate win over Galatasaray, though Barcelona needed the away goals rule to edge past Paris Saint-Germain (2-2, 1-1). The two surviving German clubs also progressed. Bayern won 2-0 both home and away against Juventus, but Dortmund, under their charismatic coach Jurgen Klopp, were lucky to beat Malaga. Already resigned to losing their German crown, Borussia had to score twice in stoppage time to beat Malaga. The first leg ended goalless in Spain but, to the shock of Dortmund's legendary 'yellow wall', Malaga took the lead through Joaquin.

Robert Lewandowski levelled before half-time but the Spanish outsiders had the away goal advantage and appeared to be progressing when substitute Eliseu put them 2-1 up with eight minutes remaining. Midfielder Marco Reus and then Felipe Santana – apparently offside – struck back for Dortmund in a style reminiscent of Manchester United in the 1999 final. Furious Malaga complained to UEFA about Scottish official Craig Thomson but in vain. Worse was to come. Two months later the Court of Arbitration for Sport upheld a one-year European club ban imposed on Malaga by UEFA for having failed to pay players' wages and tax bills on time.

The semi-finals draw was perfectly balanced: Germany against Spain in each tie – Bayern v Barcelona and Dortmund v Madrid. Neutral opinion was largely unanimous. The world's finest marksmen, Messi and Ronaldo, would be striking out towards the ultimate El Clasico confrontation in the Wembley final. All wrong. The semi-finals were virtually decided after the first legs in Germany on successive evenings, with Spain's giants battered and embarrassed. Muller scored twice in Bayern's 4-0 trouncing of Barcelona, while Polish spearhead Lewandowski, enjoying the finest occasion of his an already elite club career, scored all four Dortmund goals in their 4-1 dismissal of Madrid.

ABOVE: **JUST IN TIME BORUSSIA DORTMUND'S FELIPE SANTANA RUNS IN TO GRAB THE STOPPAGE-TIME GOAL WHICH BEATS MALAGA**

Madrid made a half-decent attempt to defy the destiny of an all-German final. They scored twice in the last seven minutes through Benzema and Ramos to set up a storming, but vain, finale. No such consolation for Barcelona who were demolished 3-0 in Nou Camp by Bayern and thus 7-0 on aggregate. Barcelona's capitulation began even before kickoff, when coach Tito Vilanova left Messi on the subs' bench. Messi was still recovering from a hamstring strain, but had scored a magnificent solo goal against Bilbao at the weekend. Even a starting presence would have been intimidating.

Spared such a challenge, Bayern produced a magnificent all-pitch effort and scored all their goals in the second half through Arjen Robben, the Dutch winger's fifth strike in eight games, Gerard Pique (own goal) and Muller. That completed Barcelona's worst aggregate defeat in the Champions League and the first time they had lost both legs of a European tie since 1987. Even better for Bayern coach Jupp Heynckes was the satisfaction that none of his players on a yellow card had collected another and he would thus have a full-strength squad at Wembley.

BELOW: **ARSENAL'S LAURENT KOSCIELNY (RIGHT) HEADS HIS TEAM'S SECOND GOAL IN THEIR VAIN ATTEMPT TO OVERCOME BAYERN IN THE ROUND OF !6 SECOND LEG IN MUNICH**

TWO DOWN, ONE TO GO, FOR GERMAN MASTERS

ABOVE: **JUST IN TIME, ARJEN ROBBEN (10) POUNCES FOR BAYERN'S LAST-MINUTE WINNING GOAL AGAINST BORUSSIA DORTMUND**

Bayern Munich landed the second leg of a terrific treble, securing Champions League glory in between German league and cup successes, after a tidal wave of attacking football overcame Borussia Dortmund in the all-German final at Wembley.

Three times previously had the UEFA Champions League Final showdown been a domestic duel. Now the Bundesliga emulated the English, Italian and Spanish championships in having the final to itself.

The 86,298 crowd, split between the yellow of Borussia and the Bavarian red, had to wait until the second half for all the goals before Bayern made amends for their final defeats in 2010 and 2012 by turning veteran coach Jupp Heynckes back into a European champion, 15 years after his success with Real Madrid.

Dortmund, having lost their league crown by a clear 25 points, were always the more physically fragile of the finalists and, ultimately, were run off their feet by a Bayern team with greater reserves of talent and stamina. Crucially, they missed Bayern-bound starlet Mario Gotze through a thigh injury.

Wembley saw none of the customary cup final cat-and-mouse football. Both clubs launched themselves forward at pace as if this were 'just another' club duel in the Ruhr or Bavaria. Dortmund, with Marco Reus wandering across the face of the Bayern defence, were the more threatening in the first quarter. Robert Lewandowski thundered in a 25-metre drive which Manuel Neuer palmed over the bar. Then Bayern's goalkeeper stuck out his left foot to defy Jakub Blaszczykowski at close range at the expense of a further corner.

Bayern raced down to the other end and might have scored themselves. Dortmund were shown to be vulnerable in the air. Franck Ribery crossed from the left and Mario Mandzukic had a header tipped over by Roman Weidenfeller. Then Javi Martinez headed inches over from the corner.

Minutes later Arjen Robben darted free on the right and should have scored rather than allow Weidenfeller to deflect the ball for a corner.

By now Dortmund coach Jurgen Klopp, a permanent presence there, was in a frenzy of tension in the technical area. He was right to be worried. The longer the game went on, the more dangerous Bayern grew. Thomas Muller glanced a header wide from yet another right-wing corner, then Robben should have scored after losing his marker Mats Hummels. Instead his toe-poke for goal was blocked by Weidenfeller's face.

Dortmund's heroic goalkeeper-captain eventually was beaten on the hour mark. The ever-willing Robben moved to the left side, exchanged passes with Ribery, then provided the inch-perfect cross so Mandzukic could pop the ball home from close range.

Eight minutes later Dortmund drew level after Dante panicked and kicked Reus in the lower stomach. Lewandowski, who had missed a penalty against Bayern in the Bundesliga, stepped aside, so Ilkay Gundogan scored from the penalty spot.

Fatigue began to shred the teams' tactical discipline, but Bayern, with superior individual class, retained the edge. Ribery and Robben kept on running defiantly at the tiring Dortmund defence. When Ribery backheeled a long ball through the heart of defence, Robben skipped over two tackles and pushed the ball wide of Weidenfeller.

Robben thus made up for his penalty miss against Chelsea and was duly voted man of the match by UEFA's technical panel. The award was handed over by Sir Alex Ferguson who had once tried, in vain, to sign him for Manchester United.

Bayern were European champions for the first time since 2001, and a well-deserved fifth occasion in all.

A delirious Robben said: 'To provide the assist for the first goal and then score your own is like a dream, it's hard to believe. This is the peak, the greatest you can achieve.

'Also, it was the only thing we still really needed after the disappointment last year against Chelsea. That's three finals and you don't want the stamp of a loser so at last we did it today and we can forget about the other things a bit.'

Not for long. Coach Heynckes, heading for retirement in the knowledge that he would be succeeded by Pep Guardiola, conceded his players, 'need to let off steam, have a party,' but cautioned: 'From Tuesday we will be preparing again for our own cup final.'

They would win that match, 3-2 against Stuttgart, to leave Guardiola with an almost impossible challenge: How do you improve on the treble?

Dortmund coach Klopp was magnanimous in defeat. At the end of the game he walked out, alone, to salute the Dortmund fans in the east end of Wembley. Then he congratulated Heynckes, as a rival 'who really deserved to have such a success'.

Only once did the mask slip as Klopp reviewed a thrilling occasion: 'What the fans did was brilliant, the whole atmosphere was brilliant, this Olympic city was brilliant, we enjoyed all the Olympic Games, the sun shone, everything was great ... only the result was rubbish.'

SATURDAY 25 MAY
WEMBLEY

BAYERN MUNICH 2
MANDZUKIC 60, ROBBEN 89

BORUSSIA DORTMUND 1
GUNDOGAN 68 PEN

HT: 0-0. ATT: 86,298
REF: RIZZOLI (ITALY)

BAYERN:
NEUER – LAHM*, BOATENG, DANTE, ALABA - JAVI MARTINEZ, SCHWEINSTEIGER – ROBBEN, MULLER, RIBERY (LUIZ GUSTAVO 89) – MANDZUKIC (GOMEZ 90).
COACH: HEYNCKES.

BORUSSIA DORTMUND:
WEIDENFELLER* – PISZCZEK, SUBOTIC, HUMMELS, SCHMELZER - BENDER (SAHIN 90), GUNDOGAN - BLASZCZYKOWSKI (SCHIEBER 90), REUS, GROSSKREUTZ - LEWANDOWSKI.
COACH: KLOPP.

*CAPTAIN

BELOW: **CUP-WINNING BAYERN COACH JUPP HEYNCKES HEADS FOR RETIREMENT AS THE HAPPIEST MAN IN EUROPEAN FOOTBALL**

MADRID'S MASTERY

Europe's big spenders did not have it all their own way along the road to the first city derby final in the history of European Champions' Cup and UEFA Champions League.

But widespread – and expensive – the changes both on the pitch and on the bench illustrated the power of impatience. Barcelona brought in Brazilian superstar Neymar, a year earlier than planned, to defy transfer rivalry from Real Madrid who splashed a world record Đ100m on Tottenham's free-scoring, wide-roaming Welsh forward Gareth Bale.

On the managerial front, Barcelona imported Argentinian 'Tata' Martino to succeed the terminally ill Tito Vilanova, Madrid persuaded Italian Carlo Ancelotti to abandon his newly-crowned French champions Paris Saint-Germain and recent Barcelona hero Pep Guardiola ended his year's sabbatical by taking over from retiring Jupp Heynckes at the European champions Bayern Munich.

Meanwhile, long-serving Arsene Wenger was a satisfied manager, still in place after 17 years, as Arsenal trounced Fenerbahce 5-0 on aggregate in the play-off round. The European federation, UEFA, was happy, too. Fenerbahce had been playing only pending an appeal to the Court of Arbitration for Sport in the long-running Turkish match-fixing saga. The

Gunners spared the European federation the uncertainties which would have been threatened by Fenerbahce's presence in the group stage draw.

Arsenal were then drawn awkwardly alongside May's runners-up Borussia Dortmund, Rafael Benitez's Napoli and Marseille. Celtic, who had famously beaten Barcelona in Glasgow the previous season, were matched with the Catalan giants once again, along with two other former winners in Milan and Ajax.

David Moyes' Champions League bow with Manchester United was scheduled against Shakhtar Donetsk, Bayer Leverkusen and Real Sociedad, while free-spending neighbours City had to confront holders Bayern once more. As for the Madrid rivals, Real landed old adversaries Juventus, while Atletico were matched with two other clubs who, like them, had also lately lifted the UEFA Cup/Europa League – Porto and Zenit St Petersburg.

All the groups may have been attractive, but they were all comparatively predictable. Bayern, with Guardiola re-jigging tactics and personnel, had an erratic first half of the season. They collected the UEFA Supercup by defeating Chelsea after a penalty shootout, but then edged Manchester City to top Group D only on head-to-head goal difference. But they were fortunate that City's new manager, Manuel Pellegrini, had misread the rules. With City winning the last game 3-2 in Munich, the Chilean stayed cautious instead of pressing for further goals. One more goal would have removed Bayern's head-to-head advantage and thus the group placings.

Easy progress was the initial, deceptive happy start for Moyes at Manchester United, who kicked off with a 4-2 win over eventual group runners-up Bayer Leverkusen. His old Everton protégé Wayne Rooney, whom he had persuaded into staying at Old Trafford, scored twice.

The tightest finish was in Group F where Dortmund, Arsenal and Napoli all ended up on 12 points, before goal difference saw the Serie A outfit relegated to the Europa League. The od men out were Marseille, who finished bottom after losing all six games.

Elsewhere, Real Madrid were undefeated ahead of Galatasaray in Group B, while Atletico were unbeaten in

RIGHT: **NO PROBLEM FOR MANAGER DAVID MOYES AS MANCHESTER UNITED WIN 5-0 AWAY TO BAYER LEVERKUSEN**

topping Group G in front of Zenit. Other group winners were Paris Saint-Germain (Group C), Chelsea (Group E) and Barcelona (Group H), followed by respective runners-up Olympiacos, Schalke and Milan.

Manchester City's interest ended in the second round against Barcelona. Pellegrini had to watch the academic second leg from the stands in Camp Nou after being suspended by UEFA for a tirade at Swedish referee Jonas Ericsson after the opening 2-0 home defeat, with goals from Leo Messi (penalty) and Dani Alves. City also finished the game with 10 men, after Martin Demichelis had been sent off for conceding the penalty by tripping his compatriot Messi on the edge of the box. The spot-kick was Messi's first goal in European competition in England.

Pellegrini accused Ericsson of being 'not impartial' and thought, bizarrely, that the referee might have been trying to make up for an error against Barcelona in a tie against AC Milan in 2012. In fact City had cause to be grateful to the officials. They would have lost more heavily, but for a bad offside decision which denied Gerard Pique another Barcelona goal.

Similar initial away wins set up quarter-final places for Paris Saint-Germain, who beat Bayer Leverkusen, Bayern against Arsenal – for whom German midfielder Mesut Ozil missed a penalty – Atletico Madrid against Milan, Borussia Dortmund against Zenit and Real Madrid at Schalke.

Chelsea and Manchester United were the only away-day failures. Chelsea drew 1-1 in Turkey, at Galatasaray, who featured old Blues warhorse Didier Drogba, while United slipped to a 2-0 defeat against Olympiacos in Athens. But both English clubs progressed to the last eight. Chelsea won 2-0 at Stamford Bridge while a hat-trick from Robin Van Persie earned United a 3-0 win over Olympiacos. Only Chelsea made

BELOW: **EASY FOR REAL MADRID AS CRISTIANO RONALDO HOLDS OFF DANY NOUNKEU TO CLAIM THEIR SIXTH GOAL AGAINST GALATASARAY**

it to the semi-final, beating Paris Saint-Germain on the away goals rule.

United were held 1-1 at home by Bayern despite the expulsion of Bastian Schweinsteiger for tripping Rooney, but then lost 3-1 in Munich to goals from Mario Mandzukic, Thomas Muller and one-time United target Arjen Robben. An unlucky 13 days later and manager Moyes himself was gone, having failed to live up to the impossibility of matching Sir Alex Ferguson.

The quarter-finals' surprise was Atletico's ousting of Barcelona. The opener, at Camp Nou, saw Atletico's Brazilian substitute Diego fire unstoppably into the top corner from 30m to open the scoring before Andres Iniesta created an equaliser for Neymar. But Atletico went on to reach their first champions' semi-final for 40 years on the strength of a lone early goal from Koke back home in a dramatic opening spell when they also hit the posts three times.

Barcelona's pursuit of a seventh successive semi-final was all over and Atletico duly went all the way to Lisbon after overcoming Chelsea in the last four. Jose Mourinho's men appeared to hold the upper hand after holding Atletico goalless in the Estadio Vicente Calderon. But they had reckoned without the mixture of skill, spirit and resilience from Diego Simeone's tightly-forged team.

Chelsea took an early lead in front of their own fans at Stamford Bridge through Atletico 'old boy' Fernando Torres after Willian had outwitted two defenders deep on the right wing. But Simeone ordered an instant response. His players raised the tempo and were rewarded with an equaliser just before half-time. Juanfran crossed from the byline, with Chelsea's five-man back line off guard, and Adrian shot home after the ball bounced over the outstretched legs of both John Terry and Ashey Cole.

Chelsea were now losing on the away goals rule, so Mourinho enacted a positive substitution, with Samuel Eto'o replacing Ashley Cole. The switch produced a goal but at the wrong end. Eto'o, back defending, tripped Diego Costa to concede a penalty which the Chelsea transfer target converted. Chelsea's faint hopes were extinguished when Arda Turan scored a simple goal from close range after Juanfran's shot rebounded down off the crossbar. Simeone indulged in a Mourinho-style gallop down the touchline in celebration.

Atletico's man of the match, however, was Belgian keeper Thibaud Courtois, on loan to them from none other than Chelsea whose hope of having him excluded from the tie was quashed by UEFA.

The other side of the draw saw Real Madrid overcome the hoodoo which had once doomed them repeatedly against German opposition. After beating Dortmund in the quarter-final, they extracted revenge over Bayern Munich for the previous season's semi-final reverse.

When Madrid won only 1-0 at home they appeared to be at the mercy of Bayern and Guardiola, who had always held the edge over them during his all-conquering years as coach of Barcelona. In Munich, however, Ancelotti scored a tactical victory to set up what the Italian described later as 'the perfect game'. Madrid won 4-0 on the night – their first victory in Munich – to sweep majestically into the final 5-0 on aggregate.

Sergio Ramos scored with two early close-range headers from almost identical set-pieces before Ronaldo struck a third which was his record 15th in 10 games in the competition. The FIFA World Player of the Year then added the coup de grace with a teasing free kick in the last minute of the match which rolled beneath the Bayern wall.

Bayern thus succumbed to the jinx that no club has proved consistently powerful enough to win the Champions League two seasons in a row. The beating was also the heaviest suffered by Pep Guardiola in his senior coaching career.

The only disappointment for Madrid coach Carlo Ancelotti was that playmaker Xabi Alonso would miss the final after collecting a first-half yellow card. Alonso was still arguing with the referee after the final whistle when the rest of his teammates were celebrating.

A delirious Gareth Bale explained: 'This is why I came to the biggest club in the world - to win trophies and play in massive games. It's a fantastic result for us. We've been working hard, got our tactics right and deserved it.'

Bayern could not argue. For the Germans, as the club's chief executive and old hero Karl-Heinz Rummenigge admitted: 'This was a debacle.'

ABOVE: **THE SAFE HANDS OF ATLETICO GOALKEEPER THIBAUD COURTOIS DENY CHELSEA'S FERNANDO TORRES**

LEFT: **SERGIO RAMOS DIVES FORWARD TO HEAD HIS AND REAL MADRID'S SECOND GOAL PAST BAYERN KEEPER MANUEL NEUER IN THE SECOND LEG OF THE SEMI-FINAL IN MUNICH AS THE SPANIARDS MARCHED TO A 4-0 WIN ON THE NIGHT IN MUNICH**

LA DECIMA ULTIMATELY

Real Madrid finally secured their record-extending 10th European champions' crown, their long-awaited *La Decima*, but they could hardly have left it later against cross-city neighbours Atletico in a high-drama showdown in Lisbon.

Real won 4-1 after two tension-stamped hours. But the trophy had so very nearly been heading to the other end of Madrid. Atletico led 1-0 until beyond the end of the 90 minutes before a stoppage-time strike by Sergio Ramos cancelled out the advantage the *Colchoneros* had seized with a 36th-minute header from defender Diego Godin – whose goal, the previous week in Barcelona, had clinched the La Liga title for them.

So much, it seemed as the clock ran down, for Real's dream of rounding up a history lesson in the Estadio Benfica. But then Atletico failed to defend Luka Modric's right-wing corner, Sergio Ramos headed home and, in extra time, Gareth Bale, Marcelo and Cristiano Ronaldo struck thrice more.

Lisbon had been the scene of the first-ever tie of the original European Champions Cup in the autumn of 1955 (between Sporting and Partizan Belgrade); the first non-Spanish winners had been Benfica, in whose new home this final was staged; to bring the final back was appropriate in the year which marked the deaths of two of Benfica's great European Cup heroes, Eusebio and Mario Coluna. Bringing it all up to date, Real were being led in their pursuit of *La Decima* by the greatest Portuguese player of his era in Cristiano Ronaldo.

All the casualties from the previous weeks were fit to enter combat, with the exception of Atletico's Arda Turan and Real's Pepe. Diego Costa was judged recovered from a hamstring strain to partner David Villa in the Atletico attack. As for Real, Karim Benzema was also fit to lead their attack while Germany's Sami Khedira took over in the heart of midfield from suspended Xabi Alonso and Raphael Varane deputised for Pepe in central defence.

Costa was at the centre of the first drama but not as he had wanted. Ten minutes sufficed for him to understand the severity of his injury and he was substituted by Adrian Lopez. Coach Diego Simeone blamed himself later for misjudging the severity of Costa's inuury.

Atletico's challenge was to raise and maintain a phenomenal workrate. But it came at a price, with the odd space in defence left untended. The 33rd minute saw the first chink in that armour. Tiago pushed the ball into a space which was filled only by the onrushing Gareth Bale. His momentum took him flying onto the penalty box, but his shot was appallingly wide.

The significance of that miss was driven home three minutes later when Godin punished Real's failure to clear a right-wing corner to claim his eighth goal of the season, all of them headers.

Ronaldo, clearly not fully fit himelf, had been virtually absent from the entire first half. But, after the break and when Di Maria was fouled again, he had a free kick opportunity. The FIFA World Player of the Year saw his shot take a deflection and force a fine save from Thibaud Courtois.

Real made nothing of the corner, pushing coach Carlo Ancelotti into a double substitution, with Marcelo and Isco replacing Fabio Coentrao and Khedira. Marcelo's arrival proved decisive as his pace down the left began to run Atletico ragged. Ronaldo and Bale both went close but not close enough.

Atletico continued to defend like demons ... until the fourth minute of stoppage time when they failed to defend a Modric

RIGHT: **SERGIO RAMOS HEADS REAL MADRID'S LAST-MINUTE EQUALISER TO EARN EXTRA TIME IN LISBON**

SATURDAY 24 MAY
ESTADIO DO BENFICA, LISBON

REAL MADRID 4
SERGIO RAMOS 90, BALE 110,
MARCELO 118, RONALDO 120 (PEN)

ATLETICO DE MADRID 1
GODIN 38

HT: 0-1. ATT: 60,976
REF: KUIPERS (HOLLAND)

REAL MADRID:
CASILLAS* - CARVAJAL, VARANE,
SERGIO RAMOS, COENTRAO (MARCELO
59) - MODRIC, KHEDIRA (ISCO 59), DI
MARIA - BALE, BENZEMA (MORATA
79), RONALDO.
COACH: ANCELOTTI.

ATLETICO DE MADRID:
COURTOIS - JUANFRAN, MIRANDA,
GODIN, FILIPE LUIS (ALDERWEIRELD
82) - RAUL GARCIA (SOSA 65), GABI*,
TIAGO, KOKE - DIEGO COSTA (ADRIAN
LOPEZ 10), VILLA.
COACH: SIMEONE.

*CAPTAIN

LEFT: **GOALKEEPER CAPTAIN
IKER CASILLAS EXPRESSES
ALL OF MADRID'S DELIGHT
AND RELIEF IN FINALLY WINNING
LA DECIMA**

corner and Ramos struck the most dramatic equaliser to force extra time.

Now, at last, Real looked more like themselves and fatigue began to eat away at Atletico's resolve. They reached the midpoint in extra time still all-square, but after Di Maria ran free on the left and crossed for Bale, with a header, to convert at long last.

Now Atletico had no option but to come out of their shell and, of course, they left bigger gaps in their defence, for they paid a high price. First, in the 117th minute, Marcelo punished them with a run through the defence and a powerful shot to finish. Ronaldo also scored, from the penalty spot, after he was tripped. It was his 17th goal of the campaign. Injury had clearly hampered him. But the great players put their stamp on the big occasions and he had achieved that, as he had promised.

Ronaldo thus secured a record of his own, his total of 17 being three goals clear of the previous single-season competition mark, shared by Jose Altafini (Milan), Ruud Van Nistelrooy (Manchester United and Lionel Messi (Barcelona).

Ancelotti, whose third triumph as a coach equalled the record of Liverpool's Bob Paisley, said: 'On my first day at the Bernabeu, in the trophy room, I said to the president [Florentino Perez]: "There's one cup missing here, the 10th, let's try to get it this year" – so we did.'

MESSI AND RONALDO SET THE STANDARD

The entire football world had eagerly awaited the ultimate *Clasico* with Barcelona and Real Madrid in the Champions League final, but Juventus had other ideas.

Throughout the second decade of the 21st century, the incomparable talents of Lionel Messi and Cristiano Ronaldo had recreated, in football terms, the rivalry described by Ernest Hemingway in *The Dangerous Summer*, which tracked the 1959 rivalry of iconic matadors Luis Miguel Domínguín and Antonio Ordóñez.

For matches, months and seasons, Messi and his Barcelona had been duelling with Ronaldo and his Real Madrid for worldwide adoration, for the greatest crowns and, personally, for the most torrential flood of goals.

Anything the one achieved, the other would emulate. Ronaldo won the FIFA World Player crown in 2008 while still a Manchester United player; Messi was runner-up. A year later, in 2009, the roles were reversed as Messi

RIGHT: **EDEN HAZARD SCORED FROM THE PENALTY SPOT DURING CHELSEA'S 6-0 GROUP G HOME VICTORY OVER MARIBOR**

won his first World Player crown with Ronaldo as runner-up. In 2010, Messi won again, with Ronaldo not even in the top three; and in 2011 it was Messi for a third time with Ronaldo once again his runner-up.

Barcelona's Andres Iniesta interrupted the sequence in 2012, courtesy of his World Cup-winning goal for Spain, and then it was back to the status quo. Ronaldo was crowned in both 2013 and 2014, with Messi his closest rival. Not even Bayern Munich and Germany's World Cup-winning goalkeeper Manuel Neuer could split them in the latter ballot.

At the start of the 2014–15 campaign both men had summer irritants to overcome. At the 2014 World Cup finals, Messi and Argentina had reached the final, only to lose 1-0 after extra time to Germany. Receiving the best player award was no consolation. Ronaldo had played the tournament virtually on one leg and had been eliminated, with Portugal, in the group stage.

As the new Champions League group stage kicked off both men could count their enduring rivalry in awards.

Messi had been Champions League top scorer four times and leading marksman in both La Liga and the European Golden Boot on three occasions. Ronaldo, three years his senior, had been top scorer in the Champions League three times, in the Spanish league twice and had also carried off the Golden Boot for leading European

league marksman on three occasions. Both had scored in two Champions League finals, regularly topped 50 goals in a season and boasted career tallies of more than 400 goals.

The initial advantage in the 2014–15 race was with Ronaldo. He was one of six Real Madrid players to top-score in the Champions League – after Alfredo Di Stefano, Ferenc Puskas, Michel, Raul and Fernando Morientes – and he underscored his prowess by scoring both Madrid's goals in their classy 2–0 victory over Sevilla in the UEFA Super Cup in Cardiff.

No one was surprised to see both Barcelona and Madrid skip through the group stage. Barcelona won five games to top Group F ahead of Paris Saint-Germain, Ajax Amsterdam and surprise qualifiers APOEL of Cyprus. The Catalans scored 15 goals (Messi scoring eight of them) and conceded five, while their one slip-up was a 3–2 defeat away to PSG. Madrid won all six of their Group B games, against Basel, Liverpool and Ludogorets Razgrad from Bulgaria. They scored 16 goals (Ronaldo five) and conceded only two.

Similarly Spanish champions Atletico Madrid commanded Group A ahead of unheralded and unfancied Juventus, but Bilbao were relegated into the Europa League. Germany was the only league to send a quartet through to the knockout stages – group winners Bayern

LEFT: **LUIS SUAREZ SCORES THE FIRST OF HIS TWO GOALS FOR BARCELONA AS THEY BEAT MANCHESTER CITY IN THE SECOND ROUND FIRST LEG**

Munich and Borussia Dortmund, plus runners-up Bayer Leverkusen and Schalke. England 'lost' Liverpool, but Arsenal, Chelsea and Manchester City all progressed.

Significantly, Arsenal and City were both 'only' runners-up, while Chelsea won Group G after reinforcing their squad by ripping star goalkeeper Thibaut Courtois, leftback Filipe Luis and prolific, £40m Diego Costa out of last season's runners-up Atletico Madrid. Chelsea, Real Madrid and Porto were the only unbeaten group winners.

Manchester City's punishment for their runners-up status was to be drawn against Barcelona for the second year running. As had been the case the previous season, Barcelona again won with something to spare. Messi set up early goals for Uruguayan Luis Suarez – on his first return to England since leaving Liverpool – and saw keeper Joe Hart save a late penalty. Sergio Aguero, his Argentina World Cup team-mate, claimed City's consolation goal in a 3-1 aggregate defeat.

Real Madrid and Ronaldo had a scary few moments before overcoming Schalke. Ronaldo and Marcelo secured a 2-0 win in the Ruhr, but sloppy defending cost Real a 4-3 home defeat, despite two goals from Ronaldo. Madrid endured a tense last six minutes after their former Dutch striker Klaas-Jan Huntelaar struck a late German winner on the night.

Complacency was even more costly for Arsenal against manager Arsene Wenger's first club, Monaco. He owned up to 'suicidal defending' as the cause for a 3-1 home defeat. The Gunners went on to record a 2-0 away victory in the second leg, but were knocked out of the competition on the away-goals rule. PSG claimed another success for France over England. Chelsea held them 1-1 at home, before the Parisians claimed a 2-2 draw at Stamford Bridge to win on away goals – despite the expulsion of Sweden spearhead Zlatan Ibrahimovic. It was the second time in three years that no English club had made it to the quarter-finals.

The remaining four slots were taken up by: Juventus (a 5-1 aggregate despatch of Dortmund); Atletico Madrid (on penalties against Leverkusen after the teams were locked at 1-1 after two matches); Porto (5-1 v Basel); and Bayern Munich (7-0 v Shakhtar). All of the Bayern goals came in the second leg, and there were seven different scorers, too.

Prospects of the ultimate Spanish Clasico were maintained by the quarter-final draw, which kept Barcelona and Madrid apart. Elsewhere, almost unnoticed, Juventus, on their way to a fourth successive Italian crown, edged Monaco 1-0 thanks to a first-leg penalty from Chilean Arturo Vidal, while Bayern recovered from a 3-1 defeat in Portugal to batter

RIGHT: **JUVENTUS STRIKER ALVARO MORATA IS UNMOVED AFTER SCORING THE GOAL THAT DEFEATED HIS FORMER CLUB REAL MADRID IN THE SEMI-FINAL SECOND LEG AT THE BERNABEU**

Porto 6-1 in the return – Poland centre-forward Robert Lewandowski scored twice.

Barcelona, to the satisfaction of coach Luis Enrique, were masterful against PSG. They won 3-1 in Paris and 2-0 at home and Messi did not score any of the five, which fell instead to Brazil superstar Neymar (three) and Suarez (two). Iniesta was creatively dominant in both legs.

Things were much tougher for Real Madrid, however. They had been drawn against cross-city rivals Atletico, who had had the better of them in every meeting between the two sides over the previous two years, with one notable exception – the previous season's Champions League final. Real had also beaten Atletico in the 1959 semi-finals and they maintained their European hegemony by winning 1-0 at home after battling to a goalless draw in the first leg at the Estadio Calderon. It was tight.

Real had been hit badly by injuries to Bale, schemer Luka Modric and France centre-forward Karim Benzema. They pressed all the way, but Atletico resisted superbly until Arda Turan was sent off in the closing stages. Gifted a little more space, Ronaldo skipped down the left and saw his low cross steered home by Javier Hernandez, who was deputizing for Benzema.

That was probably the finest moment in Chicharito's European career. He had joined Madrid on loan in January from Manchester United, with whom he had reached a nadir the previous autumn when he was substituted during a League Cup defeat by third division MK Dons.

UEFA's semi-final draw again kept the Spanish giants apart, matching Barcelona with their old boss Pep Guardiola and Bayern, while Madrid confronted Juventus, the first club to have beaten them in Madrid in Europe, all the way back in 1962. Apparently, the Berlin stage was properly set for a Barcelona-Real Madrid showdown, but Juve coach Massimiliano Allegri was plotting an ambush.

Barcelona came through surprisingly and impressively against Bayern, whose coach, Pep Guardiola, drew no immediate consolation from the knowledge that that he had laid the Barcelona foundations for his own embarrassment.

His old team won crushingly in the Camp Nou, 3-0 thanks to goals from Messi (two) and Neymar – all were scored in the final 13 minutes. They lost 3-2 in the Allianz-Arena, but carried the tie 5-3 on aggregate for a victory that was never in doubt, despite a quick start and then a late rally from the German champions.

Mehdi Benatia powered home a seventh-minute header, but a quick double from Neymar – following assists from first Lionel Messi and then Luis Suarez – effectively sank

any Bayern hopes of an improbable comeback.

The German club did at least save their honour in front of their own fans, with late strikes from Robert Lewandowski and Thomas Muller, but Guardiola knew who had made the difference, saying: 'Messi is incredible, back to his best as when I used to train him. He's the best player of all time. I can compare him with Pele.'

Madrid, noting the result, believed that the next night they would secure the right to provide the opposition to Barcelona and Messi in Berlin. They had lost their own first leg only 2-1 away to Juventus in Turin, following goals from Alvaro Morata and the former Manchester City renegade Carlos Tevez.

All they needed back in the Estadio Bernabeu was one goal. It arrived, too, in the 22nd minute, from a penalty converted by Ronaldo. Madrid led on the away-goals rule … but only for half an hour. In the 57th minute, Morata added his name to the list of discarded centre-forwards who have come home to embarrass Madrid by equalizing.

Morata, who signed for Juventus from Real Madrid the previous summer after failing to impress coach Carlo Ancelotti, brushed off a half-hearted challenge from Toni Kroos to shoot Juventus on level terms. Press as they might, Madrid found a second goal to force even extra time beyond them. Juventus, disciplined, solid and committed, and backed up by veteran Gigi Buffon in goal, were deserved winners.

Messi and Ronaldo, along with Neymar, would all finish the Champions League campaign on ten goals apiece, but the ultimate Clasico would have to wait for another day and another season.

ABOVE: **PEP GUARDIOLA, STANDING IN THE VIISTORS' TECHNICAL AREA AT THE CAMP NOU, HAS AN AIR OF RESIGNATION AS HE WATCHES HIS FORMER CLUB BARCELONA DEFEAT HIS PRESENT ONE, BAYERN MUNICH 3-0 IN THE SEMI-FINAL FIRST LEG**

BARCELONA IN A CLASS OF THEIR OWN

Barcelona secured their third Champions League title in six years and their fifth overall to provide a welcome distraction from the political chaos occurring off the pitch.

The Catalans outclassed Juventus 3-1 in Berlin's first Champions League final thanks to goals from Ivan Rakitic, Luis Suarez and Neymar. Juventus never threatened to mark the 30th anniversary of the Heysel disaster with an against-the-odds success. They were level briefly, through Alvaro Morata, but Barcelona's class and creative brilliance saw them crowned worthy European champions.

At least the occasion and the swagger of some of Barcelona's football provided a welcome respite after ten days of turbulence, in which a multi-layered corruption fire had raged through football's world federation, FIFA, and had burned down everything from the World Cup bidding process to commercial deals and even the hitherto apparently immovable president, Sepp Blatter.

UEFA's football leaders, including president Michel Platini, had taken centre stage in the FIFA crisis, but all those issues were off limits in Berlin to allow the game itself, and the most admired of club teams, to reclaim precedence. Sentiment had its place as well, in the form of Barcelona's veteran captain Xavi. He emerged from the subs' bench late on in his competition-record 151st game to carry off the cup before heading to Al Sadd in Qatar.

Juventus, resiliently as they had performed, conceded later that they had exceeded their own expectations not only in reaching the final but also by clinging on in it, despite two exhilarating bursts of Barcelona wizardry at the start of each half. In the end courage was not enough, but it never could be on the big occasion against any team with an attacking triumvirate consisting of Lionel Messi, Luis Suarez and Neymar.

Coach Massimiliano Allegri acknowledged as much at the end of his first season with Juve, regretting only the result, not the performance. Allegri, brought in after Antonio Conte took the Italy job, added: 'We can come out of this final with greater self-esteem, greater confidence and awareness of what we can do in European competition.'

Barcelona's so-called 'MSN' strike force had claimed 120 goals between them over the course of the season, yet, strangely, it was Croat midfielder Rakitic who sidefooted Barcelona ahead with little more than three minutes on the clock. With the exception of Suarez, all the other nine Barcelona outfield players contributed to the move.

They could have scored more, but Neymar shot just too high

RIGHT: **LUIS SUAREZ FOLLOWS UP TO SCORE BARCELONA'S SECOND GOAL OF THE 2015 FINAL AFTER GIGI BUFFON HAD ONLY PARRIED LIONEL MESSI'S SHOT**

SATURDAY, 6 JUNE
OLYMPIASTADION, BERLIN

BARCELONA 3
RAKITIC 4, SUAREZ 68, NEYMAR 90

JUVENTUS 1
MORATA 55

HT: 1-0. ATT: 70,442
REF: CAKIR (TURKEY)

BARCELONA:
TER STEGEN - DANI ALVES, PIQUE,
MASCHERANO, JORDI ALBA - RAKITIC
(MATHIEU 90), BUSQUETS, INIESTA*
(XAVI 78) - MESSI, SUAREZ (PEDRO
90), NEYMAR.
COACH: LUIS ENRIQUE.

JUVENTUS:
BUFFON* - LICHTSTEINER, BARZAGLI,
BONUCCI, EVRA (COMON 89) -
MARCHISIO, PIRLO, POGBA - VIDAL
(PEREYRA 79) - TEVEZ, MORATA
(LLORENTE 85).
COACH: ALLEGRI.

*CAPTAIN

LEFT: **SOUTH AMERICAN CELEBRATION TIME FOR BARCELONA IN BERLIN FOR (FROM LEFT) URUGUAY'S LUIS SUAREZ, LIONEL MESSI OF ARGENTINA AND BRAZILIAN NEYMAR**

and Dani Alves had a snap-shot palmed away by Juve's veteran goalkeeper and captain Gigi Buffon. The Catalans might even have had a penalty when Stephan Lichtsteiner blocked a Neymar cross between his forearm and his thigh.

Juventus, having emerged from an initial hurricane at a cost of only one goal, began to find their own attacking feet early in the second half when Alvaro Morata equalized after a neat backheel from Claudio Marchisio allowed Lichsteiner to cross. Carlos Tevez's initial shot, on the turn, was parried by Marc-Andre ter Stegen, but the ball fell to Morata, who fired home. Thus the former Real Madrid player was, ironically, the only Spaniard on the scoresheet.

Suddenly Juve had their tails up and their veteran playmaker, Andrea Pirlo, began to find space in which to work his own magic. But the moment was all too brief for the 'Old Lady' of Turin, as Juventus's newfound exuberance left them exposed at the back.

In the 67th minute, Barcelona broke at ferocious speed and Rakitic found Messi in space. The Argentinian ran intimidatingly at the Juve defence, unleashed a fierce low drive that Buffon could only push away and Suarez accelerated away from Patrice Evra to follow up for his seventh goal in ten games.

Almost immediately Barcelona might have had a third, but Neymar was furious to see Turkish referee Cuneyt Cakir rule the goal out on the grounds that the Brazilian superstar's flying header had deflected beyond Buffon off his own arm. Certainly his arm was outstretched, but only in the momentum of the action and, he felt, could hardly count as deliberate.

Not that he was denied for long. In the last minute of stoppage time, with Juventus strung out upfield, the former Santos forward ran away with as much time and space as he needed to enhance a scoreline that now reflected the gap between the teams more realistically: Juventus were admirable runners-up, but Barcelona were overwhelmingly deserving champions.

As man of the match Iniesta said: 'It's been a spectacular day for us, for FC Barcelona and for our supporters. Six years ago we won the treble and thought it would be impossible to repeat, yet now we've done it again. It makes my hair stand on end to look back and realize how much we have achieved.'

Barcelona, remarkably, had achieved the unique feat of becoming the only club in the 59 years of the European Cup to defeat the Dutch, English, Spanish, French, German and Italian champions in the same season.

As coach Luis Enrique said: 'This was our 60th match this season. We have lost only six and had four draws. These figures alone show this has been one of the greatest seasons of even a club like Barcelona.'

60 YEARS IN FIGURES

More than 6,000 matches have been played between the launch of the European Champions Club Cup in 1955 and the Berlin Final between Barcelona and Juventus 60 years later. The drama inbetween has created a raft of statistics which, alone, would fill several encyclopedias. One complication for statisticians has been a revising of records based only on matches since the Champions League transformation of the competition in the early 1990s.

RIGHT: **ALFREDO DI STEFANO OF REAL MADRID IN ACTION AGAINST EGYPT'S ZAMALEK IN CAIRO'S BRAND-NEW STADIUM, MARCH 1961**

Records

EUROPEAN CUP RECORDS (1955-1970)

1955-56
Semi-finals:
Real Madrid bt Milan 4-2, 1-2 (5-4 on agg)
Reims bt Hibernian 2-0, 1-0 (3-0 on agg)
Final: Real Madrid bt Reims 4-3
Top scorer: Milos Milutinovic (Partizan Belgrade), 8 goals

1956-67
Semi-finals:
Real Madrid bt Manchester United 3-1, 2-2 (5-3 on agg)
Fiorentina bt Red Star Belgrade 1-0, 0-0 (1-0 on agg)
Final: Real Madrid bt Fiorentina 2-0
Top scorer: Dennis Viollet (Manchester United), 9 goals

1957-58
Semi-finals:
Real Madrid bt Sevilla 8-0, 2-2 (10-2 on agg)
Milan bt Manchester United 1-2, 4-0 (5-2 on agg)
Final: Real Madrid bt Milan 3-2 aet
Top scorer: Alfredo Di Stefano (Real Madrid), 10 goals

1958-59
Semi-finals:
Real Madrid bt Atletico Madrid 2-1, 0-1, 2-1 (playoff, after 2-2 on agg)
Reims bt Young Boys 1-0, 0-3 (3-1 on agg)
Final: Real Madrid bt Reims 2-0
Top scorer: Just Fontaine (Reims), 10 goals

1959-60
Semi-finals:
Real Madrid bt Barcelona 3-1, 3-1 (6-2 on agg)
Eintracht Frankfurt bt Rangers 6-1, 6-3 (12-4 on agg)
Final: Real Madrid bt Eintracht Frankfurt 7-3
Top scorer: Ferenc Puskas (Real Madrid), 12 goals

1960-61
Semi-finals:
Benfica bt Rapid Vienna 3-0, 1-1 (4-1 on agg)
Barcelona bt Hamburg 1-0, 1-2, 1-0 (playoff, after 2-2 on agg)
Final: Benfica bt Barcelona 3-2
Top scorer: Jose Aguas (Benfica), 10 goals

1961-62
Semi-finals:
Benfica bt Tottenham Hotspur 3-1, 1-2 (4-3 on agg)
Real Madrid bt Standard Liege 4-0, 2-0 (6-0 on agg)
Final: Benfica bt Real Madrid 5-3
Top scorer: Heinz Strehl (Nurnberg), 8 goals

1962-63
Semi-finals:
Milan bt Dundee 5-1, 0-1 (5-2 on agg)
Benfica bt Feyenoord 0-0, 3-1 (3-1 on agg)
Final: Milan bt Benfica 2-1
Top scorer: Jose Altafini (Milan), 14 goals

1963-64
Semi-finals:
Internazionale bt Borussia Dortmund 2-2, 2-0 (4-2 on agg)
Real Madrid bt FC Zurich 2-1, 6-0 (8-1 on agg)
Final: Internazionale bt Real Madrid 3-1
Top scorers: Vladimir Kovacevic (Partizan), Sandro Mazzola (Inter), Ferenc Puskas (Real Madrid), 7 goals each

1964-65
Semi-finals:
Internazionale bt Liverpool 1-3, 3-0 (4-3 on agg)
Benfica bt Vasas Gyor 1-0, 4-0 (5-0 on agg)
Final: Internazionale bt Benfica 1-0
Top scorers: Eusebio (Benfica), Jose Torres (Benfica), 9 goals each

1965-66
Semi-finals:
Real Madrid bt Internazionale 1-0, 1-1 (2-1 on agg)
Partizan Belgrade bt Manchester United 2-0, 0-1 (2-1 on agg)
Final: Real Madrid bt Partizan Belgrade 2-1
Top scorers: Florian Albert (Ferencvaros), Eusebio (Benfica), 7 goals each

1966-67
Semi-finals:
Celtic bt Dukla Prague 3-1, 0-0 (3-1 on agg)
Internazionale bt CSKA Sofia 1-1, 1-1, 1-0 (playoff, after 2-2 on agg)
Final: Celtic bt Internazionale 2-1
Top scorers: Jurgen Piepenburg (Vorwarts), Paul Van Himst (Anderlecht), 6 goals each

1967-68
Semi-finals:
Manchester United bt Real Madrid 1-0, 3-3 (4-3 on agg)
Benfica bt Juventus 2-0, 1-0 (3-0 on agg)
Final: Manchester United bt Benfica 4-1 aet
Top scorer: Eusebio (Benfica), 6 goals

1968-69
Semi-finals:
Milan bt Manchester United 2-0, 0-1 (2-1 on agg)
Ajax bt Spartak Trnava 3-0, 0-2 (3-2 on agg)
Final: Milan bt Ajax 4-1
Top scorer: Denis Law (Manchester United), 9 goals

1969-70
Semi-finals:
Feyenoord bt Legia Warsaw 0-0, 2-0 (2-0 on agg)
Celtic bt Leeds United 1-0, 2-1 (3-1 on agg)
Final: Feyenoord bt Celtic 2-1 aet
Top scorers: Mick Jones (Leeds United), Ove Kindvall (Feyenoord), 7 goals each

FAR RIGHT: MANCHESTER UNITED CAPTAIN BOBBY CHARLTON RAISES THE EUROPEAN CUP IN TRIUMPH AT WEMBLEY IN 1968

EUROPEAN CUP RECORDS (1971–1984)

1970-71

Semi-finals:

Ajax bt Atletico Madrid 0-1, 3-0 (3-1 on agg)

Panathinaikos bt Red Star Belgrade 1-4, 3-0 (away goals, agg 4-4)

Final: Ajax bt Panathinaikos 2-0

Top scorers: Antonis Antoniadis (Panathinaikos), 10 goals

1971-72

Semi-finals:

Ajax bt Benfica 1-0, 0-0 (1-0 on agg)

Internazionale bt Celtic 0-0, 0-0 (5-4 on pens, agg 0-0)

Final: Ajax bt Internazionale 2-0

Top scorers: Johan Cruyff (Ajax), Antal Dunai (Ujpest Dozsa), Lou Macari (Celtic), Sylvester Takac (Standard Liege), 5 goals each

1972-73

Semi-finals:

Ajax bt Real Madrid 2-1, 1-0 (3-1 on agg)

Juventus bt Derby County 3-1, 0-0 (3-1 on agg)

Final: Ajax bt Juventus 1-0

Top scorer: Gerd Muller (Bayern Munich), 12 goals

1973-74

Semi-finals:

Bayern Munich bt Ujpest Dozsa 1-1, 3-0 (4-1 on agg)

Atletico Madrid bt Celtic 0-0, 2-0 (2-0 on agg)

Final: Bayern Munich bt Atletico 4-0 (replay after 1-1 aet)

Top scorers: Gerd Muller (Bayern Munich), 8 goals

1974-75

Semi-finals:

Bayern Munich bt Saint-Etienne 0-0, 2-0 (2-0 on agg)

Leeds United bt Barcelona 2-1, 1-1 (3-2 on agg)

Final: Bayern Munich bt Leeds United 2-0

Top scorers: Eduard Markarov (Ararat Yerevan), Gerd Muller (Bayern Munich), 5 goals each

1975-76

Semi-finals:

Bayern Munich bt Real Madrid 1-1, 2-0 (3-1 on agg)

Saint-Etienne bt PSV Eindhoven 1-0, 0-0 (1-0 on agg)

Final: Bayern Munich bt Saint-Etienne 1-0

Top scorer: Jupp Heynckes (Borussia Mg), 6 goals

1976-77

Semi-finals:

Liverpool bt FC Zurich 3-1, 3-0 (6-1 on agg)

Borussia Moenchengladbach bt Kiev Dynamo 0-1, 2-0 (2-1 on agg)

Final: Liverpool bt Borussia Moenchengladbach 3-1

Top scorers: Franco Cucinotta (Zurich), Gerd Muller (Bayern Munich), 5 goals each

1977-78

Semi-finals:

Liverpool bt Borussia Moenchengladbach 1-2, 3-0 (4-2 on agg)

Club Brugge bt Juventus 0-1, 2-0 (2-1 on agg)

Final: Liverpool bt Club Brugge 1-0

Top scorer: Allan Simonsen (Borussia Mg), 5 goals

1978-79

Semi-finals:

Nottingham Forest bt FC Koln 3-3, 1-0, (4-3 on agg)

Malmo bt FK Austria 0-0, 1-0 (1-0 on agg)

Final: Nottingham Forest bt Malmo 1-0

Top scorer: Claudio Sulser (Grasshopper), 11 goals

1979-80

Semi-finals:

Nottingham Forest bt Ajax 2-0, 0-1 (2-1 on agg)

Hamburg bt Real Madrid 0-2, 5-1 (5-3 on agg)

Final: Nottingham Forest bt Hamburg 1-0

Top scorer: Soren Lerby (Ajax), 10 goals

1980-81

Semi-finals:

Liverpool bt Bayern Munich 0-0, 1-1 (away goals, agg 1-1)

Real Madrid bt Internazionale 2-0, 0-1 (2-1 on agg)

Final: Liverpool bt Real Madrid 1-0

Top scorers: Terry McDermott (Liverpool), Karl-Heinz Rummenigge (Bayern Munich), Graeme Souness (Liverpool), 6 goals each

1981-82

Semi-finals:

Aston Villa bt Anderlecht 1-0, 0-0 (1-0 on agg)

Bayern Munich bt CSKA Sofia 3-4, 4-0 (7-4 on agg)

Final: Aston Villa bt Bayern Munich 1-0

Top scorer: Dieter Hoeness (Bayern Munich), 7 goals

1982-83

Semi-finals:

Hamburg bt Real Sociedad 1-1, 2-1 (3-2 on agg)

Juventus bt Widzew Lodz 2-0, 2-2 (4-2 on agg)

Final: Hamburg bt Juventus 1-0

Top scorer: Paolo Rossi (Juventus), 6 goals

1983-84

Semi-finals:

Liverpool bt Dinamo Bucharest 1-0, 2-1 (3-1 on agg)

Roma bt Dundee United 0-2, 3-0 (3-2 on agg)

Final: Liverpool bt Roma 1-1 aet, 4-2 on pens

Top scorer: Viktor Sokol (Minsk Dinamo), 6 goals

FAR RIGHT: **EMLYN HUGHES CELEBRATES AS LIVERPOOL WIN THEIR FIRST EUROPEAN CUP IN ROME IN 1977**

EUROPEAN CUP RECORDS (1985-1998)

1984-85

Semi-finals:

Juventus bt Bordeaux 3-0, 0-2 (3-2 on agg)

Liverpool bt Panathinaikos 4-0, 1-0 (5-0 on agg)

Final: Juventus bt Liverpool 1-0

Top scorers: Torbjorn Nilsson (IFK), Michel Platini (Juventus), 7 goals each

1985-86

Semi-finals:

Steaua Bucharest bt Anderlecht 0-1, 3-0 (3-1 on agg)

Barcelona bt IFK Gothenburg 0-3, 3-0 (5-4 on pens, agg 3-3)

Final: Steaua Bucharest bt Barcelona 0-0 aet, 2-0 on pens

Top scorer: Torbjorn Nilsson (IFK), 7 goals

1986-87

Semi-finals:

FC Porto bt Dynamo Kiev 2-1, 2-1 (4-2 on agg)

Bayern Munich bt Real Madrid 4-1, 0-1 (4-2 on agg)

Final: FC Porto bt Bayern Munich 2-1

Top scorer: Borislav Cvetkovic (Red Star), 7 goals

1987-88

Semi-finals:

PSV Eindhoven bt Real Madrid 1-1, 0-0 (away goals agg 1-1)

Benfica bt Steaua Bucharest 0-0, 2-0 (2-0 on agg)

Final: PSV Eindhoven bt Benfica 0-0 aet, 6-5 on pens

Top scorers: Jean-Marc Ferreri (Bordeaux), Gheorghe Hagi (Steaua), Rabah Madjer (Porto), Ally McCoist (Rangers), Michel (Real Madrid), Jose Rui Aguas (Benfica), 4 goals each

1988-89

Semi-finals:

Milan bt Real Madrid 1-1, 5-0 (6-1 on agg)

Steaua Bucharest bt Galatasaray 4-0, 1-1 (5-1 on agg)

Final: Milan bt Steaua Bucharest 4-0

Top scorer: Marco Van Basten (Milan), 9 goals

1989-90

Semi-finals:

Milan bt Bayern Munich 1-0, 1-2 (away goals agg 2-2)

Benfica bt Marseille 1-2, 1-0 (away goals agg 2-2)

Final: Milan bt Benfica 1-0

Top scorers: Jean-Pierre Papin (Marseille), Romario (PSV), 6 goals each

1990-91

Semi-finals:

Red Star Belgrade bt Bayern Munich 2-1, 2-2 (4-3 on agg)

Marseille bt Moscow Spartak 3-1, 2-1 (5-2 on agg)

Final: Red Star Belgrade bt Marseille 0-0, 5-3 on pens

Top scorers: Peter Pacult (Tirol), Jean-Pierre Papin (Marseille), 6 goals each

1991-92

Semi-finals – group-winners were deemed to be winning semi-finalists this term:

Group I: Sampdoria 8pts, Red Star 6, Anderlecht 6, Panathinaikos 4

Group II: Barcelona 9pts, Sparta Prague 6, Benfica 5, Kiev Dynamo 4

Final: Barcelona bt Sampdoria 1-0 aet

Top scorers: Jean-Pierre Papin (Marseille), Sergei Yuran (Benfica), 7 goals each

1992-93

Semi-finals – group-winners were deemed to be winning semi-finalists this term:

Group I: Marseille 9pts, Rangers 8, Club Brugge 5, CSKA Moscow 2

Group II: Milan 12pts, IFK Gothenburg 6, FC Porto 5, PSV Eindhoven 1

Final: Marseille bt Milan 1

Top scorer: Romario (PSV), 7 goals

1993-94

Semi-finals:

Milan bt Monaco 3-0 (single match)

Barcelona bt FC Porto 3-0 (single match)

Final: Milan bt Barcelona 4-0

Top scorers: Ronald Koeman (Barcelona), Wynton Rufer (Werder Bremen), 8 goals each

1994-95

Semi-finals:

Ajax bt Bayern Munich 0-0, 5-2 (5-2 on agg)

Milan bt Paris Saint-Germain 2-0, 1-0 (3-0 on agg)

Final: Ajax Amsterdam bt Milan 1-0

Top scorer: George Weah (Paris Saint-Germain), 8 goals

1995-96

Semi-finals:

Juventus bt Nantes 2-0, 2-3 (4-3 on agg)

Ajax bt Panathinaikos 0-1, 3-0 (3-1 on agg)

Final: Juventus bt Ajax 1-0

Top scorer: Jari Litmanen (Ajax), 9 goals

1996-97

Semi-finals:

Juventus bt Ajax 2-1, 4-1 (6-2 on agg)

Borussia Dortmund bt Manchester United 1-0, 1-0 (2-0 on agg)

Final: Borussia Dortmund bt Juventus 3-1

Top scorer: Ally McCoist (Rangers), 6 goals

1997-98

Semi-finals:

Juventus bt Monaco 4-1, 2-3 (6-4 on agg)

Real Madrid bt Borussia Dortmund 2-0, 0-0 (2-0 on agg)

Final: Real Madrid bt Juventus 1-0

Top scorer: Alessandro Del Piero (Juventus), 10 goals

FAR RIGHT: ONE OF THE FINEST FINAL DISPLAYS WAS STAGED BY MILAN IN BEATING BARCELONA 4-0 IN ATHENS IN 1994

CHAMPIONS LEAGUE RECORDS (1999-2012)

1998-99
Semi-finals:

Manchester United bt Juventus 1-1, 3-2 (4-3 on agg)

Bayern Munich bt Kiev Dynamo 3-3, 1-0 (4-3 on agg)

Final: Manchester United bt Bayern Munich 2-1

Top scorer: Andriy Shevchenko (Kiev Dynamo), 10 goals

1999-2000
Semi-finals:

Valencia bt Barcelona 4-1, 1-2 (5-3 on agg)

Real Madrid bt Bayern Munich 2-0, 1-2 (3-2 on agg)

Final: Real Madrid bt Valencia 3-0

Top scorers: Mateja Kezman (Partizan Belgrade), Mikhail Mikholap (Skonto Riga), 6 goals each

2000-01
Semi-finals:

Bayern Munich bt Real Madrid 1-0, 2-1 (3-1 on agg)

Valencia bt Leeds 0-0, 3-0 (3-0 on agg)

Final: Bayern Munich bt Valencia 1-1 aet, 5-4 on pens

Top scorer: Raul (Real Madrid), 7 goals

2001-02
Semi-finals:

Real Madrid bt Barcelona 2-0, 1-1 (3-1 on agg)

Bayer Leverkusen bt Manchester United 2-2, 1-1 (away goals, agg 3-3)

Final: Real Madrid bt Bayer Leverkusen 2-1

Top scorer: Ruud Van Nistelrooy (Manchester United), 10 goals

2002-03
Semi-finals:

Juventus bt Real Madrid 1-2, 3-1 (4-3 on agg)

Milan bt Internazionale 0-0, 1-1 (away goals, agg 1-1)

Final: Milan bt Juventus 0-0 aet, 3-2 on pens

Top scorer: Ruud Van Nistelrooy (Manchester United), 14 goals

2003-04
Semi-finals:

Monaco bt Chelsea 3-1, 2-2 (5-3 on agg)

Porto bt Deportivo La Coruna 0-0, 1-0 (1-0 on agg)

Final: FC Porto bt Monaco 3-0

Top scorer: Fernando Morientes (Monaco), 9 goals

2004-05
Semi-finals:

Liverpool bt Chelsea 0-0, 1-0 (1-0 on agg)

Milan bt PSV Eindhoven 2-0, 1-3 (away goals, agg 3-3)

Final: Liverpool bt Milan 3-3 aet, 3-2 on pens

Top scorer: Ruud Van Nistelrooy (Manchester United), 8 goals

2005-06
Semi-finals:

Arsenal bt Villareal 1-0, 0-0 (1-0 on agg)

Barcelona bt Milan 1-0, 0-0 (1-0 on agg)

Final: Barcelona bt Arsenal 2-1

Top scorer: Andriy Shevchenko (Milan), 9 goals

2006-07
Semi-finals:

Milan bt Manchester United 2-3, 3-0 (5-3 on agg)

Liverpool bt Chelsea 0-1, 1-0 aet (4-1 on pens, 1-1 agg)

Final: Milan bt Liverpool 2-1

Top scorer: Kaka (Milan), 10 goals

2007-08
Semi-finals:

Chelsea bt Liverpool 1-1, 3-2 (4-3 on agg)

Manchester United bt Barcelona 0-0, 1-0 (1-0 on agg)

Final: Chelsea bt Manchester United 1-1 (6-5 on penalties)

Top scorer: Cristiano Ronaldo (Manchester United), 8 goals

2008-09
Semi-finals:

Barcelona bt Chelsea 0-0, 1-1 (on away goals)

Manchester United bt Arsenal 1-0, 3-1 (4-1 on agg)

Final: Barcelona bt Manchester United 2-0

Top scorer: Lionel Messi (Barcelona), 9 goals

2009-10
Semi-finals:

Internazionale bt Barcelona 3-1, 0-1 (3-2 on agg)

Bayern Munich bt Lyon 1-0, 3-0 (4-0 on agg)

Final: Internazionale bt Bayern Munich 2-0

Top scorer: Lionel Messi (Barcelona), 8 goals

2010-11
Semi-finals:

Manchester United bt Schalke 2-0, 4-1 (6-1 on agg)

Barcelona bt Real Madrid 2-0, 1-1 (3-1 on agg)

Final: Barcelona bt Manchester United 3-1

Top scorer: Lionel Messi (Barcelona), 12 goals

2011-12
Semi-finals:

Bayern Munich bt Real Madrid 2-1, 1-2 (3-1 on penalties)

Chelsea bt Barcelona 1-0, 2-2 (3-2 on agg)

Final: Chelsea bt Bayern Munich 1-1 (4-3 on penalties)

Top scorer: Lionel Messi (Barcelona), 14 goals

FAR RIGHT: CHELSEA BECAME THE 10TH ALL-TIME WINNERS ON PENALTIES WHEN THEY BEAT BAYERN IN MUNICH IN 2012

Records

CHAMPIONS LEAGUE RECORDS (2013-2015)

2012-13
Semi-finals:
Bayern Munich bt Barcelona 4-0, 3-0 (7-0 on agg)
Borussia Dortmund bt Real Madrid 4-1, 2-0 (6-1 on agg)
Final: Bayern Munich bt Borussia Dortmund 2-1
Top scorer: Cristiano Ronaldo (Real Madrid), 12 goals

2013-14
Semi-finals:
Atletico Madrid bt Chelsea 0-0, 3-1 (3-1 on agg)
Real Madrid bt Bayern Munich 1-0, 4-0 (5-0 on agg)
Final: Real Madrid bt Atletico Madrid 4-1
Top scorer: Cristiano Ronaldo (Real Madrid), 17 goals

2014-15
Semi-finals:
Barcelona bt Bayern Munich 3-0, 2-3 (5-3 on agg)
Juventus bt Real Madrid 2-1, 1-1 (3-2 on agg)
Final: Barcelona bt Juventus 3-1
Top scorers: Lionel Messi (Barcelona), Neymar (Barcelona) and Cristiano Ronaldo (Real Madrid), 10 goals each

FAR RIGHT: **REAL MADRID HAIL THEIR RECORD-EXTENDING 10TH CHAMPIONS LEAGUE CUP WIN IN 2014**

Records

WINNERS (BY CLUB)

UEFA Champions League/European Cup:

Real Madrid 10
(1956, 1957, 1958, 1959, 1960, 1966, 1998, 2000, 2002, 2014)

Milan 7
(1963, 1969, 1989, 1990, 1994, 2003, 2007)

Barcelona 5
(1992, 2006, 2009, 2011, 2015)

Bayern Munich 5
(1974, 1975, 1976, 2001, 2013)

Liverpool 5
(1977, 1978, 1981, 1984, 2005)

Ajax 4
(1971, 1972, 1973, 1995)

Internazionale 3
(1964, 1965, 2010)

Manchester United 3
(1968, 1999, 2008)

Benfica 2
(1961, 1962)

Juventus 2
(1985, 1996)

Nottingham Forest 2
(1979, 1980)

Porto 2
(1987, 2004)

Aston Villa 1
(1982)

Borussia Dortmund 1
(1997)

Celtic 1
(1967)

Chelsea 1
(2012)

Feyenoord 1
(1970)

Hamburg 1
(1983)

Marseille 1
(1993)

PSV Eindhoven 1
(1988)

Red Star Belgrade 1
(1991)

Steaua Bucharest 1
(1986)

WINNERS (BY COUNTRY)

UEFA Champions League/European Cup:

Spain	15	Portugal	4
Italy	12	France	1
England	12	Romania	1
Germany	7	Scotland	1
Holland	6	Yugoslavia	1

All-time top scorers (Champions Lge/Cup):

Lionel Messi (Barcelona) 77
Cristiano Ronaldo (Manchester United, Real Madrid) 77
Raul (Real Madrid, Schalke) 71
Ruud van Nistelrooy (PSV Eindhoven, Manchester United, Real Madrid) 56
Thierry Henry (Monaco, Arsenal, Barcelona) 50
Alfredo Di Stefano (Real Madrid) 49
Andriy Shevchenko (Dinamo Kiev, Milan, Chelsea) 48
Eusebio (Benfica) 46
Filippo Inzaghi (Juventus, Milan) 46
Didier Drogba (Marseille, Chelsea, Galatasaray) 44

Most Appearances:

Xavi Hernandez (Barcelona) 151
Iker Casillas (Real Madrid) 150
Raul (Real Madrid, Schalke) 142
Ryan Giggs (Manchester United) 141
Clarence Seedorf (Ajax, Real Madrid, Internazionale, Milan) 125
Paul Scholes (Manchester United) 124
Roberto Carlos (Internazionale, Real Madrid, Fenerbahce) 120
Cristiano Ronaldo (Sporting Lisbon, Manchester United, Real Madrid) 115
Carles Puyol (Barcelona) 115
Thierry Henry (Monaco, Arsenal, Barcelona) 112

Single-season Top Scorer:

Cristiano Ronaldo (Real Madrid, 2013-14) 17

Most Winners Medals:

Francisco Gento (Real Madrid) 6
Alfredo Di Stefano (Real Madrid) 5
Jose Maria Zarraga (Real Madrid) 5
Paolo Maldini (Milan) 5

Wins With Three Different Clubs:

Clarence Seedorf (Ajax 1995, Real Madrid 1998, Milan 2003 and 2007)

Winners As Player and Coach:

Miguel Munoz (Real Madrid)
Giovanni Trapattoni (Milan/Juventus)
Johan Cruyff (Ajax/Barcelona)
Frank Rijkaard (Milan, Ajax/Barcelona)

Most Goals (Player) in One Tie:

Jose Altafini (Milan v US Luxembourg, 1962-63), 8 goals (5 home, 3 away)

Highest aggregate win:

18-0, Benfica v Stade Dudelange (1965-66)

FAR RIGHT: **BARCELONA'S 3-1 VICTORY OVER JUVENTUS IN THE 2015 FINAL WAS THE CLUB'S FIFTH SUCCESS IN THE EUROPEAN CUP - ONLY REAL MADRID (10) AND MILAN (7) HAVE WON THE COMPETITION ON MORE OCCASIONS**

Special appreciation for 'leg work' at home and abroad to Paddy Agnew, Alberto da Silva, Sid Lowe, Karlheinz Wild and Colin Wood. Also to Martin Corteel at Carlton Books for essential supervision, Nigel Matheson for keeping the entire project up to speed, Tom Wright for picture research beyond the call of duty and Steve Dobell for his copy-editing. Thanks are also due to John Cookman for use of his excellent programme collection.

The publishers would like to thank the following sources for their kind permission to reproduce the pictures in this book. Location indicator: T-top, B-bottom, L-left, R-right.

Getty Images: 158-159, 239; /AFP: 66; /Odd Andersen/AFP: 249TR; /Oliver Behrendt/Ullstein Bild: 252; /Giuseppe Bellini: 236; /Shaun Botterill: 223, 237, 262; /Chris Brunskill: 254; /Central Press: 49; /Chris Coleman/Manchester United: 216-217; /Helios de la Rubia/Real Madrid: 251; /Carl De Souza/AFP: 205B; /Adrian Dennis/AFP: 215, 217BR, 234-235, 259TR; /Bru Garcia/AFP: 208; /Lluis Gene/AFP: 221TR, 229, 233; /Laurence Griffiths: 224, 225, 242, 255, 277; /Alex Grimm/Bongarts: 258-259; /Alexander Hassenstein: 228; /Alexander Hassenstein/Bongarts: 244; /Mike Hewitt: 209BR; /Andreas Hillergren/AFP: 250; /Hulton Archive: 35, 62; /Josep Lago/AFP: 265; /Oliver Lang/DDP: 235BR; /Alex Livesey: 219, 226-227, 230, 232, 261; /Angel Martinez/Real Madrid: 4-5, 257; /Jamie McDonald: 218; /Jeff J Mitchell: 214; /Filippo Monteforte/AFP: 240BL; /John Peters/Manchester United: 240-241; /Dani Pozo/AFP: 264; /Tom Purslow/Manchester United: 220-221; /David Ramos: 246, 247; /Michael Regan: 260, 279; /Clive Rose: 238; /Miguel Ruiz/FC Barcelona: 263; /Sakis Savvides/AFP: 245; /Christof Stache/AFP: 248-249, 253; /Patrik Stollarz/AFP: 281; /Bob Thomas: 273; /Topical Press Agency: 11; /VI-Images: 1, 231, 243, 256, 266, 267; /Miguel Villagran/Bongarts: 222; /Wesley/Keystone: 60, 271

Press Association Images: 7, 20, 26-27, 29, 39, 48, 50, 61, 74, 86, 209BC; /Abaca Press: 163; /Matthew Ashton: 139, 167, 179TR, 192, 200; /Barratts/Alpha: 25; /Istvan Bajdat/DPA: 68; /Luca Bruno/AP: 205T; /Jon Buckle: 207; /Peter Byrne: 212; /Gareth Copley: 174-175; /David Davies: 211T; /Adam Davy: 109, 186, 213T; /Mike Egerton: 2-3, 202; /Laurence Griffiths: 143TR; /Tim Hall: 6, 14, 28, 80, 106; /Alvaro Hernandez: 164; /Jasper Juinen/AP: 203; /Thomas Kienzle/AP: 201T; /Ross Kinnaird: 119, 124-125; /Le Monde Du Sport: 162; /Christian Liewig: 108; /Paul Marriott: 125TR; /Tony Marshall: 55, 104-105, 130, 132-133, 140, 144BL, 156BL, 168-169, 171, 197, 211B, 213B; /Andrew Medichini/AP: 204; /Andrew Milligan: 190-191; /Steve Mitchell: 54, 166, 169BR; /Steve Morton: 173; /Rebecca Naden: 199B, 206; /Phil O'Brien: 112, 118, 127BR, 128-129, 275; /Tony O'Brien: 194; /Photonews: 143BR; /Nick Potts: 191TR; /Martin Ricketts: 193; /Peter Robinson: 73, 76-77, 77BR, 81, 85, 87, 89, 90, 93, 96, 97, 101, 103; /S&G: 46; /S&G/Alpha: 10, 31, 36, 38, 64, 67; /SMG: 33B, 113TL; /Neal Simpson: 116, 120-121, 144-145; /Christof Stache/AP: 210; /Michael Steele: 148, 154-155; /Studio Buzzi: 107; /Topham: 15, 17, 18, 24, 33T, 34, 42, 44, 45, 51, 268-269; /John Walton: 180-181, 184-185, 201B; /Witters: 57

Offside Sports Photography: 19; /Farabolafoto: 8; /L'Equipe: 9, 12-13, 21, 22, 23, 32, 37, 40, 41, 43, 47, 52-53, 58, 59, 63, 65, 69, 70, 71, 72, 75, 78-79, 84, 88, 91, 92, 94, 98, 99, 100, 102, 110, 111, 113TR, 120TL, 122, 123, 126-127, 131, 134, 135T, 136-137, 137BR, 138, 142, 146-147, 172, 187, 195T, 195B, 196, 199T; /Mark Leech: 83, 95, 114-115, 115, 117, 149, 150-151, 152BL, 152-153, 155TR, 156-157, 158BL, 160-161, 170, 178-179, 181TR, 182, 183, 188-189, 189BR; /Witters: 135B, 147BR, 176-177, 177BR, 185BR

Every effort has been made to acknowledge correctly and contact the source/copyright holder of each picture and Carlton Books Limited apologises for any unintentional errors or omissions, which will be corrected in further editions of this book.
Special thanks are due to Edd Griffin at Offside Sports Photography, Arnaud Jacob and Jean-Pierre Penel at Presse Sports, who greatly reduced the burdens of picture research.